Lecture Notes in Artificial Intelligence   12500

Subseries of Lecture Notes in Computer Science

More information about this subseries at http://www.springer.com/series/1244

Qiang Yang · Lixin Fan · Han Yu (Eds.)

Federated Learning

Privacy and Incentive

 Springer

Editors
Qiang Yang
WeBank
Shenzhen, China

Hong Kong University of Science
and Technology
Hong Kong, Hong Kong

Han Yu ⓘ
Nanyang Technological University
Singapore, Singapore

Lixin Fan
WeBank
Shenzhen, China

ISSN 0302-9743 ISSN 1611-3349 (electronic)
Lecture Notes in Artificial Intelligence
ISBN 978-3-030-63075-1 ISBN 978-3-030-63076-8 (eBook)
https://doi.org/10.1007/978-3-030-63076-8

LNCS Sublibrary: SL7 – Artificial Intelligence

This Springer imprint is published by the registered company Springer Nature Switzerland AG
The registered company address is: Gewerbestrasse 11, 6330 Cham, Switzerland

Preface

Machine learning (ML) has shown significant potential for revolutionizing many important applications such as fraud detection in finance, medical diagnosis in healthcare, or speech recognition in automatic customer service. The traditional approach of training ML models requires large-scale datasets. However, with rising public concerns for data privacy protection, such an approach is facing tremendous challenges. Trust establishment techniques such as blockchains can help users ascertain the origin of the data and audit their usage. Nevertheless, we still require a viable approach to extract value from such trustworthy data and fairly distribute such values to promote collaboration.

Federated learning (FL) is an emerging ML paradigm that aims to help the field of ML adapt to and thrive under the new normal of heightened data privacy concerns and distributively owned data silos. It offers a promising alternative to enable multiple participants to train a globally shared model by exchanging model information without exposing private data.

The protection of data *privacy* is often mandated by the regulatory requirements (e.g., GDPR) in business-to-consumer scenarios. Violations of such regulations can incur hefty fines amounting to the billions. Moreover, in business-to-business settings, participants from the same business sectors may be competitors. This poses further unique challenges for the design of federated *incentives* to fairly account for their contributions and sustain collaboration in the presence of competition. Research works pertaining data privacy protection and incentive mechanism design under FL settings are crucial for the formation and healthy development of FL ecosystems. This is what makes FL unique compared to existing distributed ML paradigms. Therefore, our book focuses on these two main themes.

Although FL training processes are decentralized, without exposing private data, one crux of data privacy protection is to avoid the shared model parameters being exploited by potential adversaries. In this book, we have collected multiple studies on privacy-preserving ML to show the readers potential approaches that can strengthen the privacy aspect of FL.

Despite a wealth of literature on incentive mechanism design exists, the unique settings and challenges facing FL requires meaningful extensions to these approaches. In this book, we have gathered multiple studies on motivating participants to join FL training through rewards (monetary or otherwise) in order to build a sustainable FL ecosystem.

Knowing the theories and techniques about privacy preservation and incentivization under FL is one thing, but successfully applying them in practice also requires non-trivial effort. In this book, we have also included a number of studies on the application of FL in important fields such as recommendation systems and banking.

This book consists of 19 chapters, each of which is a single-blind peer-reviewed submission. Most of the chapters are extensions from workshop or conference contributions. By providing a well-balanced collection of recent works on *privacy*, *incentive* and the *applications* of FL, the book can help readers gain a more nuanced understanding on how to build a robust and sustainable FL ecosystem and translate the research outcomes into real-world impact. The book is therefore expected to be useful for academic researchers, FL system developers as well as people interested in advanced artificial intelligence topics.

Last but not least, we would like to express our gratitude towards our amazing colleagues, specially Lanlan Chang and Jian Li from the Springer team. Without their help, the publication of this book would not be possible.

September 2020

Qiang Yang
Lixin Fan
Han Yu

Organization

Editorial Team

Qiang Yang   WeBank, China, and The Hong Kong University
of Science and Technology, Hong Kong
Lixin Fan   WeBank, China
Han Yu   Nanyang Technological University, Singapore

Program Committee

Kam Woh Ng   WeBank, China
Yilun Jin   The Hong Kong University of Science
and Technology, Hong Kong
Tianyu Zhang   WeBank, China

Contents

Privacy

Threats to Federated Learning

Lingjuan Lyu[1]([✉]), Han Yu[2], Jun Zhao[2], and Qiang Yang[3,4]

[1] National University of Singapore, Singapore, Singapore
lyulj@comp.nus.edu.sg
[2] School of Computer Science and Engineering,
Nanyang Technological University, Singapore, Singapore
{han.yu,junzhao}@ntu.edu.sg
[3] Department of AI, WeBank, Shenzhen, China
[4] Department of Computer Science and Engineering,
Hong Kong University of Science and Technology, Kowloon, Hong Kong
qyang@cse.ust.hk

Abstract. As data are increasingly being stored in different silos and societies becoming more aware of data privacy issues, the traditional centralized approach of training artificial intelligence (AI) models is facing strong challenges. Federated learning (FL) has recently emerged as a promising solution under this new reality. Existing FL protocol design has been shown to exhibit vulnerabilities which can be exploited by adversaries both within and outside of the system to compromise data privacy. It is thus of paramount importance to make FL system designers aware of the implications of future FL algorithm design on privacy-preservation. Currently, there is no survey on this topic. In this chapter, we bridge this important gap in FL literature. By providing a concise introduction to the concept of FL, and a unique taxonomy covering threat models and two major attacks on FL: 1) poisoning attacks and 2) inference attacks, we provide an accessible review of this important topic. We highlight the intuitions, key techniques as well as fundamental assumptions adopted by various attacks, and discuss promising future research directions towards more robust privacy preservation in FL.

Keywords: Federated learning · Attacks · Privacy · Robustness

1 Introduction

As computing devices become increasingly ubiquitous, people generate huge amounts of data through their day to day usage. Collecting such data into centralized storage facilities is costly and time consuming. Another important concern is data privacy and user confidentiality as the usage data usually contain sensitive information [1]. Sensitive data such as facial images, location-based services, or health information can be used for targeted social advertising and recommendation, posing the immediate or potential privacy risks. Hence, private data should not be directly shared without any privacy consideration. As societies become increasingly aware of privacy preservation, legal restrictions such

© Springer Nature Switzerland AG 2020
Q. Yang et al. (Eds.): Federated Learning, LNAI 12500, pp. 3–16, 2020.
https://doi.org/10.1007/978-3-030-63076-8_1

Table 1. Taxonomy for horizontal federated learning (HFL).

HFL	Number of participants	FL training participation	Technical capability
H2B	Small	Frequent	High
H2C	Large	Not frequent	Low

as the General Data Protection Regulation (GDPR) are emerging which makes data aggregation practices less feasible [48].

Traditional centralized machine learning (ML) cannot support such ubiquitous deployments and applications due to infrastructure shortcomings such as limited communication bandwidth, intermittent network connectivity, and strict delay constraints [26]. In this scenario, federated learning (FL) which pushes model training to the devices from which data originate emerged as a promising alternative ML paradigm [35]. FL enables a multitude of participants to construct a joint ML model without exposing their private training data [12,35]. It can handle unbalanced and non-independent and identically distributed (non-IID) data which naturally arise in the real world [34]. In recent years, FL has benefited a wide range of applications such as next word prediction [34,36], visual object detection for safety [29], etc.

1.1 Types of Federated Learning

Based on the distribution of data features and data samples among participants, federated learning can be generally classified as horizontally federated learning (HFL), vertically federated learning (VFL) and federated transfer learning (FTL) [47].

Under HFL, datasets owned by each participant share similar features but concern different users [24]. For example, several hospitals may each store similar types of data (e.g., demographic, clinical, and genomic) about different patients. If they decide to build a machine learning model together using FL, we refer to such a scenario as HFL. In this chapter, we further classify HFL into HFL to businesses (H2B), and HFL to consumers (H2C). A comparison between H2B and H2C is listed in Table 1. The main difference lies in the number of participants, FL training participation level, and technical capability, which can influence how adversaries attempt to compromise the FL system. Under H2B, there are typically a handful of participants. They can be frequently selected during FL training. The participants tend to possess significant computational power and sophisticated technical capabilities [48]. Under H2C, there can be thousands or even millions of potential participants. In each round of training, only a subset of them are selected. As their datasets tend to be small, the chance of a participant being selected repeatedly for FL training is low. They generally possess limited computational power and low technical capabilities. An example of H2C is Google's GBoard application [36].

VFL is applicable to the cases in which participants have large overlaps in the sample space but differ in the feature space, *i.e.*, different participants hold different attributes of the same records [46]. VFL mainly targets business participants. Thus, the characteristics of VFL participants are similar to those of H2B participants.

FTL deals with scenarios in which FL participants have little overlap in both the sample space and the feature space [48]. Currently, there is no published research studying threats to FTL models.

1.2   Threats to FL

FL offers a privacy-aware paradigm of model training which does not require data sharing and allows participants to join and leave a federation freely. Nevertheless, recent works have demonstrated that FL may not always provide sufficient privacy guarantees, as communicating model updates throughout the training process can nonetheless reveal sensitive information [8,37] even incur deep leakage [52], either to a third-party, or to the central server [2,36]. For instance, as shown by [3], even a small portion of gradients may reveal information about local data. A more recent work showed that the malicious attacker can completely steal the training data from gradients in a few iterations [52].

FL protocol designs may contain vulnerabilities for both (1) the (potentially malicious) server, who can observe individual updates over time, tamper with the training process and control the view of the participants on the global parameters; and (2) any participant who can observe the global parameter, and control its parameter uploads. For example, malicious participants can deliberately alter their inputs or introduce stealthy backdoors into the global model. Such attacks pose significant threats to FL, as in centralized learning only the server can violate participants' privacy, but in FL, any participant may violate the

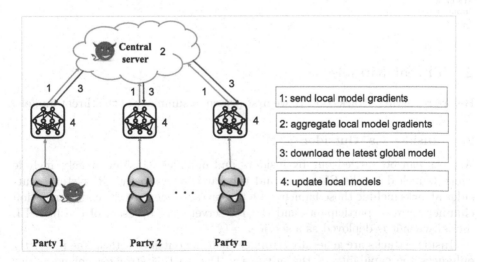

Fig. 1. A typical FL training process, in which both the (potentially malicious) FL server/aggregator and malicious participants may compromise the FL system.

privacy of other participants in the system, even without involving the server. Therefore, it is important to understand the principles behind these attacks. Existing survey papers on FL mostly focused on the broad aspect of how to make FL work [23,27,47]. In this chapter, we survey recent advances in threats to compromise FL to bridge this important gap in the artificial intelligence (AI) research community's understanding in this topic. In particular, we focus on two specific threats initiated by the insiders on FL systems: 1) poisoning attacks that attempt to prevent a model from being learned at all, or to bias the model to produce inferences that are preferable to the adversary; and 2) inference attacks that target participant privacy. The properties of these attacks are summarized in Table 2.

Table 2. A summary of attacks against server-based FL.

Attack type	Attack targets		Attacker role		FL scenario		Attack complexity		
	Model	Training data	Participant	Server	H2B	H2C	Attack iteration		Auxiliary knowledge required
							One round	Multiple rounds	
Data poisoning	YES	NO	YES	NO	YES	YES	YES	YES	YES
Model poisoning	YES	NO	YES	NO	YES	NO	YES	YES	YES
Infer class representatives	NO	YES	YES	YES	YES	NO	NO	YES	YES
Infer membership	NO	YES	YES	YES	YES	NO	NO	YES	YES
Infer properties	NO	YES	YES	YES	YES	NO	NO	YES	YES
Infer training inputs and labels	NO	YES	NO	YES	YES	NO	NO	YES	NO

2   Threat Models

Before reviewing attacks on FL, we first present a summary of the threat models.

2.1   Insider v.s. Outsider

Attacks can be carried out by insiders and outsiders. Insider attacks include those launched by the FL server and the participants in the FL system. Outsider attacks include those launched by the eavesdroppers on the communication channel between participants and the FL server, and by users of the final FL model when it is deployed as a service.

Insider attacks are generally stronger than the outsider attacks, as it strictly enhances the capability of the adversary. Due to this stronger behavior, our discussion of attacks against FL will focus primarily on the insider attacks, which can take one of the following three general forms:

1. Single attack: a single, non-colluding malicious participant aims to cause the model to miss-classify a set of chosen inputs with high confidence [4, 7];
2. Byzantine attack: the byzantine malicious participants may behave completely arbitrarily and tailor their outputs to have similar distribution as the correct model updates, making them difficult to detect [11,14,15,40,49];
3. Sybil attack: the adversaries can simulate multiple dummy participant accounts or select previously compromised participants to mount more powerful attacks on FL [4, 17].

2.2   Semi-honest v.s. Malicious

Under the semi-honest setting, adversaries are considered passive or honest-but-curious. They try to learn the private states of other participants without deviating from the FL protocol. The passive adversaries are assumed to only observe the aggregated or averaged gradient, but not the training data or gradient of other honest participants. Under the malicious setting, an active, or malicious adversary tries to learn the private states of honest participants, and deviates arbitrarily from the FL protocol by modifying, re-playing, or removing messages. This strong adversary model allows the adversary to conduct particularly devastating attacks.

2.3   Training Phase v.s. Inference Phase

Attacks at training phase attempt to learn, influence, or corrupt the FL model itself [9]. During training phase, the attacker can run data poisoning attacks to compromise the integrity of training dataset collection, or model poisoning attacks to compromise the integrity of the learning process. The attacker can also launch a range of inference attacks on an individual participant's update or on the aggregate of updates from all participants.

Attacks at inference phase are called evasion/exploratory attacks [5]. They generally do not tamper with the targeted model, but instead, either cause it to produce wrong outputs (targeted/untargeted) or collect evidence about the model characteristics. The effectiveness of such attacks is largely determined by the information that is available to the adversary about the model. Inference phase attacks can be classified into white-box attacks (i.e. with full access to the FL model) and black-box attacks (i.e. only able to query the FL model). In FL, the model maintained by the server not only suffers from the same evasion attacks as in the general ML setting when the target model is deployed as a service, the model broadcast step in FL renders the model accessible to any malicious client. Thus, FL requires extra efforts to defend against white-box evasion attacks. In this survey, we omit the discussion of inference phase attacks, and mainly focus on the training phase attacks.

3   Poisoning Attacks

Depending on the attacker's objective, poisoning attacks can be either a) random attacks and b) targeted attacks [22]. Random attacks aim to reduce the accuracy of the FL model, whereas targeted attacks aim to induce the FL model to output the target label specified by the adversary. Generally, targeted attacks is more difficult than random attacks as the attacker has a specific goal to achieve. Poisoning attacks during the training phase can be performed on the data or on the model. Figure 2 shows that the poisoned updates can be sourced from two poisoning attacks: (1) data poisoning attack during local data collection; and (2) model poisoning attack during local model training process. At a high level, both poisoning attacks attempt to modify the behavior of the target model in some undesirable way. If adversaries can compromise the FL server, then they can easily perform both targeted and untargeted poisoning attacks on the trained model.

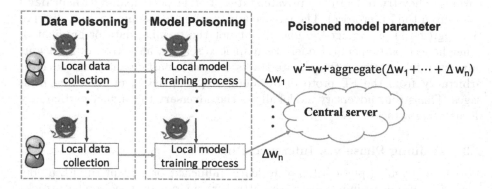

Fig. 2. Data v.s. model poisoning attacks in FL.

3.1 Data Poisoning

Data poisoning attacks largely fall in two categories: 1) clean-label [42] and 2) dirty-label [19]. Clean-label attacks assume that the adversary cannot change the label of any training data as there is a process by which data are certified as belonging to the correct class and the poisoning of data samples has to be imperceptible. In contrast, in dirty-label poisoning, the adversary can introduce a number of data sample it wishes to miss-classify with the desired target label into the training set.

One common example of dirty-label poisoning attack is the label-flipping attack [10,17]. The labels of honest training examples of one class are flipped to another class while the features of the data are kept unchanged. For example, the malicious participants in the system can poison their dataset by flipping all 1 s into 7 s. A successful attack produces a model that is unable to correctly classify 1 s and incorrectly predicts them to be 7 s. Another weak but realistic attack scenario is backdoor poisoning [19]. Here, an adversary can modify individual features or small regions of the original training dataset to embed backdoors into the model, so that the model behaves according to the adversary's objective if the input contains the backdoor features (*e.g.*, a stamp on an image).

However, the performance of the poisoned model on clean inputs is not affected. In this way, the attacks are harder to be detected.

Data poisoning attacks can be carried out by any FL participant. The impact on the FL model depends on the extent to which participants in the system engage in the attacks, and the amount of training data being poisoned. Data poisoning is less effective in settings with fewer participants like H2C.

3.2 Model Poisoning

Model poisoning attacks aim to poison local model updates before sending them to the server or insert hidden backdoors into the global model [4].

In targeted model poisoning, the adversary's objective is to cause the FL model to miss-classify a set of chosen inputs with high confidence. Note that these inputs are not modified to induce miss-classification at test time as under adversarial example attacks [45]. Rather, the miss-classification is a result of adversarial manipulations of the training process. Recent works have investigated poisoning attacks on model updates in which a subset of updates sent to the server at any given iteration are poisoned [7,11]. These poisoned updates can be generated by inserting hidden backdoors, and even a single-shot attack may be enough to introduce a backdoor into a model [4].

Bhagoji et al. [7] demonstrated that model poisoning attacks are much more effective than data poisoning in FL settings by analyzing a targeted model poisoning attack, where a single, non-colluding malicious participant aims to cause the model to miss-classify a set of chosen inputs with high confidence. To increase attack stealth and evade detection, they use the alternating minimization strategy to alternately optimize for the training loss and the adversarial objective, and use parameter estimation for the benign participants' updates. This adversarial model poisoning attack can cause targeted poisoning of the FL model undetected.

In fact, model poisoning subsumes data poisoning in FL settings, as data poisoning attacks eventually change a subset of updates sent to the model at any given iteration [17]. This is functionally identical to a centralized poisoning attack in which a subset of the whole training data is poisoned. Model poisoning attacks require sophisticated technical capabilities and high computational resources. Such attacks are generally less suitable for H2C scenarios, but more likely to happen in H2B scenarios.

4   Inference Attacks

Exchanging gradients in FL can result in serious privacy leakage [37,41,44,52]. As illustrated in Fig. 3, model updates can leak extra information about the unintended features about participants' training data to the adversarial participants, as deep learning models appear to internally recognize many features of the data that are not apparently related with the main tasks. The adversary can also save the snapshot of the FL model parameters, and conduct property inference by exploiting the difference between the consecutive snapshots, which is equal to the aggregated updates from all participants less the adversary (Fig. 4).

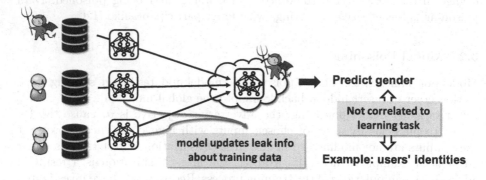

Fig. 3. Attacker infers information unrelated to the learning task.

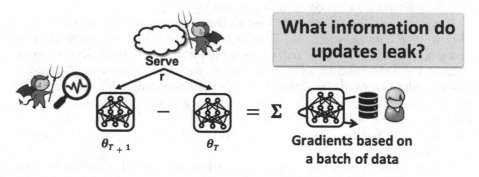

Fig. 4. Attacker infers gradients from a batch of training data.

The main reason is that the gradients are derived from the participants' private data. In deep learning models, gradients of a given layer are computed using this layer's features and the error from the layer above. In the case of sequential fully connected layers, the gradients of the weights are the inner products of the error from the layer above and the features. Similarly, for a convolutional layer, the gradients of the weights are convolutions of the error from the layer above and the features [37]. Consequently, observations of model updates can be used to infer a significant amount of private information, such as class representatives, membership as well as properties associated with a subset of the training data. Even worse, an attacker can infer labels from the shared gradients and recover the original training samples without requiring any prior knowledge about the training set [52].

4.1 Inferring Class Representatives

Hitaj *et al.* [21] devised an active inference attack called *Generative Adversarial Networks* (GAN) attack on deep FL models. Here, a malicious participant can intentionally compromise any other participant. The GAN attack exploits the real-time nature of the FL learning process that allows the adversarial participant to train a GAN that generates prototypical samples of the targeted training data which were meant to be private. The generated samples appear to come from the same distribution as the training data. Hence, GAN attack is not targeted at reconstructing actual training inputs, but only class representatives. It should be noted that GAN attack assumes that the entire training corpus for a given class comes from a single participant, and only in the special case where all class members are similar, GAN-constructed representatives are similar to the training data. This resembles model inversion attacks in the general ML settings [16]. However, these assumptions may be less practical in FL. Moreover, GAN attack is less suitable for H2C scenarios, as it requires large computation resources.

4.2 Inferring Membership

Given an exact data point, membership inference attacks aim to determine if it was used to train the model [43]. For example, an attacker can infer whether a specific patient profile was used to train a classifier associated with a disease. FL presents interesting new avenues for such attacks. In FL, the adversary's objective is to infer if a particular sample belongs to the private training data of a single participant (if target update is of a single participant) or of any participant (if target update is the aggregate). For example, the non-zero gradients of the embedding layer of a deep learning model trained on natural-language text reveal which words appear in the training batches used by the honest participants during FL model training. This enables an adversary to infer whether a given text appeared in the training dataset [37].

Attackers in an FL system can conduct both active and passive membership inference attacks [37,38]. In the passive case, the attacker simply observes the updated model parameters and performs inference without changing anything in the local or global collaborative training procedure. In the active case, however, the attacker can tamper with the FL model training protocol and perform a more powerful attack against other participants. Specifically, the attacker shares malicious updates and forces the FL model to share more information about the participants' local data the attacker is interested in. This attack, called gradient ascent attack [38], exploits the fact that SGD optimization updates model parameters in the opposite direction of the gradient of the loss.

4.3 Inferring Properties

An adversary can launch both passive and active property inference attacks to infer properties of other participants' training data that are independent of the features that characterize the classes of the FL model [37]. Property inference attacks assume that the adversary has auxiliary training data correctly labelled with the property he wants to infer. An passive adversary can only observe/eavesdrop the updates and perform inference by training a binary property classifier. An active adversary can use multi-task learning to trick the FL model into learning a better separation for data with and without the property, and thus extract more information. An adversarial participant can even infer when a property appears and disappears in the data during training (e.g., identifying when a person first appears in the photos used to train a gender classifier). The assumption in property inference attacks may prevent its applicability in H2C.

4.4   Inferring Training Inputs and Labels

The most recent work called Deep Leakage from Gradient (DLG) proposed an optimization algorithm that can obtain both the training inputs and the labels in just a few iterations [52]. This attack is much stronger than previous approaches. It can recover pixel-wise accurate original images and token-wise matching original texts. [50] presented an analytical approach called Improved Deep Leakage from Gradient (iDLG), which can certainly extract labels from the shared gradients by exploiting the relationship between the labels and the signs of corresponding gradients. iDLG is valid for any differentiable model trained with cross-entropy loss over one-hot labels, which is the general case for classification.

Inference attacks generally assume that the adversaries possess sophisticated technical capabilities and large computational resources. In addition, adversaries must be selected for many rounds of FL training. Thus, it is not suitable for H2C scenarios, but more likely under H2B scenarios. Such attacks also highlight the need for protecting the gradients being shared during FL training, possibly through mechanisms such as homomorphic encryption [48].

5   Discussions and Promising Directions

There are still potential vulnerabilities which need to be addressed in order to improve the robustness of FL systems. In this section, we outline research directions which we believe are promising.

Curse of Dimensionality: Large models, with high dimensional parameter vectors, are particularly susceptible to privacy and security attacks [13]. Most FL algorithms require overwriting the local model parameters with the global model. This makes them susceptible to poisoning and backdoor attacks, as the adversary can make small but damaging changes in the high-dimensional models without being detected. Thus, sharing model parameters may not be a strong design choice in FL, it opens all the internal state of the model to inference attacks, and maximizes the model's malleability by poisoning attacks. To address these fundamental shortcomings of FL, it is worthwhile to explore whether sharing model updates is essential. Instead, sharing less sensitive information (e.g., SIGNSGD [6]) or only sharing model predictions [13] in a black-box manner may result in more robust privacy protection in FL.

Vulnerabilities to Free-Riding Participants: In FL system, there may exist free-riders in the collaborative learning system, who aim to benefit from the global model, but do not want to contribute any real information. The main incentives for free-rider to submit fake information may include: (1) one participant may not have any data to train a local model; (2) one participant is too concerned about its privacy to release any information that may compromise privacy; (3) one participant may not want to consume any local computation power to train any model [32,33]. In the current FL paradigm [34], all participants receive the same federated model at the end of collaborative model training regardless of their contributions. This makes the paradigm vulnerable to free-riding participants [28,32,33].

Threats to VFL: In VFL [20], there may only be one participant who owns labels for the given learning task. It is unclear if all the participants have equal capability of attacking the FL model, and if threats to HFL can work on VFL. Most of the current threats still focus on HFL. Thus, threats on VFL, which is important to businesses, are worth exploring.

FL with Heterogeneous Architectures: Sharing model updates is typically limited only to homogeneous FL architectures, *i.e.*, the same model is shared with all participants. It would be interesting to study how to extend FL to collaboratively train models with heterogeneous architectures [13,18,25], and whether existing attacks and privacy techniques can be adapted to this paradigm.

Decentralized Federated Learning: Decentralized FL where no single server is required in the system is currently being studied [32,33,36,48]. This is a potential learning framework for collaboration among businesses which do not trust any third party. In this paradigm, each participant could be elected as a server in a round robin manner. It would be interesting to investigate if existing threats on server-based FL still apply in this scenario. Moreover, it may open new attack surfaces. One possible example is that the last participant who was elected as the server is more likely to effectively contaminate the whole model if it chooses to insert backdoors. This resembles the fact in server-based FL models which are more vulnerable to backdoors in later rounds of training nearing convergence. Similarly, if decentralized training is conducted in a "ring all reduce" manner, then any malicious participant can steal the training data from its neighbors.

Weakness of Current Defense: FL with secure aggregation are especially susceptible to poisoning attacks as the individual updates cannot be inspected. It is still unclear if adversarial training can be adapted to FL, as adversarial training was developed primarily for IID data, and it is still a challenging problem how it performs in non-IID settings. Moreover, adversarial training typically requires many epochs, which may be impractical in H2C. Another possible defense is based on differential privacy (DP) [30–33,36,51]. Record-level DP bounds the success of membership inference, but does not prevent property inference applied to a group of training records [37]. Participant-level DP, on the other hand, is geared to work with thousands of users for training to converge and achieving an acceptable trade-off between privacy and accuracy [36]. The FL model fails to converge with a small number of participants, making it unsuitable for H2B scenarios. Furthermore, DP may hurt the accuracy of the learned model [39], which is not appealing to the industry. Further work is needed to investigate if participant-level DP can protect FL systems with few participants.

Optimizing Defense Mechanism Deployment: When deploying defense mechanisms to check if any adversary is attacking the FL system, the FL server will need to incur extra computational cost. In addition, different defense mechanisms may have different effectiveness against various attacks, and incur different cost. It is important to study how to optimize the timing of deploying defense mechanisms or the announcement of deterrence measures. Game theoretic research holds promise in addressing this challenge.

Federated learning is still in its infancy and will continue to be an active and important research area for the foreseeable future. As FL evolves, so will the attack mechanisms. It is of vital importance to provide a broad overview of current attacks on FL so that future FL system designers are aware of the potential vulnerabilities in their designs. This survey serves as a concise and accessible overview of this topic, and it would greatly help our understanding of the threat landscape in FL. Global collaboration on FL is emerging through a number of workshops in leading AI conferences[1]. The ultimate goal of developing a general purpose defense mechanism robust against various attacks without degrading model performance will require interdisciplinary effort from the wider research community.

References

1. Abadi, M., et al.: Deep learning with differential privacy. In: CCS, pp. 308–318 (2016)
2. Agarwal, N., Suresh, A.T., Yu, F.X.X., Kumar, S., McMahan, B.: cpSGD: communication-efficient and differentially-private distributed SGD. In: NeurIPS, pp. 7564–7575 (2018)
3. Aono, Y., Hayashi, T., Wang, L., Moriai, S., et al.: Privacy-preserving deep learning via additively homomorphic encryption. IEEE Trans. Inf. Forensics Secur. **13**(5), 1333–1345 (2018)
4. Bagdasaryan, E., Veit, A., Hua, Y., Estrin, D., Shmatikov, V.: How to backdoor federated learning. CoRR, arXiv:1807.00459 (2018)
5. Barreno, M., Nelson, B., Sears, R., Joseph, A.D., Tygar, J.D.: Can machine learning be secure? In: ICCS, pp. 16–25 (2006)
6. Bernstein, J., Zhao, J., Azizzadenesheli, K., Anandkumar, A.: signSGD with majority vote is communication efficient and fault tolerant. CoRR, arXiv:1810.05291 (2018)
7. Bhagoji, A.N., Chakraborty, S., Mittal, P., Calo, S.: Analyzing federated learning through an adversarial lens. CoRR, arXiv:1811.12470 (2018)
8. Bhowmick, A., Duchi, J., Freudiger, J., Kapoor, G., Rogers, R.: Protection against reconstruction and its applications in private federated learning. CoRR, arXiv:1812.00984 (2018)

---

[1] https://www.ntu.edu.sg/home/han.yu/FL.html.

9. Biggio, B., Nelson, B., Laskov, P.: Support vector machines under adversarial label noise. In: ACML, pp. 97–112 (2011)
10. Biggio, B., Nelson, B., Laskov, P.: Poisoning attacks against support vector machines. CoRR, arXiv:1206.6389 (2012)
11. Blanchard, P., Guerraoui, R., Stainer, J., et al.: Machine learning with adversaries: Byzantine tolerant gradient descent. In: NeurIPS, pp. 119–129 (2017)
12. Bonawitz, K., et al.: Practical secure aggregation for privacy-preserving machine learning. In: CCS, pp. 1175–1191 (2017)
13. Chang, H., Shejwalkar, V., Shokri, R., Houmansadr, A.: Cronus: robust and heterogeneous collaborative learning with black-box knowledge transfer. CoRR, arXiv:1912.11279 (2019)
14. Chen, L., Wang, H., Charles, Z., Papailiopoulos, D.: Draco: Byzantine-resilient distributed training via redundant gradients. CoRR, arXiv:1803.09877 (2018)
15. Chen, Y., Su, L., Xu, J.: Distributed statistical machine learning in adversarial settings: Byzantine gradient descent. Proc. ACM Meas. Anal. Comput. Syst. 1(2), 44 (2017)
16. Fredrikson, M., Jha, S., Ristenpart, T.: Model inversion attacks that exploit confidence information and basic countermeasures. In: CCS, pp. 1322–1333 (2015)
17. Fung, C., Yoon, C.J., Beschastnikh, I.: Mitigating sybils in federated learning poisoning. CoRR, arXiv:1808.04866 (2018)
18. Gao, D., Liu, Y., Huang, A., Ju, C., Yu, H., Yang, Q.: Privacy-preserving heterogeneous federated transfer learning. In: IEEE BigData (2019)
19. Gu, T., Dolan-Gavitt, B., Garg, S.: BadNets: identifying vulnerabilities in the machine learning model supply chain. CoRR, arXiv:1708.06733 (2017)
20. Hardy, S., et al.: Private federated learning on vertically partitioned data via entity resolution and additively homomorphic encryption. CoRR, arXiv:1711.10677 (2017)
21. Hitaj, B., Ateniese, G., Pérez-Cruz, F.: Deep models under the GAN: information leakage from collaborative deep learning. In: CSS, pp. 603–618 (2017)
22. Huang, L., Joseph, A.D., Nelson, B., Rubinstein, B.I., Tygar, J.D.: Adversarial machine learning. In: Proceedings of the 4th ACM Workshop on Security and Artificial Intelligence, pp. 43–58 (2011)
23. Kairouz, P., et al.: Advances and open problems in federated learning. CoRR, arXiv:1912.04977 (2019)
24. Kantarcioglu, M., Clifton, C.: Privacy-preserving distributed mining of association rules on horizontally partitioned data. IEEE Trans. Knowl. Data Eng. 16(9), 1026–1037 (2004)
25. Li, D., Wang, J.: FedMD: heterogenous federated learning via model distillation. arXiv preprint arXiv:1910.03581 (2019)
26. Li, H., Ota, K., Dong, M.: Learning IoT in edge: deep learning for the Internet of Things with edge computing. IEEE Netw. 32(1), 96–101 (2018)
27. Li, T., Sahu, A.K., Talwalkar, A., Smith, V.: Federated learning: challenges, methods, and future directions. CoRR, arXiv:1908.07873 (2019)
28. Lingjuan Lyu, X.X., Wang, Q.: Collaborative fairness in federated learning. arxiv.org/abs/2008.12161v1 (2020)
29. Liu, Y., et al.: Fedvision: an online visual object detection platform powered by federated learning. In: IAAI (2020)
30. Lyu, L., Bezdek, J.C., He, X., Jin, J.: Fog-embedded deep learning for the Internet of Things. IEEE Trans. Ind. Inform. 15(7), 4206–4215 (2019)

31. Lyu, L., Bezdek, J.C., Jin, J., Yang, Y.: FORESEEN: towards differentially private deep inference for intelligent Internet of Things. IEEE J. Sel. Areas Commun. **38**, 2418–2429 (2020)
32. Lyu, L., Li, Y., Nandakumar, K., Yu, J., Ma, X.: How to democratise and protect AI: fair and differentially private decentralised deep learning. IEEE Trans. Dependable Secur. Comput
33. Lyu, L., et al.: Towards fair and privacy-preserving federated deep models. IEEE Trans. Parallel Distrib. Syst. **31**(11), 2524–2541 (2020)
34. McMahan, B., Moore, E., Ramage, D., Hampson, S., y Arcas, B.A.: Communication-efficient learning of deep networks from decentralized data. In: Artificial Intelligence and Statistics, pp. 1273–1282 (2017)
35. McMahan, H.B., Moore, E., Ramage, D., y Arcas, B.A.: Federated learning of deep networks using model averaging. CoRR, arXiv:1602.05629 (2016)
36. McMahan, H.B., Ramage, D., Talwar, K., Zhang, L.: Learning differentially private recurrent language models. In: ICLR (2018)
37. Melis, L., Song, C., De Cristofaro, E., Shmatikov, V.: Exploiting unintended feature leakage in collaborative learning. In: SP, pp. 691–706 (2019)
38. Nasr, M., Shokri, R., Houmansadr, A.: Comprehensive privacy analysis of deep learning: passive and active white-box inference attacks against centralized and federated learning. In: SP, pp. 739–753 (2019)
39. Pan, X., Zhang, M., Ji, S., Yang, M.: Privacy risks of general-purpose language models. In: 2020 IEEE Symposium on Security and Privacy (SP), pp. 1314–1331. IEEE (2020)
40. Pan, X., Zhang, M., Wu, D., Xiao, Q., Ji, S., Yang, M.: Justinian's GAAvernor: robust distributed learning with gradient aggregation agent. In: USENIX Security Symposium (2020)
41. Phong, L.T., Aono, Y., Hayashi, T., Wang, L., Moriai, S.: Privacy-preserving deep learning via additively homomorphic encryption. IEEE Trans. Inf. Forensics Secur. **13**(5), 1333–1345 (2018)
42. Shafahi, A., et al.: Poison frogs! Targeted clean-label poisoning attacks on neural networks. In: NeurIPS, pp. 6103–6113 (2018)
43. Shokri, R., Stronati, M., Song, C., Shmatikov, V.: Membership inference attacks against machine learning models. In: SP, pp. 3–18 (2017)
44. Su, L., Xu, J.: Securing distributed machine learning in high dimensions. CoRR, arXiv:1804.10140 (2018)
45. Szegedy, C., et al.: Intriguing properties of neural networks. CoRR, arXiv:1312.6199 (2013)
46. Vaidya, J., Clifton, C.: Privacy preserving association rule mining in vertically partitioned data. In: KDD, pp. 639–644 (2002)
47. Yang, Q., Liu, Y., Chen, T., Tong, Y.: Federated machine learning: concept and applications. ACM Trans. Intell. Syst. Technol. (TIST) **10**(2), 1–19 (2019)
48. Yang, Q., Liu, Y., Cheng, Y., Kang, Y., Chen, T., Yu, H.: Federated Learning. Morgan & Claypool Publishers, San Rafael (2019)
49. Yin, D., Chen, Y., Ramchandran, K., Bartlett, P.: Byzantine-robust distributed learning: towards optimal statistical rates. CoRR, arXiv:1803.01498 (2018)
50. Zhao, B., Mopuri, K.R., Bilen, H.: iDLG: improved deep leakage from gradients. CoRR, arXiv:2001.02610 (2020)
51. Zhao, Y., et al.: Local differential privacy based federated learning for Internet of Things. arXiv preprint arXiv:2004.08856 (2020)
52. Zhu, L., Liu, Z., Han, S.: Deep leakage from gradients. In: NeurIPS, pp. 14747–14756 (2019)

Deep Leakage from Gradients

Ligeng Zhu(✉) and Song Han

Massachusetts Institute of Technology, Cambridge, USA
{ligeng,songhan}@mit.edu

Abstract. Exchanging model updates is a widely used method in the modern federated learning system. For a long time, people believed that gradients are safe to share: *i.e.*, the gradients are less informative than the training data. However, there is information hidden in the gradients. Moreover, it is even possible to reconstruct the private training data from the publicly shared gradients. This chapter discusses techniques that reveal information hidden in gradients and validate the effectiveness on common deep learning tasks. It is important to raise people's awareness to rethink the gradient's safety. Several possible defense strategies have also been discussed to prevent such privacy leakage.

Keywords: Federated Learning · Privacy leakage · Gradients' safety

1 Introduction

Federated Learning (FL), has gained increasing attention as both data requirements and privacy concerns continue to rise [1–3]. In the Federated Learning system, the user data is not shared across the network and only model updates/gradients are transmitted. Therefore, such kind of distributed learning has been used in real-world applications where user privacy is crucial, e.g., hospital data [16] and text predictions on mobile devices [3]. Ideally, any such approach is considered as safe, as the gradients are thought less informative than the original data. Shown in Fig. 1 below, it is hard to infer from a list of numerical tensor values that the original image is a cat.

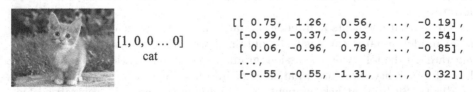

(a) Training data and label   (b) Corresponding gradients

Fig. 1. It is easy to compute gradients from the training, but not intuitive to perform vice versa. As shown in the Figure, human cannot read the cat (either image or label) from raw numerical values.

© Springer Nature Switzerland AG 2020
Q. Yang et al. (Eds.): Federated Learning, LNAI 12500, pp. 17–31, 2020.
https://doi.org/10.1007/978-3-030-63076-8_2

FL provides default participant privacy because only the gradients are shared across while the sensitive training never leaves the local device. However, is the protocol really safe? Do the gradients contain zero information about training data? If not, then how much information can we recover from them? In this section, we will explore the hidden information in the gradients and rethink the safety of gradients sharing scheme.

2   Information Leakage from Gradients

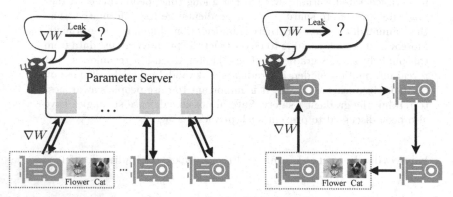

(a) Federated learning with a centralized server

(b) Federated learning without a centralized server

Fig. 2. The information leakage in two types of federated learning. The little red demon appears in the location where the leakage might happen.

From a privacy perspective, we are interested in possible leaks against an *honest-but-curious* server: It faithfully aggregates the updates from participants and delivers the updated model back, but it may be curious about the participant information and attempt to reveal it from the received updates. To study the question, we consider a key question: **What can be inferred about a participant's training dataset from the gradients shared during federated learning**?

Given that gradients and model updates are mathematically equivalent, the local model updates can easily be obtained with the gradients and the learning rate. In the following discussion, gradient-based aggregation is used without loss of generality. We care what kind of information can be inferred from the gradients. Such an attack happens in the parameter server for centralized federated learning (Fig. 2a), or any neighbours in decentralized federated learning (Fig. 2b). We focus on centralized federated learning because it is more widely used [4,5]. In this setting, several studies have been made to show that it is actually possible to infer some hidden information from the gradients.

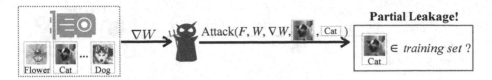

Fig. 3. Membership inference [6] in the federated setting. It uses the predicted results and ground truth labels to infer whether the record was *in* or *out* of the victim training datasets.

Membership-Inference. [6] is the basic privacy violation in this setting: Given an exact data point and pre-trained model, determine whether the data point was used to train the model. In Federated Learning, the gradients are sent to the server every round and the server thus knows the trained model based on local data. With membership-inference, the server is able to infer whether a specific data point exists in the local training set or not. In some cases, it can directly lead to privacy breaches. For example, finding that a specific patient's clinical record was used to train a model associated with a disease can reveal the fact that the patient has the disease. In practice, Melis *et al.* [7] shows that a malicious attacker can convincingly (precision 0.99) tell whether a specific location profile was used to train a gender classifier on the FourSquare location dataset [8] (Fig. 3).

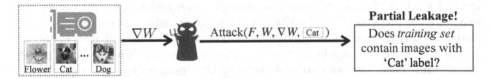

Fig. 4. Property inference [7] in the federated setting. It infers whether the victim's training set contains a data point with certain property.

Property-Inference. [7] is a similar attack: Given a pre-trained model, determine whether the corresponding training set contains a data point with certain properties. It is worth noting that the property is not necessarily related to the main task. When a model is trained to recognize gender or race on the LFW dataset [9], the property-inference can not only reveal the people's race and gender in the training set, but also tell they wear glasses or not. In practice, this also brings the potential risk of privacy leakage. It is easy to identify the patient if knowing his/her age, gender, race and glass-wearing, even the name and clinical record remain hidden.

Fig. 5. Model inversion [10] in the federated setting. It first trains a GAN model from model updates and attacker's own training data. Then it uses the GAN model to generate look alike images from the victim's updates.

Model Inversion. [10] is another powerful attack that leaks the participant privacy. The attack exploits the real-time nature of the learning process and allows the adversary to train a Generative Adversarial Network (GAN) [11] to generate a prototypical sample of the targeted training set, which was meant to private. As shown in Fig. 5, the leaked images are almost identical as the original one, because the samples generated by the GAN are intended to come from the same distributions as the training data. This attack is powerful especially when all class members look alike (e.g., face recognition).

The three attack strategies above reveal a certain level of information hidden in the gradients, but they all have their own limitations. Membership inference requires an existing data record to perform the attack. This may be hard to get when the input data is not text (e.g., image, voice). Property inference relaxes the constraints and only require a label to execute the leakage. However, the attack results only reduce the range and cannot guarantee to find a record-level identity. As for model inversion, though it can directly generate synthetic images from the statistical distribution of training data, the results are look-alike alternatives (not the original data) and only works when all class members are similar. Here we consider a more challenging question: Without prior about the training data, can we **completely** steal the training data from gradients? Conventional wisdom suggests that the answer is no, but we will show it is actually possible.

3   Training Data Leakage from Gradients

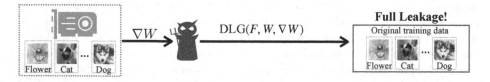

Fig. 6. Deep Leakage in federated settings. Given model updates/gradients received from victim, it aims to reserve the gradients and fully reconstructs the private training set.

While information leakage already intrudes participants' privacy in Federated Learning, we are curious about the limit of the leakage – can we completely reconstruct the private training set from shared information? Federated Learning aims to train a robust model without sharing data, but now knowing the gradients is knowing the data. This question is critical as it raises a serve challenge to the fundamental privacy assumption. In this section, we will study the challenge and demonstrate the potential risks brought by such leakage (Fig. 6).

3.1 Partial Leakage in Specific Layers

To begin with, we start with several special layers. The first one is *Fully Connected* (FC) layers. FC layers are widely used in both Neural Networks (NN) and Convolutional Neural Networks (CNN). For a biased FC layer, we can show that the corresponding input can be computed from the gradients regardless where the layer's position is and the types of preceding and succeeding layers.

Lemma 1. *Let a neural network contain a biased fully-connected layer, i.e. for the layer's input $X \in \mathbb{R}^n$, its output $Y \in \mathbb{R}^m$ is calculated as*

$$Y = WX + B \tag{1}$$

with weight $W \in \mathbb{R}^{m \times n}$ and bias $B \in \mathbb{R}^m$. The input X can reconstructed from $\frac{dL}{dW}$ and $\frac{dL}{dB}$ if there exists index i s.t. $\frac{dL}{d(B_i)} \neq 0$.

Proof 1. It is know that $\frac{dL}{d(B_i)} = \frac{dL}{dY_i} \frac{d(Y_i)}{d(W_i)} = X^T$. Therefore

$$\frac{dL}{d(W_i)} = \frac{dL}{d(Y_i)} \cdot \frac{d(Y_i)}{d(W_i)} = \frac{dL}{d(B_i)} \cdot X^T \tag{2}$$

where the Y_i, W_i and B_i denote the ith row of output Y, weights W and biases B. Thus X can be reconstructed as long as $\frac{dL}{d(B_i)} \neq 0$. $\square$

The knowledge of the derivative w.r.t. the bias $\frac{dL}{dB}$ is essential for reconstructing the layer's input. To make the leakage more general, Geiping *et al.* [12] further proved that even without biases, the input could also be reconstructed as long as a proper activation follows (e.g., ReLU). The proof procedure is similar and no optimization is required to reconstruct the training set from a fully connected network.

Even without inverting the derivatives, the gradients from some layers already indicate certain information about the input data. For example, the *Embedding* layer in language tasks only produces gradients for words appeared in the data, which reveals what words have been used in other participant's training set [7]. Another example is the *Cross Entropy* layers in classification tasks, which only generate negative gradients for class marked as corrected in the training set [13]. This property implies what the ground truth label is.

However, it is not trivial to extend to *Convolution* layers (CONV), where the dimension of features is far larger than the size of gradients. The analytical reconstruction like Lemma 1 is no longer practical. A more general attack algorithm is required for modern convolutional neural networks.

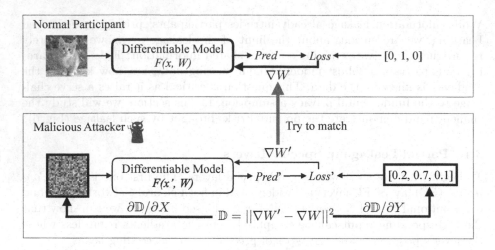

Fig. 7. The overview of DLG algorithm. Variables to be updated are marked with a bold border. While normal participants calculate ∇W to update parameter using its private training set, the malicious attacker updates its dummy inputs and labels to minimize the gradients distance. When the optimization finishes, the evil user is able to steal the training set from honest participants.

3.2 Complete Leakage from Gradients

To overcome the limitation, Zhu *et al.* [14] proposes an iterative method to **fully** reconstruct the training set, which was meant to be local and private, by only intercepting the corresponding gradients on the same neural network. The technique is named as *Deep Leakage from Gradients* (DLG), because of the "deep" threat it raises to user data's privacy.

DLG is a gradient-based feature reconstruction attack. The attacker receives the gradient update $\nabla W_{t,k}$ from other participant k at round t, and aims to steal participant k's training set $(\mathbf{x}_{t,k}, \mathbf{y}_{t,k})$ from the shared the information. Figure 7 presents how it works for federated learning on images: The algorithm first initializes a dummy image with the same resolution as real one's and a dummy label with probability representation followed by a softmax layer. DLG runs a test of this attack on the intermediate local model to compute "dummy" gradients. Note the model architecture $F()$ and weights W_t are shared by default for most federated learning applications.

Then a gradient distance loss between dummy gradients and real ones is calculated as the optimization objective. The key point of this reconstruction attack is to iteratively refine the dummy image and label so that the attacker's dummy gradients will approximate the actual gradients. When the gradient construction loss is minimized, the dummy data will also convergence to the training data with high confidence (examples shown in Sect. 3.3).

$$\mathbf{x}'^{*}, \mathbf{y}'^{*} = \arg\min_{\mathbf{x}',\mathbf{y}'} ||\nabla W' - \nabla W||^2 = \arg\min_{\mathbf{x}',\mathbf{y}'} ||\frac{\partial \ell(F(\mathbf{x}', W), \mathbf{y}')}{\partial W} - \nabla W||^2 \quad (3)$$

Algorithm 1. Deep Leakage from Gradients for Masked Language Model

Input: $F()$: Differentiable machine learning model; W: parameter weights; ∇W: gradients calculated by training data; η: learning rate used for DLG optimization.

Output: the original private training data $\mathbf{x}$ and label $\mathbf{y}$

1: **procedure** DLG(F, W, ∇W)
2:    $\mathbf{x}'_1 \leftarrow \mathcal{N}(0,1)$, $\mathbf{y}'_1 \leftarrow \mathcal{N}(0,1)$ ▷ Initialize dummy inputs and labels.
3:    **for** $i \leftarrow 1$ to n **do**
4:       $\mathbf{L}'_i = softmax(\mathbf{y}'_i)$
5:       $\nabla W'_i \leftarrow \partial \ell(F(\mathbf{x}'_i, W), \mathbf{L}'_i)/\partial W_t$ ▷ Compute dummy gradients.
6:       $\mathbb{D}_i \leftarrow ||\nabla W'_i - \nabla W||^2$
7:       $\mathbf{x}'_{i+1} \leftarrow \mathbf{x}'_i - \eta \nabla_{\mathbf{x}'_i} \mathbb{D}_i$ ▷ Update data to match gradients.
8:       $\mathbf{y}'_{i+1} \leftarrow \mathbf{y}'_i - \eta \nabla_{\mathbf{y}'_i} \mathbb{D}_i$ ▷ Update label to match gradients.
9:    **end for**
10:    **return** $\mathbf{x}'_{n+1}, \mathbf{y}'_{n+1}$
11: **end procedure**

Note that the distance $||\nabla W' - \nabla W||^2$ is differentiable w.r.t dummy inputs $\mathbf{x}'$ and labels $\mathbf{y}'$ can thus be optimized using standard gradient-based methods. Therefore this optimization requires 2nd order derivatives. A mild assumption that F is twice differentiable is made here. This holds for the majority of modern machine learning models (e.g., most neural networks) and tasks.

Iters=0 Iters=10 Iters=50 Iters=100 Iters=500 | Melis [7] | Ground Truth

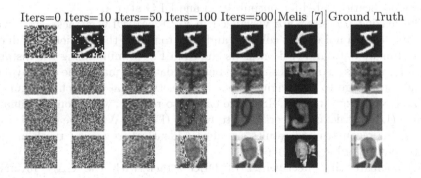

Fig. 8. The visualization showing the deep leakage on images from MNIST [15], CIFAR-100 [16], SVHN [17] and LFW [9] respectively. Our algorithm fully recovers the four images while previous work only succeeds on simple images with clean backgrounds.

3.3 DLG Attack on Image Classification

Given an image containing objects, images classification aims to determine the class of the item. The power of DLG attack is first evaluated on modern CNN architectures ResNet [18] and pictures from MNIST [15], CIFAR-100 [16], SVHN [17] and LFW [9]. Note that two changes have been made here: (1)

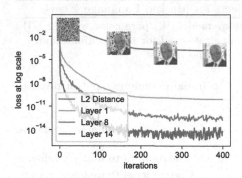
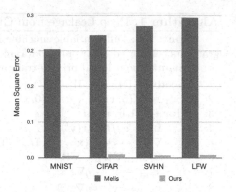

Fig. 9. Layer-i means MSE between real and dummy gradients of ith layer. When the gradients' distance gets smaller, the MSE between leaked image and the original image also gets smaller.

Fig. 10. Compassion of the MSE of images leaked by different algorithms and the ground truth. DLG method consistently outperforms previous approach by a large margin.

For model architecture, all ReLU operators are replaced with Sigmoid and the strides in CONV are removed, as our algorithm requires the model to be twice-differentiable (2) For image labels, instead of directly optimizing the discrete categorical values, we random initialize a vector with shape $N \times C$ where N is the batch size and C is the number of classes, and then take its softmax output as the classification label for optimization and DLG attack.

The leaking processes are visualized in Fig. 8. All DLG attacks start with random Gaussian noise (first column) and tried to match the gradients produced by the dummy data and real ones. As shown in Fig. 9, minimizing the distance between gradients also reduces the gap between data and makes the dummy data gradually converge to the original one. It is observed that monochrome images with a clean background (MNIST) are easiest to recover, while complex images like face (LFW) take more iterations to recover (Fig. 8). When the optimization finishes, the reconstructed results are almost identical to ground truth images, despite few negligible artifact pixels.

We compare the effectiveness of DLG attack with the GAN Inversion results [7] (discussed in Sect. 2) in Fig. 8 (visually) and Fig. 10 (numerically). The previous GAN based inversion requires the class label to be known and only works well on MNIST. On the 3rd row and 6th column of Fig. 8, though the revealed image on SVHN is still visually recognizable as digit "9", it is far different from the original training image. The cases are even worse on LFW and totally collapse on CIFAR. Figure 10 shows a numerical comparison by performing leaking and measuring the mean square error (MSE) on all dataset images. Images are normalized to the range $[0, 1]$ and DLG appears much better results (<0.03 v.s. previous >0.2) on all four datasets.

3.4   DLG Attack on Masked Language Model

Table 1. The progress of deep leakage on language tasks.

	Example 1	Example 2	Example 3
Initial Sentence	tilting fill given **less word **itude fine **nton overheard living vegas **vac **vation *f forte **dis cerambycidae ellison **don yards marne **kali	toni **enting asbestos cutler km nail **oof **dation **ori righteous **xie lucan **hot **ery at **tle ordered pa **eit smashing proto	[MASK] **ry toppled **wled major relief dive displaced **lice [CLS] us apps _ **face **bet
Iters = 10	tilting fill given **less full solicitor other ligue shrill living vegas rider treatment carry played sculptures lifelong ellison net yards marne **kali	toni **enting asbestos cutter km nail undefeated **dation hole righteous **xie lucan **hot **ery at **tle ordered pa **eit smashing proto	[MASK] **ry toppled identified major relief gin dive displaced **lice doll us apps _ **face space
Iters = 20	registration, volunteer applications, at student travel application open the; week of played; child care will be glare	we welcome proposals for tutor **ials on either core machine denver softly or topics of emerging importance for machine learning	one **ry toppled hold major ritual ' dive annual conference days 1924 apps novelist dude space
Iters = 30	registration, volunteer applications, and student travel application open the first week of september. Child care will be available	we welcome proposals for tutor **ials on either core machine learning topics or topics of emerging importance for machine learning	we invite submissions for the thirty - third annual conference on neural information processing systems
Original Text	Registration, volunteer applications, and student travel application open the first week of September. Child care will be available	We welcome proposals for tutorials on either core machine learning topics or topics of emerging importance for machine learning	We invite submissions for the Thirty-Third Annual Conference on Neural Information Processing Systems

For language tasks, DLG is evaluated on Masked Language Model (MLM) task. In each sequence, 15% of the words are replaced with a [MASK] token and MLM model attempts to predict the original value of the masked words from a given context. BERT [19] is chosen as the backbone and all hyperparameters are adopted from the official implementation[1].

Different from vision tasks where RGB inputs are continuous values, language models need to preprocess discrete words into embeddings. Therefore, on language model DLG attack is applied on embedding space and the gradients distance between dummy embeddings and real ones is minimized. After optimization finishes, the original words are derived by finding the closest entry in the embedding matrix reversely.

Table 1 exhibits the leaking history on three sentences selected from NeurIPS conference page. Similar to the vision task, DLG attack starts with randomly initialized embedding: The reconstructed results at iteration 0 is meaningless. During the optimization, the gradients produced by dummy embedding gradually match the original data's gradients and the dummy embeddings also converges to the original data's embeddings. In later iterations, part of the original sequence appears. In example 3, at iteration 20, "annual conference" shows up at iteration 30 and the leaked sentence is already close to the original one. When DLG finishes, though there are few mismatches caused by the ambiguity in tokenizing, the main content is already fully leaked.

3.5   Extensions to DLG Attack

In Algorithm 1, many factors can affect the leakage results such as the data initialization (line 2), the distance measurement between two gradients (line 6), and the optimization method (line 7 & 8). Besides these, hyper-parameters in Federated Learning like batch size and local steps also matters. In some cases, DLG may fail to reveal (e.g., with a bad initialization). To improve the stability of DLG, several approaches have been explored.

Leakage of Label Information on Classification Tasks. DLG attack is based on the belief that there is a one-to-one mapping between gradients and training data. Therefore if DLG does not discover the ground truth data, the attack will fail to converge. For tasks with cross entropy loss, Zhao *et al.* [13] proposes an analytical solution to extract the ground-truth labels from the shared gradients. When the differentiable model is trained with one-hot supervisions, the loss is computed as

$$L(X, c) = -\log \frac{e^{Y_c}}{\sum_j e^{Y_j}} \tag{4}$$

where the corresponding derivative is

$$g_i = \frac{\partial L(X, c)}{\partial Y_i} = \begin{cases} -1 + \frac{e^{Y_i}}{\sum_j e^{Y_j}}, & \text{if } i = c \\ \frac{e^{Y_i}}{\sum_j e^{Y_j}}, & \text{else} \end{cases} \tag{5}$$

---

[1] https://github.com/google-research/bert.

It is known that the softmax probability $e^{Y_c}/\sum_j e^{Y_j} \in (0,1)$. Therefore, only the index with ground truth label yields negative gradients

$$g_i \in \begin{cases} (-1,0) & \text{if } i = c \\ (0,1) & \text{else} \end{cases} \tag{6}$$

Through the observation, the ground truth label can directly obtained and the leakage process becomes more stable and efficient with the extracted label.

Choices of Gradient Distances Loss. In the original DLG algorithm, the reconstruction optimizes the euclidean distances (also known as mean squared error) between two gradients via L-BFGS optimizer.

$$\arg\min_{x \in [0,1]^n} \| \nabla_w F(x,y;w) - \nabla_w F(x*,y;w) \|_2^2 \tag{7}$$

where $x*$ indicates the original training input. Note that here the label y is assumed known via the trick introduced above. Geiping *et al.* [12] suggests that the magnitude appears not to be an important factor. Instead, the direction of gradients matters more during the leaking process. They propose to reconstruct based on cosine similarity $l(x,y) = \frac{<x,y>}{||x||||y||}$ and the optimization objective becomes

$$\arg\min_{x \in [0,1]^n} 1 - \frac{< \nabla_w F(x,y;w), \nabla_w F(x*,y;w) >}{||\nabla_w F(x,y;w)|| \nabla_w || F(x*,y;w)||} + \alpha TV(x) \tag{8}$$

The term $TV(x)$ is a simple image prior *total variation* [20]. They include this as an extra regularization to ensure the leaked results is realistic. Figure 11 shows

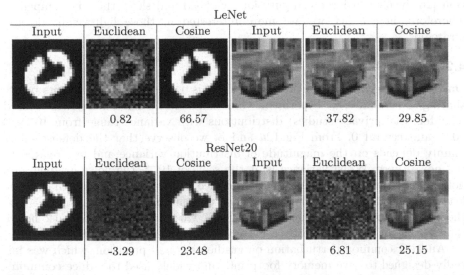

Fig. 11. Comparison between euclidean distance and cosine similarity on MNIST [15] (*Left*) and LFW [9] (*Right*) datasets. The number shown below the Figure is the PSNR (the larger the better).

the comparison between two losses. The proposed objective (Eq. 8) performs better especially complex CNN architectures.

Different Initialization. Wei *et al.* [21] analyzes the convergence of DLG on a single layer neural network, and proves that the convergence rate is $O(\frac{\|X_0 - X^*\|_2^2}{T})$, where T is the attack iterations. According to the results, the attack speed is closely related to the initialization of x_0. The default way to initialize dummy data is to sample from a uniform distribution. Though such initialization works in most scenarios [12–14], it is not optimal and sometimes may fail to converge. To address the issue, they study various initialization. The ideal initialization is to use a natural image from the same classes as the private training set. Though this initialization requires the least iterations to converge, it needs extra prior about user data, which may not always be available. As an alternative, the geometric initialization [22] is a more general approach to boost up the attack.

4 Defense Strategies

4.1 Cryptology

Cryptology can be applied to prevent the leakage: Bonawitz *et al.* [23] designs a secure aggregation protocol and Phong *et al.* [24] proposes to encrypt the gradients before sending. Among all defenses, cryptology is the most secure one and can perfectly defend the leakage in theory. However, most cryptology-based defense strategies have their limitations. Secure aggregation [23] requires gradients to be integers thus not compatible with most CNNs, secure outsourcing computation [25] only supports limited operations, and homomorphic encryption [26] involves a large computation overhead and slows the whole pipeline. Therefore, in practice we are more interested in those lightweight defense strategies.

4.2 Noisy Gradients

One straightforward attempt to defend DLG is to add noise on gradients before sharing. To evaluate, we experiment Gaussian and Laplacian noise (widely used in differential privacy studies) distributions with variance range from 10^{-1} to 10^{-4} and central 0. From Fig. 12a and b, we observe that the defense effect mainly depends on the magnitude of distribution variance and less related to the noise types. When variance is at the scale of 10^{-4}, the noisy gradients do not prevent the leak. For noise with variance 10^{-3}, though with artifacts, the leakage can still be performed. Only when the variance is larger than 10^{-2} and the noise is starting affect the accuracy, DLG will fail to execute. We also notice that Laplacian tends to slightly a better defense when both at scale 10^{-3}.

Another common perturbation on gradients is half precision, which was initially designed to save memory footprints and widely used to reduce communication bandwidth. We test two popular half precision implementations IEEE float16 (*Single-precision floating-point format*) and bfloat16 (*Brain Floating Point* [27], a truncated version of 32 bit float). Shown in Fig. 12c, unfortunately, neither half precision format is able to protect the training data.

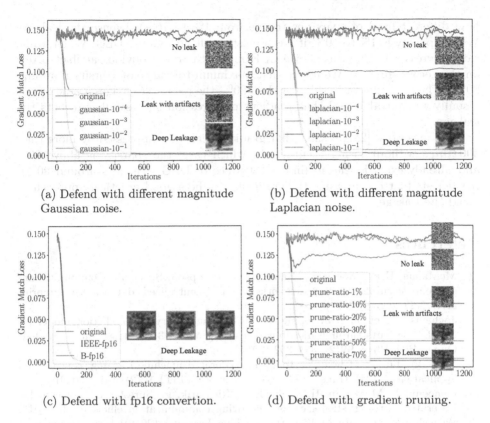

(a) Defend with different magnitude Gaussian noise.

(b) Defend with different magnitude Laplacian noise.

(c) Defend with fp16 convertion.

(d) Defend with gradient pruning.

Fig. 12. The effectiveness of various defense strategies. The corresponding accuracy is attached in Table 2.

Table 2. The trade-off between accuracy and defendability. **G**: Gaussian noise, **L**: Laplacian noise, **FP**: Floating number, **Int**: Integer quantization. ✓ means it successfully defends against DLG while ✗ means fails to defend (whether the results are visually recognizable). The accuracy is evaluated on CIFAR-100.

	Original	G-10^{-4}	G-10^{-3}	G-10^{-2}	G-10^{-1}	FP-16
Accuracy	76.3%	75.6%	73.3%	45.3%	≤1%	76.1%
Defendability	–	✗	✗	✓	✓	✗
		L-10^{-4}	L-10^{-3}	L-10^{-2}	L-10^{-1}	Int-8
Accuracy	–	75.6%	73.4%	46.2%	≤1%	53.7%
Defendability	–	✗	✗	✓	✓	✓

4.3   Gradient Compression and Sparsification

We also experimented to defend by gradient compression [28, 29]. Gradient compression prunes small gradients to zero, therefore it's more difficult for DLG to match the gradients since the optimization target also gets pruned. We evaluate how different level of sparsities (range from 1% to 70%) defense the leakage. When sparsity is 1% to 10%, it has almost no effects against DLG. When prune ratio increases to 20%, as shown in Fig. 12d, there are obvious artifact pixels on the recover images. We notice that maximum tolerance of sparsity if around 20%. When pruning ratio is larger than 20%, the recovered images are no longer visually recognizable and thus gradient compression successfully prevents the leakage.

Previous work [28,29] show that gradients can be compressed by more than 300 *times* without losing accuracy. In which case, the sparsity is above 99% and already exceeds the maximum tolerance of DLG (which is around 20%). It suggests that compressing the gradients can be a good practical approach to avoid the leakage.

References

1. McMahan, H.B., Moore, E., Ramage, D., Hampson, S., et al.: Communication-efficient learning of deep networks from decentralized data, arXiv preprint arXiv:1602.05629 (2016)
2. Jochems, A., et al.: Developing and validating a survival prediction model for NSCLC patients through distributed learning across 3 countries. Int. J. Radiat. Oncol. Biol. Phys. **99**(2), 344–352 (2017)
3. Yang, Q., Liu, Y., Chen, T., Tong, Y.: Federated machine learning: concept and applications. ACM Trans. Intell. Syst. Technol. (TIST) **10**(2), 1–19 (2019)
4. Konečný, J., McMahan, H.B., Yu, F.X., Richtarik, P., Suresh, A.T., Bacon, D.: Federated learning: strategies for improving communication efficiency. In: NIPS Workshop on Private Multi-Party Machine Learning (2016). https://arxiv.org/abs/1610.05492
5. Bonawitz, K., et al.: Towards federated learning at scale: system design. CoRR, vol. abs/1902.01046 (2019). http://arxiv.org/abs/1902.01046
6. Shokri, R., Stronati, M., Song, C., Shmatikov, V.: Membership inference attacks against machine learning models. In: 2017 IEEE Symposium on Security and Privacy (SP), pp. 3–18 IEEE (2017)
7. Melis, L., Song, C., Cristofaro, E.D., Shmatikov, V.: Exploiting unintended feature leakage in collaborative learning. CoRR, vol. abs/1805.04049 (2018). http://arxiv.org/abs/1805.04049
8. Yang, D., Zhang, D., Yu, Z., Yu, Z.: Fine-grained preference-aware location search leveraging crowdsourced digital footprints from LBSNs. In: Proceedings of the 2013 ACM International Joint Conference on Pervasive and Ubiquitous Computing, pp. 479–488 (2013)
9. Huang, G.B., Ramesh, M., Berg, T., Learned-Miller, E.: Labeled faces in the wild: a database for studying face recognition in unconstrained environments. University of Massachusetts, Amherst, Technical Report 07-49, October 2007
10. Fredrikson, M., Jha, S., Ristenpart, T.: Model inversion attacks that exploit confidence information and basic countermeasures. In: Proceedings of the 22nd ACM SIGSAC Conference on Computer and Communications Security, pp. 1322–1333. ACM (2015)
11. Goodfellow, I., et al.: Generative adversarial nets. In: Advances in Neural Information Processing Systems, pp. 2672–2680 (2014)

12. Geiping, J., Bauermeister, H., Dröge, H., Moeller, M.: Inverting gradients-how easy is it to break privacy in federated learning? arXiv preprint arXiv:2003.14053 (2020)
13. Zhao, B., Mopuri, K.R., Bilen, H.: iDLG: improved deep leakage from gradients. arXiv preprint arXiv:2001.02610 (2020)
14. Zhu, L., Liu, Z., Han, S.: Deep leakage from gradients. In: Annual Conference on Neural Information Processing Systems (NeurIPS) (2019)
15. LeCun, Y.: The mnist database of handwritten digits. http://yann.lecun.com/exdb/mnist/
16. Krizhevsky, A.: Learning multiple layers of features from tiny images. Citeseer, Technical report 2009
17. Netzer, Y., Wang, T., Coates, A., Bissacco, A., Wu, B., Ng, A.Y.: Reading digits in natural images with unsupervised feature learning (2011)
18. He, K., Zhang, X., Ren, S., Sun, J.: Deep residual learning for image recognition. In: Proceedings of the IEEE Conference on Computer Vision and Pattern Recognition, pp. 770–778 (2016)
19. Devlin, J., Chang, M., Lee, K., Toutanova, K.: BERT: pre-training of deep bidirectional transformers for language understanding. CoRR, vol. abs/1810.04805 (2018). http://arxiv.org/abs/1810.04805
20. Rudin, L.I., Osher, S., Fatemi, E.: Nonlinear total variation based noise removal algorithms. Phys. D Nonlinear Phenom. **60**(1–4), 259–268 (1992)
21. Wei, W., et al.: A framework for evaluating gradient leakage attacks in federated learning. arXiv preprint arXiv:2004.10397 (2020)
22. Rossi, F., Gégout, C.: Geometrical initialization, parametrization and control of multilayer perceptrons: application to function approximation. In: Proceedings of 1994 IEEE International Conference on Neural Networks (ICNN 1994), vol. 1, pp. 546–550. IEEE (1994)
23. Bonawitz, K., et al.: Practical secure aggregation for federated learning on user-held data. CoRR, vol. abs/1611.04482 (2016). http://arxiv.org/abs/1611.04482
24. Phong, L.T., Aono, Y., Hayashi, T., Wang, L., Moriai, S.: Privacy-preserving deep learning via additively homomorphic encryption. IEEE Trans. Inf. Forensics Secur. **13**(5), 1333–1345 (2018)
25. Hohenberger, S., Lysyanskaya, A.: How to securely outsource cryptographic computations. In: Kilian, J. (ed.) TCC 2005. LNCS, vol. 3378, pp. 264–282. Springer, Heidelberg (2005). https://doi.org/10.1007/978-3-540-30576-7_15
26. Armknecht, F.. et al.: A guide to fully homomorphic encryption, Cryptology ePrint Archive, Report 2015/1192 (2015). https://eprint.iacr.org/2015/1192
27. Tagliavini, G., Mach, S., Rossi, D., Marongiu, A., Benini, L.: A transprecision floating-point platform for ultra-low power computing. CoRR, vol. abs/1711.10374 (2017). http://arxiv.org/abs/1711.10374
28. Lin, Y., Han, S., Mao, H., Wang, Y., Dally, W.J.: Deep gradient compression: reducing the communication bandwidth for distributed training. arXiv preprint arXiv:1712.01887 (2017)
29. Tsuzuku, Y., Imachi, H., Akiba, T.: Variance-based gradient compression for efficient distributed deep learning. arXiv preprint arXiv:1802.06058 (2018)

Rethinking Privacy Preserving Deep Learning: How to Evaluate and Thwart Privacy Attacks

Lixin Fan[1], Kam Woh Ng[1], Ce Ju[1], Tianyu Zhang[1], Chang Liu[1], Chee Seng Chan[2], and Qiang Yang[1,3(✉)]

[1] WeBank, Shenzhen, China
[2] Center of Image and Signal Processing, Faculty of Computer Science and Information Technology, University of Malaya, Kuala Lumpur, Malaysia
[3] Department of Computer Science and Engineering, HKUST, Kowloon, Hong Kong
qyang@cse.ust.hk

Abstract. This chapter investigates capabilities of Privacy-Preserving Deep Learning (PPDL) mechanisms against various forms of privacy attacks. First, we propose to quantitatively measure the trade-off between model accuracy and privacy losses incurred by *reconstruction, tracing and membership attacks*. Second, a novel Secret Polarization Network (SPN) is proposed to thwart privacy attacks, which is highly competitive against existing PPDL methods. Extensive experiments showed that model accuracies are improved on average by 5–20% compared with baseline mechanisms, in regimes where data privacy are satisfactorily protected.

Keywords: Federated learning · Differential privacy · Privacy attack

1 Introduction

Federated learning aims to collaboratively train and share a deep neural network model among multiple participants, without exposing to each other information about their private training data. This is particularly attractive to business scenarios in which raw data e.g. medical records or bank transactions are too sensitive and valuable to be disclosed to other parties [14,23]. *Differential privacy* e.g. [1,18] has attracted much attentions due to its theoretical guarantee of privacy protection and low computational complexity [4,5], however, there is a fundamental trade-off between *privacy guarantee* vs *utility* of learned models, i.e. overly conservative privacy protections often significantly deteriorate model utilities (*accuracies* for classification models). Existing solutions e.g. [1,18] are unsatisfactory in our view—low ϵ privacy budget value does not necessarily lead to desired levels of privacy protection. For instance, the leakage of shared gradients may admit complete reconstruction of training data under certain circumstances [10,21,22,24], even though substantial fraction of gradients elements are truncated [18] or large random noise are added [1].

© Springer Nature Switzerland AG 2020
Q. Yang et al. (Eds.): Federated Learning, LNAI 12500, pp. 32–50, 2020.
https://doi.org/10.1007/978-3-030-63076-8_3

In order to make critical analysis and fair evaluations of different privacy preserving (PP) algorithms, we argue that one must employ an *objective* evaluation protocol to quantitatively measure privacy preserving capabilities against various forms of privacy attacks. Following a privacy adversary approach [6,15], we propose to evaluate the admitted privacy loss by three objective measures i.e. *reconstruction*, *tracing* and *membership* losses, with respect to the accuracies of protected models. To this end, Privacy-Preserving Characteristic (PPC) curves are used to delineate the trade-off, with Calibrated Averaged Performance (CAP) faithfully quantifying a given PPC curve. These empirical measures complement the theoretical bound of the privacy loss and constitute the first contribution of our work (see Fig. 5 for example PPC).

As demonstrated by experimental results in Sect. 4, the leakage of shared gradients poses serious challenges to existing PP methods [1,18,24]. Our second contribution, therefore, is a novel *secret polarization network* (SPN) and a polarization loss term, which bring about two advantages in tandem with public backbone networks—first, SPN helps to defeat privacy attacks by adding *secret, element-wise and adaptive* gradients to shared gradients; second, the added polarization loss acts as a regularization term to consistently improve the classification accuracies of baseline networks in federated learning settings. This SPN based mechanism has demonstrated strong capability to thwart three types of privacy attacks without significant deterioration of model accuracies. As summarized by CAP values in Fig. 1, SPN compares favorably with existing solutions [18] and [1] with pronounced improvements of performances against reconstruction, membership and tracing attacks.

1.1 Related Work

[1] demonstrated how to maintain data privacy by adding Gaussian noise to shared gradients during the training of deep neural networks. [18] proposed to randomly select and share a small fraction of gradient elements (those with large magnitudes) to reduce privacy loss. Although both methods [1,18] offered strong *differential privacy* (DP) guarantees [4,5], as shown by [15,24] and our empirical studies, pixel-level reconstructions of training data and disclosing of membership information raise serious concerns about potential privacy loss.

Dwork et al. [6] have formulated privacy attacks towards a database, as a series of queries maliciously chosen according to an attack strategy designed to compromise privacy. Among three privacy attacks i.e. *reconstruction*, *tracing* and *re-identification* discussed in [6], the detrimental reconstruction attack is formulated as solving a noisy system of linear equations, and reconstruction errors are essentially bounded by the worst-case accuracies of query answers (Theorem 1 in [6]). However, this formulation is not directly applicable to deep learning, since queries about private training data are not explicitly answered during the training or inferencing of DNNs.

In the context of deep learning, membership attacks was investigated in [19] while [9] demonstrated that recognizable face images can be recovered from confidence values revealed along with predictions. [15] demonstrated with both CNNs

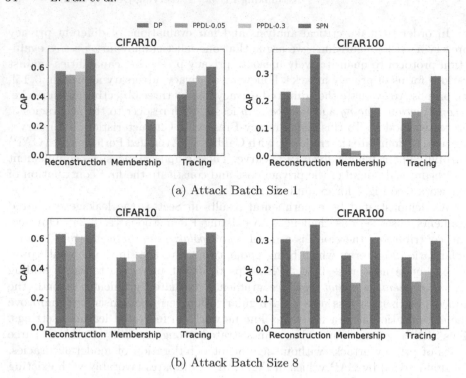

(a) Attack Batch Size 1

(b) Attack Batch Size 8

Fig. 1. Comparison of Calibrated Averaged Performances (CAPs) for the proposed SPN, PPDL [18] and DP [1] methods, against reconstruction, membership and tracing attacks (CAP the higher the better, see threat model and evaluation protocol in Sect. 2.1). (a): CIFAR10/100 models attacked with batch size 1; (b): CIFAR10/100 models attacked with batch size 8.

and RNNs that periodical gradient updates during training leaked information about *training data, features* as well as class *memberships*. Possible defences such as selective gradient sharing, reducing dimensionality, and dropout were proved to be ineffective or had a negative impact on the quality of the collaboratively trained model. Based on the assumption that activation functions are twice-differentiable, recent attacks were proposed to reconstruct training data with pixel-level accuracies [10,21,22,24]. These recent reconstruction attacks were adopted in the present work to evaluate capabilities of privacy-preserving strategies proposed in [1,15,18,24], with extensive experiments conducted over different networks and datasets (see Sect. 4).

Homomorphic-Encryption (HE) based [2,11,12] and Secure Multi-Party Computation (MPC) based privacy-preserving approaches [16,17] demonstrated strong privacy protection via encryption, but often incur significantly more demanding computational and communication costs. For instance, [2] reported 2–3 times communication overheads and [3,16] had to speed up highly-intensive computation with efficient implementations. In this chapter our work is only

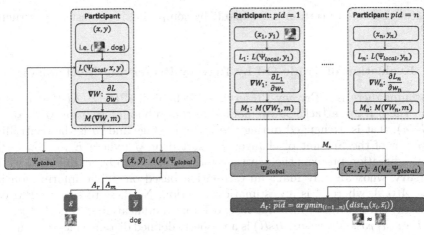

(a) **Reconstruction attacks** $\mathcal{A}_r$, with relative MSE between reconstructed and original data $\frac{\|\bar{x}-x\|}{\|x\|}$. **Membership attacks** $\mathcal{A}_m$, with categorical distance between reconstructed and original labels $dist_m(\bar{y},y)$.

(b) **Tracing attacks** $\mathcal{A}_t$, with categorical distance between recovered and actual participant IDs $dist_m(\overline{pid},p)$.

Fig. 2. Three privacy attacks considered in this chapter (see text in Sect. 2).

compared with Differential Privacy based mechanisms [1,18], and we refer readers to [20,23] for thorough reviews of HE and MPC based privacy-preserving methods therein.

2 Threat Model: Privacy Attacks on Training Data

In this chapter we consider a distributed learning scenario, in which $K(K \geq 2)$ participants collaboratively learn a multi-layered deep learning model without exposing their private training data (this setting is also known as *federated learning* [14,23]). We assume one participant is the *honest-but-curious adversary*. The adversary is honest in the sense that he/she faithfully follows the collaborative learning protocol and does not submit any malformed messages, but he/she may launch privacy attacks on the *training data* of other participants, by analyzing periodic updates to the joint model (e.g. *gradients*) during training.

Figure 2 illustrates three privacy attacks considered in this chapter. The goal of *reconstruction attack* is to recover original training data x as accurate as possible by analyzing the publicly shared gradients, which might be perturbed by privacy-preserving mechanisms. Subsequent *membership attack* and *tracing attack* are based on reconstruction attacks—for the former, membership labels are derived either directly during the reconstruction stage or by classifying reconstructed data; for the latter, the goal is to determine whether a given training data item belongs to certain participant, by comparing it against reconstructed data[1].

2.1   Evaluation of Trade-Off by Privacy Preserving Mechanism

We assume there is a Privacy-Preserving Mechanism (PPM)[2] $\mathcal{M}$ that aims to defeat the privacy attacks $\mathcal{A}$ by modifying the public information $\mathcal{G}$ to $\bar{\mathcal{G}}_m = \mathcal{M}(\mathcal{G}, m)$, that is exchanged during the learning stage and m is the controlling parameter of the amount of changes E exerted on $\mathcal{G}$ (where $E_m = \bar{\mathcal{G}}_m - \mathcal{G}$). This modification protects the private information x from being disclosed to the adversary, who can only make an estimation based on public information i.e. $\bar{x}_m = \mathcal{A}(\bar{\mathcal{G}}_m)$, where $\mathcal{A}$ is an estimation function. Needless to say, a PPM can defeat any adversaries by introducing exorbitant modification so that $dist(\bar{x}_m, x)$ is as large as possible, where $dist()$ is a properly defined distance measure such as MSE. The modification of public information, however, inevitably deteriorates the performances of global models i.e. $Acc(\bar{\mathcal{G}}_m) \leq Acc(\mathcal{G}_m)$, where $Acc()$ denotes model performances such as accuracies or any other metrics that is relevant to the model task in question. A well-designed PPM is expected to have $Acc(\bar{\mathcal{G}}_m)$ as high as possible.

We propose to plot Privacy Preserving Characteristic (PPC) to illustrate the trade-off between two opposing goals i.e. to maintain high model accuracies and low privacy losses as follows,

Definition 1 *(Privacy Preserving Characteristic). For a given Privacy-Preserving Mechanism $\mathcal{M}$, its privacy loss and performance trade-off is delineated by a set of calibrated performances i.e. $\{Acc(\bar{\mathcal{G}}_m) \cdot dist(\bar{x}_m, x) | m \in \{m_1, \cdots, m_n\}\}$, where $Acc()$ is the model performance, $dist()$ a distance measure, $\bar{\mathcal{G}}_m = \mathcal{M}(\mathcal{G}, m)$ is the modified public information, x is the private data, $\bar{x}_m = \mathcal{A}(\bar{\mathcal{G}}_m)$ is the estimation of private data by the attack and m the controlling parameter of the mechanism.*

Moreover, Calibrated Averaged Performance (CAP) for a given PPC is defined as follows,

$$CAP(\mathcal{M}, \mathcal{A}) = \frac{1}{n} \sum_{m=m_1}^{m_n} Acc(\bar{\mathcal{G}}_m) \cdot dist(\bar{x}_m, x). \tag{1}$$

Figure 5 illustrates example PPCs of different mechanisms against privacy attacks. CAP can be defined as area under a PPC. One may also quantitatively summarize PPCs with CAP—*the higher the CAP value is, the better the mechanism is at preserving privacy without compromising the model performances* (see Table 1).

---

[1] Note that membership inference in [15] is the tracing attack considered in our work.
[2] We do not restrict ourselves to privacy mechanisms considered by differential privacy[1,4,5,18].

2.2 Formulation of Reconstruction Attack

Consider a neural network $\Psi(x; w, b) : \mathcal{X} \to \mathbb{R}^C$, where $x \in \mathcal{X}$, w and b are the weights and biases of neural networks, and C is the output dimension. In a machine learning task, we optimize the parameters w and b of neural network Ψ with a loss function $\mathcal{L}(\Psi(x; w, b), y)$, where x is the input data and y is the ground truth labels. We denote the superscript $w^{[i]}$ and $b^{[i]}$ as the i-th layer weights and biases. The following theorem proves that the reconstruction of input x exists under certain conditions (proofs are given in Appendix A 5).

Theorem 1. *Suppose a multilayer neural network* $\Psi := \Psi^{[L-1]} \circ \Psi^{[L-2]} \circ \cdots \circ \Psi^{[0]}(\cdot\,; w, b)$ *is* C^1, *where the i-th layer* $\Psi^{[i]}$ *is a fully-connected layer[3] Then,* **initial input** x^* **of** Ψ **exists***, provided that: if there is an i $(1 \leq i \leq L)$ such that*

1. *Jacobian matrix* $D_x(\Psi^{[i-1]} \circ \Psi^{[i-1]} \circ \cdots \circ \Psi^{[0]})$ *around x is full-rank;*
2. *Partial derivative* $\nabla_{b^{[i]}} \mathcal{L}(\Psi(x; w, b), y)$[4] *is nonsingular.*

If assumptions in Theorem 1 are met, we can pick an index set I from row index set of $\nabla_{w^{[i]}, b^{[i]}} \mathcal{L}(\Psi(x; w, b), y)$ such that the following linear equation is well-posed,

$$B_I \cdot x = W_I,$$

where $B_I := \nabla^I_{b^{[i]}} \mathcal{L}(\Psi(x; w, b), y)$ and $W_I := \nabla^I_{w^{[i]}} \mathcal{L}(\Psi(x; w, b), y)$. According to Theorem 1, the initial input x^* is $(\Psi^{[i-1]} \circ \Psi^{[i-1]} \circ \cdots \circ \Psi^{[0]})^{-1}(x)$.

The linear system can be composed from any subsets of observed gradients elements, and the reconstruction solution exists as long as the condition of full rank matrix is fulfilled. For common privacy-preserving strategies adopted in a distributed learning scenario such as *sharing fewer gradients* or *adding noisy to shared gradients* [1,15,18], the following theorem proves that input x can be reconstructed from such a noisy linear system, if condition (2) is fulfilled.

Theorem 2. *Suppose there are perturbations* E_B, E_W *added on* B_I, W_I, *respectively, such that observed measurements* $\bar{B}_I = B_I + E_B, \bar{W}_I = W_I + E_W$. *Then, the* **reconstruction** x^* **of the initial input** x **can be determined** *by solving a noisy linear system* $\bar{B}_I \cdot x^* = \bar{W}_I$, *provided that*

$$\|B_I^{-1} \cdot E_B\| < 1; \tag{2}$$

Moreover, the relative error is bounded,

$$\frac{\|x^* - x\|}{\|x\|} \leq \frac{\kappa(B_I)}{1 - \|B_I^{-1} \cdot E_B\|} \left(\frac{\|E_B\|}{\|B_I\|} + \frac{\|E_W\|}{\|W_I\|} \right), \tag{3}$$

in which B_I^{-1} is the inverse of B_I and condition number $\kappa(B_I) := \|B_I\| \cdot \|B_I^{-1}\|$.

---

[3] Any convolution layers can be converted into a fully-connected layer by simply stacking together spatially shifted convolution kernels (see proofs in Appendix A).

[4] We write the partial derivative as a diagonal matrix that each two adjacent diagonal entries in an order are two copies of each entry in $\nabla_{b^{[i]}} \mathcal{L}(\Psi(x; w, b), y)$, see proofs in Appendix A.

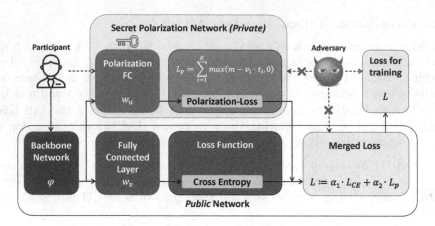

Fig. 3. Our proposed SPN architecture that consists of a public and a private network (see text in Sect. 3).

In the deep leakage approach [24], the recovery of initial image requires model parameters $\mathcal{W}$ and the corresponding gradients $\nabla\mathcal{W}$ such that a minimization of gradient differences $E_p := \|\nabla\mathcal{W}' - \nabla\mathcal{W}\|$ yields a recovery $\bar{x}$ of initial image. The minimizing error E_p introduces more errors to the noisy linear system. Therefore, for any iterative reconstruction algorithms like [24] to be successful, condition $\|B_I^{-1} \cdot E_B\| < 1$ is *necessary*. In other words, a sufficiently large perturbation $\|E_B\| > \|B_I\|$ such as Gaussian noise is *guaranteed* to defeat reconstruction attacks. To our best knowledge, (2) is the first analysis that elucidates a theoretical guarantee for thwarting reconstruction attacks like [24]. Nevertheless, existing mechanisms [1,18] have to put up with significant drops in model accuracy incurred by high levels of added noise (see Sect. 4.2).

3 Privacy Preserving with Secret Polarization Network

In [8] proved that *the reconstruction attack will not be successful if sufficiently large perturbations $\mathcal{M}(\mathcal{G}, m)$ are added to gradient $\mathcal{G}$.* We illustrate in this section a novel multi-task dual-headed networks, which leverages private network parameters and element-wise adaptive gradient perturbations to defeat reconstruction attacks and, simultaneously, maintain high model accuracies.

3.1 Secret Perturbation of Gradients via Polarization Loss

Figure 3 illustrates a Secret Polarization Network (SPN), in which fully connected polarization layers are kept private with its *parameters not shared* during the distributed learning process.

Formally, the proposed dual-headed network consists of a public and a private SPN network based on a backbone network: $\Psi\big(\varphi(\,\cdot\,; w, b); w_u, b_u\big) \oplus$

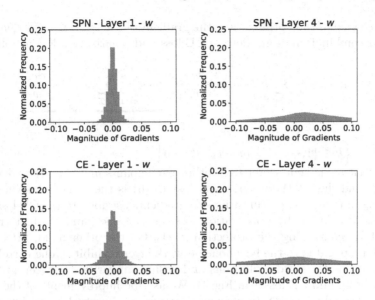

Fig. 4. Distributions of gradients at each layer. **Left:** distributions of gradients w.r.t. *weights, w* layer 1; **Right:** distributions of gradients w.r.t. *weights, w* at layer 4; **Top:** gradients by polarization loss; **Bottom:** gradients by CE loss. Cosine similarities between gradients by polarization and CE losses are (from left to right): -0.0033 and 0.1760 respectively.

$\Phi\big(\varphi(\,\cdot\,;w,b);w_v,b_v\big) : \mathcal{X} \to [0,1]^C \oplus \mathbb{R}^K$, i.e. $u \oplus v = \Psi\big(\varphi(x;w,b);w_u,b_u\big) \oplus \Phi\big(\varphi(x;w,b);w_v,b_v\big) \in [0,1]^C \oplus \mathbb{R}^K$, where $\varphi(\,\cdot\,;w,b)$ is the backbone network. The multi-task composite loss is as follows,

$$\mathcal{L}\big(\Psi \oplus \Phi, y \oplus t\big) := \alpha_1 \cdot \mathcal{L}_{CE}(u,y) + \alpha_2 \cdot \mathcal{L}_P(v,t) \tag{4}$$

$$= \alpha_1 \cdot \underbrace{\sum_{c=1}^{C} -y_c \cdot \log(u_c)}_{\text{CE loss}} + \alpha_2 \cdot \underbrace{\sum_{c=1}^{C}\sum_{k=1}^{K} \max(m - v_k \cdot t_c^k, 0)}_{\text{polarization loss}}, \tag{5}$$

where α_1 and α_2 are hyper-parameters with $\alpha_1 + \alpha_2 = 1$. y_c is an one-hot representation of labels for class c, and $t_c \in \{-1, +1\}^K$ is the target K-bits binary codes randomly assigned to each class c for $c = 1, \cdots, C$. Note that by minimizing the polarization loss [7], Hamming distances between threshold-ed outputs $Bin(v_k)$ of *intra-class* data items are minimized and, at the same time, Hamming distances are maximized for *inter-class* data items (where $Bin(v_k) \in \{-1, +1\}$, see proofs in [8]). The polarization loss therefore joints forces with the CE loss to improve the model accuracies.

At each step of the optimization, the gradient of the loss $\nabla_{w,b}\mathcal{L}(\Psi \oplus \Phi, y \oplus t)$ is a linear combination of gradient of CE loss and polarization loss as follows,

$$\nabla_{w,b}\mathcal{L} = \alpha_1 \cdot \sum_{c=1}^{C}(y_c - u_c) \cdot \frac{\partial u_c}{\partial w,b} + \underbrace{\alpha_2 \cdot \sum_{c=1}^{C}\sum_{k \in \mathcal{I}^c}(-t_c^k) \cdot \frac{\partial v_k}{\partial w,b}}_{\text{secret perturbation}}, \quad (6)$$

where $\mathcal{I}^c := \left\{ k \in \{1, \cdots, K\} \middle| m - v_k \cdot t_c^k > 0 \right\}$.

Note that w_v is kept secret from other participants including the adversary. The summand due to the polarization loss in (6) is therefore unknown to the adversaries, and acts as perturbations to gradients ascribed to the CE loss. Perturbations introduced by polarization loss, on the one hand, protect training data with α_2 controlling the protection levels. On the other hand, SPN gradients back-propagated to the backbone network layers exhibit strong correlations with CE gradients (see distributions and cosine similarities between gradients by polarization and CE losses in Fig. 4). We ascribe improvements of the model accuracies brought by SPN to element-wise adaptive perturbations introduced by polarization loss.

4   Experimental Results

4.1   Experiment Setup and Evaluation Metrics

Dataset. Popular image datasets MNIST and CIFAR10/100 are used in our experiments. Implementation of **DP** [1] method from Facebook Research Team[5] is used. Implementation[6] of **PPDL** [18] method from Torch/Lua are re-implemented in PyTorch/Python. PPDL is similar to gradient pruning which is one of the suggested protections in [24]. We only show in this chapter results with 5% and 30% of selected gradients, named respectively, as **PPDL-0.05** and **PPDL-0.3**. Implementation of **Deep Leakage** attack [24], network architecture and default setting from the official released source code[7] are used in all experiments with training batch size set as $\{1, 4, 8\}$ respectively. Following analysis in [22], we adopt *pattern-initialization* for higher reconstruction successful rates.

Relative Mean Square Error (rMSE) $(= \frac{||x^*-x||}{||x||})$ is used to measure the distances between reconstructed x^x and original data x. **Membership Distance** $(dist_m(y^*, y))$ is the *averaged categorical distances* between recovered data labels y^* and original labels y. **Tracing Distance** $(dist_t(x^*))$ is the *averaged categorical distances* between recovered participant IDs and original IDs, to which the reconstructed data x^* belongs.

---

[5] https://github.com/facebookresearch/pytorch-dp.
[6] https://www.comp.nus.edu.sg/~reza/files/PPDL.zip.
[7] https://github.com/mit-han-lab/dlg.

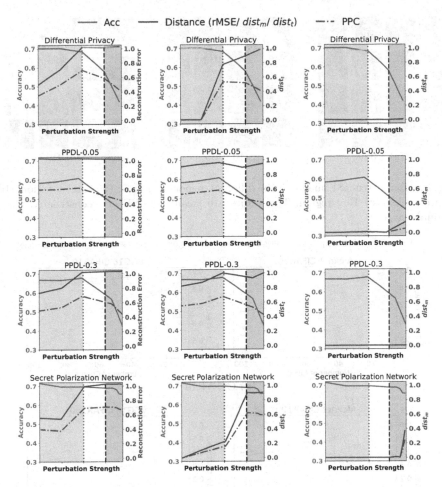

Fig. 5. Privacy-Preserving Characteristics (PPC) of different mechanisms (dash-dotted PPC curves); orange curves and y-axis (left): *Acc* of models; blue curves and y-axis (right): distances for attacks; x-axis: controlling param (perturbation strength increases from left to right). **Left to Right**: Reconstruction Attack, Tracing Attack and Membership Attack. See Fig. 6 for example reconstruction images. (Color figure online)

The averaged categorical distance $dist$ is defined as followed:

$$dist(a,b) = \frac{1}{n}\sum_{i=1}^{n}\delta(a_i, b_i) \tag{7}$$

$$\delta(a_i, b_i) = \begin{cases} 0 & \text{if } a_i = b_i \\ 1 & \text{otherwise} \end{cases} \tag{8}$$

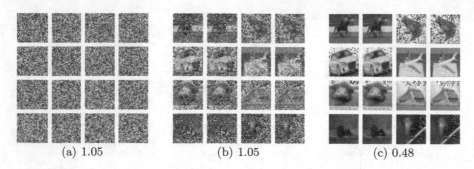

(a) 1.05   (b) 1.05   (c) 0.48

Fig. 6. Reconstructed images from different region in Fig. 5. **(a)** Green region **(b)** White region **(c)** Red region. The values are mean of rMSE of reconstructed w.r.t. original images.

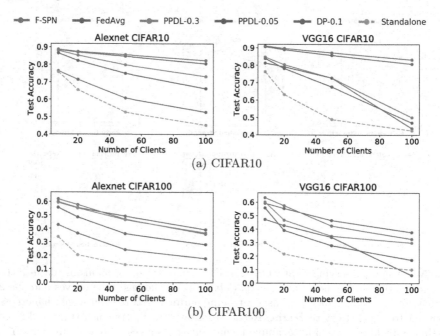

Fig. 7. Comparison of test accuracies for *standalone* local models, *FedAvg*, *PPDL-0.3*, *PPDL-0.05*, *DP-0.1* and *Federated SPN* models. Improvements over standalone models increase with the number of clients.

4.2 Comparison of Privacy Preserving Mechanisms

Figure 5 illustrates example Privacy-Preserving Characteristic (PPC) of different mechanisms against *reconstruction, membership* and *tracing* attacks, in which the controlling parameter along x-axis is the ratio m of gradient magnitudes $\mathcal{G}$ with respect to magnitudes of added perturbations E_m. It is shown that privacy attacks pose serious challenges to differential privacy based methods **DP** and **PPDL**.

Reconstruction attacks (top row): when the ratio ranges between tens to thousands in red regions, errors decrease rapidly and *pixel-level information* about original training data are almost completely disclosed (see Fig. 6c). In the white regions, increased magnitudes of perturbations lead to large reconstruction errors (rMSE ≈ 1.0) with noticeable artifacts and random noisy dots in Fig. 6b. However, model accuracies for DP and PPDL methods also decrease dramatically. Pronounced drops in accuracies (with more than 20% for CIFAR10 and 5% for MNIST) are observed when added perturbations E_m exceed magnitudes of original gradients G (in green regions), beyond which condition of reconstruction attacks is no longer fulfilled and attacks are guaranteed to be defeated (see [8] for theoretical proof and Fig. 6a).

Table 1. CAP performance with different batch size and dataset for reconstruction, membership and tracing attack. Higher better. BS = Attack Batch Size, [1] = DP, [18]* = PPDL-0.05, [18]⋆ = PPDL-0.3

BS	CIFAR10									CIFAR100								
	Reconstruction			Membership			Tracing			Reconstruction			Membership			Tracing		
	1	4	8	1	4	8	1	4	8	1	4	8	1	4	8	1	4	8
[1]	0.57	0.63	0.63	0.00	0.45	0.47	0.42	0.57	0.58	0.23	0.31	0.30	0.01	0.22	0.25	0.14	0.24	0.24
[18]*	0.55	0.55	0.55	0.00	0.37	0.44	0.50	0.50	0.50	0.18	0.18	0.18	0.02	0.13	0.16	0.16	0.16	0.16
[18]⋆	0.57	0.61	0.61	0.00	0.43	0.49	0.54	0.54	0.54	0.21	0.26	0.26	0.00	0.19	0.22	0.19	0.19	0.19
SPN	**0.69**	**0.70**	**0.70**	**0.24**	**0.50**	**0.55**	**0.60**	**0.62**	**0.64**	**0.35**	**0.35**	**0.36**	**0.17**	**0.28**	**0.31**	**0.29**	**0.30**	**0.30**

Tracing attacks (middle row): similar trends were observed for distances of tracing attacks. In addition, the distance increases as the number of participants increases.

Membership attacks (bottom row): the disclosing of memberships is more detrimental, with distances between reconstructed memberships and ground truth labels almost being zero, except for PPDL-0.05 in the green region. With the increase of the number of classes (for CIFAR100) and the training batch size (8), success rates of membership attacks dropped and the distances increased. One may mitigate membership attacks by using even larger batch sizes, as suggested in [22,24].

In a sharp contrast, Secret Polarization Network (SPN) based mechanism maintains consistent model accuracies, even though gradient magnitudes due to polarization loss exceed gradient magnitudes of original CE loss. Superior performances of SPN mechanism in this green region provide *theoretically guaranteed privacy-preserving capabilities*, and at the same time, maintain decent model accuracies to be useful in practice. This superiority is ascribed to the adaptive element-wise gradient perturbations introduced by polarization loss (see discussions near Eq. (6)).

4.3 Secret Polarization Network for Federated Learning

The dual-headed Secret Polarization Network (SPN) brought improvements in model accuracies in a federated learning setting, in which CIFAR10 and

CIFAR100 datasets are evenly distributed among all clients, resulting in small local training datasets on each client (for instance, there are only 500 CIFAR10 training data when the number of clients is 100).

Substantial performances deterioration were observed for local standalone models with large numbers of e.g. 100 clients (see Fig. 7). Since local training data are *i.i.d.*, the FedAvg algorithm [14] effectively improved the global model accuracies about 12–35% for CIFAR10 and 26–32%for CIFAR100 on AlexNet. The proposed SPN, once integrated with the FedAvg algorithm, consistently improved further model accuracies ranging between 2–3% for CIFAR10 dataset while maintaining comparable performance for CIFAR100 (around 2% drops when number of clients 100). By comparing with the same privacy guarantee (same perturbation strength) provided by DP-0.1 and SPN, SPN outperforms DP-0.1 in terms of test accuracy for CIFAR10 by 12 28% improvement while CIFAR100 by 18 22% improvement on AlexNet. SPN also outperforms PPDL-0.05 (sharing 5% gradients) and PPDL-0.3 (sharing 30% gradients) for CIFAR10 by 2–16% and 1–8% improvement respectively and CIFAR100 by 4–11% and 1–2% improvement respectively on AlexNet. Similar improvements of SPN over DP-0.1, PPDL-0.05, and PPDL-0.3 are observed on VGG16. The improvements are ascribed to element-wise gradients introduced by polarization losses (see discussion in Sect. 3), which in our view advocate the adoption of SPN in practical applications.

5   Discussion and Conclusion

The crux of differential-privacy based approaches is a trade-off between privacy vs accuracy [1, 18]. As shown in [15] and our experiments, existing defenses such as *sharing fewer gradients* and *adding Gaussian or Laplacian noise* are vulnerable to aggressive reconstruction attacks, despite the theoretical privacy guarantee [8].

We extricated from the dilemma by hiding a fraction of network parameters and gradients from the adversary. To this end, we proposed to employ a dual-headed network architecture i.e. Secret Polarization Network (SPN), which on the one hand exerts secret gradient perturbations to original gradients under attack, and on the other hand, maintains performances of the global shared model by jointing forces with the backbone network. This secret-public network configuration provides a theoretically guaranteed privacy protection mechanism without compromising model accuracies, and does not incur significant computational and communication overheads which HE/SMPC based approaches have to put up with. We find that the combination of secret-public networks provides a preferable alternative to DP-based mechanisms in application scenarios, whereas large computational and communication overheads are unaffordable e.g. with mobile or IOT devices.

As for future work, the adversarial learning nature of SPN also makes it an effective defense mechanism against adversarial example attacks. To formulate both privacy and adversarial attacks in a unified framework is one of our future directions.

Appendix A: Proofs of Reconstruction Attacks

Consider a neural network $\Psi(x; w, b) : \mathcal{X} \to \mathbb{R}^C$, where $x \in \mathcal{X}$, w and b are the weights and biases of neural networks, and C is the output dimension. In a machine learning task, we optimize the parameters w and b of neural network Ψ with a loss function $\mathcal{L}\big(\Psi(x; w, b), y\big)$, where x is the input data and y is the ground truth labels. We abbreviate loss function as $\mathcal{L}$ and denote the superscript $w^{[i]}$ and $b^{[i]}$ as the i-th layer weights and biases.

Suppose a multilayer neural network $\Psi := \Psi^{[L-1]} \circ \Psi^{[L-2]} \circ \cdots \circ \Psi^{[0]}(\,\cdot\,; w, b)$ is $\mathcal{C}^1$, where the i-th layer $\Psi^{[i]}$ is a fully-connected layer with the step forward propagation as follows,

$$o^{[i+1]} = a\big(w^{[i]} \cdot o^{[i]} + b^{[i]}\big),$$

where $o^{[i]}$, $o^{[i+1]}$, $w^{[i]}$ and $b^{[i]}$ are an input vector, an output vector, a weight matrix and a bias vector respectively, and a is the activation function in the i-th layer.

By the backpropagation, we have the matrix derivatives on $\Psi^{[i]}$ as follows,

$$\nabla_{w^{[i]}}\mathcal{L} = \nabla_{o^{[i+1]}}\mathcal{L} \cdot a'\big(w^{[i]} \cdot o^{[i]} + b^{[i]}\big) \cdot o^{[i]^T} \tag{9}$$

$$\nabla_{b^{[i]}}\mathcal{L} = \nabla_{o^{[i+1]}}\mathcal{L} \cdot a'\big(w^{[i]} \cdot o^{[i]} + b^{[i]}\big) \cdot I, \tag{10}$$

which yield the following output equations:

$$\nabla_{w^{[i]}}\mathcal{L} = \nabla_{b^{[i]}}\mathcal{L} \cdot o^{[i]^T}, \tag{11}$$

where gradients $\nabla_{w^{[i]}}\mathcal{L}$ and $\nabla_{b^{[i]}}\mathcal{L}$ are supposed to be shared in a distributed learning setting, and known to honest-and-curious adversaries who may launch reconstruction attacks on observed gradients.

Remark 1. Any convolution layers can be converted into a fully-connected layer by simply stacking together spatially shifted convolution kernels, as noted in Footnote 3. A simple illustration refers to Fig. 8 and detailed algorithm refers to a technical report [13].

Remark 2. Suppose $\nabla_{w^{[i]}}\mathcal{L} \in \mathbb{R}^{M \cdot N}$, $\nabla_{b^{[i]}}\mathcal{L} \in \mathbb{R}^M$ and $o^{[i]} \in \mathbb{R}^N$, we write

$$\nabla_{w^{[i]}}\mathcal{L} := \Big(\frac{\partial \mathcal{L}}{\partial w_{mn}^{[i]}}\Big)_{\substack{1 \le m \le M; \\ 1 \le n \le N.}}, \quad \nabla_{b^{[i]}}\mathcal{L} := \Big(\frac{\partial \mathcal{L}}{\partial b_1^{[i]}}, \cdots, \frac{\partial \mathcal{L}}{\partial b_M^{[i]}}\Big)^T, \text{ and } o^{[i]} := \Big(o_1^{[i]}, \ldots, o_N^{[i]}\Big)^T.$$

By the piecewise matrix multiplication, Eq. 11 becomes as a linear system in a formal convention as follows,

$$\frac{\partial \mathcal{L}}{\partial w_{mn}^{[i]}} = \frac{\partial \mathcal{L}}{\partial b_m^{[i]}} \cdot o_n^{[i]}, \quad \text{for } 1 \le m \le M \text{ and } 1 \le n \le N.$$

Hence, we can write the partial derivative $\nabla_{b^{[i]}}\mathcal{L}$ as an $mn \times mn$ diagonal matrix that each n adjacent diagonal entries in an order are copies of each entry, and partial derivative $\nabla_{w^{[i]}}\mathcal{L}$ as an mn-dimensional vector.

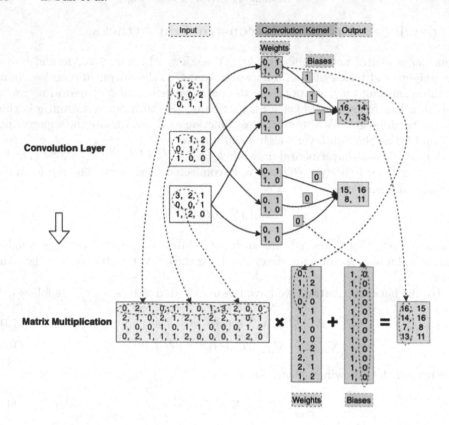

Fig. 8. A pictorial example illustrating how to switch a convolution operator to a matrix multiplication.

In the following paragraph, we always abbreviate equation coefficients $\nabla_{w^{[i]}}\mathcal{L}$ and $\nabla_{b^{[i]}}\mathcal{L}$ to $W^{[i]}$ and $B^{[i]}$ respectively.

Lemma 1. *Suppose $d^{[0]}$ and $d^{[1]},\cdots,d^{[L]}$ are dimensions of input image x and output vectors $o^{[1]},\cdots,o^{[L]}$ respectively. x and $o^{[i]}$ can be estimated by solving the following $d^{[i]}\cdot d^{[i+1]}$-dimensional linear system if it is well-posed,*

$$W^{[0]} = B^{[i]}\cdot x \tag{12}$$

$$or\ W^{[i]} = B^{[i]}\cdot {o^{[i]}}^{T},\ for\ i=1,\cdots,L-1. \tag{13}$$

Remark 3. Output vectors $o^{[1]},\cdots,o^{[L]}$ are outputs of neural networks $\Psi(\,\cdot\,;w,b)$ on input image x. However, solving Linear System (13) are always numerically unstable in that minor numerical perturbation of $B^{[i]}$ around 0 would yield the infinity solution even if it is a well-posed problem. Hence, it is not typically to directly recover input image x and output vectors $o^{[1]},\cdots,o^{[L]}$ by simple matrix computations in practice.

Lemma 2. *Assume the linear system $B \cdot x = W$ is corrupted in coefficients written as $\bar{B} \cdot \bar{x} = \bar{W}$. If B is nonsingular, we have the following inequality,*

$$||x - \bar{x}|| \le ||B^{-1}|| \cdot (||W - \bar{W}|| + ||B - \bar{B}|| \cdot ||\bar{x}||).$$

Proof. Obviously, we have

$$B \cdot (x - \bar{x}) = (W - \bar{W}) + (B - \bar{B}) \cdot \bar{x}, \tag{14}$$

which yields this lemma if B is nonsingular. □

According to Lemma 1 and Lemma 2, we have the following existing theorem.

Theorem 3. *Suppose a multilayer neural network $\Psi := \Psi^{[L-1]} \circ \Psi^{[L-2]} \circ \cdots \circ \Psi^{[0]}(\cdot\,; w, b)$ is $\mathcal{C}^1$, where the i-th layer $\Psi^{[i]}$ is a fully-connected layer. Then, **initial input x^* of Ψ exists**, provided that: if there is an i ($1 \le i \le L$) such that*

1. *Jacobian matrix $D_x(\Psi^{[i-1]} \circ \Psi^{[i-1]} \circ \cdots \circ \Psi^{[0]})$ around x is full-rank;*
2. *Partial derivative $\nabla_{b^{[i]}} \mathcal{L}(\Psi(x; w, b), y)$ is nonsingular.*

Moreover, we have the following inequality around x^*,

$$||x - x^*|| \le M \cdot ||\nabla_{w^{[i]}, b^{[i]}} \mathcal{L}(\Psi(x; w, b), y) - \nabla_{w^{[i]}, b^{[i]}} \mathcal{L}(\Psi(x^*; w, b), y)||. \tag{15}$$

Proof. WLOG, we suppose i yields that Jacobian matrix $D_x(\Psi^{[i-1]} \circ \Psi^{[i-1]} \circ \cdots \circ \Psi^{[0]})$ around x is full-rank. By the implicit function theorem, there exists a bounded inverse function $(\Psi^{[i-1]} \circ \Psi^{[i-1]} \circ \cdots \circ \Psi^{[0]})^{-1}(\cdot\,; w, b)$ around x, s.t.

$$\left|(\Psi^{[i-1]} \circ \Psi^{[i-1]} \circ \cdots \circ \Psi^{[0]})^{-1}(\cdot\,; w, b)\right| \le M^{[i]}. \tag{16}$$

Since partial derivative $\nabla_{b^{[i]}} \mathcal{L}$ is nonsingular, vector $o^{[i]}$ is solved by matrix computations in Lemma 1, and thus the initial image $x^* := (\Psi^{[i-1]} \circ \Psi^{[i-1]} \circ \cdots \circ \Psi^{[0]})^{-1}(o^{[i]})$.

By Lemma 2 and Inequality (16), in an open neighborhood of x^*, we have

$$
\begin{aligned}
||x - x^*|| &= ||(\Psi^{[i-1]} \circ \Psi^{[i-1]} \circ \cdots \circ \Psi^{[0]})^{-1}(o^{[i]}\,; w, b) - (\Psi^{[i-1]} \circ \Psi^{[i-1]} \circ \cdots \circ \Psi^{[0]})^{-1}(o^{[i]*}\,; w, b)|| \\
&\le M^{[i]} \cdot ||o^{[i]} - o^{[i]*}|| \\
&\le M^{[i]} \cdot ||\nabla_{b^{[i]}} \mathcal{L}^{-1}|| \cdot (||\nabla_{w^{[i]}} \mathcal{L}(\Psi(x; w, b), y) - \nabla_{w^{[i]}} \mathcal{L}(\Psi(x^*; w, b), y)|| \\
&\qquad + ||x^*|| \cdot ||\nabla_{b^{[i]}} \mathcal{L}(\Psi(x; w, b), y) - \nabla_{b^{[i]}} \mathcal{L}(\Psi(x^*; w, b), y)||) \\
&\le M \cdot ||\nabla_{w^{[i]}, b^{[i]}} \mathcal{L}(\Psi(x; w, b), y) - \nabla_{w^{[i]}, b^{[i]}} \mathcal{L}(\Psi(x^*; w, b), y)||,
\end{aligned}
$$

where we pick enough big number $M := M^{[i]} \cdot ||x^*|| \cdot ||\nabla_{b^{[i]}} \mathcal{L}^{-1}|| + 1$. □

Remark 4. 1) In the deep leakage approach [24], the recovery of initial image requires model parameters $\mathcal{W}$ and the corresponding gradients $\nabla \mathcal{W}$ such that a minimization of gradient differences $||\nabla \mathcal{W}' - \nabla \mathcal{W}||$ yields a recovery of initial image if the initial image exists. Our theorem provides sufficient conditions of the initial image existence, and Inequality (15) confirms the effectiveness of the deep leakage approach.

2) Essentially, deep leakage approach is a trade-off computational technique for the matrix approach in the meaning that a loss in accuracy is trade-off with the existence of approximate solution by the optimization approach. Both approaches require model parameters $\mathcal{W}$ and the corresponding gradients $\nabla\mathcal{W}$.

3) If Jacobian matrix is not full-rank or $\nabla_{b^{[i]}}\mathcal{L}$ is singular, the inverse problem is ill-posed and a minimization of gradient differences might yield multiple solutions or an infeasibility which is observed as noisy images.

If assumptions in Theorem 3 are met, we pick an index set I from row index set of $B^{[i]}$ and $W^{[i]}$ such that the following linear equation is well-posed,

$$B_I \cdot x = W_I,$$

where $B_I := B_I^{[i]}$ and $W_I := W_I^{[i]}$.

Theorem 4. *Suppose there are perturbations E_B, E_W added on B_I, W_I, respectively, such that observed measurements $\bar{B}_I = B_I + E_B, \bar{W}_I = W_I + E_W$. Then, the* **reconstruction** *x^* of the initial input x can be* **determined** *by solving a noisy linear system $\bar{B}_I \cdot x^* = \bar{W}_I$, provided that*

$$\|B_I^{-1} \cdot E_B\| < 1; \tag{17}$$

Moreover, the relative error is bounded,

$$\frac{\|x^* - x\|}{\|x\|} \leq \frac{\kappa(B_I)}{1 - \|B_I^{-1} \cdot E_B\|} \left(\frac{\|E_B\|}{\|B_I\|} + \frac{\|E_W\|}{\|W_I\|} \right), \tag{18}$$

in which B_I^{-1} is the inverse of B_I.

Proof. According to the construction, we have

$$(\bar{B}_I - B_I) \cdot x^* + B_I \cdot (x^* - x) = \bar{W}_I - W_I,$$

which yields

$$x^* - x = B_I^{-1} \cdot \left(\bar{W}_I - W_I - (\bar{B}_I - B_I) \cdot x^* \right). \tag{19}$$

Consider the relative error: since $||W_I|| \leq ||B_I|| \cdot ||x||$, Eq. (19) becomes

$$\frac{||x^* - x||}{||x||} \leq \kappa(B_I) \cdot \left(\frac{||E_B||}{||B_I||} \cdot \frac{||x^*||}{||x||} + \frac{||E_W||}{||W_I||} \right), \tag{20}$$

where condition number $\kappa(B_I) := ||B_I|| \cdot ||B_I^{-1}||$.

Moreover, according to Lemma 2, we have

$$B_I \cdot (x - x^*) = E_B \cdot x^* - E_W.$$

A simplification of the above equation, we have

$$x + (B_I^{-1} \cdot E_B - I) \cdot x^* = -B_I^{-1} \cdot E_W.$$

Take a norm on both sides, we have

$$\|x\| + \|B_I^{-1} \cdot E_B - I\| \cdot \|x^*\| \geq 0.$$

Since $\|B_I^{-1} \cdot E_B\| < 1$, we have

$$\frac{\|x^*\|}{\|x\|} \leq \frac{1}{1 - \|B_I^{-1} \cdot E_B\|}. \tag{21}$$

Combine Eq. (20) and Eq. (21), we get Eq. (18).

$\square$

Remark 5. $\|B_I^{-1} \cdot E_B\| < 1$ alone is a *necessary* condition for the iterative reconstruction algorithm to converge. In other words, a big perturbation with $\|E_B\| > \|B_I\|$, such as Gaussian noise with a sufficiently big variance, is guaranteed to defeat reconstruction attacks like [24].

References

1. Abadi, M., et al.: Deep learning with differential privacy. In: Proceedings of the 2016 ACM SIGSAC Conference on Computer and Communications Security, pp. 308–318 (2016)
2. Aono, Y., Hayashi, T., Wang, L., Moriai, S., et al.: Privacy-preserving deep learning via additively homomorphic encryption. IEEE Trans. Inf. Forensics Secur. **13**(5), 1333–1345 (2017)
3. Badawi, A.A., et al.: The AlexNet moment for homomorphic encryption: HCNN, the first homomorphic CNN on encrypted data with GPUs. CoRR abs/1811.00778 (2018). http://arxiv.org/abs/1811.00778
4. Dwork, C.: Differential privacy. Automata, languages and programming, pp. 1–12 (2006)
5. Dwork, C., McSherry, F., Nissim, K., Smith, A.: Calibrating noise to sensitivity in private data analysis. In: Halevi, S., Rabin, T. (eds.) TCC 2006. LNCS, vol. 3876, pp. 265–284. Springer, Heidelberg (2006). https://doi.org/10.1007/11681878_14
6. Dwork, C., Smith, A., Steinke, T., Ullman, J.: Exposed! A survey of attacks on private data. Annu. Rev. Stat. Appl. **4**, 61–84 (2017)
7. Fan, L., Ng, K.W., Ju, C., Zhang, T., Chan, C.S.: Deep polarized network for supervised learning of accurate binary hashing codes. In: Bessiere, C. (ed.) Proceedings of the Twenty-Ninth International Joint Conference on Artificial Intelligence, IJCAI-20, pp. 825–831. International Joint Conferences on Artificial Intelligence Organization, July 2020. https://doi.org/10.24963/ijcai.2020/115. https://doi.org/10.24963/ijcai.2020/115. Main track
8. Fan, L., Ng, K.W., Ju, C., Zhang, T., Liu, C., Chan, C.S., Yang, Q.: Rethinking privacy preserving deep learning: how to evaluate and thwart privacy attacks (2020). http://arxiv.org/abs/2006.11601
9. Fredrikson, M., Jha, S., Ristenpart, T.: Model inversion attacks that exploit confidence information and basic countermeasures. In: Proceedings of the 22nd ACM SIGSAC Conference on Computer and Communications Security, pp. 1322–1333 (2015)

10. Geiping, J., Bauermeister, H., Dröge, H., Moeller, M.: Inverting gradients-how easy is it to break privacy in federated learning? arXiv preprint arXiv:2003.14053 (2020)
11. Gilad-Bachrach, R., Dowlin, N., Laine, K., Lauter, K., Naehrig, M., Wernsing, J.: CryptoNets: applying neural networks to encrypted data with high throughput and accuracy. In: International Conference on Machine Learning, pp. 201–210 (2016)
12. Hardy, S., et al.: Private federated learning on vertically partitioned data via entity resolution and additively homomorphic encryption. arXiv preprint arXiv:1711.10677 (2017)
13. Ma, W., Lu, J.: An equivalence of fully connected layer and convolutional layer (2017)
14. McMahan, H.B., Moore, E., Ramage, D., Hampson, S., y Arcas, B.A.: Communication-efficient learning of deep networks from decentralized data. In: Proceedings of the 20th International Conference on Artificial Intelligence and Statistics (AISTATS) (2017). http://arxiv.org/abs/1602.05629
15. Melis, L., Song, C., De Cristofaro, E., Shmatikov, V.: Exploiting unintended feature leakage in collaborative learning. In: 2019 IEEE Symposium on Security and Privacy (SP), pp. 691–706. IEEE (2019)
16. Mohassel, P., Rindal, P.: ABY3: a mixed protocol framework for machine learning. In: Proceedings of the 2018 ACM SIGSAC Conference on Computer and Communications Security, pp. 35–52 (2018)
17. Rouhani, B.D., Riazi, M.S., Koushanfar, F.: DeepSecure: scalable provably-secure deep learning. In: Proceedings of the 55th Annual Design Automation Conference, pp. 1–6 (2018)
18. Shokri, R., Shmatikov, V.: Privacy-preserving deep learning. In: Proceedings of the 22nd ACM SIGSAC Conference on Computer and Communications Security, pp. 1310–1321 (2015)
19. Shokri, R., Stronati, M., Song, C., Shmatikov, V.: Membership inference attacks against machine learning models. In: 2017 IEEE Symposium on Security and Privacy (SP), pp. 3–18 (2017)
20. Tanuwidjaja, H.C., Choi, R., Kim, K.: A survey on deep learning techniques for privacy-preserving. In: International Conference on Machine Learning for Cyber Security, pp. 29–46 (2019)
21. Wang, Z., Song, M., Zhang, Z., Song, Y., Wang, Q., Qi, H.: Beyond inferring class representatives: user-level privacy leakage from federated learning. In: IEEE INFOCOM 2019-IEEE Conference on Computer Communications, pp. 2512–2520 (2019)
22. Wei, W., et al.: A framework for evaluating gradient leakage attacks in federated learning. arXiv preprint arXiv:2004.10397 (2020)
23. Yang, Q., Liu, Y., Chen, T., Tong, Y.: Federated machine learning: concept and applications. ACM Trans. Intell. Syst. Technol. (TIST) **10**(2), 12 (2019)
24. Zhu, L., Liu, Z., Han, S.: Deep leakage from gradients. In: Wallach, H.M., Larochelle, H., Beygelzimer, A., d'Alché-Buc, F., Fox, E.B., Garnett, R. (eds.) NeurIPS, pp. 14747–14756 (2019). http://papers.nips.cc/paper/9617-deep-leakage-from-gradients

Task-Agnostic Privacy-Preserving Representation Learning via Federated Learning

Ang Li$^{(\boxtimes)}$, Huanrui Yang, and Yiran Chen

Department of Electrical and Computer Engineering, Duke University, Durham, USA
{ang.li630,huanrui.yang,yiran.chen}@duke.edu

Abstract. The availability of various large-scale datasets benefits the advancement of deep learning. These datasets are often crowdsourced from individual users and contain private information like gender, age, etc. Due to rich private information embedded in the raw data, users raise the concerns on privacy leakage from the shared data. Such privacy concerns will hinder the generation or use of crowdsourcing datasets and lead to hunger of training data for new deep learning applications. In this work, we present *TAP*, a task-agnostic privacy-preserving representation learning framework to protect data privacy with anonymized intermediate representation. The goal of this framework is to learn a feature extractor that can hide the privacy information from the intermediate representations; while maximally retaining the original information embedded in the raw data for the data collector to accomplish unknown learning tasks. We adopt the federated learning paradigm to train the feature extractor, such that learning the extractor is also performed in a privacy-respecting fashion. We extensively evaluate TAP and compare it with existing methods using two image datasets and one text dataset. Our results show that TAP can offer a good privacy-utility tradeoff.

Keywords: Task-agnostic · Privacy-preserving · Representation learning · Federated learning

1 Introduction

Deep learning has achieved unprecedented success in many applications, such as computer vision [11,16] and natural language processing [2,28,36]. Such success of deep learning partially benefits from various large-scale datasets (e.g., ImageNet [5], MS-COCO [20], etc.), which can be used to train powerful deep neural networks (DNN). The datasets are often crowdsourced from individual users to train DNN models. For example, companies or research institutes that want to implement face recognition systems may collect the facial images from employees or volunteers. However, those data that are crowdsourced from individual users for deep learning applications often contain private information such as gender,

© Springer Nature Switzerland AG 2020
Q. Yang et al. (Eds.): Federated Learning, LNAI 12500, pp. 51–65, 2020.
https://doi.org/10.1007/978-3-030-63076-8_4

age, etc. Unfortunately, the data crowdsourcing process can be exposed to serious privacy risks as the data may be misused by the data collector or acquired by the adversary. It is recently reported that many large companies face data security and user privacy challenges. The data breach of Facebook, for example, raises users' severe concerns on sharing their personal data. These emerging privacy concerns hinder generation or use of large-scale crowdsourcing datasets and lead to hunger of training data of many new deep learning applications. A number of countries are also establishing laws to protect data security and privacy. As a famous example, the new European Union's General Data Protection Regulation (GDPR) requires companies to not store personal data for a long time, and allows users to delete or withdraw their personal data within 30 days. It is critical to design a data crowdsourcing framework to protect the privacy of the shared data while maintaining the utility for training DNN models.

Existing solutions to protect privacy are struggling to balance the trade-off between privacy and utility. An obvious and widely adopted solution is to transform the raw data into task-oriented features, and users only upload the extracted features to corresponding service providers, such as Google Now and Google Cloud. Even though transmitting only features are generally more secure than uploading raw data, recent developments in model inversion attacks [6,7,23] have demonstrated that adversaries can exploit the acquired features to reconstruct the raw image, and hence the person on the raw image can be re-identified from the reconstructed image. In addition, the extracted features can also be exploited by an adversary to infer private attributes, such as gender, age, etc. Ossia *et al.* [29] move forward by applying dimentionality reduction and noise injection to the features before uploading them to the service provider. However, such approach leads to unignorable utility loss. Inspired by Generative Adversarial Networks (GAN), several adversarial learning approaches [13,18,21,27] have been proposed to learn obfuscated features from raw images. Unfortunately, those solutions are designed for known primary learning tasks, which limits their applicability in the data crowdsourcing where the primary learning task may be unknown or changed when training a DNN model. The need of collecting large-scale crowdsourcing dataset under strict requirement of data privacy and limited applicability of existing solutions motivates us to design a privacy-respecting data crowdsourcing framework: the raw data from the users are locally transformed into an intermediate representation that can remove the private information while retaining the discriminative features for primary learning tasks.

In this work, we propose TAP – a task-agnostic privacy-preserving representation learning framework for data crowdsourcing. The ultimate goal of this framework is to learn a feature extractor that can remove the privacy information from the extracted intermediate features while maximally retaining the original information embedded in the raw data for primary learning tasks. However, training the feature extractor also requires to crowdsource data from individual users. In order to keep data private, we adopt the federated learning (FL) [15] method for training the feature extractor. FL is a popular distributed machine learning framework that enables a number of participants to train a

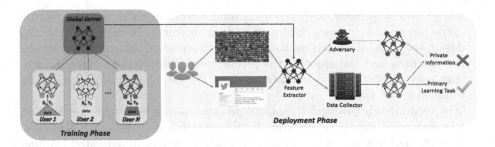

Fig. 1. The overview of TAP.

shared global model collaboratively without transferring their local data. A central server coordinates the FL process, where each participant communicates only the model parameters with the central server while keeping local data private. By applying FL, we can train the feature extractor with decentralized data in a privacy-preserving way.

As Fig. 1 illustrates, there are two phases of applying TAP: the *training phase* and the *deployment phase*. In the training phase, we train the feature extractor in a federated fashion. In the deployment phase, users can locally run the learned feature extractor and submit only those intermediate representations to the data collector instead of submitting the raw data. The data collector then trains DNN models using these collected intermediate representations, but both the data collector and the adversary cannot accurately infer any protected private information. Compared with existing adversarial learning methods [13, 18, 21, 27], TAP does not require the knowledge of the primary learning task and, hence, directly applying existing adversarial training methods becomes impractical. It is challenging to remove all concerned private information that needs to be protected while retaining everything else for unknown primary learning tasks. To address this issue, we design a hybrid learning method to learn the anonymized intermediate representation. This learning method is performed locally by each participating user in federated learning process. The learning purpose is two-folded: (1) hiding private information from features; (2) maximally retaining original information. Specifically, we hide private information from features by performing our proposed privacy adversarial training (PAT) algorithm, which simulates the game between an adversary who makes efforts to infer private attributes from the extracted features and a defender who aims to protect user privacy. The original information are retained by applying our proposed MaxMI algorithm, which aims to maximize the mutual information between the feature of the raw data and the union of the private information and the retained feature. In summary, our key contributions are the follows:

- We propose TAP – a task-agnostic privacy-preserving representation learning framework for data crowdsourcing without the knowledge of any specific primary learning task. By applying TAP, the learned feature extractor can hide private information from features while maximally retaining the information of the raw data.

- We propose a privacy adversarial training algorithm to enable the feature extractor to hide privacy information from features. In addition, we also design the MaxMI algorithm to maximize the mutual information between the raw data and the union of the private information and the retained feature, so that the original information from the raw data can be maximally retained in the feature.
- We quantitatively evaluate the utility-privacy tradeoff with applying TAP on two real-world datasets, including both image and text data. We also compare the performance of two synchronization strategies in federated learning process.

The rest of this chapter is organized as follows. Section 2 reviews the related work. Section 3 describes the framework overview and details of core modules. Section 4 evaluates the framework. Section 5 concludes this chapter.

2   Related Work

Data Privacy Protection: Many techniques have been proposed to protect data privacy, most of which are based on various anonymization methods including k-anonymity [35], l-diversity [23] and t-closeness [19]. However, these approaches are designed for protecting sensitive attributes in a static database and hence, are not suitable to our addressed problem – data privacy protection in the online data crowdsourcing for training DNN models. Differential privacy [1,3,8,9,32,33] is another widely applied technique to protect privacy of an individual's data record, which provides a strong privacy guarantee. However, the privacy guarantee provided by differential privacy is different from the privacy protection offered by TAP in data crowdsourcing. The goal of differential privacy is to add random noise to a user's true data record such that two arbitrary true data records have close probabilities to generate the same noisy data record. Compared with differential privacy, our goal is to hide private information from the features such that an adversary cannot accurately infer the protected private information through training DNN models. Osia *et al.* [29] leverage a combination of dimensionality reduction, noise addition, and Siamese fine-tuning to protect sensitive information from features, but it does not offer the tradeoff between privacy and utility in a systematic way.

Visual Privacy Protection: Some works have been done to specifically preserve privacy in images and videos. De-identification is a typical privacy-preserving visual recognition approach to alter the raw image such that the identity cannot be visually recognized. There are various techniques to achieve de-identification, such as Gaussian blur [26], identity obfuscation [26], etc. Although those approaches are effective in protecting visual privacy, they all limit the utility of the data for training DNN models. In addition, encryption-based approaches [10,38] have been proposed to guarantee the privacy of the data, but they require specialized DNN models to directly train on the encrypted data. Unfortunately, such encryption-based solutions prevent general dataset release and introduce substantial computational overhead. All the above practices only consider protecting privacy in specific data format, i.e., image and video, which limit their applicability across diverse data modalities in the real world.

Tradeoff Between Privacy and Utility Using Adversarial Networks: With recent advances in deep learning, several approaches have been proposed to protect data privacy using adversarial networks and simulate the game between the attacker and the defender who defend each other with conflicting utility-privacy goals. Pittaluga *et al.* [31] design an adversarial learning method for learning an encoding function to defend against performing inference for specific attributes from the encoded features. Seong *et al.* [27] introduce an adversarial network to obfuscate the raw image so that the attacker cannot successfully perform image recognition. Wu *et al.* [37] design an adversarial framework to explicitly learn a degradation transform for the original video inputs, aiming to balance between target task performance and the associated privacy budgets on the degraded video. Li *et al.* [18] and Liu *et al.* [21] propose approaches to learn obfuscated features using adversarial networks, and only obfuscated features will be submitted to the service provider for performing inference. Attacker cannot train an adversary classifier using collected obfuscated features to accurately infer a user's private attributes or reconstruct the raw data. The same idea behind the above solutions is that using adversarial networks to obfuscate the raw data or features, in order to defending against privacy leakage. However, those solutions are designed to protect privacy information while targeting some specified learning tasks, such as face recognition, activity recognition, etc. Our proposed TAP provides a more general privacy protection, which does not require the knowledge of the primary learning task.

Differences Between TAP and Existing Methods: Compared with prior arts, our proposed TAP has two distinguished features: (1) a more general approach that be applied on different data formats instead of handling only image data or static database; (2) require no knowledge of primary learning tasks.

3   Framework Design

3.1   Overview

There are three parties involved in the crowdsourcing process: *user, adversary,* and *data collector*. Under the strict requirement of data privacy, a data collector offers options to a user to specify any private attribute that needs to be protected. Here we denote the private attribute specified by a user as u. According to the requirement of protecting u, the data collector will learn a feature extractor $E_\theta(z|x, u)$ that is parameterized by weight θ, which is the core of TAP. The data collector distributes the data collecting request associated with the feature extractor to users. Given the raw data x provided by a user, the feature extractor can locally extract feature z from x while hiding private attribute u. Then, only extracted feature z will be shared with the data collector, which can train DNN models for primary learning tasks using collected z. An adversary, who may be an authorized internal staff of the data collector or an external hacker, has access to the extracted feature z and aims to infer private attribute u based on z. We assume an adversary can train a DNN model via collecting z, and then the trained model takes a user's extracted feature z as input and infers the user's private attribute u.

The critical challenge of TAP is to learn the feature extractor, which can hide private attribute from features while maximally retaining original information from the raw data. Note that we train the feature extractor via federated learning to defend against the privacy leakage.

The ultimate goal of the feature extractor $E_\theta(\cdot)$ is two-folded:

- **Goal 1:** make sure the extracted features conveys no private attribute;
- **Goal 2:** retain as much information of the raw data as possible to maintain the utility for primary learning tasks.

To achieve the above goals, we design a hybrid learning method to train the feature extractor, including the *privacy adversarial training (PAT)* algorithm and the *MaxMI* algorithm. The hybrid learning method is performed locally by each participant in federated learning process. In particular, we design the PAT algorithm to achieve Goal 1, which simulates the game between an adversary who makes efforts to infer private attributes from the extracted features and a defender who aims to protect user privacy. By applying PAT to optimize the feature extractor, we enforce the feature extractor to hide private attribute u from extracted features z. Additionally, we propose the MaxMI algorithm to achieve Goal 2. By performing MaxMI to train the feature extractor, we can enable the feature extractor to maximize the mutual information between the information of the raw data x and the joint information of the private attribute u and the extracted feature z.

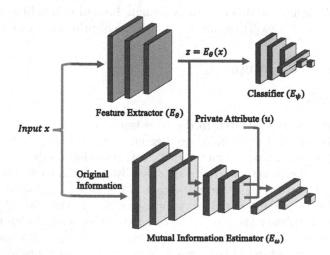

Fig. 2. The hybrid learning method performed by each participant in federated learning.

As Fig. 2 shows, there are three neural network modules in the hybrid learning method: *feature extractor* $E_\theta(\cdot)$, *adversarial classifier* $E_\psi(\cdot)$ and *mutual information estimator* $E_\omega(\cdot)$. These three modules are parameterized with θ, ψ, and ω, respectively. The feature extractor is the one we aim to learn by performing the proposed hybrid learning algorithm. The adversarial classifier simulates an adversary in the PAT algorithm, aiming to infer private attribute u from the eavesdropped features. The mutual information estimator is adopted in MaxMI algorithm to measure the mutual information between the raw data x and the joint distribution of the private attribute u and the extracted feature z. All three modules are end-to-end trained by each participant using our proposed hybrid learning method.

3.2   Privacy Adversarial Training Algorithm

We design the PAT algorithm to achieve Goal 1. Formally, we can formulate Goal 1 as:

$$\min_\theta I(z; u), \tag{1}$$

where $I(z; u)$ represents the mutual information between z and u. It is widely accepted in the previous works that precisely calculating the mutual information between two arbitrary distributions are likely to be infeasible [30]. Therefore, we replace the mutual information objectives in Eq. 1 with their upper bounds for effective optimization. For Goal 1, we utilize the mutual information upper bound derived in [34] as:

$$I(z; u) \le \mathbb{E}_{q_\theta(z)} D_{KL}(q_\theta(u|z)\|p(u)), \tag{2}$$

for any distribution $p(u)$. Note that the term $q_\theta(u|z)$ in Eq. (2) is hard to estimate and hence we instead replace the KL divergence term with its lower bound by introducing a conditional distribution $p_\psi(u|z)$ parameterized with ψ. It was shown in [34] that:

$$\mathbb{E}_{q_\theta(z)} \left[\log p_\psi(u|z) - \log p(u)\right]$$
$$\le \mathbb{E}_{q_\theta(z)} D_{KL}(q_\theta(u|z)\|p(u)) \tag{3}$$

Hence, Eq. 1 can be rewritten as an adversarial training objective function:

$$\min_\theta \max_\psi \mathbb{E}_{q_\theta(z)} \left[\log p_\Psi(u|z) - \log p(u)\right], \tag{4}$$

As $\log p(u)$ is a constant number that is independent of z, Eq. 4 can be further simplified to:

$$\max_\theta \min_\psi -\mathbb{E}_{q_\theta(z)} \left[\log p_\psi(u|z)\right], \tag{5}$$

which is the cross entropy loss of predicting u with $p_\psi(u|z)$, i.e., $CE\left[p_\psi(u|z)\right]$. This objective function can be interpreted as an adversarial game between an adversary p_ψ who tries to infer u from z and a defender q_θ who aims to protect the user privacy.

Based on the above formulation, the PAT algorithm is designed by simulating the game between an adversary who makes efforts to infer private attributes from the extracted features and a defender who aims to protect user privacy. We can apply any architecture to both the feature extractor and the classifier based on the requirement of data format and the primary learning task. The performance of the classifier (C) is measured using the cross-entropy loss function as:

$$\mathcal{L}(C) = CE(y, u) = CE(E_\Psi(E_\theta(x), u), \tag{6}$$

where $CE\,[\cdot]$ stands for the cross entropy loss function. When we simulate an adversary who tries to enhance the accuracy of the adversary classifier as high as possible, the classifier needs to be optimized by minimizing the above loss function as:

$$\Psi = \arg\min_\Psi \mathcal{L}(C). \tag{7}$$

On the contrary, when defending against private attribute leakage, we train the feature extractor in PAT that aims to degrade the performance of the classifier. Consequently, the feature extractor can be trained using Eq. 8 when simulating a defender:

$$\theta = \arg\max_\theta \mathcal{L}(C). \tag{8}$$

Based on Eqs. 7 and 8, the feature extractor and the classifier can be jointly optimized using Eq. 9:

$$\theta, \Psi = \arg\max_\theta \min_\Psi \mathcal{L}(C), \tag{9}$$

which is consistent with Eq. 5.

3.3 MaxMI Algorithm

For Goal 2, we propose MaxMI algorithm to make the feature extractor retain as much as information from the raw data as possible, in order to maintain the high utility of the extracted features. Similarly, we also formally define Goal 2 based on the mutual information as:

$$\max_\theta I(x; z|u). \tag{10}$$

In order to avoid any potential conflict with the objective of Goal 1, we need to mitigate counting in the information where u and x are correlated. Therefore, the mutual information in Eq. 10 is evaluated under the condition of private attribute u. Note that

$$I(x; z|u) = I(x; z, u) - I(x; u). \tag{11}$$

Since both x and u are considered fixed under our setting, $I(x; u)$ will stay as a constant during the optimization process of feature extractor f_θ. Therefore, we can safely rewrite the objective of Goal 2 as:

$$\max_\theta I(x; z, u), \tag{12}$$

which is to maximize the mutual information between x and joint distribution of z and u. In addition, we adopt the previously proposed Jensen-Shannon mutual information estimator [12,25] to estimate the lower bound of the mutual information I(x; z,u). The lower bound is formulated as follows:

$$\mathcal{I}(x; z, u) \geq \mathcal{I}_{\theta,\omega}^{(JSD)}(x; z, u)$$
$$:= \mathbb{E}_x \left[-sp(-E_\omega(x; f_\theta(x), u)) \right] - \mathbb{E}_{x,x'} \left[sp(E_\omega(x'; f_\theta(x), u)) \right], \qquad (13)$$

where x' is an random input data sampled independently from the same distribution of x, $sp(z) = log(1+e^z)$ is the softplus function and E_ω is a discriminator modeled by a neural network with parameters ω. Hence, to maximally retain the original information, the feature extractor and the mutual information estimator can be optimized using Eq. 14:

$$\theta, \omega = \arg \max_\theta \max_\omega \mathcal{I}_{\theta,\omega}^{(JSD)}(x; z, u). \qquad (14)$$

Considering the difference of x, z and u in dimensionality, we feed them into the E_ω from different layers as illustrated in Fig. 2. For example, the private attribute u may be a binary label, which is represented by one bit. However, x may be high dimensional data (e.g., image), and hence it is not reasonable feed both x and u from the first layer of E_ω.

Finally, the feature extractor is trained by alternatively performing PAT algorithm and MaxMI algorithm. As aforementioned, we also introduce an utility-privacy budget λ to balance the tradeoff between protecting privacy and retaining the original information. Therefore, combining Eq. 9 and 14, the objective function of training the feature extractor can be formulated as:

$$\theta, \psi, \omega = \arg \max_\theta (\lambda \min_\psi \mathcal{L}(C) + (1 - \lambda) \max_\omega \mathcal{I}_{\theta,\omega}^{(JSD)}(x; z, u)), \qquad (15)$$

where $\lambda \in [0, 1]$ serves as a utility-privacy budget. A larger λ indicates a stronger privacy protection, while a smaller λ allowing more original information to be retained in the extracted features.

3.4   Federated Learning

We adopt the federated learning method to train the feature extractor, each participant will perform the proposed hybrid learning method locally. Algorithm 1 summarizes the federated learning method of TAP. Within each training batch, each participant performs PAT algorithm and MaxMI algorithm to update ψ and ω, respectively. Then, the parameter of feature extractor θ will be updated according to Eq. 15. The server performs aggregations on θ, ψ, and ω via FedAvg [24] to update corresponding global parameters $\hat{\theta}$, $\hat{\psi}$, and $\hat{\omega}$, respectively.

Algorithm 1. Federated Learning Algorithm of TAP.

Output: $\hat{\theta}$
Server:
  initialize the global model $\hat{\theta}$, $\hat{\psi}$, and $\hat{\omega}$
  $k \leftarrow \max(N \times K, 1)$ $\triangleright$ N available participants, random sampling rate K
  $S_t \leftarrow \{C_1, \ldots, C_k\}$ $\triangleright$ randomly selected k participants indexed by k
  for each round $t = 1, 2, \ldots$ **do**
    for each participant $k \in S_t$ **in parallel do**
      $\hat{\theta} = \frac{1}{k}\sum_{i=1}^{i=k}\theta$, $\hat{\psi} = \frac{1}{k}\sum_{i=1}^{i=k}\psi$, $\hat{\omega} = \frac{1}{k}\sum_{i=1}^{i=k}\omega$
    end for
  end for
Participant:
  for every epoch **do**
    for every batch **do**
      $\mathcal{L}(C) \rightarrow$ update ψ (performing PAT)
      $-\mathcal{I}_{\theta,\omega}^{JSD}(x; z, u) \rightarrow$ update ω (performing MaxMI)
      $-\lambda\mathcal{L}(C) - (1 - \lambda)\mathcal{I}_{\theta,\omega}^{JSD}(x; z, u) \rightarrow$ update θ
    end for
  end for

---

4 Evaluation

In this section, we evaluate TAP's performance on two real-world datasets, with a focus on the utility-privacy tradeoff. We also compare the impact of different synchronization strategies in federated learning on the performance.

4.1 Experiment Setup

We evaluate TAP, especially the learned feature extractor, on one image dataset and one text dataset. We apply mini-batch technique in training with a batch size of 64, and adopt the AdamOptimizer [14] with an adaptive learning rate in the hybrid learning procedure. We adopt the same model architecture configurations as presented in [17]. In terms of the federated learning, we assume there are 100 available clients, and only 20 participants are randomly selected to participate in each training around. For evaluating the performance, given a primary learning task, a simulated data collector trains a normal classifier using features processed by the learned feature extractor. The utility and privacy of the extracted features $E_\theta(x)$ are evaluated by the classification accuracy of primary learning tasks and specified private attribute, respectively. We adopt CelebA [22] and the dialectal tweets dataset (DIAL) [4] for the training and testing of TAP.

4.2 Evaluations on CelebA

Impact of the Utility-Privacy Budget λ: An important step in the hybrid learning procedure (see Eq. 15) is to determine the utility-privacy budget λ. In our experiments, we set 'young' and 'gender' as the private labels to protect in

CelebA, and consider detecting 'gray hair' and 'smiling' as the primary learning tasks to evaluate the utility. To determine the optimal λ, we evaluate the utility-privacy tradeoff on CelebA by setting different λ. Specifically, we evaluate the impact of λ with four discrete choices of $\lambda \in \{1, 0.9, 0.5, 0\}$. As Fig. 3 illustrates, the classification accuracy of primary learning tasks will increase with a smaller λ, but the privacy protection will be weakened. Such phenomenon is reasonable, since the smaller λ means hiding less privacy information in features but retaining more original information from the raw data according to Eq. 15. For example, in Fig. 3 (a), the classification accuracy of 'gray hair' is 82.17% with $\lambda = 1$ and increases to 90.35% by setting $\lambda = 0$; the classification accuracy of 'young' is 67.75% and 82.34% with decreasing λ from 1 to 0, respectively. Overall, $\lambda = 0.9$ is an optimal utility-privacy budget for experiment settings in CelebA.

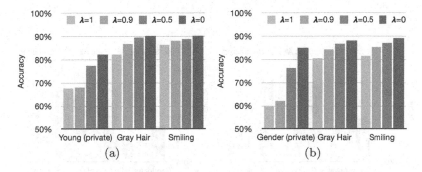

Fig. 3. The impact of the utility-privacy budget λ on CelebA

Impact of the Different Synchronization Strategies: In our study, we train the feature extractor using the proposed federated learning method. There are three parameter sets for the feature extractor (θ), the classifier (ψ), and the mutual information estimator (ω) need to be communicated between the central server and clients. In this experiment, we compare two types of synchronization strategies in federate learning process: **Sync All** synchronizes all the three parameter sets between the each client and the central server; **Sync FE** synchronizes only the feature extractor (θ) between the each client and the central server. In addition, we also compare these two synchronization strategies of the federated learning method with the **Centralized** method, where the feature extractor is trained in a centralized way rather than the federated fashion. In this experiment, the private labels and primary learning tasks in CelebA are set as same as the above experiments. In addition, we set $\lambda = 0.9$ when training the feature extractor.

Figure 4 shows the experiment results on CelebA. In general, the Centralized method outperforms the other two federated learning methods in terms of the privacy-utility tradeoff. However, Sync All only has a slight performance decrease compared with the Centralized method, but the federated learning method can mitigate the privacy leakage due to data movement compared with the Centralized method. For example, in Fig. 4 (a), the classification accuracy of 'gray hair' is 87.97% with the Centralized method and decreases to 86.96% by applying the Sync All strategy in federated learning. In addition, the privacy-utility tradeoff when applying the Sync FE strategy is slightly degraded compared with applying the Sync All strategy. For example, in Fig. 4 (b), the classification accuracy of 'gray hair' is 84.21% with the Sync All strategy and decreases to 81.56% by applying the Sync FE strategy; the classification accuracy of 'gender' is 62.18% and 65.75% when switching the strategy from Sync All to Sync FE, respectively. Moreover, by synchronizing the feature extractor only instead of all the three parameter sets, the communication costs can be reduced by about two thirds in both upload and download streams. The trade-off between improving communication efficiency and offering better privacy-utility tradeoff should be considered case-by-case.

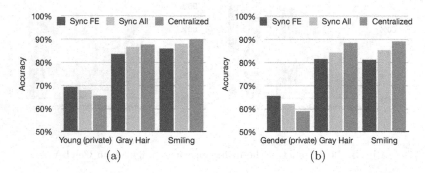

Fig. 4. The impact of the synchronization strategies on CelebA

4.3   Evaluation on DIAL

To quantitatively evaluate the utility-privacy tradeoff of TAP on DIAl, we choose 'race' as the private attribute that needs to be protected and predicting 'mentioned' as the primary learning task. The binary mention task is to determine if a tweet mentions another user, i.e., classifying conversational vs. non-conversational tweets. Similar to the experiment settings in CelebA, we evaluate the utility-privacy tradeoff on DIAL by setting different λ with four discrete choices of $\lambda \in \{1, 0.9, 0.5, 0\}$. As Fig. 5 shows, the classification accuracy of primary learning tasks will increase with a smaller λ, but the privacy protection will be weakened, showing the same phenomenon as the evaluations on CelebA. For example, the classification accuracy of 'mentioned' is 65.31% with $\lambda = 1$ and increases to 75.12% by setting $\lambda = 0$, and the classification accuracy of 'race' increases by 20.35% after changing λ from 1 to 0.

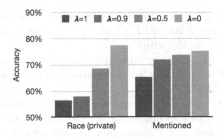

Fig. 5. The impact of the utility-privacy budget λ on DIAL.

5 Conclusion

We proposed a task-agnostic privacy-preserving representation learning framework TAP. A feature extractor is learned via federated learning to hide privacy information features and maximally retain original information from the raw data. By applying TAP, a user can locally extract features from the raw data using the learned feature extractor, and the data collector will acquire the extracted features only to train a DNN model for the primary learning tasks. Evaluations on two benchmark datasets show that TAP offers a desired privacy-utility tradeoff, indicating the usability of proposed framework.

Acknowledgement. This work was supported in part by NSF-1822085 and NSF IUCRC for ASIC membership from Ergomotion. Any opinions, findings, conclusions or recommendations expressed in this material are those of the authors and do not necessarily reflect the views of NSF and their contractors.

References

1. Avent, B., Korolova, A., Zeber, D., Hovden, T., Livshits, B.: Blender: enabling local search with a hybrid differential privacy model. In: 26th USENIX Security Symposium (USENIX Security 17), pp. 747–764 (2017)
2. Bahdanau, D., Cho, K., Bengio, Y.: Neural machine translation by jointly learning to align and translate. arXiv preprint arXiv:1409.0473 (2014)
3. Bassily, R., Smith, A.: Local, private, efficient protocols for succinct histograms. In: Proceedings of the Forty-seventh Annual ACM Symposium on Theory of Computing, pp. 127–135 (2015)
4. Blodgett, S.L., Green, L., O'Connor, B.: Demographic dialectal variation in social media: a case study of African-american English. arXiv preprint arXiv:1608.08868 (2016)
5. Deng, J., Dong, W., Socher, R., Li, L.J., Li, K., Fei-Fei, L.: ImageNet: a large-scale hierarchical image database. In: 2009 IEEE Conference on Computer Vision and Pattern Recognition, pp. 248–255. IEEE (2009)
6. Dosovitskiy, A., Brox, T.: Generating images with perceptual similarity metrics based on deep networks. In: Advances in Neural Information Processing Systems, pp. 658–666 (2016)

7. Dosovitskiy, A., Brox, T.: Inverting visual representations with convolutional networks. In: Proceedings of the IEEE Conference on Computer Vision and Pattern Recognition, pp. 4829–4837 (2016)
8. Duchi, J.C., Jordan, M.I., Wainwright, M.J.: Local privacy and statistical minimax rates. In: 2013 IEEE 54th Annual Symposium on Foundations of Computer Science, pp. 429–438. IEEE (2013)
9. Erlingsson, U., Pihur, V., Korolova, A.: RAPPOR: randomized aggregatable privacy-preserving ordinal response. In: Proceedings of the 2014 ACM SIGSAC Conference on Computer and Communications Security, pp. 1054–1067 (2014)
10. Gilad-Bachrach, R., Dowlin, N., Laine, K., Lauter, K., Naehrig, M., Wernsing, J.: CryptoNets: applying neural networks to encrypted data with high throughput and accuracy. In: International Conference on Machine Learning, pp. 201–210 (2016)
11. He, K., Zhang, X., Ren, S., Sun, J.: Deep residual learning for image recognition. In: Proceedings of the IEEE Conference on Computer Vision and Pattern Recognition, pp. 770–778 (2016)
12. Hjelm, R.D., et al.: Learning deep representations by mutual information estimation and maximization. arXiv preprint arXiv:1808.06670 (2018)
13. Kim, T.h., Kang, D., Pulli, K., Choi, J.: Training with the invisibles: obfuscating images to share safely for learning visual recognition models. arXiv preprint arXiv:1901.00098 (2019)
14. Kingma, D.P., Ba, J.: Adam: a method for stochastic optimization. arXiv:1412.6980, December 2014
15. Konecny, J., McMahan, H.B., Yu, F.X., Richtarik, P., Suresh, A.T., Bacon, D.: Federated learning: strategies for improving communication efficiency. arXiv preprint arXiv:1610.05492 (2016)
16. Krizhevsky, A., Sutskever, I., Hinton, G.E.: ImageNet classification with deep convolutional neural networks. In: Advances in Neural Information Processing Systems, pp. 1097–1105 (2012)
17. Li, A., Duan, Y., Yang, H., Chen, Y., Yang, J.: TIPRDC: task-independent privacy-respecting data crowdsourcing framework for deep learning with anonymized intermediate representations. In: Proceedings of the 26th ACM SIGKDD International Conference on Knowledge Discovery & Data Mining, KDD 2020, pp. 824–832. Association for Computing Machinery, New York (2020). https://doi.org/10.1145/3394486.3403125
18. Li, A., Guo, J., Yang, H., Chen, Y.: DeepObfuscator: adversarial training framework for privacy-preserving image classification. arXiv preprint arXiv:1909.04126 (2019)
19. Li, N., Li, T., Venkatasubramanian, S.: t-closeness: privacy beyond k-anonymity and l-diversity. In: 2007 IEEE 23rd International Conference on Data Engineering, pp. 106–115. IEEE (2007)
20. Lin, T.-Y., et al.: Microsoft COCO: common objects in context. In: Fleet, D., Pajdla, T., Schiele, B., Tuytelaars, T. (eds.) ECCV 2014. LNCS, vol. 8693, pp. 740–755. Springer, Cham (2014). https://doi.org/10.1007/978-3-319-10602-1_48
21. Liu, S., Du, J., Shrivastava, A., Zhong, L.: Privacy adversarial network: representation learning for mobile data privacy. Proc. ACM Interact. Mob. Wearable Ubiquitous Technol. **3**(4), 1–18 (2019)
22. Liu, Z., Luo, P., Wang, X., Tang, X.: Deep learning face attributes in the wild. In: Proceedings of International Conference on Computer Vision (ICCV), December 2015

23. Mahendran, A., Vedaldi, A.: Understanding deep image representations by inverting them. In: Proceedings of the IEEE Conference on Computer Vision and Pattern Recognition, pp. 5188–5196 (2015)
24. McMahan, B., Moore, E., Ramage, D., Hampson, S., y Arcas, B.A.: Communication-efficient learning of deep networks from decentralized data. In: Artificial Intelligence and Statistics, pp. 1273–1282 (2017)
25. Nowozin, S., Cseke, B., Tomioka, R.: f-GAN: training generative neural samplers using variational divergence minimization. In: Advances in Neural Information Processing Systems, pp. 271–279 (2016)
26. Oh, S.J., Benenson, R., Fritz, M., Schiele, B.: Faceless person recognition: privacy implications in social media. In: Leibe, B., Matas, J., Sebe, N., Welling, M. (eds.) ECCV 2016. LNCS, vol. 9907, pp. 19–35. Springer, Cham (2016). https://doi.org/10.1007/978-3-319-46487-9_2
27. Oh, S.J., Fritz, M., Schiele, B.: Adversarial image perturbation for privacy protection a game theory perspective. In: 2017 IEEE International Conference on Computer Vision (ICCV), pp. 1491–1500. IEEE (2017)
28. Oord, A.v.d., et al.: WaveNet: a generative model for raw audio. arXiv preprint arXiv:1609.03499 (2016)
29. Osia, S.A., et al.: A hybrid deep learning architecture for privacy-preserving mobile analytics. IEEE Internet Things J. **7**, 4505–4518 (2020)
30. Peng, X.B., Kanazawa, A., Toyer, S., Abbeel, P., Levine, S.: Variational discriminator bottleneck: improving imitation learning, inverse RL, and GANs by constraining information flow. arXiv preprint arXiv:1810.00821 (2018)
31. Pittaluga, F., Koppal, S., Chakrabarti, A.: Learning privacy preserving encodings through adversarial training. In: 2019 IEEE Winter Conference on Applications of Computer Vision (WACV), pp. 791–799. IEEE (2019)
32. Qin, Z., Yang, Y., Yu, T., Khalil, I., Xiao, X., Ren, K.: Heavy hitter estimation over set-valued data with local differential privacy. In: Proceedings of the 2016 ACM SIGSAC Conference on Computer and Communications Security, pp. 192–203 (2016)
33. Smith, A., Thakurta, A., Upadhyay, J.: Is interaction necessary for distributed private learning? In: 2017 IEEE Symposium on Security and Privacy (SP), pp. 58–77. IEEE (2017)
34. Song, J., Kalluri, P., Grover, A., Zhao, S., Ermon, S.: Learning controllable fair representations. arXiv preprint arXiv:1812.04218 (2018)
35. Sweeney, L.: k-anonymity: a model for protecting privacy. Int. J. Uncertain. Fuzziness Knowl. Based Syst. **10**(05), 557–570 (2002)
36. Wu, Y., et al.: Google's neural machine translation system: bridging the gap between human and machine translation. arXiv preprint arXiv:1609.08144 (2016)
37. Wu, Z., Wang, Z., Wang, Z., Jin, H.: Towards privacy-preserving visual recognition via adversarial training: a pilot study. In: Ferrari, V., Hebert, M., Sminchisescu, C., Weiss, Y. (eds.) ECCV 2018. LNCS, vol. 11220, pp. 627–645. Springer, Cham (2018). https://doi.org/10.1007/978-3-030-01270-0_37
38. Yonetani, R., Naresh Boddeti, V., Kitani, K.M., Sato, Y.: Privacy-preserving visual learning using doubly permuted homomorphic encryption. In: Proceedings of the IEEE International Conference on Computer Vision, pp. 2040–2050 (2017)

Large-Scale Kernel Method for Vertical Federated Learning

Zhiyuan Dang[1,2] ⓘ, Bin Gu[1] ⓘ, and Heng Huang[1,3(✉)] ⓘ

[1] JD Finance America Corporation, Mountain View, CA 94043, USA
zhiyuandang@gmail.com, jsgubin@gmail.com, henghuanghh@gmail.com
[2] Xidian University, Xi'an 710071, China
[3] University of Pittsburgh, Pittsburgh, PA 15260, USA

Abstract. For nowadays real-world data mining task, multiple data holders usually maintain the different feature part of the common data which is called as vertically partitioned data. Accompanying by the emerging demand of privacy persevering, it is hard to do data mining over this kind of vertically partitioned data by legacy machine learning methods. In consideration of less literature for non-linear learning over kernels, in this chapter, we propose a vertical federated kernel learning (VFKL) method to train over the vertically partitioned data. Specifically, we first approximate the kernel function by the random feature technique, and then federatedly update the predict function by the special designed doubly stochastic gradient without leaking privacy in both data and model. Theoretically, our VFKL could provide a sublinear convergence rate, and guarantee the security of data under the common semi-honest assumption. We conduct numerous experiments on various datasets to demonstrate the effectiveness and superiority of the proposed VFKL method.

Keywords: Vertical federated learning · Kernel method · Stochastic gradient descent · Random feature approximation · Privacy preservation

1 Introduction

To be suitable for various data in modern society, current data mining applications face new challenges. Data now always distribute in multiple data holders (such as private finance and E-business companies, hospitals and government branches) where each one keeps its different feature part. In such situation, this kind of data is called vertical partitioned data [21]. For a practical example, a digital finance company, an E-business company, and a bank maintain different information from the same person. The digital finance company keeps online consumption, loan, and repayment information. The E-business company keeps online shopping information. The bank has customer information such as average monthly deposit, account balance, account statement. If the person applies for

© Springer Nature Switzerland AG 2020
Q. Yang et al. (Eds.): Federated Learning, LNAI 12500, pp. 66–80, 2020.
https://doi.org/10.1007/978-3-030-63076-8_5

a loan to the digital finance company, the digital finance company might assess the credit risk of this financial loan by collaboratively utilizing the information stored in these three parts.

However, with the policy of the government and the commercial profit requirement of the company, it is impractical to directly access the data from other holders. Specifically, aim to answer the emerging concerns about personal privacy from users, the European Union draw up the General Data Protection Regulation (GDPR) [8]. As for the company, on the one hand, users' data is the valuable property, therefore, the company have an obligation to protect it. The recent data leakage from Facebook has attracted wide protests [1]. On the other hand, the real user data is useful for the company to train a superior commercial learning model (such as recommendation model). Therefore, it is necessary to do federated learning over vertical partitioned data without leaking privacy.

Nowadays, researchers have proposed numerous vertical federated learning algorithms in various fields, for example, linear regression [9,10,14,20], k-means clustering [23], logistic regression [13,16], random forest [15], XGBoost [4], support vector machine (SVM) [27], cooperative statistical analysis [7] and association rule-mining [22]. From the optimization view, Wan et al. [24] proposed privacy-preservation gradient descent algorithm for vertically partitioned data. Zhang et al. [28] proposed a feature-distributed SVRG algorithm for high-dimensional linear classification.

However, current federated learning algorithms are training based the assumption that the learning models are implicitly linearly separable, i.e., $f(x) = \mathcal{G} \circ h(x)$ [24], where $\mathcal{G}$ is any differentiable function, $h(x)$ is a linearly separable function with the form of $\sum_{\ell=1}^{m} h^{\ell}(w_{g_\ell}, x_{g_\ell})$ and $\{g_1, g_2, \ldots, g_m\}$ is a features partition. However, it is widely known that non-linear models could achieves superior performance than linear ones. Therefore, almost all we mentioned above methods are constrained by linearly separable assumption and then have limited performance. Kernel methods are a vital branch of non-linear learning approaches. The kernel methods are always formulated as the form: $f(x) = \sum_{i}^{N} \alpha_i k(x_i, x)$ which do not satisfy the assumption of implicitly linear separability, where $k(\cdot, \cdot)$ is a kernel function. To the best of our knowledge, PP-SVMV [27] is the only privacy-preserving non-linear kernels method to learn vertically partitioned data. Nevertheless, PP-SVMV [27] has to gather the local kernel matrices from different workers and then sum them as a global kernel matrix, which leads to high communication cost. Thus, it still challenging to efficiently and scalably train over vertically partitioned data by kernel methods without disclosing privacy.

In order to solve this problem, in this chapter, we propose a novel vertically partitioned federated kernel learning (VFKL) method to train over the vertically partitioned data. Specifically, we first approximate the kernel function by the random feature technique, and then federatedly update the predict function by the special designed doubly stochastic gradient without leaking privacy in both data and model. Theoretically, our VFKL could provide a sublinear convergence rate (near $\mathcal{O}(1/t)$), and guarantee the security of data under the common semi-honest assumption (*i.e.*, Assumption 2). We conduct numerous experiments on various datasets to demonstrate the effectiveness and superiority of the proposed VFKL method. This chapter extends the content of our KDD paper [11].

2   Brief Review of Doubly Stochastic Kernel Methods

In this section, we first introduce the random feature approximation technique, and then give a brief review of doubly stochastic gradient (DSG) algorithm, finally, discuss between DSG and our VFKL. DSG [5,12,25] is a scalable and efficient kernel method which uses the doubly stochastic gradients *w.r.t.* samples and random features to update the kernel function. We extend DSG to vertically partitioned data scenario, and then propose VFKL method.

2.1   Problem Formulation

Given a training set $\{(x_i, y_i)\}_{i=1}^{N}$, where $x_i \in \mathbb{R}^d$ and $y_i \in \{+1, -1\}$ for binary classification or $y_i \in \mathbb{R}$ for regression. We denote $l(u, y)$ as a convex loss function (such as square loss, hinge loss and logistic loss). Given a positive definite kernel function $k(\cdot, \cdot)$ and the corresponding reproducing kernel Hilbert spaces (RKHS) $\mathcal{H}$ [2], kernel methods usually try to find a predictive function $f \in \mathcal{H}$ for solving the following optimization problem:

$$\arg\min_{f \in \mathcal{H}} \mathcal{L}(f) = \mathbb{E}_{(x,y)} l(f(x), y) + \frac{c}{2}\|f\|_{\mathcal{H}}^2, \tag{1}$$

where $c > 0$ is a regularization parameter.

2.2   Random Feature Approximation

Random feature [17,18] is a powerful technique to scale kernel methods. It utilizes the intriguing duality between positive definite kernels which are continuous and shift invariant (*i.e.*, $k(x_i, x_j) = k(x_i - x_j)$) and stochastic processes as shown in Theorem 1.

Theorem 1 ([19]). *A continuous, real-valued, symmetric and shift-invariant function $k(x_i, x_j) = k(x_i - x_j)$ on $\mathbb{R}^d$ is a positive definite kernel if and only if there is a finite non-negative measure $\mathbb{P}(\omega)$ on $\mathbb{R}^d$, such that*

$$k(x_i - x_j) = \int_{\mathbb{R}^d} e^{i\omega^T(x_i - x_j)} d\mathbb{P}(\omega) \tag{2}$$

$$= \int_{\mathbb{R}^d \times [0,2\pi]} 2\cos(\omega^T x_i + b)\cos(\omega^T x_j + b) d(\mathbb{P}(\omega) \times \mathbb{P}(b)),$$

where $\mathbb{P}(b)$ is a uniform distribution on $[0, 2\pi]$, and $\phi_\omega(x) = \sqrt{2}\cos(\omega^T x + b)$.

According to Theorem 1, for effective computation, we approximate the kernel function with Monte-Carlo sampling as follow:

$$k(x_i - x_j) \approx \frac{1}{D} \sum_{z=1}^{D} \phi_{\omega_z}(x_i)\phi_{\omega_z}(x_j) = \phi_\omega(x_i)\phi_\omega(x_j), \qquad (3)$$

where D is the number of random feature and $\omega_z \in \mathbb{R}^d$ are drawn from $\mathbb{P}(\omega)$, for convenience, w in last equality is stacked into a matrix, i.e., $\omega \in \mathbb{R}^{d \times D}$. Specifically, for Gaussian RBF kernel $k(x_i, x_j) = \exp(-||x_i - x_j||^2/2\sigma^2)$, $\mathbb{P}(\omega)$ is a Gaussian distribution with density proportional to $\exp(-\sigma^2||\omega||^2/2)$. For the Laplace kernel [26], this yields a Cauchy distribution. Notice that computing random feature map ϕ requires to compute a linear combination of the raw input features, which can be partitioned vertically. This character makes random feature approximation well-suited for the federated learning setting.

2.3   Doubly Stochastic Gradient

Based on the definition of the function $f \in \mathcal{H}$, we easily obtain $\nabla f(x) = \nabla \langle f, k(x, \cdot)\rangle_\mathcal{H} = k(x, \cdot)$, and $\nabla||f||^2_\mathcal{H} = \nabla \langle f, f\rangle_\mathcal{H} = 2f$. Consequently, the stochastic gradient of $\nabla f(x)$ w.r.t. the random feature ω can be rewritten as the following (4):

$$\nabla \hat{f}(x) = \hat{k}(x, \cdot) = \phi_\omega(x)\phi_\omega(\cdot). \qquad (4)$$

Given a randomly sampled instance (x_i, y_i), and a random feature ω_i, the doubly stochastic gradient of the loss function $l(f(x_i), y_i)$ on RKHS w.r.t. the sampled instance (x_i, y_i) and the random feature ω_i can be formulated as follows.

$$\xi(\cdot) = l'(f(x_i), y_i)\phi_{\omega_i}(x_i)\phi_{\omega_i}(\cdot). \qquad (5)$$

Since $\nabla||f||^2_\mathcal{H} = 2f$, the stochastic gradient of $\mathcal{L}(f)$ can be formulated as follows:

$$\hat{\xi}(\cdot) = \xi(\cdot) + cf(\cdot) = l'(f(x_i), y_i)\phi_{\omega_i}(x_i)\phi_{\omega_i}(\cdot) + cf(\cdot). \qquad (6)$$

Note that we have $\mathbb{E}_{(x,y)}\mathbb{E}_\omega\hat{\xi}(\cdot) = \nabla \mathcal{L}(f)$. According to the stochastic gradient (6), we can update the solution by stepsize η_t. Then, let $f_1(\cdot) = \mathbf{0}$, we have that:

$$f_{t+1}(\cdot) = f_t(\cdot) - \eta_t\,(\xi(\cdot) + cf(\cdot)) = \sum_{i=1}^{t} -\eta_i \prod_{j=i+1}^{t} (1 - \eta_j c)\zeta_i(\cdot) \qquad (7)$$

$$= \sum_{i=1}^{t} -\eta_i \prod_{j=i+1}^{t} (1 - \eta_j c)l'(f(x_i), y_i)\phi_{\omega_i}(x_i)\phi_{\omega_i}(\cdot) = \sum_{i=1}^{t} \alpha_i^t \phi_{\omega_i}(\cdot)$$

According to (7), the function $f(\cdot)$ could be viewed as the weighted sum about $\phi_{\omega_i}(\cdot)$ where the weights are α_i^t, for $i = 1, \cdots, t$. Same to the kernel model form $f(x) = \sum_i^N \alpha_i k(x_i, x)$ mentioned in Section.1, the predictive function $f(x)$ in (7) do not satisfy the assumption of implicitly linear separability.

Discussion. The key that DSG could be extended to vertical partitioned data scenario is that the computation of random features can be *linearly separable*. Therefore, we compute the partitioned random feature of the vertical partitioned data in local worker, and when we need the entire kernel function to compute the global functional gradient, we could easily reconstruct the entire random feature from local workers by summing local random feature.

3   Vertical Federated Kernel Learning

In this section, we provide the non-linear problem restatement in vertical partitioned data scenario. Then, we give the overall method structure. Finally, we provide the detailed description of our VFKL algorithm.

3.1   Problem Restatement

As mentioned previously, in numerous real-world data mining and machine learning applications, the training instance (x, y) is divided vertically into m parts, *i.e.*, $x = [x_{g_1}, x_{g_2}, \ldots, x_{g_m}]$, and $x_{g_\ell} \in \mathbb{R}^{d_\ell}$ is stored on the ℓ-th worker and $\sum_{\ell=1}^{m} d_\ell = d$. According to whether the label is included in a worker, we divide the workers into two types: one is active worker and the other is passive worker, where the active worker is the data provider who holds the label of a instance, and the passive worker only has the input of a instance. The active worker would be a dominating server in federated learning, while passive workers play the role of clients [4]. We let S_ℓ denote the data stored on the ℓ-th worker, where the labels y_i are distributed on active workers. S_ℓ includes parts of labels $\{y_i\}_{i=1}^{l}$. Thus, our goal in this chapter can be presented as follows.

Goal. Solving the nonlinear learning problem (1) by collaborating with these active workers and passive workers on the vertically partitioned data $\{S_\ell\}_{\ell=1}^{m}$ while keeping data privacy.

3.2   Method Structure

Same to the vertical federated learning setting, each worker keeps its local vertically partitioned data. Figure 1 presents the system structure of VFKL. As we mentioned above, the main idea of VFKL is that the computation of the random features can be vertically divided. Specifically, we give detailed descriptions of data privacy, model privacy and tree-structured communication, respectively, as follows:

- **Data Privacy:** To keep the vertically partitioned data privacy, we need to divide the computation of the value of $\phi_{\omega_i}(x_i) = \sqrt{2}\cos(\omega_i^T x_i + b)$ to avoid transferring the local data $(x_i)_{g_\ell}$ to other workers. Specifically, we send a random seed to the ℓ-th worker. Once the ℓ-th worker receive the random seed, it can generate the random direction ω_i uniquely according to the random

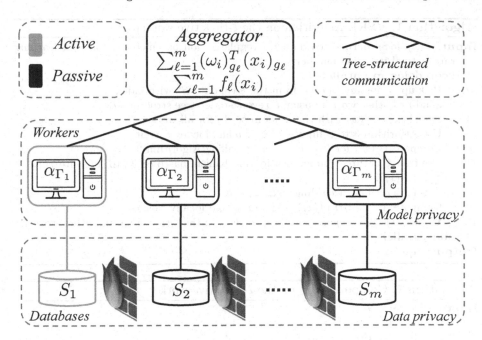

Fig. 1. System structure of VFKL.

seed. Thus, we can locally compute $(\omega_i)_{g_\ell}^T (x_i)_{g_\ell} + b$ which avoids directly transferring the local data $(x_i)_{g_\ell}$ to other workers for computing $\omega_i^T x_i + b$. In the next section, we will discuss it is hard to infer any $(x_i)_{g_\ell}$ according to the value of $(\omega_i)_{g_\ell}^T (x_i)_{g_\ell} + b$ from other workers.

– **Model Privacy:** The model coefficients α_i are stored in different workers separately and privately. According to the location of the model coefficients α_i, we partition the model coefficients $\{\alpha_i\}_{i=1}^t$ as $\{\alpha_{\Gamma_\ell}\}_{\ell=1}^m$, where α_{Γ_ℓ} denotes the model coefficients at the ℓ-th worker, and Γ_ℓ is the set of corresponding iteration indices. We do not directly transfer the local model coefficients α_{Γ_ℓ} to other workers. To compute $f(x)$, we locally compute $f_\ell(x) = \sum_{i \in \Gamma_\ell} \alpha_i \phi_{\omega_i}(x)$ and transfer it to other worker, and $f(x)$ can be reconstructed by summing over all the $f_\ell(x)$. It is difficult to infer the local model coefficients α_{Γ_ℓ} based on the value of $f_\ell(x)$ if $|\Gamma_\ell| \geq 2$. Thus, we achieve the model privacy.

– **Tree-Structured Communication:** Zhang et al. [28] proposed an efficient tree-structured communication mechanism to get the global sum which is faster than the simple strategies of star-structured communication [24] and ring-structured communication [27]. We adopt this mechanism for efficiently and privately accumulating the local results from different workers.

Algorithm. To extend DSG to federated learning on vertically partitioned data while keeping data privacy, we need to carefully design the procedures of computing $\omega_i^T x_i + b$, $f(x_i)$ and the solution updates, which are presented in detail as follows.

Algorithm 1. VFKL Algorithm on the ℓ-th active worker

Input: $\mathbb{P}(\omega)$, local normalized data S^ℓ, regularization parameter c, constant learning
rate η, total iteration number t.

1: **keep doing in parallel**
2:    Pick up an instance $(x_i)_{g_\ell}$ from the local data S^ℓ with index i.
3:    Send i to other workers using a reverse-order tree structure T_0.
4:    Sample $\omega_i \sim \mathbb{P}(\omega)$ with the random seed i for all workers.
5:    Use Algorithm 3 to compute $\omega_i^T x_i + b$ and locally save it.
6:    Compute $f_{\ell'}(x_i)$ for $\ell' = 1, \ldots, m$ by calling Algorithm 2.
7:    Use tree-structured communication mechanism based on T_0 to compute $f(x_i) = \sum_{\ell=1}^m f_\ell(x_i)$.
8:    Compute $\phi_{\omega_i}(x_i)$ according to $\omega_i^T x_i + b$.
9:    Compute $\alpha_i = -\eta \left(l'(f(x_i), y_i) \phi_{\omega_i}(x_i) \right)$ and locally save α_i.
10:    Update $\alpha_j = (1 - \eta c)\alpha_j$ for all previous j in the ℓ-th worker and other workers.
11: **end parallel loop**
Output: α_{Γ^ℓ}.

Algorithm 2. Compute $f_\ell(x)$ on the ℓ-th active worker

Input: $\mathbb{P}(\omega)$, α_{Γ^ℓ}, Γ_ℓ, x.

1: Set $f_\ell(x) = 0$.
2: **for each** $i \in \Gamma_\ell$ **do**
3:    Sample $\omega_i \sim \mathbb{P}(\omega)$ with the random seed i for all workers.
4:    Obtain $\omega_i^T x + b$ if it is locally saved, otherwise compute $\omega_i^T x + b$ by using Algorithm 3.
5:    Compute $\phi_{\omega_i}(x)$ according to $\omega_i^T x + b$.
6:    $f_\ell(x) = f_\ell(x) + \alpha_i \phi_{\omega_i}(x)$
7: **end for**
Output: $f_\ell(x)$

---

1. **Computing $\omega_i^T x_i + b$:** We generate the random direction ω_i according to a same random seed i and a probability measure $\mathbb{P}$ for each worker. Thus, we can locally compute $(\omega_i)_{g_\ell}^T (x_i)_{g_\ell}$. To keep $(x_i)_{g_\ell}$ private, instead of directly transferring $(\omega_i)_{g_\ell}^T (x_i)_{g_\ell}$ to other workers, we randomly generate b_ℓ uniformly from $[0, 2\pi]$, and transfer $(\omega_i)_{g_\ell}^T (x_i)_{g_\ell} + b_\ell$ to another worker. After all workers have calculated $(\omega_i)_{g_\ell}^T (x_i)_{g_\ell} + b_\ell$ locally, we can get the global sum $\sum_{\hat{\ell}=1}^m \left((\omega_i)_{g_{\hat{\ell}}}^T (x_i)_{g_{\hat{\ell}}} + b_{\hat{\ell}} \right)$ efficiently and safely by using a tree-structured communication mechanism based on the tree structure T_1 for workers $\{1, \ldots, m\}$ [28].

Currently, for the ℓ-th worker, we get multiple values of b with m times. To recover the value of $\sum_{\hat{\ell}=1}^m \left((\omega_i)_{g_{\hat{\ell}}}^T (x_i)_{g_{\hat{\ell}}} \right) + b$, we pick up one $b_{\ell'}$ from $\{1, \ldots, m\}/\{\ell\}$ as the value of b by removing other values of $b_{\hat{\ell}}$ (*i.e.*, removing $\bar{b}_{\ell'} = \sum_{\hat{\ell} \neq \ell'} b_{\hat{\ell}}$). In order to prevent leaking any information of b_ℓ, we use

---

Algorithm 3. Compute $\omega_i^T x_i + b$ on the ℓ-th active worker

---

Input: ω_i, x_i

$\{//$ This loop asks multiple workers running in parallel.$\}$

1: **for** $\hat{\ell} = 1, \ldots, m$ **do**

2:    Compute $(\omega_i)_{g_{\hat{\ell}}}^T (x_i)_{g_{\hat{\ell}}}$ and randomly generate a uniform number $b_{\hat{\ell}}$ from $[0, 2\pi]$ with the seed $\sigma_{\hat{\ell}}(i)$.

3:    Calculate $(\omega_i)_{g_{\hat{\ell}}}^T (x_i)_{g_{\hat{\ell}}} + b_{\hat{\ell}}$.

4: **end for**

5: Use tree-structured communication mechanism based on the tree structure T_1 for workers $\{1, \ldots, m\}$ to compute $\Delta = \sum_{\hat{\ell}=1}^{m} \left((\omega_i)_{g_{\hat{\ell}}}^T (x_i)_{g_{\hat{\ell}}} + b_{\hat{\ell}} \right)$.

6: Pick up $\ell' \in \{1, \ldots, m\}/\{\ell\}$ uniformly at random.

7: Use tree-structured communication mechanism based on the totally different tree structure T_2 for workers $\{1, \ldots, m\}/\{\ell'\}$ to compute $\bar{b}_{\ell'} = \sum_{\hat{\ell} \neq \ell'} b_{\hat{\ell}}$.

Output: $\Delta - \bar{b}_{\ell'}$.

---

a *totally different tree structure* T_2 for workers $\{1, \ldots, m\}/\{\ell'\}$ (please see Definition 1) to compute $\bar{b}_{\ell'} = \sum_{\hat{\ell} \neq \ell'} b_{\hat{\ell}}$. The detailed procedure of computing $\omega_i^T x_i + b$ is summarized in Algorithm 3.

Definition 1 (Two Different Trees). *For two tree structures T_1 and T_2, they are totally different if there does not exist a subtree with more than one leaf which belongs to both of T_1 and T_2.*

2. **Computing $f(x_i)$:** According to (7), we have that $f(x_i) = \sum_{i=1}^{t} \alpha_i^t \phi_{\omega_i}(x_i)$. However, α_i^t and $\phi_{\omega_i}(x_i)$ are stored in different workers. Thus, we first locally compute $f_\ell(x_i) = \sum_{i \in \Gamma_\ell} \alpha_i^t \phi_{\omega_i}(x_i)$ which is summarized in Algorithm 2. By using a tree-structured communication mechanism, we can get the global sum $\sum_{\ell=1}^{m} f_\ell(x_i)$ efficiently which is equal to $f(x_i)$ (please see Line 7 in Algorithm 1).

3. **Updating Rules:** Since α_i^t are stored in different workers, we use a communication mechanism with a reverse-order tree structure to update α_i^t in each workers by the coefficient $(1 - \eta c)$ (please see Line 10 in Algorithm 1).

Based on these key procedures, we summarize our overall VFKL algorithm in Algorithm 1. Different to the diminishing learning rate used in DSG, our VFKL uses a constant learning rate η which can be implemented more easily in the parallel computing environment. However, the convergence analysis for constant learning rate is more difficult than the one for diminishing learning rate. We give the theoretic analysis in the following section.

4   Theoretical Analysis

In this section, we provide the convergence, security and complexity analysis of the proposed VFKL. All detailed proofs are provided in KDD [11] Appendix[1].

---

[1] https://drive.google.com/open?id=1ORqXDM1s1eiA-XApy4oCpGhAnhFbrqKn.

4.1　Convergence Analysis

As the basis of our analysis, our first lemma states that the output of Algorithm 3 is actually equal to $\omega_i^T x + b$.

Lemma 1. *The output of Algorithm 3 (i.e., $\sum_{\hat{\ell}=1}^{m} \left((\omega_i)_{g_{\hat{\ell}}}^T (x)_{g_{\hat{\ell}}} + b_{\hat{\ell}} \right) - \bar{b}_{\ell'}$ is equal to $\omega_i^T x + b$, where each $b_{\hat{\ell}}$ and b are drawn from a uniform distribution on $[0, 2\pi]$, $\bar{b}_{\ell'} = \sum_{\hat{\ell} \neq \ell'} b_{\hat{\ell}}$, and $\ell' \in \{1, \dots, q\}/\{\ell\}$.*

Based on Lemma 1, we can conclude that the federated learning algorithm (*i.e.*, VFKL) can produce the same doubly stochastic gradients as that of a DSG algorithm with constant learning rate. Thus, under Assumption 1, we can prove that VFKL converges to the optimal solution almost at a rate of $\mathcal{O}(1/t)$ as shown in Theorem 2. Note that the convergence proof of the original DSG algorithm in [5] is limited to diminishing learning rate.

Assumption 1. *Suppose the following conditions hold.*

1. *There exists an optimal solution, denoted as f_*, to the problem (1).*
2. *We have an upper bound for the derivative of $l(u, y)$ w.r.t. its 1st argument, i.e., $|l'(u, y)| < M$.*
3. *The loss function $l(u, y)$ and its first-order derivative are L-Lipschitz continuous in terms of the first argument.*
4. *We have an upper bound κ for the kernel value, i.e., $k(x, x') \leq \kappa$. We have an upper bound ϕ for random feature mapping, i.e., $|\phi_\omega(x)\phi_\omega(x')| \leq \phi$.*

Theorem 2. *Set $\epsilon > 0$, $\min\{\frac{1}{c}, \frac{\epsilon c}{4M^2(\sqrt{\kappa} + \sqrt{\phi})^2}\} > \eta > 0$, for Algorithm 1, with $\eta = \frac{\epsilon \vartheta}{8\kappa B}$ for $\vartheta \in (0, 1]$, under Assumption 1, we will reach $\mathbb{E}\left[|f_t(x) - f_*(x)|^2\right] \leq \epsilon$ after*

$$t \geq \frac{8\kappa B \log(8\kappa e_1/\epsilon)}{\vartheta \epsilon c} \tag{8}$$

iterations, where $B = \left[\sqrt{G_2^2 + G_1} + G_2\right]^2$, $G_1 = \frac{2\kappa M^2}{c}$, $G_2 = \frac{\kappa^{1/2} M (\sqrt{\kappa} + \sqrt{\phi})}{2c^{3/2}}$ and $e_1 = \mathbb{E}[\|h_1 - f_*\|_{\mathcal{H}}^2]$.

Remark 1. Based on Theorem 2, we have that for any given data x, the evaluated value of f_{t+1} at x will converge to that of a solution close to f_* in terms of the Euclidean distance. The rate of convergence is almost $\mathcal{O}(1/t)$, if eliminating the $\log(1/\epsilon)$ factor. Even though our algorithm has included more randomness by using random features, this rate is nearly the same as standard SGD. As a result, the efficiency of the proposed algorithm is guaranteed.

4.2　Security Analysis

We discuss the data security (in other words, prevent local data on one worker leaked to or inferred by other workers) of VFKL under the *semi-honest* assumption which is commonly used in previous works [4, 13, 24].

Assumption 2 (Semi-honest Security). *All workers will follow the protocol or algorithm to perform the correct computations. However, they may retain records of the intermediate computation results which they may use later to infer the data of other workers.*

Because each worker knows the parameter ω given a random seed, we can have a linear system of $o_j = (\omega_j)_{g_\ell}^T (x_i)_{g_\ell}$ with a sequence of trials of ω_j and o_j. It has the potential to infer $(x_i)_{g_\ell}$ from the linear system of $o_j = (\omega_j)_{g_\ell}^T (x_i)_{g_\ell}$ if the sequence of o_j is also known. We call it inference attack. Please see its formal definition in Definition 2. In this part, we will prove that VFKL can prevent inference attack (*i.e.*, Theorem 3).

Definition 2 (Inference Attack). *An inference attack on the ℓ-th worker is to infer a certain feature group g of sample x_i which belongs to other workers without directly accessing it.*

Theorem 3. *Under the semi-honest assumption, the VFKL algorithm can prevent inference attack.*

As discussed above, the key of preventing the inference attack is to mask the value of o_j. As described in lines 2–3 of Algorithm 3, we add an extra random variable $b_{\hat{\ell}}$ into $(\omega_j)_{g_\ell}^T (x_i)_{g_\ell}$. Each time, the algorithm only transfers the value of $(\omega_i)_{g_\ell}^T (x_i)_{g_\ell} + b_{\hat{\ell}}$ to another worker. Thus, it is impossible for the receiver worker to directly infer the value of o_j. Finally, the ℓ-th active worker gets the global sum $\sum_{\hat{\ell}=1}^m \left((\omega_i)_{g_{\hat{\ell}}}^T (x_i)_{g_{\hat{\ell}}} + b_{\hat{\ell}} \right)$ by using a tree-structured communication mechanism based on the tree structure T_1. Thus, lines 2–4 of Algorithm 3 keeps data privacy.

As proved in Lemma 1, lines 5–7 of Algorithm 3 is to get $\omega_i^T x + b$ by removing $\bar{b}_{\ell'} = \sum_{\hat{\ell} \neq \ell'} b_{\hat{\ell}}$ from the sum $\sum_{\hat{\ell}=1}^m \left((\omega_i)_{g_{\hat{\ell}}}^T (x_i)_{g_{\hat{\ell}}} + b_{\hat{\ell}} \right)$. To prove that VFKL can prevent the inference attack, we only need to prove that the calculation of $\bar{b}_{\ell'} = \sum_{\hat{\ell} \neq \ell'} b_{\hat{\ell}}$ in line 7 of Algorithm 3 does not disclose the value of $b_{\hat{\ell}}$ or the sum of $b_{\hat{\ell}}$ on a node of tree T_1, which is indicated in Lemma 2.

Lemma 2. *In Algorithm 3, if T_1 and T_2 are totally different tree structures, for any worker $\hat{\ell}$, there is no risk to disclose the value of $b_{\hat{\ell}}$ or the sum of $b_{\hat{\ell}}$ to other workers.*

4.3 Complexity Analysis

The computational complexity for one iteration of VFKL is $\mathcal{O}(dmt)$. The total computational complexity of VFKL is $\mathcal{O}(dmt^2)$. Further, the communication cost for one iteration of VFKL is $\mathcal{O}(mt)$, and the total communication cost of VFKL is $\mathcal{O}(mt^2)$. The details of deriving the computational complexity and communication cost of VFKL are provided in Appendix.

5   Experiments

In this section, we first present the experimental setup, and then provide the experimental results and discussions.

5.1   Experimental Setup

Design of Experiments. To demonstrate the superiority of VFKL on federated kernel learning with vertically partitioned data, we compare VFKL with PP-SVMV [27], which is the state-of-the-art algorithm of the field. Additionally, we also compare with SecureBoost [4], which is recently proposed to generalize the gradient tree-boosting algorithm to federated scenarios. Moreover, to verify the predictive accuracy of VFKL on vertically partitioned data, we compare with oracle learners that can access the whole data samples without the federated learning constraint. For the oracle learners, we use state-of-the-art kernel classification solvers, including LIBSVM [3] and DSG [5]. Finally, we include FD-SVRG [24], which uses a linear model, to comparatively verify the accuracy of VFKL.

Table 1. The benchmark datasets used in the experiments.

Datasets	Features	Size
gisette	5,000	6,000
a9a	123	48,842
real-sim	20,958	72,309
epsilon	2,000	400,000
defaultcredit	23	30,000
givemecredit	10	150,000

Implementation Details. Our experiments were performed on a 24-core two-socket Intel Xeon CPU E5-2650 v4 machine with 256GB RAM. We implemented our VFKL in python, where the parallel computation was handled via MPI4py [6]. We utilized the SecureBoost algorithm through the official unified framework[2]. The code of LIBSVM is provided by [3]. We used the implementation[3] provided by [5] for DSG. We modified it to constant learning rate case. Our experiments use the following binary classification datasets as described below.

---

[2] The framework code is available at https://github.com/FederatedAI/FATE.
[3] DSG code: https://github.com/zixu1986/Doubly_Stochastic_Gradients.

Datasets. We summarizes the datasets used in experiment (including four binary classification datasets and two real-world financial datasets) at Table 1. The first four datasets are obtained from LIBSVM website[4], the defaultcredit dataset is from UCI[5], and the givemecredit dataset is from Kaggle[6]. We split the dataset as 3:1 for train and test partition, respectively. Note that in the experiments of the *real-sim*, *givemecredit* and *epsilon* datasets, PP-SVMV always runs out of memory, which means this method only works when the number of instance is below around 45,000 when using the computation resources specified above. Since the training time is beyond 15 h, the result of SecureBoost algorithm on *epsilon* dataset is absent.

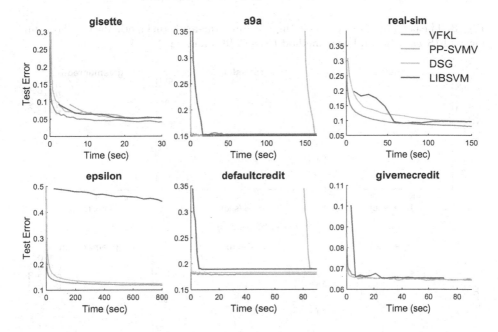

Fig. 2. The results of binary classification above the comparison methods.

5.2 Results and Discussions

We provide the test errors *v.s.* training time picture on four state-of-the-art kernel methods in Fig. 2. Obviously, our algorithm always achieves fastest convergence rate compared to other state-of-art kernel methods.

We also present the test errors of three state-of-the-art kernel methods, treeboosting method (SecureBoost), linear method (FD-SVRG) and our VFKL in

---

[4] Datasets can be found at https://www.csie.ntu.edu.tw/~cjlin/libsvmtools/data sets/.
[5] https://archive.ics.uci.edu/ml/datasets/default+of+credit+card+clients.
[6] https://www.kaggle.com/c/GiveMeSomeCredit/data.

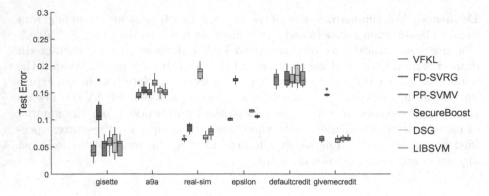

Fig. 3. The boxplot of test errors of three state-of-the-art kernel methods, tree-boosting method (SecureBoost), linear method (FD-SVRG) and our VFKL.

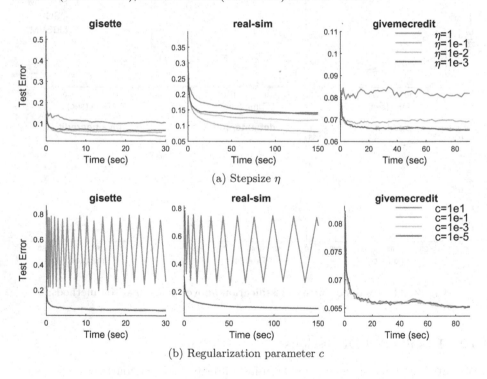

(a) Stepsize η

(b) Regularization parameter c

Fig. 4. The sensitive results of hyper-parameters on our VFKL methods.

Fig. 3. All results are averaged over 10 different train-test split trials. From the plot, we find that our VFKL always achieves lowest test error and variance. In addition, tree-boosting method SecureBoost performs poor in high-dimensional datasets such as *real-sim*. It is easy to found that linear method normally has worse results than other kernel methods.

Finally, we provide the sensitive results of hyper-parameters such as the stepsize η and the regularization parameter c in Fig. 4. At experiments, we select η from the interval $[1 : 1e^{-3}]$ and c from the interval $[1e^1 : 1e^{-5}]$. According to the results, our method always achieves better performance at smaller stepsize eta. And our method seems not sensitive to smaller regularization parameter.

6 Conclusion

To do privacy-preservation federated learning over vertically partitioned data is raring in current data mining application. In this chapter, we proposed VFKL algorithm to deal with vertically partitioned data, which breaks the limitation of implicitly linear separability used in the existing federated learning algorithms. We proved that VFKL has a sublinear convergence rate, and can guarantee data security under the semi-honest assumption. To the best of our knowledge, VFKL is the first efficient and scalable privacy-preservation federated kernel method. Extensive experimental results show that VFKL is more efficient than the existing state-of-the-art kernel methods particularly in high dimensional data while retaining a similar generalization performance.

References

1. Badshah, N.: Facebook to contact 87 million users affected by data breach. The Guardian) (2018). https://www.theguardian.com/technology/2018/apr/08/facebook-to-contact-the-87-million-users-affected-by-data-breach
2. Berlinet, A., Thomas-Agnan, C.: Reproducing Kernel Hilbert Spaces in Probability and Statistics. Springer, New York (2011)
3. Chang, C.C., Lin, C.J.: LIBSVM: a library for support vector machines. ACM Trans. Intell. Syst. Technol. **2**, 1–27 (2011). Software. http://www.csie.ntu.edu.tw/~cjlin/libsvm
4. Cheng, K., Fan, T., Jin, Y., Liu, Y., Chen, T., Yang, Q.: SecureBoost: a lossless federated learning framework. arXiv preprint arXiv:1901.08755 (2019)
5. Dai, B., Xie, B., He, N., Liang, Y., Raj, A., Balcan, M.F.F., Song, L.: Scalable kernel methods via doubly stochastic gradients. In: Advances in Neural Information Processing Systems, pp. 3041–3049 (2014)
6. Dalcin, L.D., Paz, R.R., Kler, P.A., Cosimo, A.: Parallel distributed computing using Python. Adv. Water Resour. **34**(9), 1124–1139 (2011)
7. Du, W., Atallah, M.J.: Privacy-preserving cooperative statistical analysis. In: Seventeenth Annual Computer Security Applications Conference, pp. 102–110. IEEE (2001)
8. EU: Regulation (EU) 2016/679 of the European parliament and of the council on the protection of natural persons with regard to the processing of personal data and on the free movement of such data, and repealing directive 95/46/EC (general data protection regulation) (2016). https://eur-lex.europa.eu/legal-content/EN/TXT
9. Gascón, A., et al.: Secure linear regression on vertically partitioned datasets. IACR Cryptology ePrint Archive **2016**, 892 (2016)

10. Gascón, A., et al.: Privacy-preserving distributed linear regression on high-dimensional data. Proc. Priv. Enhancing Technol. **2017**(4), 345–364 (2017)
11. Gu, B., Dang, Z., Li, X., Huang, H.: Federated doubly stochastic kernel learning for vertically partitioned data. In: Proceedings of the 26th ACM SIGKDD International Conference on Knowledge Discovery & Data Mining on Applied Data Science Track. ACM (2020)
12. Gu, B., Huo, Z., Huang, H.: Asynchronous doubly stochastic group regularized learning. In: International Conference on Artificial Intelligence and Statistics, pp. 1791–1800 (2018)
13. Hardy, S., et al.: Private federated learning on vertically partitioned data via entity resolution and additively homomorphic encryption. arXiv preprint arXiv:1711.10677 (2017)
14. Karr, A.F., Lin, X., Sanil, A.P., Reiter, J.P.: Privacy-preserving analysis of vertically partitioned data using secure matrix products. J. Off. Stat. **25**(1), 125 (2009)
15. Liu, Y., Liu, Y., Liu, Z., Zhang, J., Meng, C., Zheng, Y.: Federated forest. arXiv preprint arXiv:1905.10053 (2019)
16. Nock, R., et al.: Entity resolution and federated learning get a federated resolution. arXiv preprint arXiv:1803.04035 (2018)
17. Rahimi, A., Recht, B.: Random features for large-scale kernel machines. In: Advances in Neural Information Processing Systems, pp. 1177–1184 (2008)
18. Rahimi, A., Recht, B.: Weighted sums of random kitchen sinks: replacing minimization with randomization in learning. In: Advances in Neural Information Processing Systems, pp. 1313–1320 (2009)
19. Rudin, W.: Fourier Analysis on Groups, vol. 121967. Wiley, Hoboken (1962)
20. Sanil, A.P., Karr, A.F., Lin, X., Reiter, J.P.: Privacy preserving regression modelling via distributed computation. In: Proceedings of the tenth ACM SIGKDD International Conference on Knowledge Discovery and Data Mining, pp. 677–682. ACM (2004)
21. Skillicorn, D.B., Mcconnell, S.M.: Distributed prediction from vertically partitioned data. J. Parallel Distrib. Comput. **68**(1), 16–36 (2008)
22. Vaidya, J., Clifton, C.: Privacy preserving association rule mining in vertically partitioned data. In: Proceedings of the Eighth ACM SIGKDD International Conference on Knowledge Discovery And Data Mining, pp. 639–644. ACM (2002)
23. Vaidya, J., Clifton, C.: Privacy-preserving k-means clustering over vertically partitioned data. In: Proceedings of the Ninth ACM SIGKDD International Conference on Knowledge Discovery and Data Mining, pp. 206–215 (2003)
24. Wan, L., Ng, W.K., Han, S., Lee, V.: Privacy-preservation for gradient descent methods. In: Proceedings of the 13th ACM SIGKDD International Conference on Knowledge Discovery and Data Mining, pp. 775–783. ACM (2007)
25. Xie, B., Liang, Y., Song, L.: Scale up nonlinear component analysis with doubly stochastic gradients. In: Advances in Neural Information Processing Systems, pp. 2341–2349 (2015)
26. Yang, J., Sindhwani, V., Fan, Q., Avron, H., Mahoney, M.W.: Random laplace feature maps for semigroup kernels on histograms. In: Proceedings of the IEEE Conference on Computer Vision and Pattern Recognition, pp. 971–978 (2014)
27. Yu, H., Vaidya, J., Jiang, X.: Privacy-preserving SVM classification on vertically partitioned data. In: Ng, W.-K., Kitsuregawa, M., Li, J., Chang, K. (eds.) PAKDD 2006. LNCS (LNAI), vol. 3918, pp. 647–656. Springer, Heidelberg (2006). https://doi.org/10.1007/11731139_74
28. Zhang, G.D., Zhao, S.Y., Gao, H., Li, W.J.: Feature-distributed SVRG for high-dimensional linear classification. arXiv preprint arXiv:1802.03604 (2018)

Towards Byzantine-Resilient Federated Learning via Group-Wise Robust Aggregation

Lei Yu[✉] and Lingfei Wu

IBM Research, Yorktown Heights, NY, USA
Lei.Yu1@ibm.com, wuli@us.ibm.com

Abstract. Federated learning (FL) is a distributed machine learning approach where many participants collaboratively train a model while keeping the training data decentralized. The distributed setting makes FL vulnerable to Byzantine failures and malicious participants, leading to unusable models or compromised model with backdoor. Although several robust statistics based methods have been proposed to address the robustness of FL against Byzantine failures, recent works has shown the insufficiency of their defenses because that non-i.i.d data distribution and high variance of gradients among participants in practical FL settings disrupt their common assumptions. To address this problem, we propose a simple but efficient group-wise robust aggregation framework, which clusters model parameters into different groups and applies robust aggregation with-in each cluster. We apply our framework with a number of popular Byzantine-robust aggregation methods, and evaluate its resiliency against the attack that can successfully circumvent these methods in their original settings. Our experimental results demonstrate that the group-wise robust aggregation effectively improves the robustness against Byzantine failures and highlights the effect of clustering for addressing the gap between practical FL and theoretical assumptions of robust statistics based defense.

Keywords: Federated learning · Byzantine attacks · Robustness · Machine learning security · Poisoning attack

1 Introduction

Federated Learning (FL) is a recent approach of distributed machine learning that attracts significant attentions from both industry and academia [7,9], because of its advantages on data privacy and large-scale deployment. In FL, the training dataset is distributed among many participants (e.g., mobile phones, IoT devices or organizations). Each participant maintains a local model with its local training dataset and collaboratively updates a global model under the coordination of a central server. By keeping the training datasets locally along with data owners, FL mitigates data privacy risks while enabling the harvest of

© Springer Nature Switzerland AG 2020
Q. Yang et al. (Eds.): Federated Learning, LNAI 12500, pp. 81–92, 2020.
https://doi.org/10.1007/978-3-030-63076-8_6

decentralized information and computing resources. Despite of its significance and advantages, FL can be vulnerable to various kinds of failures and attacks. The participants can behave arbitrarily during the learning process, which is typically modeled as Byzantine failure, due to software crashes, faulty hardware, or compromised devices by malicious attackers. Therefore, the updates from a participant can deviate arbitrarily from true values, which can create major degradation in learning performance [5] and vulnerable models that suffers evasion attacks [11] and backdoor attacks [3].

In FL, the coordinator computes a new global model via aggregation of the model updates from every participant round by round. A standard aggregation function is to compute the mean of local model parameters received from participants [9]. It has been shown that the mean aggregation is not Byzantine resilient, in the sense that the global model can be arbitrarily deviated even if only one participant is compromised [5]. To improve the robustness of FL against Byzantine failures of certain participants, a number of works have been proposed [1,5,10,13,14] to replace the mean aggregation with a robust estimate of the mean, such as median [14], Trimmed mean [14], Krum [5] and Bulyan [10]. Their theoretical analysis have shown provable robustness against Byzantine failure.

All the robust aggregation based defenses lie some important basis assumptions: the data samples are independent and identically distributed (i.i.d.) among participants and so as well for model parameters; the variance of model parameters between different participants is limited such that large changes on model parameters can be removed with robust estimates. However, those two assumptions often do not hold in practical FL settings. A fundamental characteristic of FL in realistic applications is unbalanced and non-i.i.d partitioning of data across different participants. Previous work [6] has shown that the error rate of models trained with robust aggregation increases with the degree of non-i.i.d, which indicates the ineffectiveness of robust aggregation when the FL setting has highly non-i.i.d data. For the second assumption, recent work [4] showed that the variance is indeed high enough even for simple datasets which allows sufficient malicious changes to subvert the final model.

To combat the mismatch between the basis assumed by robust aggregation and realistic FL settings, in this chapter we propose a group-wise aggregation framework. In our approach, every round the coordinator runs a clustering algorithm on the model updates from different participants and group similar model updates into different clusters. Robust aggregation is applied to each cluster to estimate the average center of the cluster. The global model is updated as the aggregation of all cluster centers, each of which is weighted by its cluster size or an evaluation score.

Intuitively, the group-wise aggregation addresses the mismatch mentioned above to a certain extent. For the i.i.d assumption, through clustering the model parameters in the same group share similar values and thus more likely they are from dataset with similar or identical distributions. The robust aggregation is performed group-wise, which allows the aggregation to yield a good estimator for the desired cluster average center. For the second variance assumption, the clustering reduces with-in cluster variance of model parameters, which limits the malicious changes to each cluster center. The final weighted average of different clusters further limits the malicious inference from Byzantine participants. Our experiment result shows that our framework improves the resiliency against Byzantine participants.

2   Background and Problem Statement

2.1   System Model

A standard FL training process [7] repeats a number of steps round by round until the training is stopped:

- Participant selection: The coordinator selects m number of participants that meet certain eligibility requirements such as the mobile phones with battery powered. Each participant is denoted by p_i, which has a local training dataset D_i.
- Broadcast: The coordinator sends the current global model parameters $\mathbf{w}$ to all m participants.
- Local model update: Each participant p_i aims to solve the optimization problem $\min_{\mathbf{w}_i} F(\mathbf{w}_i, D_i)$ where the model parameters $\mathbf{w}_i$ is initialized with global model parameters $\mathbf{w}$ and F is the objective loss function that measures the accuracy of the predictions made by the model $\mathbf{w}_i$ on each data point. A popular method to solve the optimization problem is stochastic gradient descent, which in each iteration t updates $\mathbf{w}_i$ by $\mathbf{w}'_i = \mathbf{w}_i - \gamma \frac{\partial F(\mathbf{w}_i, B_t)}{\partial \mathbf{w}_i}$ where B_t is a batch of random samples from D_i and γ is learning step size.
- Aggregation: The coordinator collects local models from every participant and aggregate them via an aggregation function $\mathcal{A}$ as $\mathbf{w}' = \mathcal{A}(\mathbf{w}_1, \ldots, \mathbf{w}_m)$
- Model update: The global model is updated, i.e., $\mathbf{w} \leftarrow \mathbf{w}'$.

A variant of local model update step is the participant p_i sends the difference $\Delta \mathbf{w}_i = \mathbf{w} - \mathbf{w}_i$ to the coordinator and the aggregation step instead computes $\mathbf{w}' = \mathbf{w} - \mathcal{A}(\Delta \mathbf{w}_1, \ldots, \Delta \mathbf{w}_m)$ which is equivalent to $\mathcal{A}(\mathbf{w}_1, \ldots, \mathbf{w}_m)$ for certain aggregations such as average [9] and coordinate-wise median aggregation [14].

Notation. In the rest of the chapter we use the following notations: Let $\mathcal{S}_w$ be the set $\{\mathbf{w}_i : i \in [m]\}$, d be the number of dimensions (parameters) of the model, and $(\mathbf{w}_i)_j$ be the j-th dimension parameter of $\mathbf{w}_i$ $(j \in [d])$.

2.2   Byzantine Failure and Attack Model

We consider Byzantine failure model [8] for participants in FL setting, which means that some participants may behave completely arbitrarily and send any model parameters to the coordinator. We assume the coordinator is trusted and secure, which means the computation at the coordinator server is always correct.

However, with arbitrary local model updates as input, the learned global model can deviate arbitrarily from an intact learning result.

The Byzantine failures can be caused either by non-malicious reasons such as unreliable network communication and software crash on participant devices, or malicious participants that aim to subvert the normal learning process through model poisoning attacks. The malicious failures are generally more damaging than non-malicious ones, since the adversaries can have capability to construct sophisticated, coordinated and undetectable attacks with maximizing their objectives.

There are two types of model poisoning attacks, to which it has been shown FL is vulnerable, untargeted poisoning attacks [6,10] and targeted poisoning attacks [2,4,12]. The goal of untargeted poisoning attack is to prevent the global model from reaching good accuracy or even convergence. It incurs a high error rate indiscriminately for testing examples. For targeted poisoning attacks, the adversary manipulates the model the training time such that it produces attacker-targeted prediction at the inference time for some particular testing examples, e.g. predicting a spam with some specific text as non-spam. Because this type of attacks only affect a small set of testing examples of interest while maintaining the overall accuracy, they are also known as backdoor attacks.

Because the participants in FL may be IoT devices, mobile phones etc., it is easy for an attacker to join the learning process with multiple devices fully under his control. In this chapter we assume the adversary can control up to f participants ($f < m$), and we call them malicious participants. The adversary has full access to the machine learning model, local training datasets, FL training plan at every malicious participants. Moreover, malicious participants can conclude with each other under the adversary's coordination in poisoning attacks. Also, in accordance with Kerckhoffs's principle, we assume the attacker has full knowledge of the defense mechanism used by FL.

2.3   Robust Aggregation Based Defense

In this section we provide an overview of the state-of-the-art defense mechanisms for FL using robust aggregation. It is worth to note that these methods are proposed in the context of distributed learning with synchronous SGD, in which the coordinator estimates the average of gradients collected from participants and use it to update the global model with a gradient descent step. It is actually equivalent to collecting and aggregating local model parameters when the same learning rate is used at the participants. Following our system model, we interpret each method with regard to model parameters.

Median [14]: It computes coordinate-wise median of local parameters across different participants. Formally, the aggregation can be expressed as

$$\mathcal{A}_{med}(\mathcal{S}_w) = \left\{ x_j = median(\{(\mathbf{w}_i)_j : i \in [m]\}) : j \in [d] \right\}$$

Trimmedmean [14]: It computes coordinate-wise trimmed mean at each dimension of the model parameter. It can be represented as

$$\mathcal{A}_{trimmedmean}(\mathcal{S}_w) = \left\{ x_j = \frac{1}{|U_j|} \sum_{i \in U_j} (\mathbf{w}_i)_j : j \in [d] \right\}$$

where U_j is the indices of elements in the vector $\{(\mathbf{w}_i)_j : i \in [m]\}$. The definition of U_j can vary: in [14] it can be obtained by removing the largest and smallest k elements from $\{(\mathbf{w}_i)_j : i \in [m]\}$, which means $|U_j| = m - 2k$; in [10] U_j is defined as the indices of top $m - 2k$ values in the vector $\{(\mathbf{w}_i)_j : i \in [m]\}$ that are closest to the median of the vector. They aim to defend against up to $f = \lceil \frac{m}{2} \rceil - 1$ malicious participants.

Krum [5]: Krum chooses one from the m local models that has minimum average distance to its $n - f - 2$ closest neighbors as the global model. The model parameter that differ significantly with its nearest parameters are outliers and discarded. Formally it can written as:

$$\mathcal{A}_{Krum}(\mathcal{S}_w) = (\mathbf{w}_i : i = argmin_{i \in [m]} \sum_{i \to j} ||w_i - w_j||^2)$$

where $i \to j$ represents the set of $\mathbf{w}_j$ that are $n - f - 2$ closest vectors to $\mathbf{w}_i$. Similarly, it is also designed to defend against up to $\lceil \frac{m}{2} \rceil - 1$ malicious participants.

Bulyan [10]: Due to the high dimensionality of the model parameters, the Euclidean distance may not capture the disagreement between two model parameters on a single coordinate. Therefore, the malicious participant can introduce a large change on a single parameter without significantly affecting the Euclidean distance, and render Krum ineffective. El Mhamdi et al. [10] proposed Bulyan to address this issue. Specifically, Bulyan first applies Krum iteratively to select a set of $n - 2f$ probably good candidates from $\mathcal{S}_w$. After that, Bulyan aggregates the candidates' model parameters with coordinate-wise robust aggregation such as TrimmedMean. By discarding outlying coordinates with TrimmedMean, it overcomes the above issue.

2.4 Why Defense Fails

Recent works [4,6,10] have shown that the defense mechanisms such as Krum, Trimmedmean, and Bulyan can be successfully defeated by carefully constructed attacks. The reasons for their failures fall into two categories.

– Non-IID data and high variance of model parameters disrupt the common assumption of Byzantine-robust aggregation methods [4,6]. The robust aggregation methods described above all assume i.i.d data (thus i.i.d gradient) among participants such that the averaging of model parameters can yield a good estimator. However, in practical FL settings the data can be highly unbalanced and Non-IID, which render the robust estimators less robust than

---

Algorithm 1: Group-wise Robust Aggregation Framework

Input: model updates $\{\Delta\mathbf{w}_i = \mathbf{w} - \mathbf{w}_i : i \in [m]\}$, current model $\mathbf{w}$

1 $\{C_i : i \in [k]\} \leftarrow Clustering(\{\Delta\mathbf{w}_i = \mathbf{w} - \mathbf{w}_i : i \in [m]\})$;

2 **for** $i \in [k]$ **do**

3 $\quad \mathbf{c}_i \leftarrow \mathcal{A}_{robust}(C_i)$;

4 $\quad a_i \leftarrow Scoring(\mathbf{c}_i)$;

5 **end**

6 $\Delta\mathbf{w} \leftarrow \frac{1}{\sum_{i \in [k]} a_i} \sum_{i \in [k]} a_i \mathbf{c}_i$;

7 **return** $\mathbf{w} - \Delta\mathbf{w}$

---

assumed theoretically. Most robust aggregation methods also assume that the variance of model parameters among benign participants are sufficiently bounded and malicious changes within that bound are not able to subvert the global model. As pointed out by [4], however, the variance can be high enough in practice (caused by Non-IID data and randomness of mini-batch SGD), which provides the attacker a large room to craft byzantine updates to deviate the global model as far as possible from the correct ones. The attack against Krum and Trimmedmean proposed in [6] searches the maximal possible model deviation that can be accepted and the inherent high variance ensures the attack a high chance to find the solution.

– Under the high dimensionality of model parameters, the l_p norm distance criteria is not sufficient for measuring deviation of model parameters from the unbiased one [10]. Therefore, l_p norm distance based outlier detection and robust aggregation (e.g. Krum) may not achieve desired resiliency against the attacks which: 1).exploit large deviation on a single dimension of model parameters, which can be sufficient enough to achieve desired malicious objective but without affect much the Euclidean distances with benign models; 2), for the infinite norm, only modify non-maximal coordinates to deviate the global model without substantially affecting the distance.

3 Group-Wise Robust Aggregation Framework

Our group-wise robust aggregation framework aims to improve the resiliency of robust aggregation against the adversarial attacks that exploit the weakness described in the previous section. In the framework, the updates of model parameters from participants $\{\Delta\mathbf{w}_i = \mathbf{w} - \mathbf{w}_i : i \in [m]\}$ are clustered into different groups by similarity. Each cluster of model updates is further aggregated with a robust aggregation method to compute a cluster center. The final model update is a weighted average of cluster centers. Algorithm 1 gives a formal description of our framework. It also has a scoring function to weight each cluster center and the final model update is a weighted combination of all cluster centers.

The clustering step is to reduce in-cluster variance of model parameters, for improving the resiliency of robust aggregation per-cluster. In realistic FL setting, each participant has its own source to collect or generate his local dataset. Thus, we can assume that each participant draw samples from one of data distributions independently. Yet, considering a large-scale FL setting with many participants, for each data distribution, there are multiple participants of which the local dataset is drawn from it. Following this assumption, the clustering of model updates by similarity is expected to implicitly group their source participants by the similarity of underlying data distributions, which means within a cluster data among participants satisfies i.i.d.

As a result of clustering, there are two cases for malicious participants: 1) they may be spread among groups or 2) majority of them are clustered into one group where the attacker try to deviate the cluster center from the correct one. In the first case, the number of malicious participants in a cluster can be small, the robust aggregation can effectively eliminate their impact. In the second case, the malicious updates can collectively drive the cluster center to the target desired by the attacker. However, they have very limited effect on other clusters of which the majority is benign. Since the global model update is computed as the sum of the cluster centers with each weighted by a scoring function, the deviation introduced by malicious participants can be further reduced.

3.1   Algorithm Details

Clustering: For the clustering of model parameter updates, we consider the popular k-means algorithm for cluster analysis. It is an iterative approach to partition n data points to k clusters. It minimizes within-cluster variances, which helps to deal with large variance weakness of existing robust aggregation methods. It requires a specified number of clusters k, which indicates a trade-off between resiliency and model quality, which we will discuss later.

Robust Aggregation per Cluster: Within each cluster, we can apply existing robust aggregation method such as Trimmed mean, Median, Krum and Bulyan to compute the center of the cluster. The reduced variance within each cluster improves the robustness of these methods and achieve a good estimate of correct cluster centers.

Scoring and Weighted Sum of Cluster Centers: The framework uses a scoring function to weight the quality and importance of each cluster center. A straightforward scoring function is to compute $a_i = \frac{|C_i|}{m}$ for cluster center c_i, i.e., each cluster is weighted by its normalized cluster size. Larger cluster size means that the corresponding center has more participants that support it. Another approach is to individually evaluate the model that is only updated with a single cluster center by the change of loss function over a small validation dataset. The cluster center with a higher accuracy or loss reduction is assigned with a higher weight. In this way, we further limit the impact of compromised clusters.

On one end, when $k = 1$ which means no group partitioning, our framework falls back to the original robust aggregation methods that work on the whole set of participants. On the other end which has $k = m$, each participant forms a cluster on its own and aggregation on a single point is itself. Therefore, the framework just computes the simple average aggregation of all local updates, but usually achieve the best model quality compared with robust aggregation methods under no attacks. We demonstrate that by have multiple clusters $1 < k < m$, our approach can achieve better resiliency than existing defenses based on robust aggregation, while in the case of no malicious participants it can achieve better accuracy.

Security Analysis:
To understand the resiliency of our framework, we consider a simple case with $k = 2$ and present an informal analysis. Suppose in our framework $\mathcal{A}(\mathbf{S})$ can defend against up to $\lceil \frac{|S|}{2} \rceil - 1$ malicious inputs in $\mathbf{S}$. We can show with clustering can be strictly stronger than without clustering. Without clustering, $\mathcal{A}$ fails when there are $\lceil \frac{m}{2} \rceil$ malicious participants. With clustering, it may not completely fail even there are $\lceil \frac{m}{2} \rceil$ malicious participants. If the clustering is a random partition of input data, in each cluster the malicious participants can take up to half of members and all clusters are compromised. In this case the resiliency is equivalent to the case of no clustering. However, in our framework the inputs are clustered by similarity. Because state-of-the-art attacks tend to let one targeted Byzantine update accepted via having all other malicious updates to support it, they have a larger chance to be grouped together. As a result, only one cluster center is compromised and another cluster center is intact. With a scoring function to evaluate their quality, the benign cluster center is assigned with higher weight and the global model can get closer to the true result. For a formal analysis, we leave it to our future work.

4   Evaluation

We evaluate the resiliency of our framework against the attacks recently proposed that evades all state-of-the-art robust aggregation based defenses [4] within different scenarios.

4.1   Experiment Setup

Our experiment follows the set-up in most previous defense and attack works [4, 10,14].

Datasets: We consider two datasets: MNIST and CIFAR10. MNIST includes 60,000 training examples and 10,000 testing examples, each of which is an 28×28 grayscale image of hand-written digits. CIFAR10 consists of 32×32 color images with three channels (RGB) in 10 classes including ships, planes, dogs and cats. Each class has 6000 images. There are 50,000 examples for training and 10,000 for testing.

Models and FL: We choose the same model architectures for the classification task on the two datasets and the same FL setting as the previous work [4]. For

MNIST, we use a simple feed-forward neural network that has a 100-dimensional hidden layer with ReLU activation and train it with cross-entropy objective. For CIFAR10, we use a 7-layer CNN with cross-entropy objective.

The models are trained with $m = 51$ participants in the Federated learning. Each participant performs one iteration of SGD on a batch of examples. For simplicity, in our experiments the gradients are broadcast and aggregated, which is equivalent to using model differences. By default, FL runs for 300 epochs and remembers the global model with maximal accuracy among all epochs.

Attack: At default we set $f = 12$ malicious participants, about 24% of total participants. We apply the untargeted model poisoning attack with the same parameter settings as [4]. The untargeted model poisoning attack, also referred to as convergence attack in [4], aims to make the global model to suffer high testing error rate, with small changes to model parameters. The attack searches the model changes within a perturbation range $(\mu - z\sigma, \mu + z\sigma)$ where μ and σ are the average and standard deviation of benign model updates, which can be estimated by the attacker with all the controlled malicious participants. z is determined in the way that there are s non-malicious participants reside farther away from the mean than malicious participants, so the defense prefer to select malicious model updates. With assuming normal distribution, z can be calculated accordingly by using cumulative standard normal distribution function. With 12 malicious ones out of 51 participants, we have $z = 1.5$.

Framework Setup: Our experiment chooses k-means as the clustering algorithm with $k = 10$ at default, and simply use cluster size based weight for combining cluster centers. We combine our framework with different robust aggregation functions, so there are three variants of our framework: GroupRA, GroupRA-Median, and GroupRA-Trimmed Mean. Each uses trivial average and two robust aggregation methods Median and Trimmed Mean respectively. The trivial average aggregation result is simply the cluster centers that can be directly obtained by k-means. They are also very similar to Krum that chooses the vector that has minimum sum of squared Euclidean distance with $n - f - 2$ nearest neighbors. Therefore, we do not consider the combination of our framework with Krum and Bulyan in this work. In addition, we observed the framework with Median and Trimmed Mean already outperform Krum and Bulyan in our experiment.

4.2 Experiment Results

Untargeted Model Poisoning Attack. We applied the untargeted model poisoning attack, and compared the resilience of existing defenses with our framework by measuring the maximal accuracy achieved during the training process. Result can be found in Table 1. With no defense, we can see the attack can reduce the model accuracy by about 10% for MNIST and 28% for CIFAR10. All the robust aggregation based defenses cannot improve accuracy at all compared with the no defense case. What is even worse is they achieve less accuracy than no defense, which confirms the previous results in [4]. We conjecture that it could be caused by i.i.d assumption of robust aggregation. The local models trained on non-i.i.d data may have large variance. The average combines models trained with data from different distributions, but the robust aggregation may regard some updates as outliers and remove them in the aggregation, which causes significant information loss.

Our framework GroupRA with different aggregation methods all achieve better accuracy than existing defense mechanisms. More importantly, on MNIST dataset, it achieves a higher accuracy than no defense in contrast to robust aggregation. It demonstrates that our framework indeed improves the resiliency against the untargeted poisoning attack.

Table 1. Untargeted model poisoning attack results

	MNIST	CIFAR10
No Attack	97.2	55.8
No Defense	87.84	27.14
Median	87.52	21.7
Trimmed Mean	84.28	23.05
Krum	79.59	25.79
Bulyan	85.83	22.91
GroupRA	**91.31**	**26.45**
GroupRA-Median	91.06	24.97
GroupRA-Trimmed Mean	90.89	26.16

Effect of Number of Clusters k. We evaluate the effect of k on the resiliency of GroupRA on MNIST. The results are presented in Table 2. We qualitatively discussed the behavior with k ranging from 1 to m in the previous section. Here we look into the specific behavior quantitatively. For GroupRA, the mean aggregation of all cluster centers is used. Thus, the result with $k = 1$ is equivalent as $k = m$. At the same time, we observe that the resiliency (indicated by testing accuracy) show a trend from increment to decrement, which indicates that an optimal k exists in between for the best resiliency.

Table 2. Untargeted model poisoning attack results on MNIST

k	1	2	3	4	5	6	10	20	51
GroupRA	87.84	90.28	90.71	90.81	91.02	91.23	**91.31**	90.97	87.8

5   Conclusion and Future Work

In this chapter we overview the existing robust aggregation based defense and discuss their vulnerabilities caused by inherent characteristics of federated learning: no-i.i.d data, high variance among local models, and high dimensionality of model parameters. To address these problems, we propose a new defense framework with group-wise robust aggregation to improve the robustness. Our experiment demonstrate that applying robust aggregation with our framework effectively improves the resiliency against powerful attacks that evades all state-of-the-art defenses.

There are a number of directions we will examine in our future work.

- Our experimental work demonstrates the benefit of clustering and group-wise robust aggregation for improving resiliency. However, it is essential to understand the effect of clustering and if the framework has any provable robustness against Byzantine failure.
- Our experiment shows optimal k number of cluster exist for strongest resiliency. It is highly correlated with underlying data distribution among participants and can vary among different learning scenarios and even across rounds due to participants may leave and join dynamically. At the same time, the clustering can be costly, especially for high dimensional models. Therefore, it is important to effectively identify the best k or try clustering without pre-specifying k such as DBSCAN.
- In this chapter we use simple sum combination of cluster centers weighted by cluster sizes. We are considering how to exploit the cluster structure and different scoring functions to produce more robust results.

References

1. Gaavernor, J.: Robust distributed learning with gradient aggregation agent. In: 29th USENIX Security Symposium (USENIX Security 20). USENIX Association, Aug 2020
2. Bagdasaryan, E., Veit, A., Hua, Y., Estrin, D., Shmatikov, V.: How To Backdoor Federated Learning, July 2018
3. Bagdasaryan, E., Veit, A., Hua, Y., Estrin, D., Shmatikov, V.: How to backdoor federated learning. In: Chiappa, S., Calandra, R. (eds.) Proceedings of the Twenty Third International Conference on Artificial Intelligence and Statistics. Proceedings of Machine Learning Research, vol. 108, pp. 2938–2948. PMLR, 26–28 Aug 2020
4. Baruch, G., Baruch, M., Goldberg, Y.: A little is enough: circumventing defenses for distributed learning. In: Wallach, H., Larochelle, H., Beygelzimer, A., d Alché-Buc, F., Fox, E., Garnett, R. (eds.) Advances in Neural Information Processing Systems, vol. 32, pp. 8635–8645. Curran Associates, Inc. (2019)
5. Blanchard, P., El Mhamdi, E.M., Guerraoui, R., Stainer, J.: Machine learning with adversaries: Byzantine tolerant gradient descent. In: Advances in Neural Information Processing Systems. vol. 2017-Decem, pp. 119–129 (2017)
6. Fang, M., Cao, X., Jia, J., Gong, N.Z.: Local Model Poisoning Attacks to Byzantine-Robust Federated Learning (2020)

7. Kairouz, P., et al.: Advances and Open Problems in Federated Learning, December 2019
8. Lamport, L., Shostak, R., Pease, M.: The Byzantine generals problem. ACM Trans. Program. Lang. Syst. **4**(3), 382–401 (1982)
9. McMahan, H.B., Moore, E., Ramage, D., Hampson, S., Arcas, B.A.y.: Communication-efficient learning of deep networks from decentralized data. In: Proceedings of the 20th International Conference on Artificial Intelligence and Statistics, AISTATS 2017, February 2016
10. Mhamdi, E.M.E., Guerraoui, R., Rouault, S.: The hidden vulnerability of distributed learning in Byzantium. In: 35th International Conference on Machine Learning, ICML 2018, vol. 8, 5674–5686, February 2018
11. Szegedy, C., et al.: Intriguing properties of neural networks. In: International Conference on Learning Representations (2014)
12. Xie, C., Huang, K., Chen, P.Y., Li, B.: DBA: distributed backdoor attacks against federated learning, September 2020
13. Xie, C., Koyejo, O., Gupta, I.: Zeno: distributed stochastic gradient descent with suspicion-based fault-tolerance. In: 36th International Conference on Machine Learning, ICML 2019, June 2019, pp. 11928–11944, May 2018
14. Yin, D., Chen, Y., Ramchandran, K., Bartlett, P.: Byzantine-robust distributed learning: towards optimal statistical rates. In: 35th International Conference on Machine Learning, ICML 2018, vol. 13, pp. 8947–8956. International Machine Learning Society (IMLS), Mar 2018

Federated Soft Gradient Boosting Machine for Streaming Data

Ji Feng[1,2](✉), Yi-Xuan Xu[1,3](✉), Yong-Gang Wang[2], and Yuan Jiang[3]

[1] Baiont Technology, Nanjing, China
{fengji,xuyixuan}@baiontcapital.com
[2] Sinovation Ventures AI Institute, Beijing, China
{fengji,wangyonggang}@chuangxin.com
[3] National Key Laboratory for Novel Software Technology,
Nanjing University, Nanjing, China
{xuyx,jiangy}@lamda.nju.edu.cn

Abstract. Federated learning has received wide attention in both academic and industrial communities recently. Designing federated learning models applicable on the streaming data has received growing interests since the data stored within each participant may often vary from time to time. Based on recent advancements on soft gradient boosting machine, in this work, we propose the federated soft gradient boosting machine framework applicable on the streaming data. Compared with traditional gradient boosting methods, where base learners are trained sequentially, each base learner in the proposed framework can be efficiently trained in a parallel and distributed fashion. Experiments validated the effectiveness of the proposed method in terms of accuracy and efficiency, compared with other federated ensemble methods as well as its corresponding centralized versions when facing the streaming data.

Keywords: Federated learning · Gradient boosting · Streaming data

1 Introduction

Gradient boosting machine (GBM) has proven to be one of the best tools for descrete data modeling [11]. Its efficient implementations such as XGBoost [4], LightGBM [17] and CatBoost [25] are still the dominant tools for real-world applications ranging from click through rate (CTR) prediction [15], collaborative filtering [2], particles discovery [1], and many more.

Recently, there have been many attempts trying to marry the power of gradient boosting and deep learning. For instance, multi-layered gradient boosting decision trees [9] is the first non-differentiable system while having the capability of learning distributed representations, which was considered only achievable using neural networks. However, just like other GBMs, each base leaner has to be trained after the previous base learners, making the whole system less efficient in terms of parallel computing.

© Springer Nature Switzerland AG 2020
Q. Yang et al. (Eds.): Federated Learning, LNAI 12500, pp. 93–107, 2020.
https://doi.org/10.1007/978-3-030-63076-8_7

Soft gradient boosting machine (sGBM) [8], on the other hand, is the first differentiable gradient boosting system that all base learners can be simultaneously trained, a huge gain in terms of the training efficiency. To do so, the sGBM first wires multiple differentiable base learners together, and injects both local and global objectives inspired from gradient boosting. Since the whole structure is differentiable, all base learners can then be jointly optimized, achieving a linear speed-up compared to the original GBM. When using differentiable soft decision trees as the base learner, such device can be regarded as an alternative version of the (hard) gradient boosting decision trees (GBDT) with extra benefits, especially on handling the streaming data.

Federated learning is considered to be the next generation of distributed learning [28]. It has several benefits compared to the traditional distributed systems (e.g., MapReduce [6] and Ray), such as less communication costs and more advanced data privacy protection guarantees of local nodes. Such system is best practiced when facing non-iid data from multiple data sources, each with strong privacy concerns. In this work, we propose the federated soft gradient boosting framework, aiming to provide a more efficient distributed implementation of sGBM while keeping all the benefits of federated learning and GBMs.

The rest of the paper is organized as follow: First, some related works are discussed; Second, preliminaries are discussed to make the chapter more self-contained; Third, the problem setting and details on the proposed method are presented; Finally, experiment results on the proposed method are reported, and we conclude in the last section.

2   Related Work

Federated learning is a framework recently proposed by Google [22], which is capable of building a learning model based on the local data distributed across different participants. Meanwhile, the local data on each participant remain private, and is invisible to other participants. It has already been successfully applied to several applications such as Gboard for query suggestions [14]. Federated learning can be roughly categorized into three classes [28]: Horizontal federated learning (HFL) focuses on the scenarios where each participant has different samples in the same feature space; Vertical federated learning (VFL) focuses on the scenarios where participants are with different feature spaces; Federated transfer learning (FTL) locates in the intersection of horizontal and vertical federated learning [21], where data in different participants may have different feature spaces and label spaces. Throughout the paper, we focus on the horizontal federated learning setting.

Gradient Boosting Machine (GBM) is a sequential ensemble algorithm that can be used to optimize any differentiable loss function [30]. Base learners in GBM are fitted in an iterative fashion. Concretely, at each iteration, a new base learner is fitted to bridge the gap between the output of fitted base learners in GBM and the ground-truth. The entire learning procedure of GBM can be interpreted as conducting gradient descent in the functional space [11]. The decision tree extension of GBM, Gradient Boosting Decision Tree (GBDT), is one of the most widely-used ensemble algorithms in the literature. Efficient implementations on GBDT, such as XGBoost [4], LightGBM [17], and CatBoost [25], achieve excellent predictive performance on a broad range of real-world tasks such as particle discovery [1], click through rate prediction [15], and many more. Recently, Feng et al. shows that GBDT can also be used for learning distributed representations [9], which is originally believed to be the special properties of neural networks. Due to the fact that base learners in GBM are fitted sequentially, the original GBM suffers from large training costs. Furthermore, it cannot be directly applied to the streaming data as base learners cannot be modified once they were fitted. More recently, the soft Gradient Boosting Machine (sGBM) is proposed [8], which is able to jointly fit all base learners by assuming that they are differentiable. Apart from achieving competitive performance to the traditional GBMs, sGBM also greatly reduces the training costs by fitting all base learners jointly.

Recently, there have been growing interests on extending GBM to the framework of federated learning. SecureBoost is a seminal tree-based gradient boosting algorithm that solves the vertical federated learning problem [5]. It is able to achieve the same performance as the non-federated version of decision tree based GBM that requires all local data to be aggregated before the training stage. SecureGBM is another GBM framework that focuses on the scenarios in federated learning where participants may have different features, and only one participant owns the ground-truth [10]. Li et al. proposes a novel gradient boosting decision tree model for horizontal federated learning, which achieves much higher training efficiency through a relaxation on the privacy constraints [19]. However, to the best of our knowledges, there is no work on studying the federated version of GBM applicable on the streaming data.

3 Preliminaries

To make our work more self-contained, we give a detailed introduction on related topics in this section: (1) Horizontal federated learning; (2) Gradient boosting machine (GBM) and soft gradient boosting machine (sGBM).

3.1 Horizontal Federated Learning

Federated learning is able to build a learning model using distributed datasets across all participants without any leakage on the private datasets [28]. Both the theoretical studies and experiments show that the privacy and security problems can be greatly mitigated using federated learning. For horizontal federated learning, a standard procedure on building a federated model can be roughly summarized as four steps: (1) Each participant builds a model using local data, and sends the model parameters or training gradients to the coordinator (e.g., a central server) after encryptions; (2) The coordinator aggregates all local parameters or training gradients to updated the federated model; (3) The coordinator broadcasts the updated model to all participants after model encryptions; (4)

Each participant updates the local model after receiving the shared model from the coordinator. The procedure above can be iteratively conducted for many rounds to achieve better performance. Figure 1 is a graphical illustration on building a federated model in horizontal federated learning.

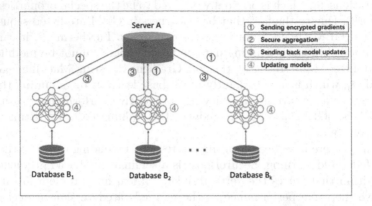

Fig. 1. A paradigm of horizontal federated learning (HFL) [28].

For many applications in federated learning, a central problem is how to effectively utilize the training data arriving in a streaming fashion [16]. A federated learning model applicable on the streaming data is able to improve the performance on both learning tasks and security, as the transmission costs between participants and the coordinator, and inconsistencies in dynamically evolving datasets can both be greatly reduced.

3.2 GBM and sGBM

Gradient boosting machine (GBM) is a popularly-used ensemble algorithm in the literature [11]. Given M base learners $\{h_m\}_{m=1}^M$, with each of them parametrized by $\{\boldsymbol{\theta}_m\}_{m=1}^M$, the goal of GBM is to determine their parameters such that the additive output of all base learners $\sum_{m=1}^M h_m(\mathbf{x}; \boldsymbol{\theta}_m)$ is able to minimize a predefined empirical loss function l over the training dataset $\{\mathbf{x}^i, y^i\}_{i=1}^N$. Formally,

$$\boldsymbol{\theta}_1^*, \boldsymbol{\theta}_2^*, \cdots, \boldsymbol{\theta}_M^* = \underset{\boldsymbol{\theta}_1, \boldsymbol{\theta}_2, \cdots, \boldsymbol{\theta}_M}{\arg\min} \sum_{i=1}^N l(y^i, \sum_{m=1}^M h_m(\mathbf{x}^i; \boldsymbol{\theta}_m)). \tag{1}$$

The original GBM determines the learner parameter $\boldsymbol{\theta}_m$ in a sequential way, resulting in a total number of M training iterations [11]. Concretely, during the m-th iteration, the learner parameter $\boldsymbol{\theta}_m^*$ is determined by:

$$\boldsymbol{\theta}_m^* = \underset{\boldsymbol{\theta}_m}{\arg\min} \sum_{i=1}^N (r_m^i - h_m(\mathbf{x}^i; \boldsymbol{\theta}_m))^2, \tag{2}$$

where r_m^i denotes the residual defined in GBM, defined as the negative gradient of the loss function with respect to the additive output of fitted base learners before h_m. Therefore, the learning target of the m-th base learner in gradient boosting can be considered as a regression problem on a new training dataset $\{\mathbf{x}^i, r_m^i\}_{m=1}^M$ using the squared error. Once the learner parameter $\boldsymbol{\theta}_m^*$ is determined, the training procedure of GBM moves on to the next iteration.

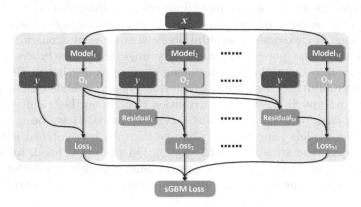

Soft Gradient Boosting Machine (sGBM)

Fig. 2. The graphical illustration on soft gradient boosting machine [8].

On the other hand, sGBM jointly fits all base learners based on the assumption that base learners are differentiable. To be brief, given the output of all base learners on a sample $\mathbf{x}^i$: $\{o_1^i, o_2^i, \cdots, o_M^i\}$, sGBM then simultaneously computes the residuals for all base learners. For the m-th base learner, its residual r_m^i on a sample $\mathbf{x}^i$ is defined as follows:

$$r_m^i = -\frac{l(y^i, \sum_{j=0}^{m-1} o_j^i)}{\sum_{j=0}^{m-1} o_j^i}, \tag{3}$$

where o_0^i is a pre-defined null output, and returns zero for any given input $\mathbf{x}^i$. Therefore, the residual for a base learner in sGBM is defined as the negative gradient of the additive output of base learners before it with respect to the loss function. Note that a key difference on the definition of residual between GBM and sGBM is that sGBM does not require a base learner to first be fitted before computing the residual for subsequent base learners. Given the set $\{o_1^i, o_2^i, \cdots, o_M^i\}$, the residuals for all base learners $\{r_1^i, r_2^i, \cdots, r_M^i\}$ can be computed in parallel. Given the computed residuals $\{r_m^i\}_{m=1}^M$, a final sGBM loss on each sample $\mathbf{x}^i$ is then defined as:

$$\mathcal{L}^i = \sum_{m=1}^M (o_m^i - r_m^i)^2. \tag{4}$$

Assuming that all base learners are differentiable, sGBM then is able to adopt the error back-propagation and online optimization techniques (e.g., stochastic gradient descent) to simultaneously update parameters for all base learners. Figure 2 presents the computation graph of sGBM to obtain a final loss $\mathcal{L}$.

3.3 Streaming Data

With a rapid growth on the volume of datasets (e.g., ImageNet [7], COCO [20]), it becomes increasingly difficult to deploy learning models under the traditional offline setting. For example, computation devices in many scenarios have very limited computation power and memory storage (e.g., smartphones, wireless sensors, and many more), making deploying learning models in the offline setting onto them prohibitively expensive. Meanwhile, these methods cannot properly handle the concept drift, such as distribution changes on the training data [13]. As a result, many algorithms focusing on streaming data have been developed. For example, models lying in the offline setting can be combined with model reuse to handle the streaming data [26,29]. On the other hand, models that can be directly fitted using some variants of online optimization techniques can naturally adapt to the streaming data, such as the deep neural network.

4   The Proposed Method

In this section, we formally present the proposed Fed-sGBM. First, the problem setting is presented; Second, details on the training stage of Fed-sGBM are introduced; Third, we introduce the extension of Fed-sGBM when using decision trees as the base learner. We conclude this section with a discussion on the communication costs of Fed-sGBM.

4.1   Problem Setting

In the section, we formally introduce the problem setting. Given K participants $\{P_1, P_2, \cdots, P_K\}$, with each of them equipped with a local dataset $\mathcal{D}_k$, the problem is to build a GBM model based on all local datasets $\{\mathcal{D}_k\}_{k=1}^{K}$ with the existence of a coordinator C. Meanwhile, it is required that the local dataset of each participant remains private to the coordinator and other participants. Following [5], we make the assumption that the coordinator C is trustable, and the communication between C and each participant P_k is securely encrypted using schemes such as homomorphic encryption. Furthermore, each local dataset $\mathcal{D}_k$ evolves with the time. Upon a new local dataset $\mathcal{D}_k^{(t)}$ arriving at the time t, the old dataset $\mathcal{D}_k^{(t-1)}$ will be instantly discarded and no longer available for the training stage. Such streaming setting is more realistic in the real-world because participants in federated learning can be cheap devices such as smartphones, which are unable to store a large volume of local data. Figure 3 is a graphical illustration on our problem setting.

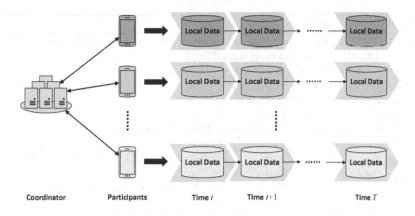

Fig. 3. Graphical illustration of local participants over time

4.2 Federated Soft Gradient Boosting Machine

Gradient Boosting Machine is a powerful ensemble algorithm that achieves excellent predictive performance on many real-world problems [23]. However, it cannot be directly applied to our problem setting illustrated above because of its inherently sequential training procedure: a base learner is required to be fixed before fitting the next base learner. We propose to extend the sGBM onto the framework of federated learning to solve the targeted problem, where base learners can be trained in a parallel and distributed fashion. Our results are a novel GBM model under the framework of federated learning. The rest of this section focuses on the training details on the proposed `Fed-sGBM`.

First, the training stage of `Fed-sGBM` is initiated by the coordinator C. After determining the kind of base learner and the number of base learners M, the coordinator then builds M base learners of the specified type $\{h_m\}_{m=1}^M$, and the learner parameters $\{\boldsymbol{\theta}_m\}_{m=1}^M$ are randomly initialized. Second, the model parameters are updated iteratively for a total number of T rounds via the communications between the coordinator and all participants. At last, the coordinator aggregates the local model parameters from all participants, and computes a final model via learner-wise model averaging:

$$h_m(\mathbf{x}; \boldsymbol{\theta}_m) = \frac{1}{K} \sum_{k=1}^K h_{m,k}(\mathbf{x}; \boldsymbol{\theta}_{m,k}) \ \forall m \in \{1, 2, \cdots, M\}, \tag{5}$$

where $h_{m,k}(\mathbf{x}; \boldsymbol{\theta}_{m,k})$ denotes the parameter of the m-th base learner in the participant P_k. To prevent the local datasets from leaking, the communications between the coordinator and participants are restricted to transmitting the model parameters. Furthermore, the homomorphic encryption is used to improve the security on transmissions.

Concretely, at each round t, each participant P_k first receives a copy of model parameters from the coordinator C via broadcasting. After then, each participant splits the local dataset into non-overlapping batches $\{B_1, B_2, \cdots, B_{|\mathcal{B}|}\}$ for

---

Algorithm 1: Training stage of Fed-sGBM

Input: Number of rounds T, learner parameters from the coordinator
$\{\boldsymbol{\theta}_m\}_{m=1}^M$, local training data $\{\mathcal{D}_k\}_{k=1}^K$
Output: Updated model parameters $\{\boldsymbol{\theta}_m^*\}_{m=1}^M$

1 **for** $t = 1, 2, \cdots, T$ **do**
2   // The side of participants
3   **for** $k = 1, 2, \cdots, K$ **do**
4   Receive the learner parameters from the coordinator:
        $\boldsymbol{\theta}_{m,k} \leftarrow \boldsymbol{\theta}_m \ \forall m \in \{1, 2, \cdots, M\}$;
5   Split the local training data $\mathcal{D}_k$ into batches: $\mathcal{B} \leftarrow \{B_1, B_2, \cdots, B_{|\mathcal{B}|}\}$;
6   **for** $b = 1, 2, \cdots, |\mathcal{B}|$ **do**
7   Conduct data forward: $o_m^i \leftarrow \sum_{j=0}^{m-1} h_j(\mathbf{x}^i; \boldsymbol{\theta}_{m,k}) \ \forall \mathbf{x}^i \in B_b$;
8   Compute the residual: $r_m^i \leftarrow -\frac{\partial l(y^i, o_m^i)}{\partial o_m^i} \ \forall \mathbf{x}^i \in B_b$;
9   Compute the training loss on the current data batch:
          $\mathcal{L}_{b,k} \leftarrow \sum_{\mathbf{x}^i \in B_b} \sum_{m=1}^M (o_m^i - r_m^i)^2$;
10   Update $\{\boldsymbol{\theta}_{m,k}\}_{m=1}^M$ w.r.t $\mathcal{L}_{b,k}$ using gradient descent ;
11   **end**
12   Send $\{\boldsymbol{\theta}_{m,k}\}_{m=1}^M$ to the coordinator C ;
13   **end**
14   // The side of the coordinator
15   Receive parameters from all participants: $\{\boldsymbol{\theta}_{m,k}\}_{k=1}^K \ \forall m \in \{1, 2, \cdots, M\}$;
16    $\boldsymbol{\theta}_m \leftarrow \frac{1}{K} \sum_{k=1}^K \boldsymbol{\theta}_{m,k} \ \forall m \in \{1, 2, \cdots, M\}$;
17 **end**
18 $\{\boldsymbol{\theta}_m^*\}_{m=1}^M \leftarrow \{\boldsymbol{\theta}_m\}_{m=1}^M$;
19 Return $\{\boldsymbol{\theta}_m^*\}_{m=1}^M$;

---

efficient model updating. For each batch of data, a training loss defined in Eq. (4) is first computed. After then, each participant adopts error back-propagation and first-order optimization techniques to update local model parameters, following the routine in sGBM [8]. At last, the updated model parameters is transmitted to the coordinator after encryptions. Upon receiving model parameters from all participants, the coordinator uses model averaging to compute a final model as in Eq. (5), and the training stage moves to the next round. Algorithm 1 presents details on the training stage of Fed-sGBM.

Since the local model on the side of participants can be efficiently updated in a mini-batch fashion using back propagation, the proposed Fed-sGBM can be naturally applied to the streaming data. Suppose that at time t, a new batch of data $\mathcal{D}_k^{(t)}$ arrives at the participant P_k and replaces the old data $\mathcal{D}_k^{(t-1)}$, there is no need for the participant to train a new local model from scratch. The only modification needs to be made is to update parameters on the batches of the new data $\mathcal{D}_k^{(t)}$. All base learners in the existing local model then can be jointly trained to adapt to the newly-coming batch of data.

According to the Algorithm 1, the communication cost between the coordinator and each participant is $2 \times T \times M \times |\boldsymbol{\theta}|$, where M is the number of base learners in `Fed-sGBM`, $|\boldsymbol{\theta}|$ denotes the size of model parameters. As an ensemble algorithm in federated learning, a larger value of M is able to effectively improve the overall performance of `Fed-sGBM`, yet the communication cost also increases linearly. Therefore, a trade-off exists between the performance of `Fed-sGBM` and the communication cost.

4.3 Federated Soft Gradient Boosting Decision Tree

Decision tree models, such as Classification And Regression Tree (CART) [3], are popularly used as the base learner in gradient boosting. State-of-the-art gradient boosting decision tree (GBDT) libraries such as XGBoost [4], LightGBM [17], and CatBoost [25] achieve excellent predictive performance on a variety number of real-world tasks. Due to the fact that building a single decision tree is a one-pass procedure that requires all data to first be aggregated before training, extending GBDTs to the horizontal federated learning setting is non-trivial. In this section, we extend the proposed `Fed-sGBM` to the cases where tree-based model is used as the base learner, and the result is a novel GBDT model for horizontal federated learning: `Fed-sGBDT`.

Concretely, a novel soft decision tree model is used in `Fed-sGBDT` to ensure that the entire model can still be updated using back propagation [12]. Compared to classic tree-based models that assign each sample to a single leaf node, soft decision tree assigns each sample to all leaf nodes with different probabilities. To achieve this, each internal node in the soft decision tree is equipped with a logistic regression model that splits each sample to its child nodes with different probabilities. The output of the entire model on a sample is the weighted average of predictions from all leaf nodes, where weights correspond to the probabilities assigned to each leaf node. Due to the fact that the soft decision tree is differentiable, it can be naturally integrated into the proposed `Fed-sGBM`, leading to the proposed `Fed-sGBDT`. Since the entire `Fed-sGBDT` model can still be trained using online optimization techniques such as stochastic gradient descent, it is capable of quickly adapting to the streaming data.

5 Experiment

Experiments are divided into five sub-sections, and the goals are to validate that: (1) The proposed method is an effective ensemble algorithm for horizontal federated learning; (2) The proposed method applies well to the streaming data setting in federated learning, which are frequently encountered in the real-world.

First, we introduce the setup of the experiments; Second, we compare the performance of `Fed-sGBM` with different contenders; After then, we investigate the performance under different number of participants and base learners, separately; At last, the performance of `Fed-sGBM` on the streaming data is presented.

5.1 Experiment Setup

Dataset. Three benchmark datasets on classification are selected to evaluate the performance of `Fed-sGBM`: *Letter*, *MNIST*, and *CIFAR-10*. *Letter* is a dataset that contains samples belonging to 26 capital letters in the English alphabet. Each sample is associated with 16 features that contain statistical information such as edge counts. *MNIST* is a dataset on handwritten digit recognition, and each sample corresponds to a gray image of size 28×28. *CIFAR-10* is another image classification dataset with 10 classes, and each sample is a colorful image of size $3 \times 32 \times 32$. All datasets are normalized to its mean and unit variance before the training stage. Table 1 presents basic statistics on the datasets used.

Table 1. Basic statistics on the datasets used

Dataset name	# Training	# Evaluating	# Features	# Classes
Letter	16000	4000	16	26
MNIST	60000	10000	28×28	10
CIFAR-10	50000	10000	$3 \times 32 \times 32$	10

Base Learner. Three different kinds of base learners are included to evaluate `Fed-sGBM`: *SoftTree*, *MLP*, and *CNN*. For *SoftTree*, we set the tree depth as 5. We also use a regularization term introduced in [12] during the training stage to encourage the *SoftTree* to exploit its leaf nodes. The coefficient of this regularization term is set as 0.001. For *MLP*, since it is difficult to find the best network architecture for each dataset in practice, we directly use the architecture reported in the literature [31]. Concretely, the architecture of *MLP* on *Letter* dataset is Input $- 70 - 50 -$ Output, and the architecture on *MNIST* and *CIFAR-10* dataset is Input $- 512 - 512 -$ Output. For *CNN*, we adopt a modified version of LeNet-5 [18] with Relu activation and dropout [27].

Computation. All experiments are conducted on a single machine with 32GB RAM, a Xeon E5-2650v4 CPU, and a RTX-2080Ti GPU. We implement the `Fed-sGBM` using PyTorch [24]. The distributed communication package Torch-Distributed is used to simulate the distributed setting in federated learning.

Simulation. Given K participants exist in federated learning, we split the training data into K non-overlapping parts with relatively equal size, and each part is treated as the local dataset on a participant P_k.

5.2 Performance Comparison

In this section, we evaluate the performance of `Fed-sGBM` as an ensemble algorithm in federated learning. For performance comparison, we also report the results of `Fed-Voting`, sGBM [8], and the original GBM [11]. In `Fed-Voting`, the coordinator and all participants jointly learn a voting-based ensemble model without sharing the local data. Notice that sGBM and GBM requires local data from all participants, and cannot be directly applied to the federated learning setting. We keep the type of base learner same in three methods, and set the number of base learner as 10. The number of participants in Fed-sGBM and Fed-Voting is set as 2. Experiment results on different configurations of datasets and base learners are presented in Table 2. The performance of *CNN* on the *Letter* dataset is ignored since it cannot be applied to tabular datasets.

According to Table 2, it can be observed that the performance of Fed-sGBM is slightly worse than sGBM, which is reasonable considering that the Fed-sGBM is trained in a distributed fashion. On the other hand, the performance of Fed-sGBM outperforms Fed-Voting by a large margin on different configurations of base learner and dataset except the Tree@Letter, validating its effectiveness as a general ensemble method in federated learning.

Table 2. Performance comparison between Fed-sGBM and different baselines

Configuration	Fed-sGBM	Fed-Voting	sGBM	GBM
Tree@Letter	88.43	94.88	89.15	87.43
MLP@Letter	94.10	89.78	95.60	95.83
Tree@MNIST	96.37	94.34	97.02	95.88
MLP@MNIST	98.82	97.44	98.70	98.49
CNN@MNIST	99.52	99.04	99.53	99.34
Tree@CIFAR-10	50.70	41.57	51.86	50.92
MLP@CIFAR-10	58.10	51.62	57.46	55.89
CNN@CIFAR-10	74.92	71.97	75.02	74.68

5.3 Performance Under Different Number of Base Learners

In this section, we investigate the performance of Fed-sGBM when increasing the number of base learners. The goal is to validate that increasing the number of base learners is able to effectively improve the performance of Fed-sGBM.

Based on the datasets and base learners presented above, we set the number of base learners as $\{1, 5, 10, 15, 20\}$, and evaluate the testing accuracy of Fed-sGBM. The experiment results are presented in Fig. 4. It can be shown that the testing accuracy of Fed-sGBM consistently increases on all combinations of datasets and base learners with more base learners added. The experiment results validate our claims: increasing the number of base learners effectively improves the performance of Fed-sGBM on different datasets.

5.4 Performance Under Different Number of Participants

In this section, we evaluate the performance of Fed-sGBM with different number of participants existing in federated learning. The goal is to validate that the performance of Fed-sGBM is robust to the number of participants.

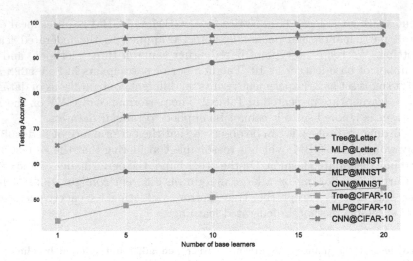

Fig. 4. Performance of `Fed-sGBM` with different number of base learners

Concretely, we train a shared `Fed-sGBM` model when there are $\{2, 3, 4\}$ participants in federated learning, respectively. The experiment results are presented in Fig. 5. According to the experiment results, it can be observed that the performance of `Fed-sGBM` only deteriorates slightly on three datasets with more participants added. Since the volume of the local dataset on each participant decreases drastically based on our experiment setup, the experiment results validate that the performance of `Fed-sGBM` is robust to the number of participants. Notice that the performance of `Fed-sGBM` even improves with the number of participants increasing when using the *MLP* base learner on *CIFAR-10* dataset. We conjecture that the reason is that the procedure of obtaining a jointly learned `Fed-sGBM` model can be considered as one kind of ensemble on all local models (i.e., model averaging). Therefore, the final performance of `Fed-sGBM` improves with more participants added, despite the fact that each participant has less volume of training data.

5.5   Performance on Streaming Data

In this section, we evaluate the performance of `Fed-sGBM` under the streaming data setting in federated learning. Given a dataset, we first randomly split the training part into 5 non-overlapping batches to simulate the streaming data setting. At each time t ($t = 1, 2, \cdots, 5$), each participant P_k will receive a newly-coming batch of data $\mathcal{D}_k^{(t)}$, and the local model will then be fitted on $\mathcal{D}_k^{(t)}$. We report the performance of `Fed-sGBM` on the testing data after the shared model is fitted on each batch of data from all participants, leading to a total number of five testing accuracy records. The experiment results on three combinations of base learner and dataset (MLP@Letter, Tree@MNIST, CNN@CIFAR-10) are presented in Table 3. The number of base learners and participants in `Fed-sGBM` is set as 10 and 2, separately.

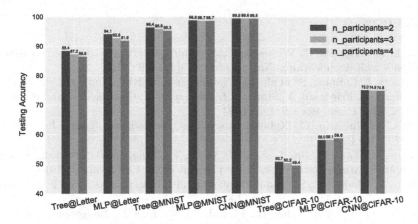

Fig. 5. Performance of `Fed-sGBM` with different number of participants

Table 3. Performance of `Fed-sGBM` on the streaming data setting

Learner@Dataset	Timestamp ID				
	1	2	3	4	5
MLP@Letter	79.00	83.75	85.00	86.78	86.93
Tree@MNIST	94.57	95.62	96.34	96.73	96.73
CNN@CIFAR-10	60.77	62.12	63.54	64.92	65.45

According to the experiment results in Table 3, it can be observed that the performance of `Fed-sGBM` consistently improves with more batches of data coming. Meanwhile, a better performance can also be achieved by tuning the parameters and training the local model on each batch of data for more epochs. Such results cannot be easily achieved by the original GBM because at each time t, a new model has to be trained from scratch, with the learned local model before totally wasted.

6 Conclusion

In this chapter, we propose a novel gradient boosting model for horizontal federated learning. The proposed method is able to utilize local datasets from all participants to efficiently build a shared model without any leakage on the local data. Compared to existing works on combining gradient boosting with federated learning, the proposed `Fed-sGBM` can be applied onto the streaming data, and is robust to the number of participants in federated learning. Extensive experiments are conducted to evaluate the performance of `Fed-sGBM` as an ensemble algorithm in the framework of federated learning, along with the performance on streaming data.

References

1. Baldi, P., Sadowski, P., Whiteson, D.: Searching for exotic particles in high-energy physics with deep learning. Nat. Commun. **5**(1), 1–9 (2014)
2. Bennett, J., Lanning, S., et al.: The Netflix prize. In: KDD Cup 2007, vol. 35 (2007)
3. Breiman, L., Friedman, J., Stone, C.J., Olshen, R.A.: Classification and Regression Trees. CRC Press, Boca Raton (1984)
4. Chen, T., Guestrin, C.: Xgboost: a scalable tree boosting system. In: SIGKDD, pp. 785–794 (2016)
5. Cheng, K., Fan, T., Jin, Y., Liu, Y., Chen, T., Yang, Q.: Secureboost: a lossless federated learning framework. arXiv preprint arXiv:1901.08755 (2019)
6. Dean, J., Ghemawat, S.: MapReduce: simplified data processing on large clusters. Commun. ACM **51**(1), 107–113 (2008)
7. Deng, J., Dong, W., Socher, R., Li, L.J., Li, K., Li, F.F.: ImageNet: a large-scale hierarchical image database. In: CVPR, pp. 248–255 (2009)
8. Feng, J., Xu, Y.X., Jiang, Y., Zhou, Z.H.: Soft gradient boosting machine. arXiv preprint arXiv:2006.04059 (2020)
9. Feng, J., Yu, Y., Zhou, Z.H.: Multi-layered gradient boosting decision trees. In: NIPS, pp. 3551–3561 (2018)
10. Feng, Z., et al.: SecureGBM: secure multi-party gradient boosting. In: IEEE International Conference on Big Data, pp. 1312–1321. IEEE (2019)
11. Friedman, J.H.: Greedy function approximation: a gradient boosting machine. Ann. Stat. **29**, 1189–1232 (2001)
12. Frosst, N., Hinton, G.: Distilling a neural network into a soft decision tree. arXiv preprint arXiv:1711.09784 (2017)
13. Gama, J., Žliobaitė, I., Bifet, A., Pechenizkiy, M., Bouchachia, A.: A survey on concept drift adaptation. ACM Comput. Surv. **46**(4), 1–37 (2014)
14. Hard, A., et al.: Federated learning for mobile keyboard prediction. arXiv preprint arXiv:1811.03604 (2018)
15. He, X., et al.: Practical lessons from predicting clicks on ads at Facebook. In: International Workshop on Data Mining for Online Advertising, pp. 1–9 (2014)
16. Kairouz, P., et al.: Advances and open problems in federated learning. arXiv preprint arXiv:1912.04977 (2019)
17. Ke, G., et al.: LightGbm: a highly efficient gradient boosting decision tree. In: NIPS, pp. 3146–3154 (2017)
18. LeCun, Y., Bottou, L., Bengio, Y., Haffner, P.: Gradient-based learning applied to document recognition. IEEE **86**(11), 2278–2324 (1998)
19. Li, Q., Wen, Z., He, B.: Practical federated gradient boosting decision trees. In: AAAI, pp. 4642–4649 (2020)
20. Lin, T.-Y.: Microsoft COCO: common objects in context. In: Fleet, D., Pajdla, T., Schiele, B., Tuytelaars, T. (eds.) ECCV 2014. LNCS, vol. 8693, pp. 740–755. Springer, Cham (2014). https://doi.org/10.1007/978-3-319-10602-1_48
21. Liu, Y., Chen, T., Yang, Q.: Secure federated transfer learning. arXiv preprint arXiv:1812.03337 (2018)
22. McMahan, B., Moore, E., Ramage, D., Hampson, S., y Arcas, B.A.: Communication-efficient learning of deep networks from decentralized data. In: Artificial Intelligence and Statistics, pp. 1273–1282 (2017)
23. Natekin, A., Knoll, A.: Gradient boosting machines, a tutorial. Front. Neurorobotics **7**, 21 (2013)

24. Paszke, A., et al.: Pytorch: an imperative style, high-performance deep learning library. In: NIPS, pp. 8026–8037 (2019)
25. Prokhorenkova, L., Gusev, G., Vorobev, A., Dorogush, A.V., Gulin, A.: Catboost: unbiased boosting with categorical features. In: NIPS, pp. 6638–6648 (2018)
26. Shalev-Shwartz, S.: Online learning and online convex optimization. Foundations Trends Mach. Learn. **4**(2), 107–194 (2011)
27. Srivastava, N., Hinton, G., Krizhevsky, A., Sutskever, I., Salakhutdinov, R.: Dropout: a simple way to prevent neural networks from overfitting. J. Mach. Learn. Res. **15**(1), 1929–1958 (2014)
28. Yang, Q., Liu, Y., Chen, T., Tong, Y.: Federated machine learning: concept and applications. ACM Trans. Intell. Syst. Technol. **10**(2), 1–19 (2019)
29. Zhao, P., Cai, L.-W., Zhou, Z.-H.: Handling concept drift via model reuse. Mach. Learn. **109**(3), 533–568 (2019). https://doi.org/10.1007/s10994-019-05835-w
30. Zhou, Z.H.: Ensemble Methods: Foundations and Algorithms. CRC Press, Boca Raton (2012)
31. Zhou, Z.H., Feng, J.: Deep forest. In: IJCAI, pp. 3553–3559 (2017)

Dealing with Label Quality Disparity
in Federated Learning

Yiqiang Chen[1,2(✉)], Xiaodong Yang[1,2], Xin Qin[1,2], Han Yu[3], Piu Chan[4],
and Zhiqi Shen[3]

[1] The Beijing Key Laboratory of Mobile Computing and Pervasive Device,
Institute of Computing Technology, Chinese Academy of Sciences, Beijing, China
{yqchen,yangxiaodong,qinxin18b}@ict.ac.cn
[2] University of Chinese Academy of Sciences, Beijing, China
[3] Nanyang Technological University, Singapore, Singapore
{han.yu,zqshen}@ntu.edu.sg
[4] Xuanwu Hospital, Capital Medical University, Beijing, China
pbchan@hotmail.com

Abstract. Federated Learning (FL) is highly useful for the applications
which suffer silo effect and privacy preserving, such as healthcare, finance,
education, etc. Existing FL approaches generally do not account for dis-
parities in the quality of local data labels. However, the participants tend
to suffer from label noise due to annotators' varying skill-levels, biases
or malicious tampering. In this chapter, we propose an alternative approach to address this challenge. It maintains a small set of benchmark
samples on the FL coordinator and quantifies the credibility of the participants' local data without directly observing them by computing the
mutual cross-entropy between performance of the FL model on the local
datasets and that of the participant's local model on the benchmark
dataset. Then, a credit-weighted orchestration is performed to adjust
the weight assigned to participants in the FL model based on their credibility values. By experimentally evaluating on both synthetic data and
real-world data, the results show that the proposed approach effectively
identifies participants with noisy labels and reduces their impact on the
FL model performance, thereby significantly outperforming existing FL
approaches.

Keywords: Federated Learning · Label quality · Credit-weighted

1 Introduction

With the development of edge computing, the growth of End-Edge-Cloud systems makes the collection and processing of massive amounts of personal data a
possibility. This has raised privacy concerns and may hinder the development of
such technologies if not addressed. Federated Learning (FL) has emerged to be
a useful machine learning paradigm to help leverage personal data in a privacy-
preserving manner [9]. Under FL, multiple participants collaborate to train an

© Springer Nature Switzerland AG 2020
Q. Yang et al. (Eds.): Federated Learning, LNAI 12500, pp. 108–121, 2020.
https://doi.org/10.1007/978-3-030-63076-8_8

FL model without exchanging raw data. Nevertheless, one key challenge that remains open and hinders wide spread adoption of FL, especially in the health-care domain, is label quality disparity.

The quality of labels in participants' local datasets influences the performance of the FL model. Existing FL approaches implicitly assume that there is no significant difference among the quality of labels from local datasets [3]. Thus, popular FL approaches such as FedAvg treat model parameters from different participants equally [6]. Due to difference in the annotators' skills, biases or malicious tampering, label noise is common in data collected by FL systems [10,12]. Taking healthcare as an example, hospitals across China are at a different level and there are generally more cases of mis-diagnosis in smaller hospitals than in better-staffed larger hospitals, even if the patient cases are the same. Apparently, a noisy-label participant can negatively impact the learned model in FL since it gives the wrong knowledge [3]. What makes it more challenging is that the noisy participant is hard to be detected for the raw data is forbidden to share in the FL setting, let alone the noisy participant can be not self-aware. Therefore, enabling the FL system to effectively detect and deal with label quality disparity is of vital importance to its success.

In this chapter, we propose Federated Opportunistic Computing (FOC) app-roach to address this challenging problem. It is designed to identify participants with noisy labels and aggregate their model parameters into the FL model in an opportunistic manner. FOC works for the cross-silo federated settings. It main-tains a small set of benchmark samples in the central coordinator, which is not enough to train a strong model. During the FL training process, the local model (which is trained on the local data in each participant) and the FL model (which is the aggregated model) on the coordinator will form a Twin Network, where both of them share the same model architecture but different parameters. By defining a mutual cross-entropy loss of the Twin Network, the credibility of each participant's data can be measured, which is then used to determine the extent to which the corresponding participant is allowed to participate in FL. In each round, FOC performs credibility-weighted orchestration on the coordinator to avoid update corruption. The term "Opportunistic" is used to indicate that a participant model is not aggregated into the FL model by simple averaging (as in the case of FedAvg [5]), but weighted by its credibility.

To evaluate FOC, we firstly test it on a synthetic human activity recognition dataset in which labels are tampered in different ways in a subset of the par-ticipants. Then, it is tested on a real-world dataset from hospitals with diverse label qualities for detecting Parkinson's Disease symptoms. The experimental results show that FOC can detect participants with noisy labels and reduce their impact on the FL model performance more effectively compared to existing FL approaches.

2   Related Work

Label noise is a common problem in machine learning and may lead to label quality disparity across the participants in the federated learning. Unlike the non-IID problem in federated learning that participants may have different data distributions but with correct labels, label quality disparity instead focuses on the situation where the labels may be inconsistent even if the participants are given the same set of instances.

In the conventional machine learning settings, there are two categories of methods to deal with this problem: 1) at the data level and 2) at the algorithm level. At the data level, existing methods generally aim to sanitize the noisy labels to mitigate their impact. Cretu et al. [2] used small slices of the training data to generate multiple models and produce provisional labels for each input. This is used to determine if noisy labels are present. Xie et al. [8] designed Byzantine-robust aggregators to defend against label-flipping data poisoning attacks on convolutional neural networks. However, Koh et al. [4] recently found that a federated approach to data sanitization is still vulnerable to data poisoning attacks.

At the algorithm level, existing methods generally aim to train noise-tolerant models. Natarajan et al. [7] studied the impact of label noise in binary classification from a theoretical perspective, and proposed a simple weighted surrogate loss to establish a strong empirical risk bounds. Since deep learning models can easily overfit to the label noise, Zhang et al. [13] used meta-learning to train deep models, where synthetic noisy labels were generated to updates the model before the conventional gradient updates. Nevertheless, these existing methods cannot be directly applied in the context of federated learning as they require access to raw data.

In FL, label noise is also related to non-IID issue. Zhao et al. [14] found that the non-IID participants produced a poor global model in FL since the large Earth Mover's Distance (EMD) among the participants' data made their models diverse. However, the proposed data sharing strategy requires more communication and risks diluting the participants' information. Furthermore, the calculation of EMD requires the FL coordinator to have access to participants raw data, which is not permissible under FL settings.

To the best of our knowledge, there is currently no published work on mitigating the impact of label noise under FL settings.

3 Traditional FL Model Training

Under FL, the training data are distributed among K participants, each storing a subset of the training data $\mathcal{D}_k = (\mathcal{X}_k, \mathcal{Y}_k)$, $k = 1, \ldots, K$. Each participant trains its local model $\mathcal{M}^k$ by minimizing the loss function on its own dataset only and any raw data exchange between participants is forbidden.

Many different machine learning algorithms can be trained with FL [9]. For simplicity of exposition, we use the convolutional neural networks (CNN) architecture as the basis to train an FL classification model in this chapter. In this context, the cross entropy as the objective function which needs to be minimized:

$$\mathcal{L} = -\frac{1}{n_k} \sum_{i=1}^{n_k} y_i \log P(y_i | x_i). \tag{1}$$

$|n_k|$ denotes the amount of the training data owned by the k-th participant. After that, the FL coordinator collects the model updates from the participants, and aggregates them to form the new global FL model $\mathcal{M}^s$. The most widely used FL aggregation method is the Federated Averaging FedAvg algorithm [6], which is given by:

$$\mathcal{M}_t^s = \sum_{k=1}^{K} \frac{n_k}{n} \mathcal{M}_t^k \tag{2}$$

where $\mathcal{M}_t^s$ denotes the FL model updates at time t, n is the total amount of data used for FL model training by the participants involved, $n = \sum_{k=1}^{K} n_k$.

Apparently, in the traditional FL model training, all the data labels are assumed to be absolutely correct. While such setting is meaningful, it can be far from practical situations where each participant can have a large variety of data which may be incorrectly annotated.

4   The Proposed FOC Approach

The proposed FOC approach quantifies label noise in the dataset from each FL participant under horizontal federated learning. It measures the quality of each participant's data and aggregates their local model updates into the FL model in an opportunistic manner. For clarity, we only present the case where each participant sends local model updates to the coordinator in plaintext. Nevertheless, added protection mechanism, such as homomorphic encryption and secret sharing, can be added into FOC following methods explained in [9].

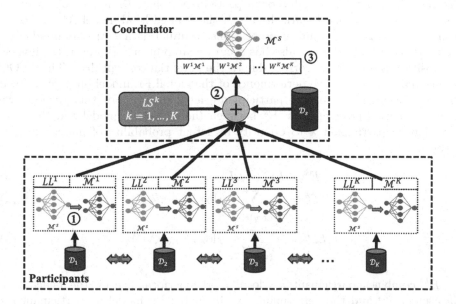

Fig. 1. The pipeline of FOC.

The pipeline of FOC is shown in Fig. 1. Once each participant has received the current global model from the FL coordinator, and sent the local model updates to the FL coordinator after training on the local dataset:

1. Each participant i evaluates the global FL model on its own local dataset, and sends the evaluation result, LL^i, to the FL coordinator along with its model updates.
2. The FL coordinator evaluates each participant i's local model M^i one by one on the small set of benchmark dataset and records the model performance as LS^i.
3. Once the corresponding LL^i value is received by the FL coordinator, it computes the mutual cross-entropy loss between LL^i and LS^i to produce a credibility measure which reflects the quality of participant i's local labels.
4. Finally, the credibility measure for each participant i is used as its weight in a weighted `FedAvg` operation to produce a new global FL model.

In the following parts of this section, we provide more details on the FOC pipeline.

4.1   Participant Label Quality Measurement

Since there is no prior knowledge about the participant label quality, FOC considers a small set of benchmark samples $\mathcal{D}_s = (\mathcal{X}_s, \mathcal{Y}_s)$ in the FL coordinator, where there is little noise (i.e., the instances are labeled accurately). This may require working closely with specialists in the target field, which is beyond the scope of this chapter. Once this requirement is satisfied, then given a benchmark dataset $\mathcal{D}_s$ in the FL coordinator, a participant's data $\mathcal{D}_k$ follows an identical distribution to the benchmark dataset if the trained local model $\mathcal{M}^k$ performs well on $\mathcal{D}_s$. As $\mathcal{D}_s$ has accurate annotations, a similar data distribution indicates that the participant dataset also has accurate annotations. However, the inverse proposition is not always correct due to the potential concept drift. Thus, FOC additionally considers the performance of the global FL model on a given local dataset, in order to measure participants' label quality. For this purpose, we define a mutual cross-entropy E^k between the global FL model and the local model from participant k to quantify its latent probability of noise, which is given by:

$$E^k = LS^k + LL^k \tag{3}$$

$$LS^k = - \sum_{(x,y) \in \mathcal{D}_s} y \log P(y|x; \mathcal{M}^k) \tag{4}$$

$$LL^k = - \sum_{(x,y) \in \mathcal{D}_k} y \log P(y|x; \mathcal{M}^s) \tag{5}$$

E^k combines participant k's local model performance on the benchmark dataset (LS^k) and the performance of the global FL model on participant k's local dataset (LL^k). There are three possible cases when analyzing E^k:

- **Small E^k**: A small E^k indicates that the local data follows a similar distribution as the benchmark dataset, meaning that participant k's dataset possesses accurate labels.
- **Large E^k**: If both the global FL model and the local model perform badly when tested on each other's dataset, it will result in a large E^k. This means the participant's dataset follows a different data distribution compared to the benchmark dataset. Thus, participant k is likely to possess noisy labels.
- **Medium E^k**: If either one of the two models performs badly, it will lead to a medium E^k. In this case, it is not sufficient to determine that participant k has noisy labels. If the local model is the one with poor performance, it means that the local dataset is not large enough to train a good model; if the global FL model is the one with poor performance, it means that there exist noisy labels in other participants which contribute to training the FL model.

Therefore, the mutual cross-entropy loss is strongly correlative with the quality of participant's data label. For normalization, we define a participant k's *credibility* C^k to reflect the quality of their local data labels, as:

$$C^k = 1 - \frac{e^{\alpha E^k}}{\sum_i e^{\alpha E^i}}. \tag{6}$$

α is the temperature during the normalization. With this measure, we propose an opportunistic model aggregation for FL, which is based on the participants' credibility to improve the traditional `FedAvg`.

4.2 Opportunistic FL Model Aggregation

To leverage the measured participant's credibility, we rewrite the `FedAvg` model aggregation rule from Eq. 2 as:

$$\mathcal{M}_t^s = \sum_{k=1}^{K} W_{t-1}^k \mathcal{M}_t^k. \tag{7}$$

Unlike `FedAvg`, the aggregation weight for each participant not only is related to the amount of local instances, but also involves the participants' credibility values which may vary in different rounds. Given the participant credibility value C_t^k is assigned to participant k in round t, W_t^k is defined as:

$$W_t^k = \frac{n_k C_t^k}{\sum_{i=1}^{K} n_i C_t^i}. \tag{8}$$

As the mutual cross-entropy is based on both the local models and the global one at round t, the opportunistic aggregation is weighted by the latest credibility values which is calculated at round $t - 1$. Note that since $\sum_{k=1}^{K} W_{t+1}^k = 1$, the convergence of the proposed FOC approach is guaranteed as long as the `FedAvg` algorithm in Eq. 2 converges.

Communication Cost. During the training, FOC requires two communications per round: 1) broadcasting the global model, and 2) participants submit local model parameter updates to the FL coordinator for aggregation. During the broadcasting, the central coordinator sends the current FL model $\mathcal{M}^s$ to all the participants. During the aggregation, all or part of the K participants send their local model parameters, $(LL^k, \mathcal{M}^k), k = 1, \ldots, K$, to the FL coordinator. Compared with `FedAvg`, the only item that needs to be transmitted in addition to model parameters is the performance value of the global FL model on each local dataset.

5   Experimental Evaluation

5.1   Experiment Settings

We evaluated the proposed FOC by the experiments in the cross-silo scenarios. Two healthcare-related datasets are adopted in our experiments. They are:

- **USC-HAD** [11]: This dataset is a public benchmark dataset for human activity recognition, which contains 12 most common types of human activities in daily life from 14 subjects. The activity data were captured by a 6-axis inertial sensor worn by the subjects on their front right hip. The data were collected over 84 h (Fig. 2a).
- **PD-Tremor** [1]: This dataset was collected from Parkinson's Disease (PD) patients by measuring their tremor, which is one of the most typical motor symptoms. The subject was required to hold a smartphone for 15 s in a relaxing status. The hand motion data were collected by sensors embedded in the smartphone including the accelerometer and the gyroscope. Data was collected from 99 subjects in 3 hospitals (Fig. 2b).

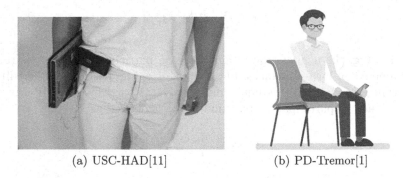

(a) USC-HAD[11]   (b) PD-Tremor[1]

Fig. 2. Two testbed datasets.

A sliding-window is employed to preprocess and segment the data stream. A convolutional neural network (CNN) is used to train a model through Stochastic

Gradient Descent (SGD), where each axis of the multi-modal sensors is regarded as a channel. We compare FOC with the traditional FedAvg in our experiments. The dataset is split into the training set and the testing set. Accuracy of the global FL model on the testing set is used as the evaluation metric.

5.2   Evaluation on the Synthetic Dataset

In this experiment, we study the negative impact of noisy participants in federated learning. USC-HAD is a dataset in which all the samples are correctly annotated. To simulate a federated learning setting, the whole dataset is divided into 5 parts, one of which is selected at random to be the benchmark dataset on the FL coordinator and the others are distributed to the participants. To synthesize a noisy participant, one of the 4 participants is randomly selected and all its labels are randomized.

There are two scenarios for federated learning: one is referred to as "Normal", where all the four participants are annotated with correct labels; the other is referred to as "Noisy", where one of participants has noisy labels. The testing accuracy comparison between FedAvg and FOC under these two scenarios is shown in Fig. 3. It can be observed that under the "Normal" scenario, FOC and FedAvg achieved a similar performance in terms of accuracy. In this sense, FedAvg can be regarded as a special case of FOC, which assumes all the participants are 100% trustworthy. Under the "Noisy" scenario, due to incorrect labels of the noisy participant, some valuable information is lost and performance degradation is significant for both FedAvg and FOC. Since all the local models including that from the noisy participant are aggregated indiscriminately in FedAvg, its performance is poorer than FOC. Through noisy participant detection and opportunistic model aggregation, FOC alleviates the impact of the noisy participant by assigning a lower aggregation weight, which results in the advantage over FedAvg by 5.82% in terms of accuracy.

The opportunistic aggregation weights produced by FOC for the 4 participants when convergence are shown in Fig. 4. As the data on normal participants follows an identical data distribution, they are assigned almost equal weight during FL model aggregation. However, the weight for the noisy participant which has been significantly reduced by FOC, shows that the proposed method can correctly detect noisy participant and take appropriate actions.

Figure 5 shows the training loss comparison during each FL training round with a same learning rate setting. The training loss at round t is defined as the average loss of K participants, which can be calculated as:

$$l_{fl}^t = \frac{1}{K} \sum_{k=1}^{K} \mathcal{L}(\mathcal{M}_t^k, \mathcal{D}_k) \tag{9}$$

$\mathcal{L}$ is the cross-entropy loss in our experiments.

Both FedAvg and FOC take longer time to converge under the "Noisy" scenario compared to under the "Normal" scenario. Nevertheless, the convergence rate of FOC under both scenarios is faster than that of FedAvg. Because of the

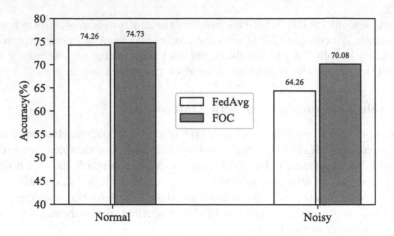

Fig. 3. The test accuracy comparison on USC-HAD.

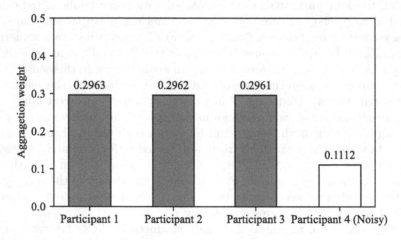

Fig. 4. The weights assigned to the participants by FOC.

incorrect labels, the data distribution of the noisy participants is different from the others, resulting in larger Earth Mover's Distance values and diverse model parameters [14]. Thus, during the aggregation in the coordinator under FOC, the global model is less impacted by the noisy participant due to its reduced weight.

Another evidence for the reduced impact of the noisy participant on the FL model is that the final loss achieved by FOC is larger than that of FedAvg. This is because the global FL model under FOC does not fit the noisy data as well as the normal data, which results in a larger training loss on the noisy data. In other words, FOC is capable of avoiding over-fitting the noisy data.

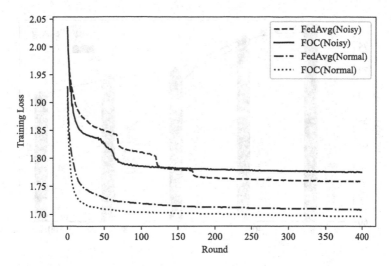

Fig. 5. The training loss comparison results on USC-HAD.

Furthermore, we explore and analyze the performance of FOC in the "Noisy" scenario with different noisy degree. To quantify the degree of noise, a metric is defined as:

$$D = \frac{|\hat{y} \neq y|}{|y|} \tag{10}$$

where $\hat{y}$ indicates the label used in training and y indicates the correct label. The comparative result of FOC and FedAvg is shown in Fig. 6.

When D is low, e.g. 20%, the noisy labels are overwhelmed by the local data and the noisy participant has nearly no negative impact on the FL model. Thus, FedAvg shows a similar performance to FOC. With the increment of D, more labels are randomized in the participant and the FL model gets more influence and worsen its performance in terms of testing accuracy. However, since FOC learns a lower weight for the noisy participant, it shows more robustness than FedAvg, especially when D is as large as over 60%. The learned weights of noisy participant under different Ds are given in Fig. 7. With more noise, the participant gains a lower weight for model aggregation, which makes FOC outperform FedAvg.

5.3 Evaluation on the Real-World Dataset

In this section, we evaluate FOC onto a real-world practical dataset for Parkinson's Disease symptom recognition, PD-Tremor, by comparing it with the popular FedAvg approach.

Among the three hospitals from which this dataset was collected, two of them are top-tier hospitals, and the third one is considered a lower-tier hospital. We regard each hospital as a participant in the federation. All the data are annotated by doctors from the 3 hospitals. As doctors from the lower-tier hospital tend to

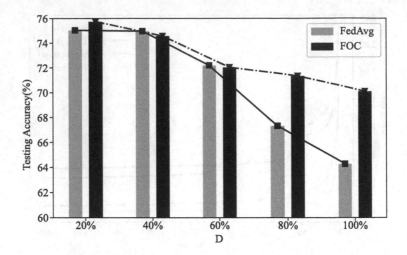

Fig. 6. Testing accuracy under different noise degree.

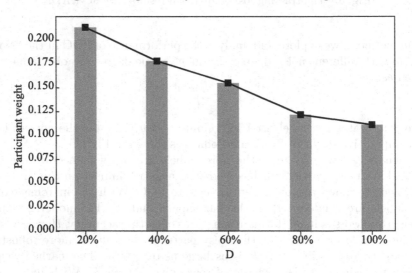

Fig. 7. Noisy participant's weight under different noise degree.

be less experienced and are more likely to make wrong annotations, we test FOC on this dataset to evaluate its effectiveness.

To collect a set of benchmark samples, two experts were invited to make consistent annotations on a sample dataset. The benchmark samples are divided into two parts. One of them is used as the benchmark dataset on the FL coordinator; and the other is used as the test set.

The results in terms of testing accuracy and participant weights in FOC are shown in Figs. 8 and 9, respectively. "Base" denotes the base model trained with the benchmark dataset.

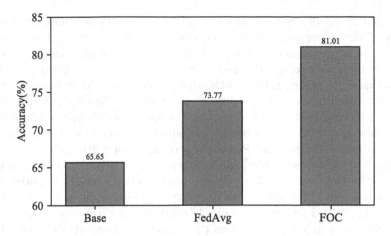

Fig. 8. The test accuracy comparison on PD-Tremor.

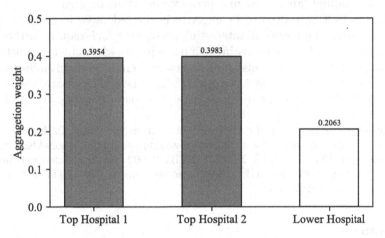

Fig. 9. The weights assigned to the hospitals by FOC.

It can be observed that both FL-based approaches, FOC and `FedAvg`, are able to learn more information from the participants and train stronger models. FOC outperformed `FedAvg` in terms of accuracy by 7.24%, which also confirmed our suspicion that there are noises in the participants. By observing the opportunistic weight of each participant, we find that the lower-tier hospital is assigned a smaller weight, which indicates that its data are of low-quality and contain noisy labels.

6   Conclusions and Future Work

Label quality disparity is an important challenge facing today's federated learning field. So far, it remains open. Noisy labels in FL participants can corrupt the learned FL model. Since under FL, sensitive local data cannot be transmitted out of the owner participant's data store in order to protect user privacy. This makes the problem of noisy local labels even more challenging to resolve. In this chapter, we propose the Federated Opportunistic Computing (FOC) to address this challenging problem. FOC maintains a small set of benchmark samples in the coordinator. A novel mutual cross-entropy based credibility score is designed to compute the label quality of a participant's dataset without requiring access to raw data. Based on the measured credibility, we further proposed a modification to the popular `FedAvg` algorithm to opportunistically aggregate participant model updates into a global FL model. In this way, only a parameter which carries the local loss is extra communicated. Extensive experiments on both synthetic and real-world data demonstrated significant advantage of FOC over `FedAvg`. With FOC, we empower FL systems to effectively identify participants with noisy label and improve their model training strategy to mitigate the negative effects. To the best of our knowledge, it is the first FL approach capable of handling label noisy in a privacy preserving manner.

Although FOC is proved to be effective in the federated learning with label quality disparity, there are still interesting problems which require further investigation. For example, how to distinguish participants who maliciously attack the FL system by faking their labels and those facing genuine difficulties in providing correct labels is an important issue which affects how these participants should be dealt with. In subsequent research, we will focus on tackling this problem.

Acknowledgments. Thank the clinical doctors from the China Parkinson Alliance for supporting the data acquisition. This work was supported by National Key Research & Development Plan of China No. 2017YFB1002802; Natural Science Foundation of China No. 61972383; Research & Development Plan in Key Field of Guangdong Province No. 2019B010109001.

References

1. Chen, Y., Yang, X., Chen, B., Miao, C., Yu, H.: PdAssist: objective and quantified symptom assessment of Parkinson's disease via smartphone. In: 2017 IEEE International Conference on Bioinformatics and Biomedicine (BIBM), pp. 939–945. IEEE (2017)
2. Cretu, G.F., Stavrou, A., Locasto, M.E., Stolfo, S.J., Keromytis, A.D.: Casting out demons: sanitizing training data for anomaly sensors. In: The 2008 IEEE Symposium on Security and Privacy (SP 2008), pp. 81–95. IEEE (2008)
3. Kairouz, P., et al.: Advances and open problems in federated learning. CoRR. p. arXiv:1912.04977 (2019)
4. Koh, P.W., Steinhardt, J., Liang, P.: Stronger data poisoning attacks break data sanitization defenses. CoRR, arXiv:1811.00741 (2018)
5. McMahan, B., Moore, E., Ramage, D., Hampson, S., y Arcas, B.A.: Communication-efficient learning of deep networks from decentralized data. In: Artificial Intelligence and Statistics, pp. 1273–1282 (2017)
6. McMahan, H.B., Moore, E., Ramage, D., y Arcas, B.A.: Federated learning of deep networks using model averaging. Page arXiv:1602.05629 (2016)

7. Natarajan, N., Dhillon, I.S., Ravikumar, P.K., Tewari, A.: Learning with noisy labels. In: Proceedings of the 27th Conference on Neural Information Processing Systems (NeurIPS 2013), pp. 1196–1204 (2013)

8. Xie, C., Koyejo, S., Gupta, I.: Zeno: distributed stochastic gradient descent with suspicion-based fault-tolerance. In: Proceedings of the 36th International Conference on Machine Learning (ICML 2019), pp. 6893–6901 (2019)

9. Yang, Q., Liu, Y., Cheng, Y., Kang, Y., Chen, T., Yu, H.: Federated Learning. Morgan & Claypool Publishers, San Rafael (2019)

10. Zeni, M., Zhang, W., Bignotti, E., Passerini, A., Giunchiglia, F.: Fixing mislabeling by human annotators leveraging conflict resolution and prior knowledge. Proc. ACM Interact. Mob. Wearable Ubiquitous Technol. $3(1)$, 32 (2019)

11. Zhang, M., Sawchuk, A.A.: USC-HAD: a daily activity dataset for ubiquitous activity recognition using wearable sensors. In: Proceedings of the 2012 ACM Conference on Ubiquitous Computing (UbiComp 2012), pp. 1036–1043. ACM (2012)

12. Zhang, W.: Personal context recognition via skeptical learning. In: Proceedings of the 28th International Joint Conference on Artificial Intelligence (IJCAI 2019), pp. 6482–6483 (2019)

13. Zhang, W., Wang, Y., Qiao, Y.: MetaCleaner: learning to hallucinate clean representations for noisy-labeled visual recognition. In: Proceedings of the 2019 IEEE Conference on Computer Vision and Pattern Recognition (CVPR 2019), pp. 7373–7382 (2019)

14. Zhao, Y., Li, M., Lai, L., Suda, N., Civin, D., Chandra, V.: Federated learning with Non-IID data. CoRR, arXiv:1806.00582 (2018)

Incentive

FedCoin: A Peer-to-Peer Payment System for Federated Learning

Yuan Liu[1]($\boxtimes$), Zhengpeng Ai[1], Shuai Sun[1], Shuangfeng Zhang[1], Zelei Liu[2], and Han Yu[2]

[1] Software College, Northeastern University Shenyang,
Shenyang 110169, Liaoning, China
liuyuan@swc.neu.edu.cn, im@aizhengpeng.cn,
sunshuai.edu@gmail.com, 1971161@stu.neu.edu.cn
[2] School of Computer Science and Engineering, Nanyang Technological University,
Singapore 639798, Singapore
{zelei.liu,han.yu}@ntu.edu.sg
http://www.blockchain-neu.com

Abstract. Federated learning (FL) is an emerging collaborative machine learning method to train models on distributed datasets with privacy concerns. To properly incentivize data owners to contribute their efforts, Shapley Value (SV) is often adopted to fairly and quantitatively assess their contributions. However, the calculation of SV is time-consuming and computationally costly. In this chapter, we propose Fed-Coin, a blockchain-based peer-to-peer payment system for FL to enable a feasible SV based profit distribution. In FedCoin, blockchain consensus entities calculate SVs and a new block is created based on the proof of Shapley (PoSap) protocol. It is in contrast to the popular BitCoin network where consensus entities "mine" new blocks by solving meaningless puzzles. Based on the computed SVs, we propose a scheme for dividing the incentive payoffs among FL participants with non-repudiation and tamper-resistance properties. Experimental results based on real-world data show that FedCoin can promote high-quality data from FL participants through accurately computing SVs with an upper bound on the computational resources required for reaching block consensus. It opens opportunities for non-data owners to play a role in FL.

Keywords: Federated learning · Blockchain · Shapley value

1 Introduction

Nowadays, many businesses generate a large volume of data through connecting massive end devices, and machine learning (ML) supported decision-making systems boost novel and intelligent applications [21,24]. With changing regulatory

Supported by the National Natural Science Foundation for Young Scientists of China under Grant No. 61702090 and No. 61702084; 111 Project (B16009); Nanyang Technological University, Nanyang Assistant Professorship (NAP).

Q. Yang et al. (Eds.): Federated Learning, LNAI 12500, pp. 125–138, 2020.
https://doi.org/10.1007/978-3-030-63076-8_9

scene, ML is facing increasingly difficult challenges with respect to the usage of such data [20]. Data are often owned by multiple distributed entities, which are often sensitive and not feasible to be stored in a centralized server without violating privacy protection laws. In recent years, federated learning (FL) has emerged as a promising solution to these challenges [13,14,22].

In FL, each entity trains its local model and contributes the model parameter gradients to a central server towards a more powerful global model. Compared with centralized ML methods, FL not only reduces communication costs by transmitting model updates instead of raw data, but also reduces the computational costs of the server by leveraging computing power from participants. Moreover, as local data never leaves its owner, FL improves user privacy [3,16].

From the above description, it is clear that FL participants are making significant contributions towards the FL model. Thus, in order to sustain an FL community, it is important for FL participants to be properly incentivized. For this to happen, FL participants must be treated fairly [23]. Existing FL incentive schemes generally agree that fair treatment of FL participants shall be based on a fair assessment of their contributions to the FL model [9]. Currently, the most widely adopted method for fair assessment of FL participant contribution is that of Shapley Values (SVs) [8,19].

SV is a popular notion in fairly distributing profits among a coalitional contributors. It has been applied in various fields, ranging from economics, information theory, and ML. The reason for its broad application is that the SV divides the payoff with attractive properties such as fairness, individual rationality, and additivity. However, SV based distribution solution often takes exponential time to compute with a complexity of $\mathcal{O}(n!)$ where n is the number of data items. Even though the computational complexity can be reduced through approximating SV with marginal error guarantees [8], it is still computationally costly.

In order to help FL systems compute SVs to support sustainable incentive schemes, we propose a blockchain-based peer-to-peer payment system *FedCoin*. The Shapley value of each FL participant, reflecting its contribution to the global FL model in a fair way, is calculated by the Proof of Shapley (PoSap) consensus protocol which replaces the traditional hash-based protocol in existing proof of work (PoW) based blockchain systems. All the payments are recorded in the block in an immutable manner. Under FedCoin, paying out incentives to FL participants does not need to rely on a central FL server. Based on this, FedCoin provides a decentralized payment scheme for FL so that incentives for all participants can be delivered in third-party-free manner with nonrepudiation and tamper-resistance properties.

Extensive experiments based on real-world data show that FedCoin is able to properly determine FL participants' Shapley Value-based contributions to the global FL model with an upper bound on the computational resources required for reaching consensus. To the best of our knowledge, FedCoin is the first attempt to leverage the blockchain technology in federated learning incentive scheme research. It opens up new opportunities for entities which has computational resources but without local data to contribute to federated learning.

2   Related Work

The incentive mechanism design is an important research direction in the field of federated learning [9,22]. In [10], the contract theory is employed to improve the accuracy of model training considering the unreliable data contributors. A consortium blockchain architecture is applied to build a decentralized reputation system. In [11], a Stackelberg-game based incentive mechanism is designed to optimize the utilities of both FL participants and the FL server. These works focus on optimizing the rewards for self-interested FL participants and FL customers who pay to use the FL model. Our study is compatible with these works in terms of determining the payment budget for the FL customers.

In field of ML, SV has also be studied widely for various purpose. SV can be applied in feature selection, ranking the importance of training data, which is further applied in explaining the behavior of ML models [15]. Since the computation complexity is $\mathcal{O}(n!)$, approximations of SV also attract many attentions. In [1], a polynomial-time approximation of SV is proposed for deep neural network. Group sampling based approximation is studied in [8]. In this work, our objective is not to decrease the computational complexity, but to establish a scheme so that distributed computational resources, which are otherwise wasted, can be leveraged to help FL systems calculate SVs.

Blockchain has been widely applied in addressing the security problems in FL applications [5,9,22]. FLChain [2] and BlockFL [12,13] have been proposed to record and verify the local model parameter updates in the temper-resistant manner. A blockchain-based FL was proposed in [18] so as to remove the need for an FL server. A blockchain-based trust management system was proposed in [10] to assist FL server to select reliable and high quality data owners as FL participants. These blockchain systems are used as immutable ledgers to record local gradients and aggregate them in a trusted manner. Our work will adopt the blockchain network as a computational engine and payment distribution ledger, which is the first of its kind in the current literature.

3   Preliminaries

For a typical FL scenario, we take $\mathcal{F}^i(w) = \ell(x_i, y_i; w_t)$ as the loss of prediction on a sample (x_i, y_i) with model parameters w at the t-th round. The parameters w_t is a d-dimensional vector. We assume that there are K participants, and each participant has a local data set $\mathcal{D}_k$ with $n_k = |\mathcal{D}_k|$. The overall dataset is $\mathcal{D} = \{\mathcal{D}_1, \ldots, \mathcal{D}_K\}$ with $n = |\mathcal{D}| = \sum_{k=1}^{K} n_k$. The objective function to be optimized is:

$$\min_{w \in \mathcal{R}^d} \mathcal{F}(w) \quad \text{where} \quad \mathcal{F}(w) = \frac{1}{n} \sum_{k=1}^{K} \sum_{i \in \mathcal{D}_k} \mathcal{F}^i(w) \tag{1}$$

This optimization problem is generally solved by stochastic gradient descent (SGD) [7] based methods. For example, based on the current model w_t, the federated averaging algorithm [16] computes the average gradient $g_k^t = \frac{1}{n_k} \sum_{i \in \mathcal{D}_k} \nabla \mathcal{F}_i(w^t)$ on the local data of participant k. Each participant updates its local model $w_{t+1}^k \leftarrow w_t - \eta g_k^t$, and the FL server aggregates the local models as the global FL model.

$$w_{t+1} \leftarrow \mathcal{A}(\{w_{t+1}^k | k = 1, \ldots, K\}) \tag{2}$$

where $\mathcal{A}$ is an aggregation function.

4   FedCoin

There are two networks of participants in our system: 1) the FL network, and 2) the peer-to-peer blockchain network (Fig. 1). A *FL model requester* or FL training task requester refers to the entities who need to train an FL network and with a budget of V. In the FL network, there is a centralized server, referred as *FL server*, in coordinating the executing of model training and receiving payment V from the FL model requester.

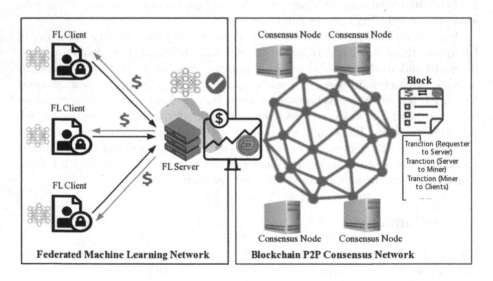

Fig. 1. Overview of the proposed model

The distributed data owners, called as *FL participants*, participate in a collaborative training task and receive a payment V. Each FL participant trains its local model and submits the parameter updates to the FL server. The FL server plays three roles. Firstly, it publishes a training task to FL participants with price TrainPrice. Secondly, it aggregates local updates through a secure aggregation protocol [4] and earns a computation payment (ComPrice). Thirdly, it transfer a processing fee SapPrice to the blockchain network to enlist its members' help in calculating the FL model. The total payment of the task (TrainPrice + ComPrice + SapPrice) should be not greater than V in order to sustain payment balance without relying on external transfer of values into this system.

After each global model update epoch, the FL server publishes a task to calculate the contribution of each FL participant. The consensus nodes in blockchain network then collaboratively calculate SVs, and the block winner receives a payment of TrainPrice+SapPrice. The winner then divides TrainPrice to FL participants according to their respective SVs by creating transactions in the blockchain. In our current design, we only reward participants with positive contributions, but refrain from penalizing participants with negative contributions. All the transactions are recorded in the new block and further updated to the chain.

Therefore, the connection between the FL network and the blockchain network is a special type of task. The task includes the received local update set $W = \{w_k | k = 1, \ldots, K\}$, the aggregation function $\mathcal{A}$, the loss function $\mathcal{F}(w)$, and SapPrice and TrainPrice for each update round. Note that SapPrice and TrainPrice decreases as the number of training rounds increases, and the total payment for training can be divided among the rounds equally or not. Without loss of generality, the following description focuses on a single training round.

4.1 Shapley Value Based Blockchain Consensus

Upon receiving a Shapley value calculation task from the FL network, the miners in the blockchain network are to calculate the SV vector $S = [s_k]_{k \in [1,K]}$ where s_k is the SV of the participant in providing $w_k \in W$. Each miner independently calculates the SV vector following Algorithm 1. Since the objective of the mining process is to competitively calculate SV vectors so as to prove the miner's computation power, we name the algorithm as "Proof of Shapley (PoSap)". The input of Algorithm 1 comes from the task specifications from the FL network. The output is a new generated block.

In Algorithm 1, a miner first initializes the SV vector as an all-zero vector, and sets the calculation iteration number as 0 (Line 1–2). The SV computation continues as long as one of the following two conditions are satisfied: 1) there is no new block received; or 2) the received block fails to pass the verification which is specified in Algorithm 2 (Line 3). The SV calculation process is described in Line 4 to Line 13. The miner initializes a temporary SV vector S_t to record the calculated value in this iteration (Line 4). Then, the miner randomly generates a rank of the K FL participants (Line 5). According to the rank, an SV of the first entity is calculated as in Line 6, which is the contribution of the entity to the loss function (Line 6)). For the next entity i, the Shapley value is calculated as its marginal contribution (Line 7–10). S is updated by averaging all the previous iterations and the current S_t (Line 11). The iteration time is then incremented by 1 (Line 12). Then, the entity broadcast S and *time* (Line 13).

Whenever a miner receives S and *time*, the miner calculates the average results $\overline{S}$ of all the received S (Line 16). Then, the miner calculates the

---

Algorithm 1: Proof of Shapley (PoSap)

Input: $\mathcal{F}$: Loss function;
$\quad\quad\quad$ $\mathcal{A}$: Aggregation function;
$\quad\quad\quad$ W: Contribution of FL participants in size K;
$\quad\quad\quad$ D: Difficulty in Mining;
Output: Blk: a new block

1   Initialize $S = [s_k = 0 | k = 1, \ldots, K]$;
2   time=0;
3   **while** *No received Blk OR !VerifyBlock(Blk)* **do**
4      $S_t = [s_k = 0 | k = 1, \ldots, K]\%$ temporary store S
5   Random generate a rank $R = [r_k | k = 1, \ldots, K]$;
6      $S_t(R(1)) = \mathcal{F}(\mathcal{A}(W(R(1))))$;
7   **for** *i from 2 to K* **do**
8          $S_t(R(i)) = \mathcal{F}(\mathcal{A}(W(R(1:i))))$;
9          $S_t(R(i)) = S_t(R(i)) - \sum_{j=1}^{i-1} S_t(R(j))$;
10   **end**
11      $S = \frac{S \times time + S_t}{time + 1}$;
12   time=time+1;
13   Broadcast S and time;
14   **end**
15   **if** *Receive a new S* **then**
16   Average the Received S to $\overline{S} = \frac{\sum time \times S}{\sum time}$;
17   **if** $\|S - \overline{S}\|_p \leq D$ **then**
18   Create a new block Blk after longest chain;
19   Broadcast Blk;
20   **return** Blk;
21   **end**
22   **end**
23   **if** *Receive a new Blk* **then**
24   **if** *VerifyBlock(Blk)==ture* **then**
25   Update Blk to its chain;
26   **return** Blk;
27   **end**
28   **end**

P-distance between its own S and $\overline{S}$. When the distance is no greater than the mining difficulty D, the miner becomes the winner and generates a new block Blk (Line 18). The difficulty D is adapted dynamically as explained in Sect. 4.2. The illustration of the Shapley based verification is shown in Fig. 2. The new block is then appended to the current longest chain.

Whenever a miner receives a new block Blk, the miner verifies this block according to Algorithm 2. Once the verification passes, the block is appended to the miner's chain, and the mining process terminates (Line 23–28).

The structure of a block is shown in Fig. 3, including block header and block body. The block header includes seven pieces of information, Table 1 presents

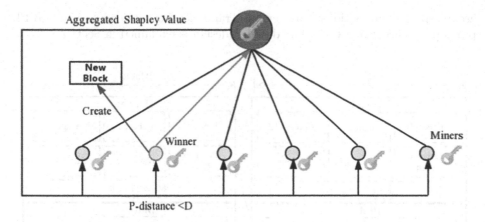

Fig. 2. Shapley valued based consensus protocol

Algorithm 2: VerifyBlock (new Blk)

Input: Blk: Received new block;

$\quad\quad\overline{S}$: Local average of received Shapley Value;

$\quad\quad D$: Difficulty in Mining;

Output: ValuationResult: True OR False

1 $S_t = Blk.S;\ \overline{S}_t = Blk.\overline{S};$

2 **if** $\|S_t - \overline{S}_t\|_p \leq D$ **then**

3 $\quad$ **if** $\|\overline{S} - \overline{S}_t\|_p \leq D$ **then**

4 $\quad\quad$ **if** $Blk.ID\geq$ *longest chain length* **then**

5 $\quad\quad\quad$ | **return** ValuationResult=ture;

6 $\quad\quad$ **end**

7 $\quad\quad$ **else**

8 $\quad\quad\quad$ | **return** ValuationResult=false;

9 $\quad\quad$ **end**

10 $\quad$ **end**

11 $\quad$ **else**

12 $\quad\quad$ | **return** ValuationResult=false;

13 $\quad$ **end**

14 **end**

15 **else**

16 $\quad$ | **return** ValuationResult=false;

17 **end**

---

the explanation about each header item. The block body records two types of data: (1) The task specification including all the inputs for Algorithm 1; and (2) The transactions in the blockchain network. Here, a transaction is denoted as a certain amount of FedCoins transferred from a user account to another, which is similar to that in BitCoin [17]. The block winner has the privilege to create special transactions: transferring TrainPrice from its own account to FL participants according to $\overline{S}$. The detailed design is explained in Sect. 4.3.

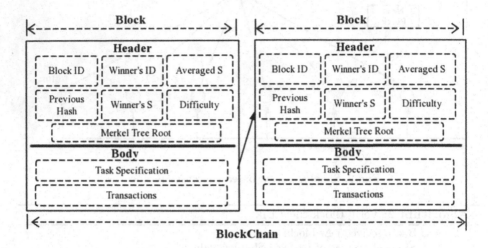

Fig. 3. Block structure in FedCoin

Table 1. Explanation of Block Header

Type	Explanations
Block ID	The block height
Winner's ID	Identity of the block generator
Averaged S	The calculated Shapley vector in Line 15 of Algorithm 1
Previous Hash	Hash of previous block based on a hash function, e.g. SHA 256
Winner's S	The Shapley vector calculated by the winner
Difficulty	The required difficulty D
Merkel Tree Root	Root of Merkel tree organized with transactions in block body

The verification procedure is described as in Algorithm 2. Three conditions must be satisfied for a block to successfully pass the verification. The first condition is $\|S_t - \overline{S}_t\|_p \le D$ which aims to verify whether the winner has generated the block with a valid SV calculation result. The second condition is $\|\overline{S} - \overline{S}_t\|_p \le D$ which requires that the $\overline{S}$ value of the block should be close enough to the local aggregated S. $\overline{S}$ should be equal to $\overline{S}_t$ when the blockchain network is synchronized. In an asychronized network, this condition requires that the winner should aggregate a sufficient number of results from other entities. Thirdly, the current block ID should be the largest to ensure that only the longest chain is acceptable. This longest chain principle can effectively avoid forking, resulting in consistent chain status in a distributed network.

4.2 Dynamic Mining Difficulty

The difficulty level in mining new blocks can be adapted dynamically. There are two main factors influencing the difficulty updates: 1) the total mining power of the miners and 2) the speed of generating a block. Given the same mining power, the difficulty level should be decreased as the block generation speed increases. Given the same block generation speed, the difficulty level should be increased as the mining power increases. Difficulty update can be achieved by deploying a smart contract. For example, in BitCoin, a block is generated in every ten minutes and the difficulty level is updated in every two-week duration.

4.3 The Payment Scheme

With the FedCoin system in place, an FL model requester starts by depositing V FedCoins at the FL server. The value of V shall be no greater than the value of the FL model for the requester. To divide V among FL participants, blockchain miners, and the FL server, all the entities should register a transaction account. The value of V is then divided into three parts.

- TrainPrice: payments to the FL participants;
- ComPrice: payment to the FL sever for processing the model aggregation;
- SapPrice: payments to the blockchain network miners for calculating the Shapley value of each participant.

The division can be determined by a pre-agreed smart contract. For example, the division contract could specify that TrainPrice:ComPrice:SapPrice $= 7:1:2$. Then, TrainPrice $= 0.7V$, ComPrice $= 0.1V$, and SapPrice $= 0.2V$. The specific payment scheme is shown in Algorithm 3.

In Algorithm 3, a model training task is successfully accepted by the FL server whenever the server receives payment V from the FL model requester. The payment of V is confirmed when the transfer transaction (requester $\xrightarrow{V}$ server) is recorded in the blockchain. The server then calculates TrainPrice and SapPrice and leaving ComPrice $=$ V-TrainPrice-SapPrice as its own payment for processing the task (Line 2). The training task is then published to FL participants with price TrainPrice (Line 3). When the training task is completed, the server then publishes a SV calculation task to the blockchain network with price SapPrice (Line 4–6). As the blockchain network completes the task by successfully mining a new block, the server creates a transaction to transfer TrainPrice + SapPrice to the block winner. The block winner creates the transactions in dividing Train-Price to the FL participants with positive Shapley value. All the transactions as well as submitted unconfirmed transactions are stored in the new block.

5 Analysis

Under FedCoin, the decentralized payment scheme is reliable based on the security of proposed PoSap consensus protocol. Each miner who successfully calculate the sufficiently converging SV is allowed to record a set of transactions and

---

Algorithm 3: The Payment Scheme in FedCoin

Input: V: The value paid by a model requester;
  $\overline{S}$: The final aggragated Shapley Value;
Output: An allocation of V

1 **while** *FL server receives V from a model requester* **do**
2   Calculate TrainPrice and SapPrice;
3   Publish traing task with price TrainPrice;
4   **if** *The model is well trained* **then**
5   Publish a Shapley task to blockchain network with pirce SapPrice;
6   **end**
7 **end**
8 **while** *a new block is mined* **do**
9   FL server transfers TrainPrice+SapPrice to the block winner; **for** *each FL participant i* **do**
10   **if** $S_i > 0$ **then**
11         $p_i = \frac{S_i}{\sum_{S_j > 0} S_j}$TrainPrice;
12   block winner transfers p_i to i;
13   **end**
14   **end**
15 **end**

---

receive payment from the FL server. The more mining power (i.e. resources) a miner applies, the higher its chances to become a block winner. PoSap provides incentives for miners to contribute their resources to the system, and is essential to the decentralized nature of the proposed payment system.

The security of PoSap is also similar to that of the BitCoin system. Empirical evidence shows that Bitcoin miners may form pools in order to decrease the variance among their incomes. Within such pools, all members contribute to the solution of each cryptopuzzle, and share the rewards proportionally to their contributions. Ideally, a feasible payment system should be designed to resist the formation of large mining pools. Bitcoin system has been shown to be vulnerable when a mining pool attracts more than 50% of the miners. Similarly, the proposed system can also only resist upto 50% of the miners colluding.

Next we discuss how our system fares against the selfish mining strategy [6].

Observation 1. *When the FL server processes FL training model requests sequentially, it is not rational for colluders to follow the selfish mining strategy.*

According to Algorithm 3, each public block winner is paid by the FL server before creating a new block containing the block reward payment transactions. When the training task is processed one by one, if a selfish miner becomes the winner but does not publish this result immediately, it cannot receive the block rewards. Meanwhile, the selfish miner cannot mine the next block without publishing its private block since the next SV task must wait for the completion of payment in the current block in the setting of sequentially training models.

Observation 2. *When the FL server processes FL training model requests in parallel, and all the miners have the same block propagation delay to the FL server, the expected revenue for selfish miner is greater than that for honest miners when the selfish pool attracts more then 25% of the total mining power in the blockchain network.*

If the tasks are published in parallel, a selfish miner can reserve a block and continue to mine the next block. The state transition and revenue analysis is same as that in [6], resulting the condition of the threshold of selfish pool's mining power to be 1/4 under the condition of the same propagation delay to the FL server. Thus, processing FL training model requests in parallel under the proposed scheme is not recommended.

6   The Demonstration System

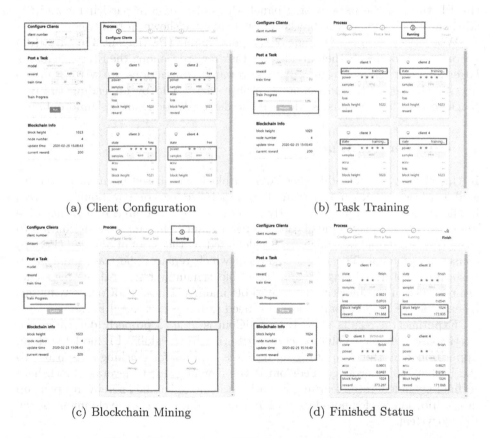

(a) Client Configuration　　　　　　(b) Task Training

(c) Blockchain Mining　　　　　　(d) Finished Status

Fig. 4. The interfaces of the demonstration system

FedCoin is demonstrated on a well-known digit classification dataset - MNIST - which includes 70,000 images, with a widely used software environment - TensorFlow - to perform federated digit classification tasks. The network participants are generated based on Dockers. Participants can independantly communicate with each other by sending messages, performing FL training tasks or Shapley value calculation tasks following PoSap to sustain a full copy of the blockchain. The total computation power is equal to that of our simulation platform (CPU Interl i7-7700, GPU 2G, RAM 8g, ROM 1t, SSD 256M). We adopt `FedAvg` [4] for FL model aggregation. It averages the collected local model parameters to derive the global FL model parameters.

The FedCoin system interface can be divided into four panels: 1) setting panel (Fig. 4(a)), 2) task specification panel (Fig. 4(b)), 3) control panel (Fig. 4(c)), and 4) presentation panel (Fig. 4(d)). In the setting panel, a user can set the number of participants and the initial dataset of each participant. In the task specification panel, the task model for each FL participant can be selected from a list of classification models (e.g., CNN). The payment and training time for the task are also specified in this panel. In the control panel, a user can commence the FL task. In the presentation panel, the status of each participant and the statistic information of the blockchain network are shown in real time.

When the mining is over, one of the participants (Participant 3 in Fig. 4(d)) becomes the winner. It then divides the task rewards among the FL participants based on their Shapley values. All the rewards transactions are written in the new block and all the participants update their chain by appending the new block to their local chains. A video of the demonstration can be found online[1].

7   Chapter Summary

In this chapter, we introduce FedCoin - a blockchain-based payment system to enable a federated learning system. It can mobilize free computational resources in the community to perform costly computing tasks required by FL incentive schemes. The Shapley value of each FL participant, reflecting its contribution to the global FL model in a fair way, is calculated by the proof of Shapley (PoSap) consensus protocol. The proposed PoSap which replaces the traditional hash-based protocol in existing Bitcoin based blockchain systems. All the payments are recorded in the block in an immutable manner. Under FedCoin, paying out incentives to FL participants does not need to rely on a central FL server.

Experimental results show that FedCoin is able to properly determine FL participants' Shapley Value-based contribution to the global FL model with an upper bound on the computational resource required for reaching consensus. To the best of our knowledge, FedCoin is the first attempt to leverage blockchain technology in federated learning incentive scheme research. Thereby, it opens up new opportunities for non-data owners to contribute to the development of the FL ecosystem.

---

[1] https://youtu.be/q2706lpR8NA.

References

1. Ancona, M., Öztireli, C., Gross, M.H.: Explaining deep neural networks with a polynomial time algorithm for Shapley value approximation. In: Proceedings of the 36th International Conference on Machine Learning, ICML 2019, 9–15 June 2019, Long Beach, California, USA, pp. 272–281 (2019)
2. Bao, X., Su, C., Xiong, Y., Huang, W., Hu, Y.: FLChain: a blockchain for auditable federated learning with trust and incentive. In: Proceedings of 5th International Conference on Big Data Computing and Communications, BIGCOM, pp. 151–159 (2019)
3. Bonawitz, K., et al.: Towards federated learning at scale: system design. CoRR abs/1902.01046 (2019)
4. Bonawitz, K., et al.: Practical secure aggregation for privacy-preserving machine learning. In: Proceedings of ACM SIGSAC Conference on Computer and Communications Security CCS, pp. 1175–1191 (2017)
5. Dillenberger, D., et al.: Blockchain analytics and artificial intelligence. IBM J. Res. Dev. **63**, 1–5 (2019)
6. Eyal, I., Sirer, E.G.: Majority is not enough: bitcoin mining is vulnerable. Commun. ACM **61**(7), 95–102 (2018)
7. Goodfellow, I., Bengio, Y., Courville, A.: Deep Learning. MIT Press, Cambridge (2016)
8. Jia, R., et al.: Towards efficient data valuation based on the Shapley value. In: Proceedings of the 22nd International Conference on Artificial Intelligence and Statistics AISTATS 2019, pp. 1167–1176 (2019)
9. Kairouz, P., McMahan, H.B., Avent, B., et al.: Advances and open problems in federated learning. CoRR abs/1912.04977 (2019)
10. Kang, J., Xiong, Z., Niyato, D., Xie, S., Zhang, J.: Incentive mechanism for reliable federated learning: a joint optimization approach to combining reputation and contract theory. IEEE Internet Things J. **6**(6), 10700–10714 (2019)
11. Khan, L.U., et al.: Federated learning for edge networks: resource optimization and incentive mechanism. CoRR abs/1911.05642 (2019)
12. Kim, H., Park, J., Bennis, M., Kim, S.L.: Blockchained on-device federated learning. IEEE Commun. Lett. **24**, 1279–1283 (2019)
13. Kim, H., Park, J., Bennis, M., Kim, S.: Blockchained on-device federated learning. IEEE Commun. Lett. **24**(6), 1279–1283 (2020)
14. Li, T., Sahu, A.K., Talwalkar, A., Smith, V.: Federated learning: challenges, methods, and future directions. IEEE Signal Process. Mag. **37**(3), 50–60 (2020)
15. Li, Y., Cui, X.: Shapley interpretation and activation in neural networks. CoRR abs/1909.06143 (2019)
16. McMahan, B., Moore, E., Ramage, D., Hampson, S., y Arcas, B.A.: Communication-efficient learning of deep networks from decentralized data. In: Proceedings of the 20th International Conference on Artificial Intelligence and Statistics AISTATS, pp. 1273–1282 (2017)
17. Nakamoto, S., et al.: Bitcoin: a peer-to-peer electronic cash system. Working Paper (2008)
18. Ramanan, P., Nakayama, K., Sharma, R.: Baffle: Blockchain based aggregator free federated learning. arXiv preprint arXiv:1909.07452 (2019)
19. Song, T., Tong, Y., Wei, S.: Profit allocation for federated learning. In: Proceedings of the 2019 IEEE International Conference on Big Data (IEEE BigData 2019) (2019)

20. Tamburri, D.A.: Design principles for the general data protection regulation (GDPR): a formal concept analysis and its evaluation. Inf. Syst. **91**, 101469 (2020)
21. Verbraeken, J., Wolting, M., Katzy, J., Kloppenburg, J., Verbelen, T., Rellermeyer, J.S.: A survey on distributed machine learning. ACM Comput. Surv. **53**, 1–33 (2020)
22. Yang, Q., Liu, Y., Chen, T., Tong, Y.: Federated machine learning: concept and applications. ACM Trans. Intell. Syst. Technol. (TIST) **10**(2), 12 (2019)
23. Yu, H., et al.: A fairness-aware incentive scheme for federated learning. In: Proceedings of the 3rd AAAI/ACM Conference on Artificial Intelligence, Ethics, and Society (AIES-2020) (2020)
24. Zhang, Q., Yang, L.T., Chen, Z., Li, P.: A survey on deep learning for big data. Inf. Fusion **42**, 146–157 (2018)

Efficient and Fair Data Valuation
for Horizontal Federated Learning

Shuyue Wei[1], Yongxin Tong[1(✉)], Zimu Zhou[2], and Tianshu Song[1]

[1] SKLSDE Lab, BDBC and IRI, Beihang University, Beijing, China
{weishuyue,yxtong,songts}@buaa.edu.cn
[2] School of Information Systems, Singapore Management University,
Singapore, Singapore
zimuzhou@smu.edu.sg

Abstract. Availability of big data is crucial for modern machine learning applications and services. Federated learning is an emerging paradigm to unite different data owners for machine learning on massive data sets without worrying about data privacy. Yet data owners may still be reluctant to contribute unless their data sets are fairly valuated and paid. In this work, we adapt Shapley value, a widely used data valuation metric to valuating data providers in federated learning. Prior data valuation schemes for machine learning incur high computation cost because they require training of extra models on all data set combinations. For efficient data valuation, we approximately construct all the models necessary for data valuation using the gradients in training a single model, rather than train an exponential number of models from scratch. On this basis, we devise three methods for efficient contribution index estimation. Evaluations show that our methods accurately approximate the contribution index while notably accelerating its calculation.

Keywords: Federated learning · Data valuation · Incentive mechanism · Shapley value

1 Introduction

The success of modern machine learning is largely attributed to the availability of massive data. Although machine learning systems' appetite for data continue to grow, free access to massive data is becoming difficult. On the one hand, data providers have realized the value of data and are unwilling to contribute their data for free. On the other hand, regulations such as the General Data Protection Regulation (GDPR) [4] impose strict restrictions on raw data access.

To comply with the regulations on raw data access, machine learning production is shifting to federated learning, a paradigm that trains a global model across multiple data providers without sharing their raw data [3,9,11,15]. Of our particular interest is horizontal federated learning, where the data set of every data provider has the same attributes [15]. Horizontal federated learning

© Springer Nature Switzerland AG 2020
Q. Yang et al. (Eds.): Federated Learning, LNAI 12500, pp. 139–152, 2020.
https://doi.org/10.1007/978-3-030-63076-8_10

is common in practice. For example, a medical company may want to develop a new medical image classification technique for pneumonia by acquiring the corresponding patient data from multiple hospitals.

To motivate data owners to contribute their data for model training, incentive mechanisms are necessary. In commercial machine learning production, data providers often get profits based on the valuation of their data sets. Pioneer studies [5,7,8] have proposed the adoption of the Shapley value, a classical concept in game theory [12], for fair valuation of data points in machine learning.

To this end, we investigate data valuation for federated learning, a critical step to enable federated learning in commercial machine learning applications. We instantiate Shapley value from general machine learning to federated learning and define the Contribution Index (CI), a metric to evaluate the contribution of the data set of each data provider on training the global model. However, directly calculating the CI by definition is time-consuming because it involves accessing the accuracy of models trained on *all possible combinations* of data sets. For example, if a company trains a model via federated learning with n data providers (*i.e.*, in effect, the model is trained on the union of the n data sets) for applications, it needs to train another $2^n - 2$ models via federated learning simply for valuation of the n data providers.

In this work, we explore efficient data valuation schemes for horizontal federated learning. Our key observation is that the gradients during federated learning on the *union* of the data sets suffice to approximately construct the models learned on *all combinations* of the data sets, which are necessary data valuation. Therefore, valuation of data providers only involves training the global model for applications. No extra model training on other combinations of data sets are necessary, which saves notable computation overhead.

The main contributions of this work are summarized as follows.

- We instantiate the Shapley value for federated learning and define the Contribution Index (CI) to quantify contributions of data providers in federating learning.
- We design three approximate algorithms to efficiently calculate the CIs without extra model training on all data set combinations.
- We verify the effectiveness and efficiency of our algorithms in various settings. Experimental results show that our algorithms closely approximate the exact CI while accelerating its calculation by 2 to 14×.

A preliminary version of this work can be found in [14] and we make following new contributions: *(i)* We design a new algorithm TMR, which is more effective and efficient by overcoming the drawbacks of MR. *(ii)* We conduct extensive experiments to study the effectiveness and efficiency of the new algorithm.

In the rest of this chapter, we define our problem in Sect. 2, introduce our efficient data valuation algorithms in Sect. 3, present their evaluations in Sect. 4 and finally conclude our work in Sect. 5.

2   Background and Problem Definition

In this section, we define the Contribution Index (CI), a valuation metric for data providers in federated learning. The metric is an adaptation of the general Shapley value [13] to federated model training, as explained below.

2.1   Federated Learning

In federated learning [11], a server trains a global model with n data providers (a.k.a participants), each with data set $D_i, i \in N = \{1, 2, \cdots, n\}$. The model is trained iteratively. Each round $t \in \{0, 1, \cdots, R-1\}$ works as follows.

- Step 1: The server sends a global model $M^{(t)}$ to all the participants.
- Step 2: Each participant, take participant i as an example, trains $M^{(t)}$ based on its own data D_i and returns the updated sub-model $M_i^{(t)}$ to the server.
- Step 3: The server integrates the sub-models $\{M_i^{(t)} | i \in N\}$ and gets a new global model $M^{(t+1)}$ for the next round. Specifically, the server first calculates the gradient of each participant $\Delta_i^{(t+1)} = M_i^{(t)} - M^{(t)}$. Then the overall gradient is calculated as the weighted average of all participants' gradients: $\Delta^{(t+1)} = \sum_{i=1}^{n} \frac{|D_i|}{\sum_{i=1}^{n} |D_i|} \cdot \Delta_i^{(t+1)}$, where $|D_i|$ is the size of training data D_i. Finally the global model for the next round $M^{(t+1)} = M^{(t)} + \Delta^{(t+1)}$.

Note that during each round of model training, the gradients of all participants are calculated based on the *same* global model, which offers a common reference to compare and evaluate the contribution of different participants. Our main contribution is to exploit these gradients for data evaluation *during model training* rather than data valuation by training and evaluating extra models.

2.2   Contribution Index for Participant Valuation

We define the Contribution Index (CI) to evaluate the contribution of each participant on the global model in federated learning. Our CI metric is an instance of the general concept of the Shapley value [13].

The Sharply value is widely used for data evaluation. Assume a cooperative game [12] with n agents and a utility function $U : S \to \mathbf{R}^+, S \subseteq N$, where N is the set of agents and $U(S)$ measures the utility of a subset of agents S. The Shapley value [13] assigns each agent a reward based on their utility as follows:

$$\phi_i = C \cdot \sum_{S \subseteq N \setminus \{i\}} \frac{U(S \cup \{i\}) - U(S)}{\binom{n-1}{|S|}} \tag{1}$$

In federated learning, we can consider each participant as an agent and the accuracy of the global model as the utility function. Accordingly, we can define the Contribution Index for each participant in federated learning as follows.

Definition 1 (Contribution Index (CI)). *Assume n participants with data sets $D_1, D_2, \cdots, D_n$, a machine learning algorithm $\mathcal{A}$ and a test set T. We use D_S which is a multi-set to denote $\cup_{i \in S} D_i$ where $S \subseteq N = \{1, 2, \cdots, n\}$. A model trained on D_S by algorithm $\mathcal{A}$ is denoted by $M_S(\mathcal{A})$, or M_S for abbreviation. The accuracy of M evaluated on test set T is denoted by $U(M, T)$, or $U(M)$ for abbreviation. We use $\phi(\mathcal{A}, D_N, T, D_i)$, or ϕ_i for abbreviation, to denote the contribution index of D_i in the context of $D_N, \mathcal{A}$ and T, which is defined as:*

$$\phi(\mathcal{A}, D_N, T, D_i) = C \cdot \sum_{S \subseteq N \setminus \{i\}} \frac{U(M_{S \cup \{i\}}) - U(M_S)}{\binom{n-1}{|S|}} \qquad (2)$$

The definition of CI inherits the desirable properties of Shapley value for fair data valuation. *(i)* If D_j has no effect on the accuracy of algorithm $\mathcal{A}$ on test set T, the CI of D_j is zero, *i.e.*, if for any subset $S \subseteq N$ we have $U(M_S) = U(M_{S \cup \{j\}})$, then $\phi_j = 0$. *(ii)* If D_i and D_j have the same contribution on the accuracy of $\mathcal{A}$ on test set T, their CIs are the same, *i.e.*, if for any subset $S \subseteq N \setminus \{i, j\}$ we have $U(M_{S \cup \{i\}}) = U(M_{S \cup \{j\}})$, then $\phi_i = \phi_j$. *(iii)* CI is linear with respect to test set T, *i.e.*, for any two disjoint test sets T_1, T_2 and any $i \in N = \{1, 2, \cdots, n\}$, we have $\phi(\mathcal{A}, D_N, T_1 \cup T_2, D_i) = \phi(\mathcal{A}, D_N, T_1, D_i) + \phi(\mathcal{A}, D_N, T_2, D_i)$.

2.3   Inefficiency of Contribution Index Calculation

Directly calculating Shapley value by definition can be computation-expensive, because it requires calculating the utility of all agent combinations. In the context of CI, quantifying the utility of one combination of participant data sets means training a model using this data set combination and evaluating its accuracy on the test set. If there are n participants, we have to quantify the utility for $2^n - 1$ combinations of participant data sets. Note that the model training on each data set combination is the same as the federated learning workflow in Sect. 2.1 (R rounds). However, in addition to training one model using all the participant data sets, we need to train $2^n - 2$ extra models to calculate the CIs naively based on Definition 1.

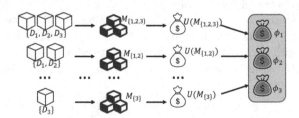

Fig. 1. An illustration of directly calculating CIs by definition for 3 participants.

Figure 1 shows the process of calculating CIs for three participants. We first train a model using the data sets of all the 3 participants and get the utility

$U(M_{\{1,2,3\}})$. Then we quantify the utilities of combinations of 2 participants, $U(M_{\{1,2\}})$, $U(M_{\{1,3\}})$ and $U(M_{\{2,3\}})$. Finally we train models using the data sets of each participant individually, and get the utilities $U(M_{\{1\}})$, $U(M_{\{2\}})$ and $U(M_{\{3\}})$. The CI of each participant is calculated based on these 7 utilities. In this example, 6 extra models, $\{M_{\{1,2\}}, M_{\{1,3\}}, M_{\{2,3\}}, M_{\{1\}}, M_{\{2\}}, M_{\{3\}}\}$, are trained to calculate the CIs.

3 Efficient Contribution Index Calculation

As mentioned in Sect. 2, directly calculating CI based on Definition 1 incurs heavy computation overhead for its need to train an exponential number of extra models. In this section, we present three efficient CI calculation methods exploiting the gradients during federated learning. The overall idea is to use the participants' gradients returned to the server to *approximately construct* the models trained on different data set combinations, which are essential to calculate the CIs of each participant. As next, we explain our three CI calculation methods in detail.

3.1 One-Round Reconstruction (OR)

Our first method, One-Round Construction (OR), gathers the gradients updated by the participants in different training rounds and aggregates them according to all the subsets $S \subseteq N = \{1, 2, \cdots, n\}$. Then it approximately constructs all the models $\{M_S | S \subseteq N\}$ using these aggregated gradients. Figure 2 illustrates its workflow.

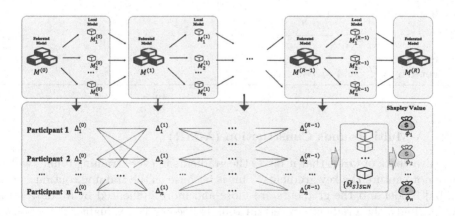

Fig. 2. Schematic diagram for One-Round Construction.

Algorithm 1 presents the details of OR. In line 2 we initialize a global model $M^{(0)}$ and constructed models $\{\widetilde{M}_S^{(0)} | S \subseteq N\}$ based on different nonempty subsets $S \subseteq N$ using the same randomized model. In lines 3–12, in each training round, the server first distributes an initial model $M^{(t)}$ to each participant in line 4 and then receives the updated sub-models $\{M_i^{(t)}\}_{i=1,2,\cdots,n}$ from the participants in line 5. In line 6, the gradients of the participants $\{\Delta_i^{(t)}\}_{i=1,2,\cdots,n}$ are calculated for model aggregation. In line 7, the global model is updated according to Step 3 in Sect. 2.1. In lines 8–11, we construct $\widetilde{M}_S^{(t+1)}$ approximately based on the gradients from the participants. Specifically, for each $S \subseteq N$, we calculate the corresponding gradients by weighted averaging according to the data size in line 9 and use the aggregated gradients to update the corresponding model in line 10. In lines 13–15, the CIs of different participants are calculated. Specifically, for each participant i, we calculate its CI based on Definition 1 using the models constructed in line 14.

Algorithm 1. One-Round (OR)

1: $N \leftarrow \{1, 2, \cdots, n\}$
2: Initialize $M^{(0)}, \{\widetilde{M}_S^{(0)} | S \subseteq N\}$
3: **for** each round $t \leftarrow 0, 1, 2, ..., R-1$ **do**
4:    Send $M^{(t)}$ to all the participants
5:    $M_i^{(t)} \leftarrow Update(i, M^{(t)})$ for participant $i \in N$
6:    $\Delta_i^{(t+1)} \leftarrow M_i^{(t)} - M^{(t)}$ for participant $i \in N$
7:    $M^{(t+1)} \leftarrow M^{(t)} + \sum_{i \in N} \frac{|D_i|}{\sum_{i \in N} |D_i|} \cdot \Delta_i^{(t+1)}$
8:    **for** each subset $S \subseteq N$ **do**
9:       $\Delta_S^{(t+1)} \leftarrow \sum_{i \in S} \frac{|D_i|}{\sum_{i \in S} |D_i|} \cdot \Delta_i^{(t+1)}$
10:      $\widetilde{M}_S^{(t+1)} \leftarrow \widetilde{M}_S^{(t)} + \Delta_S^{(t+1)}$
11:   **end for**
12: **end for**
13: **for** i $\leftarrow 1, 2, ..., n$ **do**
14:    $\phi_i = C \cdot \sum_{S \subseteq N \setminus \{i\}} \frac{U(\widetilde{M}_{S \cup \{i\}}^{(R)}) - U(\widetilde{M}_S^{(R)})}{\binom{n-1}{|S|}}$
15: **end for**
16: **return** $M^{(R)}$ and $\phi_1, \phi_2, ..., \phi_n$

3.2 λ-Multi-Rounds Construction (λ-MR)

One drawback of OR is that it mixes the gradients in every training round, which may not capture the key gradients. This is because as the training continues, the global model and the gradients are more and more influenced by all data sets. Accordingly, the gradients in certain rounds become less valuable. In response, we propose to differentiate the gradients in different rounds and devise a second CI estimation method, λ-Multi-Rounds Construction (λ-MR).

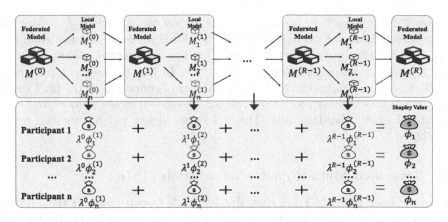

Fig. 3. Schematic diagram for λ-Multi-Rounds Construction.

Algorithm 2. λ-Multi-Rounds (λ-MR)

1: $N \leftarrow \{1, 2, \cdots, n\}$
2: Initialize $M^{(0)}, \{\widetilde{M}_S^{(0)} | S \subseteq N\}$
3: **for** each round $t \leftarrow 0, 1, 2, ..., R - 1$ **do**
4: $\quad M_i^{(t)} \leftarrow Update(i, M^{(t)})$ for participant $i \in N$
5: $\quad \Delta_i^{(t+1)} \leftarrow M_i^{(t)} - M^{(t)}$ for participant $i \in N$
6: $\quad M^{(t+1)} \leftarrow M^{(t)} + \sum_{i \in N} \frac{|D_i|}{\sum_{i \in N} |D_i|} \cdot \Delta_i^{(t+1)}$
7: $\quad$ **for** each subset $S \subseteq N$ **do**
8: $\quad\quad \Delta_S^{(t+1)} \leftarrow \sum_{i \in S} \frac{|D_i|}{\sum_{i \in S} |D_i|} \cdot \Delta_i^{(t+1)}$
9: $\quad\quad \widetilde{M}_S^{(t+1)} \leftarrow M^{(t)} + \Delta_S^{(t+1)}$
10: $\quad$ **end for**
11: $\quad$ **for** i $\leftarrow 1, 2, ..., n$ **do**
12: $\quad\quad \phi_i^{(t+1)} = C \cdot \sum_{S \subseteq N \backslash \{i\}} \frac{U(\widetilde{M}_{S \cup \{i\}}^{(t+1)}) - U(\widetilde{M}_S^{(t+1)})}{\binom{n-1}{|S|}}$
13: $\quad$ **end for**
14: **end for**
15: $\phi_i = \sum\limits_{t=1}^{R} \lambda^t \cdot \frac{\phi_i^{(t)}}{\sum_{i=1}^{n} \phi_i^{(t)}}$ for participant $i \in N$
16: **return** $M^{(R)}$ and $\phi_1, \phi_2, ..., \phi_n$

Figure 3 illustrates the idea of λ-MR. Instead of estimating CIs all at once, λ-MR estimates a set of CIs in each training round, which are then aggregated into the final CIs. In each round, λ-MR constructs the models related to different data set combinations using the gradients on the global model of the current round. Then it calculates the CIs based on Definition 1 by evaluating the accuracy of these constructed models on the test set. The weighted average of these sets of CIs from different training rounds are considered as the final CIs.

Algorithm 2 shows the details of λ-MR. Lines 1–6 show the calculation of the global model, which is the same as in Algorithm 1. The key difference is embodied in lines 7–15. In lines 7–10, we approximately construct models $\widetilde{M}_S^{(t+1)}$ based on the gradients from the participants and the global model in the last round. In lines 11–13, we estimate the *normalized* CI of the constructed models in the t_{th} round, which is referred to as round-CI $\phi_i^{(t+1)}$. In line 15, we use a parameter $\lambda \in (0,1)$ (a decay factor) to control the weights of round-CIs in the final result. The idea is that in later rounds of training, the global model is more and more influenced by all the data sets. Thus, we give higher weights for the earlier rounds.

3.3   Truncated Multi-Rounds Construction (TMR)

This subsection presents Truncated Multi-Rounds Construction (TMR), a third CI estimation algorithm which improves λ-MR from two aspects. *(i)* We take the accuracy of each round into consideration and assign higher weights to the training rounds with higher accuracy when performing weighted averaging. The rationale is that, at the very beginning of the training, the randomly initialized models cannot well indicate contributions of the participants. With the increase of accuracy, the accuracy improvement of models then start to reflect the contributions of the participants. *(ii)* We eliminate unnecessary model construction to improve efficiency. Due to the decay factor λ, the weights of round-CIs in the last few rounds are negligible. Thus we only construct and evaluate models which have an effective impact on the final result.

Algorithm 3. Truncated Multi-Rounds (TMR)

1: $N \leftarrow \{1, 2, \cdots, n\}$
2: Initialize $M^{(0)}, \{\widetilde{M}_S^{(0)} | S \subseteq N\}$
3: **for** each round $t \leftarrow 0, 1, 2, ..., R-1$ **do**
4:      $M_i^{(t)} \leftarrow Update(i, M^{(t)})$ for participant $i \in N$
5:      $\Delta_i^{(t+1)} \leftarrow M_i^{(t)} - M^{(t)}$ for participant $i \in N$
6:      $M^{(t+1)} \leftarrow M^{(t)} + \sum_{i \in N} \frac{|D_i|}{\sum_{i \in N} |D_i|} \cdot \Delta_i^{(t+1)}$
7:      **if** $\lambda^t > \delta$ **then**
8:          **for** each subset $S \subseteq N$ **do**
9:              $\Delta_S^{(t+1)} \leftarrow \sum_{i \in S} \frac{|D_i|}{\sum_{i \in S} |D_i|} \cdot \Delta_i^{(t+1)}$
10:             $\widetilde{M}_S^{(t+1)} \leftarrow M^{(t)} + \Delta_S^{(t+1)}$
11:         **end for**
12:         **for** i $\leftarrow 1, 2, ..., n$ **do**
13:             $\phi_i^{(t+1)} = C \cdot \sum_{S \subseteq N \setminus \{i\}} \frac{U(\widetilde{M}_{S \cup \{i\}}^{(t+1)}) - U(\widetilde{M}_S^{(t+1)})}{\binom{n-1}{|S|}}$
14:         **end for**
15:     **end if**
16: **end for**
17: $\phi_i = \sum_{t=1}^{\lfloor \frac{\lg \delta}{\lg \lambda} \rfloor} \lambda^t \cdot \frac{U(M^{(t)}) \cdot \phi_i^{(t)}}{\sum_{i=1}^n \phi_i^{(t)}}$ for participant $i \in N$
18: **return** $M^{(R)}$ and $\phi_1, \phi_2, ..., \phi_n$

Algorithm 3 explains the details of TMR. Lines 1–6 show the calculation of the global model, which is the same as in Algorithm 1 and Algorithm 2. The key difference from λ-MR lies in line 7 and line 17. In line 7, once the round-CIs are negligible to the final result, we do not construct or evaluate the models. In line 17, we use the decay factor λ and the accuracy in various rounds to control the weights of round-CIs in the final result.

4   Evaluation

This section presents the evaluations of our proposed methods.

4.1   Experimental Setup

Data Sets. We experiment on the MNIST data set [10]. It contains 60,000+ training images and 10,000+ testing images for handwritten digits 0 to 9. Since the number of training images for each digit varies from 5421 to 6742, we randomly pick 5421 images for each digit so that each digit has the same amount of training images. Similarly, we randomly pick 892 testing images for each digit. Hence the sizes of the training and test set are 54210 and 8920, respectively.

Training Setups. Since the data sets owned by participants may vary in size, distribution and quality, we evaluate our methods using the following settings.

- **Same-Size-Same-Distribution.** We randomly split the training set into five partitions of the same size. The number of images with the same label is the same among the five partitions.
- **Same-Size-Different-Distribution.** We randomly split the training set into five partitions of the same size. Participant 1 has 40% of label '0', 40% of label '1' and the data points with the remaining eight labels share the remaining 20% of data provider 1's data. The training set of the other four participants can be generated in a similar way.
- **Different-Size-Same-Distribution.** We randomly split the training set into five partitions with their ratios of data size 2:3:4:5:6. The number of images with the same label is the same among the five partitions.
- **Same-Size-Noisy-Label.** We randomly split the training set into five partitions of the same size. Each partition also has the same amount of images with the same label. We then change 0%, 5%, 10%, 15%, 20% of the labels of the five partitions into one of other nine labels with equal probability.
- **Same-Size-Noisy-Image.** We randomly split the training set into five partitions of the same size. We generate the Gaussian noise with mean 0 and variance 1, and then multiply the noise by 0.00, 0.05, 0.10, 0.15 and 0.20 respectively to get different levels of noise. Finally we add different levels of noise to all the input images.

Compared Algorithms. We compare the following algorithms.

- **Exact.** It directly calculates the CIs of the participants according to Definition 1. Specifically, it trains models based on different combinations of the data sets and these models are evaluated on the test set.
- **Extended-TMC-Shapley.** It is an extension of a state-of-the-art data valuation scheme for general machine learning [5]. We extend Algorithm 1 Truncated Monte Carlo Shapley (TMC-Shapley) of [5] to federated learning. Extended-TMC-Shapley first samples a random permutation π of all $n!$ permutations of $1, 2, \cdots, n$ which is denoted by Π. Then it trains models based on permutation π and calculates the CI of each participant according to

$$\phi_i = \mathbb{E}_{\pi \sim \Pi}[U(M_{\pi_i}) - U(M_{\pi_{i-1}})]. \tag{3}$$

where π_i is the set of the first i numbers in π and thus M_{π_i} means the model trained on the first i data sets in permutation π.
- **Extended-GTB.** It is an extension of another state-of-the-art data valuation scheme for general machine learning [8]. We extend Algorithm 1 Group Testing Based SV Estimation of [8] as follows. It samples some subsets S of $N = \{1, 2, \cdots, n\}$ and trains models M_S. Based on the accuracy of these models, it solves a feasibility problem to estimate the CIs of each participant under some constraints. The feasibility problem is solved by Mathematica 11.2 [6]. If the feasibility problem has no solutions, we relax the constraints until it has one. We set the same convergence condition for Extended-GTB and Extended-TMC-Shapley. The results of models trained on different combinations of the data sets are recorded for reuse as well.
- **One-Round.** Our Algorithm 1 in Sect. 3.1.
- **λ-Multi-Rounds.** Our Algorithm 2 in Sect. 3.2.
- **Truncated Multi-Rounds.** Our Algorithm 3 in Sect. 3.3.

Note that at the beginning of training, the global model may perform poorly since it is randomly initialized. Consequently, some CIs may be negative. In this case, we adopt the egalitarianism and assign each participant the same CI.
Evaluation Metrics. We compare the performance of different algorithms using the following metrics.

- **CI Calculation Time.** We evaluate the efficiency of CI calculation using the time to calculate CIs. The time of model training is excluded.
- **CI Estimation Error.** We evaluate the effectiveness of different approximate CI estimation algorithms using the mean absolute error (MAR):

$$MAR = \frac{\sum_{i=1}^{n} |\phi_i - \phi_i^*|}{n}, \tag{4}$$

where $\phi_1^*, \phi_2^*, \cdots, \phi_n^*$ denote the *normalized* CIs of the n participants estimated by an approximate algorithm, and $\phi_1, \phi_2, \cdots, \phi_n$ denote the *normalized* CIs calculated according to Definition 1.

Implementation. All the algorithms are implemented in python 3.6 with TensorFlow [2] 1.14.0 and TensorFlow Federated [1] 0.8.0. The experiments are conducted on a machine with Intel(R) Xeon(R) Platinum 8163 CPU @ 2.50 GHz and 32 GB main memory.

4.2   Experimental Results

We present the experimental results in the five settings in sequel.

Results on Same-Size-Same-Distribution. Figure 4(a) plots the time cost of different methods. OR has the lowest time cost. λ-MR and TMR takes twice time as OR to calculate CIs. All of our three methods are more efficient than the methods with extra model retraining. For comparison, the time cost of Extended-GTB and Exact is 6–15× as OR and TMR. Figure 4(b) compares the MAR of different methods. The MAR of OR, λ-MR and TMR are almost to 0, *i.e.*, the CIs estimated via our methods are almost the same as the exact values. The MAR of Extended-TMC-Shapley is 17.3× of that of TMR. Extended-GTB also performs poorly in estimation error.

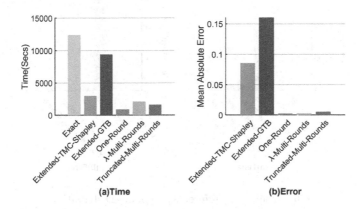

Fig. 4. Results on Same-Size-Same-Distribution.

Results on Same-Size-Different-Distribution. From Fig. 5(a), OR is still the fastest, and TMR is still the second fastest. Extended-TMC-Shapley incurs a high time cost in case of Same-Size-Different-Distribution. Its time cost is

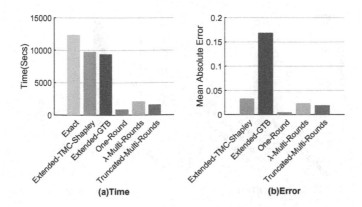

Fig. 5. Results on Same-Size-Different-Distribution.

9.2× higher than OR and 4.5× higher than TMR. From Fig. 5(b), OR performs better than the others in estimation error. The CIs estimated by OR are almost as accurate as the exact one. With much lower calculation time, TMR and λ-MR are still more accurate than Extended-TMC-Shapley and Extended-GTB. Overall, OR and TMR outperform the others in this setting as well.

Results on Different-Size-Same-Distribution. From Fig. 6(a), OR and TMR still have much lower time cost than the others. From Fig. 6(b), OR and TMR also approximate the exact CIs well and outperform the others in terms of estimation error. Extended-TMC-Shapley is less accurate and Extended-GTB's performance is unsatisfactory.

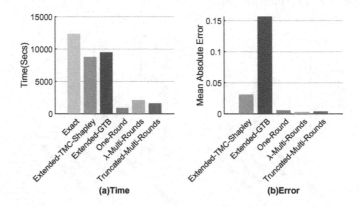

Fig. 6. Results on Different-Size-Same-Distribution.

Results on Same-Size-Noisy-Label From Fig. 7(a), OR and TMR are the most efficient. From Fig. 7(b), we can observe that OR's MAR decline obliviously. The MAR of λ-MR and TMR is stable. The MAR of Extended-TMC-Shapley is 1.5× of TMR and the MAR of Extended-GTB is 7.3× of TMR. OR is more accurate than Extended-GTB but worse than Extended-TMC-Shapley.

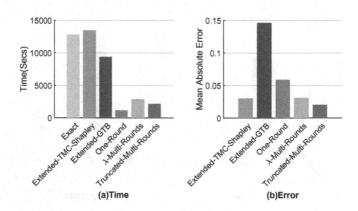

Fig. 7. Results on Same-Size-Noisy-Label.

The results indicate that OR may be sensitive to noisy labels. In contrast, TMR is robust to noisy labels and is more accurate than other approximate algorithms.

Results on Same-Size-Noisy-Image. Overall, OR is slightly better than TMR in time cost while TMR is slightly better than OR in estimation error (see Fig. 8). Both OR and TMR are notably better than the two baseline algorithms. From Fig. 8(b), the MAR of Extended-TMC-Shapley is 6.9× larger than TMR and the MAR of Extended-GTB is 28.6× larger than TMR.

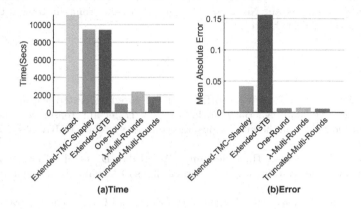

Fig. 8. Results on Same-Size-Noisy-Image.

4.3   Summary of Results

Our main experimental findings are as below.

– **CI Calculation Time.** Extended-TMC-Shapley and Extended-GTB are the most time consuming. They are similar in time efficiency. The cost time of our OR and TMR algorithms are consistently fast in different settings. OR is better than TMR.
– **CI Estimation Error.** Our TMR algorithm has low estimation errors in all settings and the error. Our OR algorithm approximates the exact CIs best in most settings. However, it is sensitive to the noisy labels. Extended-TMC-Shapley and Extended-GTB perform the worst.

5   Conclusion

In this chapter, we study data valuation metrics for federated learning. We define the Contribution Index, a Shaply valued based metric to quantify the contribution of data providers on training a global model via federated learning. Naively calculating the contribution index by definition is computation-intensive since it involves training a series of models on all data set combinations. For efficient Contribution Index calculation, we exploit the gradients in the training of the global model to construct all the models necessary for Contribution Index, thus avoiding training an exponential number of models simply for data valuation. Following this idea, we design three efficient Contribution Index estimation methods. Evaluations on MNIST show that our methods accurately approximate the exact Contribution Index while accelerating its calculation by 2 to 14 times.

Acknowledgment. We are grateful to reviewers for their constructive comments. This is partially supported by the National Key Research and Development Program of China under Grant No. 2018AAA0101100 and the National Science Foundation of China (NSFC) under Grant No. 61822201 and U1811463. Yongxin Tong is the corresponding author of this chapter.

References

1. Tensorflow federated. www.tensorflow.org/federated/federated_learning
2. Abadi, M., Agarwal, A., Barham, P., Brevdo, E., et al.: TensorFlow: large-scale machine learning on heterogeneous distributed systems. CoRR abs/1603.04467 (2016)
3. Bonawitz, K., Eichner, H., Grieskamp, W., Huba, D., et al.: Towards federated learning at scale: system design. In: Proceedings of Machine Learning and Systems (2019)
4. European Parliament, The Council of the European Union: The general data protection regulation (GDPR) (2016). https://eugdpr.org
5. Ghorbani, A., Zou, J.Y.: Data shapley: equitable valuation of data for machine learning. In: Proceedings of the 36th International Conference on Machine Learning, pp. 2242–2251 (2019)
6. Wolfram Research, Inc.: Mathematica, version 11.2 (2017)
7. Jia, R., Dao, D., Wang, B., Hubis, F.A., et al.: Efficient task-specific data valuation for nearest neighbor algorithms. Proc. VLDB Endow. **12**(11), 1610–1623 (2019)
8. Jia, R., Dao, D., Wang, B., Hubis, F.A., et al.: Towards efficient data valuation based on the shapley value. In: The 22nd International Conference on Artificial Intelligence and Statistics, pp. 1167–1176 (2019)
9. Kairouz, P., McMahan, H.B., Avent, B., Bellet, A., et al.: Advances and open problems in federated learning. CoRR abs/1912.04977 (2019)
10. LeCun, Y., Cortes, C., Burges, C.J.: The MNIST Database (1998). http://yann.lecun.com/exdb/mnist/
11. McMahan, B., Moore, E., Ramage, D., Hampson, S., et al.: Communication-efficient learning of deep networks from decentralized data. In: Proceedings of the 20th International Conference on Artificial Intelligence and Statistics, pp. 1273–1282 (2017)
12. Myerson, R.B.: Game Theory. Harvard University Press, Cambridge (2013)
13. Shapley, L.S.: A value for n-person games. Ann. Math. Stud. **28**, 307–317 (1953)
14. Song, T., Tong, Y., Wei, S.: Profit allocation for federated learning. In: IEEE International Conference on Big Data, pp. 2577–2586 (2019)
15. Yang, Q., Liu, Y., Chen, T., Tong, Y.: Federated machine learning: concept and applications. ACM Trans. Intell. Syst. Technol. (TIST) **10**(2), 12 (2019)

A Principled Approach to Data Valuation for Federated Learning

Tianhao Wang[1], Johannes Rausch[2], Ce Zhang[2], Ruoxi Jia[3(✉)], and Dawn Song[4]

[1] Harvard University, Cambridge, USA
tianhaowang@fas.harvard.edu
[2] ETH Zurich, Zürich, Switzerland
{johannes.rausch,ce.zhang}@inf.ethz.ch
[3] Virginia Tech, Blacksburg, USA
ruoxijia@vt.edu
[4] UC Berkeley, Berkeley, USA
dawnsong@gmail.com

Abstract. Federated learning (FL) is a popular technique to train machine learning (ML) models on decentralized data sources. In order to sustain long-term participation of data owners, it is important to fairly appraise each data source and compensate data owners for their contribution to the training process. The Shapley value (SV) defines a unique payoff scheme that satisfies many desiderata for a data value notion. It has been increasingly used for valuing training data in centralized learning. However, computing the SV requires exhaustively evaluating the model performance on every subset of data sources, which incurs prohibitive communication cost in the federated setting. Besides, the canonical SV ignores the order of data sources during training, which conflicts with the sequential nature of FL. This chapter proposes a variant of the SV amenable to FL, which we call the *federated Shapley value*. The federated SV preserves the desirable properties of the canonical SV while it can be calculated without incurring extra communication cost and is also able to capture the effect of participation order on data value. We conduct a thorough empirical study of the federated SV on a range of tasks, including noisy label detection, adversarial participant detection, and data summarization on different benchmark datasets, and demonstrate that it can reflect the real utility of data sources for FL and has the potential to enhance system robustness, security, and efficiency. We also report and analyze "failure cases" and hope to stimulate future research.

Keywords: Data valuation · Federated learning · Shapley value

1 Introduction

Building high-quality ML models often involves gathering data from different sources. In practice, data often live in silos and agglomerating them may be

© Springer Nature Switzerland AG 2020
Q. Yang et al. (Eds.): Federated Learning, LNAI 12500, pp. 153–167, 2020.
https://doi.org/10.1007/978-3-030-63076-8_11

intractable due to legal constraints or privacy concerns. FL is a promising paradigm which can obviate the need for centralized data. It directly learns from sequestered data sources by training local models on each data source and distilling them into a global federated model. FL has been used in applications such as keystroke prediction [8], hotword detection [22], and medical research [3].

A fundamental question in FL is how to value each data source. FL makes use of data from different entities. In order to incentivize their participation, it is crucial to fairly appraise the data from different entities according to their contribution to the learning process. For example, FL has been applied to financial risk prediction for reinsurance [1], where a number of insurance companies who may also be business competitors would train a model based on all of their data and the resulting model will create certain profit. In order to prompt such collaboration, the companies need to concur with a scheme that can fairly divide the earnings generated by the federated model among them.

The SV has been proposed to value data in recent works [6,10,11]. The SV is a classic way in coopereative game theory to distribute total gains generated by the coalition of a set of players. One can formulate ML as a cooperative game between different data sources and then use the SV to value data. An important reason for employing the SV is that it *uniquely* possesses a set of appealing properties desired by a data value notion: it ensures that (1) *all* the gains of the model are distributed among data sources; (2) the values assigned to data owners accord with their actual contributions to the learning process; and (3) the value of data accumulates when used multiple times.

Despite the appealing properties of the SV, it cannot be directly applied to FL. By definition, the SV calculates the average contribution of a data source to every possible subset of other data sources. Thus, evaluating the SV incurs prohibitive communication cost when the data is decentralized. Moreover, the SV neglects the order of data sources, yet in FL the importance of a data source could depend on when it is used for training. For instance, in order to ensure convergence, the model updates are enforced to diminish over time (e.g., by using a decaying learning rate); therefore, intuitively, the data sources used toward the end of learning process could be less influential than those used earlier. Hence, a new, principled approach to valuing data for FL is needed.

In this chapter, we propose *the federated SV*, a variant of the SV designed to appraise decentralized, sequential data for FL. The federated SV can be determined from local model updates in each training iteration and therefore does not incur extra communication cost. It can also capture the effect of participation order on data value as it examines the performance improvement caused by each subset of players following the actual participation order in the learning process. Particularly, the federated SV preserves the desirable properties of the canonical SV. We present an efficient Monte Carlo method to compute the federated SV. Furthermore, we conduct a thorough empirical study on a range of tasks, including noisy label detection, adversarial participant detection, and data summarization on different benchmark datasets, and demonstrate that the federated SV can reflect the actual usefulness of data sources in FL. We also report and analyze cases in which the proposed federated SV can be further improved and hope to stimulate future research on this emerging topic.

2   Related Work

Various data valuation schemes have been studied in the literature, and from a practitioner's point of view they can be classified into query-based pricing that attaches prices to user-initiated queries [18,28]; data attribute-based pricing that builds a price model depending on parameters such as data age and credibility using public price registries [9]; and auction-based pricing that sets the price dynamically based on auctions [21,25]. However, one common drawback of the existing strategies is that they cannot accommodate the unique properties of data as a commodity; for instance, the value of a data source depends on the downstream learning task and the other data sources used for solving the task.

The SV uniquely satisfies the properties desired by a data value notion. The use of the SV for pricing personal data can be traced back to [4,16] in the context of marketing survey, collaborative filtering, recommendation systems, and networks. Despite the desirable properties of the SV, computing the SV is known to be expensive. In its most general form, the SV can be #P-complete to compute [5]. The computational issue becomes even more serious when the SV is used to value training data for ML, because calculating it requires re-training models for many times. Most of the recent work on the SV-based data valuation has been focused on the centralized learning setting and improving its computational efficiency [6,10,11,13]. Two important assumptions of the canonical SV are that the training performance on every combination of data points is measurable and that the performance does not depend on the order of training data. These two assumptions are plausible for centralized learning because the entire data is accessible to the coordinator and the data is often shuffled before being used for training. However, they are no longer valid for the federated setting.

Existing work on pricing data in FL can be roughly categorized into two threads. One thread of work [14,15] studies the mechanism design to incentivize participation given the disparity of data quality, communication bandwidth, and computational capability among different participants. In these works, the authors assume that the task publisher (i.e., the coordinator) has some prior knowledge about the data quality of a participant and design an optimal contract to maximize the utility of the coordinator subject to rationality constraints of individual participants. However, it remains a question how to precisely characterize data quality in FL. Another thread of work investigates the way to measure data quality and share the profit generated by the federated model according to the data quality measurement. [29] and [27] apply the canonical SV to value each data source; however, as discussed earlier, the direct application of the SV is intractable in practice due to the decentralized data and conceptually flawed due to the sequential participation of participants. Recently, [30] has studied at the intersection of two threads by proposing a fair profit sharing scheme while considering individual costs incurred by joining FL as well as the mismatch between contribution and payback time. Our work can be potentially integrated with their work to better characterize the data contribution.

3   Data Valuation Based on SV

Cooperative game theory studies the behaviors of coalitions formed by game players. Formally, a cooperative game is defined by a pair (I, ν), where $I = \{1, \ldots, N\}$ denotes the set of all players and $\nu : 2^N \to \mathbb{R}$ is the utility function, which maps each possible coalition to a real number that describes the utility of a coalition, i.e., how much collective payoff a set of players can gain by forming the coalition. One of the fundamental questions in cooperative game theory is to characterize the importance of each player to the overall cooperation. The SV [26] is a classic method to distribute the total gains generated by the coalition of all players. The SV of player i with respect to the utility function ν is defined as the average marginal contribution of i to coalition S over all $S \subseteq I \setminus \{i\}$:

$$s_i^\nu = \frac{1}{N} \sum_{S \subseteq I \setminus \{i\}} \frac{1}{\binom{N-1}{|S|}} [\nu(S \cup \{i\}) - \nu(S)] \tag{1}$$

We suppress the dependency on ν when the utility used is clear and use s_i to represent the value allocated to player i.

The formula in (1) can also be stated in the equivalent form:

$$s_i = \frac{1}{N!} \sum_{\pi \in \Pi(I)} [\nu(P_i^\pi \cup \{i\}) - \nu(P_i^\pi)] \tag{2}$$

where $\pi \in \Pi(I)$ is a permutation of players and P_i^π is the set of players which precede player i in π. Intuitively, imagine all players join a coalition in a random order, and that every player i who has joined receives the marginal contribution that his participation would bring to those already in the coalition. To calculate s_i, we average these contributions over all the possible orders.

Applying these game theory concepts to data valuation, one can think of the players as data contributors and the utility function $\nu(S)$ as a performance measure of the model trained on the set of training data S. The SV of each data contributor thus measures its importance to learning an ML model. The following desirable properties that the SV *uniquely* possesses motivate many prior works [4,6,10,12,13,16] to adopt it for data valuation.

1. **Group Rationality**: The value of the model is completely distributed among all data contributors, i.e., $\nu(I) = \sum_{i \in I} s_i$.
2. **Fairness**: (1) Two data contributors who are identical with respect to what they contribute to a dataset's utility should have the same value. That is, if data contributor i and j are equivalent in the sense that $\nu(S \cup \{i\}) = \nu(S \cup \{j\}), \forall S \subseteq I \setminus \{i, j\}$, then $s_i = s_j$. (2) Data contributor with zero marginal contributions to all subsets of the dataset receive zero payoff, i.e., if $\nu(S \cup \{i\}) = 0, \forall S \subseteq I \setminus \{i\}$, then $s_i = 0$.

3. **Additivity**: The values under multiple utilities sum up to the value under a utility that is the sum of all these utilities: $s_i^{\nu_1} + s_i^{\nu_2} = s_i^{\nu_1+\nu_2}$ for $i \in I$.

The *group rationality* property states that any rational group of data contributors would expect to distribute the full yield of their coalition. The *fairness* property requires that the names of the data contributors play no role in determining the value, which should be sensitive only to how the utility function responds to the presence of a seller. The *additivity* property facilitates efficient value calculation when data are used for multiple applications, each of which is associated with a specific utility function. With additivity, one can compute value shares separately for each application and sum them up.

There are two assumptions underlying the definition of the SV:

1. **Combinatorially Evaluable Utility**: The utility function can be evaluated for every combination of players;
2. **Symmetric Utility**: The utility function does not depend on the order of the players.

Both of the assumptions are plausible for centralized learning. Since the entire data is accessible to the coordinator, it is empowered to evaluate the model performance on the data from an arbitrary subset of contributors. Furthermore, in centralized learning, the data is often shuffled before being used for training. Hence, it is reasonable to consider the model performance to be independent the order of data points in the training set. In the next section, we will argue that these two assumption are no longer valid for FL and propose a variant of the SV amenable to the federated setting.

4   Valuing Data for FL

4.1   Federated Shapley Value

A typical FL process executes the following steps repeatedly until some stopping criterion is met: (1) The coordinator samples a subset of participants; (2) The selected participants download the current global model parameters from the coordinator; (3) Each selected participant locally computes an update to the model by training on the local data; (4) The coordinator collects an aggregate of the participant updates; (5) The coordinator locally updates the global model based on the aggregated update computed from the participants that participate in the current round.

Let I be the set of participants that participate in at least one round of the FL process. Our goal is to assign a real value to each participant in I to measure its contribution to learning the model. Suppose the learning process lasts for T rounds. Let the participants selected in round t be I_t and we have $I = I_1 \cup \cdots \cup I_T$.

In FL, different participants contribute to the learning process at different time and the performance of the federated model depends on the participation order of participants. Clearly, the symmetric utility assumption of the SV does not hold. Moreover, FL is designed to maintain the confidentiality of participants' data and in each round, only a subset of participants are selected and upload their model updates. Hence, the coordinator can only know the model performance change caused by adding a participant's data into the subset of participants' data selected earlier. However, computing the SV requires the ability to evaluate the model performance change for every possible subset of participants. Unless the participants are able to bear considerable extra communication cost, the combinatorially evaluable utility assumption is invalid for FL. Hence, the SV cannot be used to value the data of different participants in the federated setting.

We propose a variant of the SV amenable to the federated setting. The key idea is to characterize the aggregate value of the set of participants in the same round via the model performance change caused by the addition of their data and then use the SV to distribute the value of the set to each participant. We will call this variant *the federated SV* and its formal definition is given below. We use $\nu(\cdot)$ to denote the utility function which maps any participants' data to a performance measure of the model trained on the data. Note that unlike in the canonical SV definition where $\nu(\cdot)$ takes a set as an input, the argument of $\nu(\cdot)$ is an ordered sequence. For instance, $U(A + B)$ means the utility of the model that is trained on A's data first, then B's data. Furthermore, let $I_{1:t-1}$ be a shorthand for $I_1 + \cdots + I_{t-1}$ for $t \geq 2$ and $\emptyset$ for $t = 1$.

Definition 1 (The Federated Shapley Value). *Let $I = \{1, \cdots, N\}$ denote the set of participants selected by the coordinator during a T-round FL process. Let I_t be the set of participants selected in round t and $I_t \subseteq I$. Then, the federated SV of participant i at round t is defined as*

$$s_t^\nu(i) = \frac{1}{|I_t|} \sum_{S \subseteq I_t \setminus \{i\}} \frac{1}{\binom{|I_t|-1}{|S|}} \left[\nu(I_{1:t-1} + (S \cup \{i\})) - \nu(I_{1:t-1} + S) \right] \; if \; i \in I_t \quad (3)$$

and $s_t(i) = 0$ otherwise. The federated SV takes the sum of the values of all rounds:

$$s^\nu(i) = \sum_{t=1}^{T} s_t(i) \tag{4}$$

We will suppress the dependency of the federated SV $s^\nu(i)$ on ν whenever the underlying utility function is self-evident.

Due to the close relation between the canonical SV and the federated SV, one can expect that the federated variant will inherit the desirable properties of the canonical SV. Indeed, Theorem 1 shows that the federated SV preserves the group rationality, fairness, as well as additivity.

Theorem 1. *The federated SV defined in (4) uniquely possesses the following properties:*

1. Instantaneous group rationality: $\sum_{i \in I_t} s_t(i) = \nu(I_{1:t}) - \nu(I_{1:t-1})$.

2. *Fairness: (1) if* $\nu(I_{1:t-1} + (S \cup \{i\})) = \nu(I_{1:t-1} + (S \cup \{j\}))$, $\forall S \subseteq I_t/\{i,j\}$
   for some round t, then $s_t(i) = s_t(j)$. *(2)* $\nu(I_{1:t-1} + (S \cup \{i\})) = \nu(I_{1:t-1} + S)$,
   $\forall S \subseteq I_t/\{i\}$ *for some round t, then* $s_t(i) = 0$.
3. *Additivity:* $s^{\nu_1 + \nu_2}(i) = s^{\nu_1}(i) + s^{\nu_2}(i)$ *for all* $i \in I$.

The proof of the theorem follows from the fact that the federated Shapley value calculates the Shapley value for the players selected in each round which distributes the performance difference from the previous round.

By aggregating the instantaneous group rationality equation over time, we see that the federated SV also satisfies the *long-term* group rationality:

$$\sum_{i=1}^{N} s(i) = U(I_1 + \cdots + I_T) \tag{5}$$

The *long-term* group rationality states that the set of players participates in a T-round FL process will divide up the final yield of their coalition.

4.2   Estimating the Federated SV

Similar to the canonical SV, computing the federated SV is expensive. Evaluating the exact federated SV involves computing the marginal utility of every participant to every subset of other participants selected in each round (see Eq. 3). To evaluate $U(I_{1:t-1} + S)$, we need to update the global model trained on $I_{1:t-1}$ with the aggregate of the model updates from S and calculate the updated model performance. The total complexity is $\mathcal{O}(T2^m)$, where m is the maximum number of participants selected per round. In this section, we present efficient algorithms to approximate the federated SV. We say that $\hat{s} \in \mathbb{R}^N$ is a (ϵ, δ)-approximation to the true SV $s = [s_1, \cdots, s_N]^T \in \mathbb{R}^N$ if $Pr[|||\hat{s}_i - s_i||_\infty \le \epsilon] \ge 1 - \delta$. These algorithms utilize the existing approximation methods developed for the canonical SV [12,23] to improve the efficiency of per-round federated SV calculation.

The idea of the first approximation algorithm is to treat the Shapley value of a participant as its expected contribution to the participants before it in a random permutation using Eq. 2 and use the sample average to approximate the expectation. We will call this algorithm *permutation sampling-based approximation* hereinafter and the pseudocode is provided in Algorithm 2. An application of Hoeffding bound indicates that to achieve (ϵ, δ)-approximation in each round of updating, the number of utility evaluations required for T rounds is $Tm(\frac{2r^2}{\epsilon^2}) \log(\frac{2m}{\delta})$.

The second approximation algorithm makes use of the group testing technique [11] to estimate the per-round federated SV and we will call this algorithm *group testing-based approximation*. In our scenario, each "test" corresponds to evaluating the utility of a subset of participant updates. The key idea of the algorithm is to intelligently design the sampling distribution of participants' updates so that we can calculate Shapely differences between the selected participants from the test results with high-probability bound on the error. Based on the result in [11], the number of tests required to estimate the Shapley differences up to $(\frac{\epsilon}{C_\epsilon}, \frac{\delta}{C_\delta})$ is $T_1 = \frac{4}{(1-q_{tot}^2)h(\frac{2\epsilon}{ZrC_\epsilon(1-q_{tot}^2)})} \log(\frac{C_\delta(m-1)}{2\delta})$, where $h(u) = (1+u)\log(1+u) - u$ and other variables are defined in Algorithm 3. We can then take any participant i and estimate the corresponding SV using the permutation sampling-based approximation, denote it as s_*. Then, the SV of all other $m-1$ users can be estimated using the estimated difference of the SV with participant i (we choose the mth participant as the pivot participant in the pseudo-code in Algorithm 4). The number of utility evaluation required for estimating s_* up to $(\frac{(C_\epsilon-1)\epsilon}{C_\epsilon}, \frac{(C_\delta-1)\delta}{C_\delta})$ is $T_2 = \frac{4r^2C_\epsilon^2}{(C_\epsilon-1)^2\epsilon^2} \log(\frac{2C_\delta}{(C_\delta-1)\delta})$. C_ϵ, C_δ are chosen so that $T_1 + T_2$ are minimized. Algorithm 1, 2, 3, and 4 present the pseudo-code for both permutation sampling and group testing.

If we treat ϵ, δ as constant, $T_1 + T_2 \sim \mathcal{O}((\log m)^2)$ while permutation sampling-based approximation is $\mathcal{O}(m\log m)$. Therefore, when the number of selected participants in each round is large, group testing-based approximation is significantly faster than permutation sampling-based one. One the other hand, when the number of selected participants is small, permutation sampling-based approximation is more preferable since its utility evaluation complexity tends to have a smaller constant.

Algorithm 1: Federated SV Estimation.

input : N - available participants, C - fraction of selected participants in each round, `ParticipantUpdate` - function for participant's local update, e.g. SGD

output : $(\hat{s}_1, \hat{s}_2, \dots, \hat{s}_N)$ - estimated SV for all participants

1 Initialize global model w_0; initialize $\hat{S}_i \leftarrow 0$ for $i = 1\dots N$.
2 **for** each round $t = 0, 1, \dots,$ **do**
3    $m \leftarrow \max(C \cdot N)$
4    $C_t \leftarrow$ random set of m participants
5   **for** each participant $k \in C_t$ in parallel **do**
6      $w_{t+1}^k \leftarrow$ `ParticipantUpdate`(k, w_t)
7   **end**
8    $\hat{S}[C_t] \leftarrow \hat{S}[C_t] + $ RoundSVEstimation$(\{w_{t+1}^k\}, w_t)$
9    $w_{t+1} \leftarrow \frac{1}{m}\sum_{k=1}^m w_{t+1}^k$
10 **end**
11 **return** $\hat{S}$

Algorithm 2: RoundSVEstimation estimates the SV s_t for selected participants at round t using permutation sampling

input : $\{w_{t+1}^i\}_{i=1}^m$ - selected participants' updates in round $t+1$, w_t - global model in round t, $U(\cdot) \in [0, r]$ - utility function, ϵ, δ - approximation parameter

output : $(\hat{s}_1, \dots, \hat{s}_m)$ - estimated SV for selected participants

12 $T \leftarrow \frac{2r^2}{\epsilon^2}\log(\frac{2m}{\delta})$
13 $U_{prev} \leftarrow U(w_t)$
14 Initialize $\hat{s}_i \leftarrow 0$ for $i = 1\dots m$.
15 **for** $t = 1\dots T$ **do**
16   Uniformly sample a permutation S of set $\{w_{t+1}^i\}_{i=1}^m$.
17   **for** $i = 1\dots m$ **do**
18      $\hat{s}_i \leftarrow \hat{s}_i + (U(w_t + S[:i]) - U_{prev})$
19      $U_{prev} \leftarrow U(w_t + S[:i])$
20   **end**
21 **end**
22 $\hat{s} \leftarrow \hat{s}/T$
23 **return** $\hat{s}$

Algorithm 3: RoundSVEstimation estimates the SV s_t for selected participants at round t using group testing

input : $\{w_{t+1}^i\}_{i=1}^m$ - selected participants' updates in round $t+1$, w_t - global model in round t, $U(\cdot) \in [0, r]$ - utility function, ϵ, δ - approximation parameter, C_ϵ, C_δ - tradeoff parameters

output : $(\hat{s}_1, \dots, \hat{s}_m)$ - estimated SV for selected participants

24 $U_{tot} \leftarrow U(w_t + \{w_{t+1}^i\}_{i=1}^m)$
25 $Z \leftarrow 2\sum_{k=1}^{m-1}\frac{1}{k}$
26 $q(k) \leftarrow \frac{1}{k}(\frac{1}{k} + \frac{1}{m-k})$ for $k = 1\dots m-1$.
27 $q_{tot} \leftarrow \frac{m-2}{m}q(1) + \sum_{k=2}^{m-1}q(k)[1 + \frac{2k(k-m)}{m(m-1)}]$
28 $T \leftarrow \frac{4}{(1-q_{tot}^2)h(\frac{2\epsilon}{ZrC_\epsilon(1-q_{tot}^2)})}\log(\frac{C_\delta(m-1)}{2\delta})$
29 Initialize $(a)_{ti} \leftarrow 0, t = 1\dots T, i = 1\dots m$.
30 **for** $t = 1\dots T$ **do**
31   Draw $k_t \sim q(k)$
32   Uniformly sample a length-k_t sequence S from $\{1, \dots, m\}$.
33    $a_{ti} \leftarrow 1$ for all $i \in S$
34    $B_t \leftarrow U(w_t + S)$
35 **end**
36 $C_{ij} \leftarrow \frac{Z}{T}\sum_{t=1}^T B_t(A_{ti} - A_{tj})$ for $i = 1\dots m, j = 1\dots m$.
37 $\hat{s} \leftarrow$ DiffToSV(C_{ij})

Algorithm 4: DiffToSV recovers the SV s_t for selected participants at round t from the estimated difference C_{ij}.

38 $T \leftarrow \frac{4r^2C_\epsilon^2}{(C_\epsilon-1)^2\epsilon^2}\log(\frac{2C_\delta}{(C_\delta-1)\delta})$
39 $\hat{s}_* \leftarrow 0$
40 **for** $t = 1\dots T$ **do**
41   Uniformly sample a subset S from $\{1, \dots, m-1\}$
42    $\hat{s}_* \leftarrow \hat{s}_* + \frac{1}{T}(U(w_t + S \cup \{m\}) - U(w_t + S))$
43 **end**
44 **for** $i = 1\dots m$ **do**
45    $\hat{s}_i = \hat{s}_* + C_{im}$
46 **end**
47 **return** $\hat{s} = (\hat{s}_1, \dots, \hat{s}_m)$

5   Empirical Study

In this section, we conduct the first empirical evaluation on a range of real-world FL tasks with different datasets to study whether the proposed data value notion can reflect the real utility of data. The tasks include noisy data detection, adversarial participant removal and data summarization. We would expect that a good data value notion will assign low value to participants with noisy, adversarial, and low-quality data, which will in turn help us remove those participants.

5.1   Baseline Approaches

We will compare the federated SV with the following two baselines.

Federated Leave-One-Out. One natural way to assign the contribution to a participant update i at round t is by calculating the model performance change when the participant is removed from the set of participants selected at round t, i.e., $loo_t(i) = U(I_{1:t}) - U(I_{1:t-1} + I_t/\{i\})$, and $loo_t(i) = 0$ if participant i is not selected in round t. The Leave-One-Out (LOO) value for FL takes the sum of the LOO values of all rounds: $loo(i) = \sum_{t=1}^{T} loo_t(i)$.

Random. The random baseline does not differentiate between different participants' contribution and just randomly selects participants to perform a given task.

In the figures, we will use Fed. LOO and Fed. SV to denote federated leave-one-out and federated Shapley Value approach, respectively.

5.2   Experiment Setting

For each task, we perform experiments on the MNIST [20] as well as the CIFAR10 dataset [19]. Following [24], we study two ways of partitioning the MNIST data over participants: **IID**, where the data is shuffled, and then partitioned into 100 participants each receiving 600 examples, and **Non-IID**, where we first sort the data by digit label, divide it into 200 shards of size 300, and assign each of 100 participants 2 shards. For MNIST, we train a simple multilayer-perceptron (MLP) with 2-hidden layers with 200 neurons in each layer and ReLu activations as well as a simple CNN. For all experiments on CIFAR10, we train a CNN with two 5×5 convolution layers (the first with 32 channels, the second with 64, each followed by 2×2 max pooling), a fully connected layer with 512 neurons with ReLu activation, and a final softmax output layer. In each round of training, we randomly select 10 participants out of 100, unless otherwise specified. We run 25 rounds for training on MNIST, achieving up to 97% and 92% global model accuracy for the IID and the non-IID setting, respectively. For CIFAR10, we run up to 50 to 200 rounds of training. We achieve up 77% and 70% test accuracy in IID and non-IID setting, respectively, for 200 rounds of training. As a side note, the state-of-the-art models in [17] can achieve test accuracy of 99.4% for CIFAR10; nevertheless, our goal is to evaluate the proposed data value notion rather than achieving the best possible accuracy. We use the permutation sampling approach in Algorithm 2 to estimate the Shapley value in all experiments since the number of participants is small.

5.3 Noisy Label Detection

Labels in the real world are often noisy due to annotators' varying skill-levels, biases or malicious tampering. We show that the proposed data value notion can help removing the noisy participants. The key idea is to rank the participants according to their data value, and drop the participants with the lowest values.

We set 20 participants' local data to be noisy where noise flipping ratio is 10% for MNIST, and 3% for CIFAR10. The performances of different data value measures are illustrated in Fig. 1a and 1b. We inspect the label of participant's local training instances that have the lowest scores, and plot the change of the fraction of detected noisy participants with the fraction of the inspected participants. We can see that when the training data is partitioned in IID setting, federated LOO and federated SV perform similarly. However, in the Non-IID setting, the federated SV outperforms federated LOO. We conjecture that this is because for Non-IID participants, the trained local models tend to overfit, diverge from the global model, and exhibit low accuracy. In comparison with the federated SV, federated LOO only computes the marginal contribution of a participant to the largest subset of other selected participants and therefore the noisy participants are harder to be identified by federated LOO.

We also find that, with the number of training rounds increases, the total contribution of participants in each round will decrease, as shown in Fig. 2a. This makes sense since the federated SV satisfies instantaneous group rationality in Theorem 1, and the improvement of global model's utility will slowdown when it is close to convergence. That is, it is relatively easy to improve the global model's utility in earlier rounds, while harder to further improve the utility in later rounds. Hence, the contribution of participants selected in early rounds is inflated. This inspires us to consider a variant of data value measures, which normalize the per-round data values by their norms and then aggregate them across all rounds. The performance of noisy label detection with the normalized versions of federated SV and federated LOO is shown in Fig. 1c and 1d. As we can see, it is much easier to separate noisy participants from benign participants with the normalized version of data value notions. However, the normalized federated SV no longer preserves the group rationality and additivity property. We leave developing more detailed analysis of different variants of data value as future work.

5.4 Backdoor Attack Detection

Motivated by privacy concerns, in FL, the coordinator is designed to have no visibility into a participant's local data and training process. This lack of transparency in the agent updates can be exploited so that an adversary controlling a small number of malicious participants can perform a *backdoor attack*. The

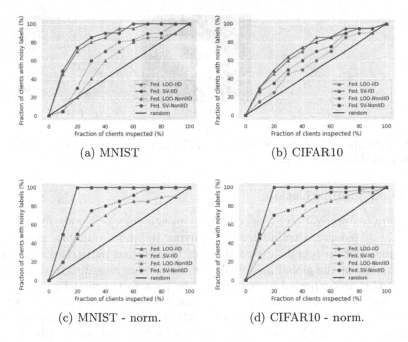

(a) MNIST   (b) CIFAR10

(c) MNIST - norm.   (d) CIFAR10 - norm.

Fig. 1. Experiment results of (a) (b) noisy label detection; (c) (d) noisy label detection with normalized federated LOO/SV.

adversary's objective is to cause the jointly trained global model to misclassify a set of chosen inputs, i.e. it seeks to poison the global model in a targeted manner, while also ensures that the global model has a good performance on the clean test data. We focus on backdoor attacks based on the model replacement paradigm proposed by [2].

For CIFAR10, following the settings in [2], we choose the feature of vertically stripped walls in the background (12 images) as the backdoor. For MNIST, we implement pixel-pattern backdoor attack in [7]. We set the ratio of the participants controlled by the adversary to be 30%. We mix backdoor images with benign images in every training batch (20 backdoor images per batch of size 64) for compromised participants, following the settings in [2].

In Fig. 3a and 3b, we show the success rate of backdoor detection with respect to the fraction of checked participants. Both of the figures indicate that federated SV is a more effective than federated LOO for detecting compromised participants. In the Non-IID setting, both compromised participants and some benign participants tend to have low contribution on the main task performance, which makes the compromised participants more difficult to be identified by the low data values. Hence, we also test the performance of normalized version of federated SV/LOO for this task and Fig. 3c and 3d show that the performance improves a lot compared with the original definitions.

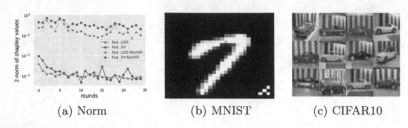

(a) Norm   (b) MNIST   (c) CIFAR10

Fig. 2. (a) Norm of contribution varies with different rounds for MNIST-IID; (b) (c) illustrations of backdoor image

5.5   Data Summarization

In our data summarization experiments, we investigate whether the federated SV can facilitate federated training by identifying the most valuable participants. Per communication round, a percentage of the selected participants is ignored for the update of the global model. We use data value measures to dismiss participants that are expected to contribute the least to the model accuracy. The data values are calculated on a separate validation set, which contains 1000 and 800 random samples for MNIST and CIFAR10, respectively. During each communication round of FL, we compute the data value summands. After training has finished, we compute the total data value.

We then repeat training, while maintaining an identical selection of participants per round. During each round, we dismiss a certain fraction $q \in [0, 0.1, \ldots, 0.9]$ of the selected participants. We compute and average the results for the random baseline three times per run.

We train a small CNN model on the MNIST dataset. The CNN consists of two 5×5 convolution layers, each followed with 2×2 max pooling and ReLu activations. Two fully connected layers (input, hidden and output dimensions of 320, 50, 10, respectively) with intermediate ReLu activation follow the second convolution layer. We apply dropout on the second convolution and first fully connected layer. For CIFAR10, we operate on 1000-dimensional feature vectors extracted with an imagenet-pretrained MobileNet v2 mode.[1] We train a MLP with 2-hidden layers with 1000 neurons in each layer and ReLu activations.

We evaluate our algorithm for FL of 10 rounds on MNIST and 100 rounds on CIFAR10. The results of our experiments are shown in Fig. 4. For the MNIST IID case, the federated SV approach outperforms both baselines. While it also consistently outperforms the random baseline in the non-IID setting, federated LOO achieves higher test accuracies for lower fractions of dismissed samples. Here, analysis of the federated SV per participant shows that it tends to be higher for participants that are selected throughout the FL. Furthermore, we observe that participants that were sampled few times also are more likely to have a negative federated SV, compared to the IID setting. We hypothesize that this bias negatively affects the performance of the federated SV-based summarization in the non-IID setting.

---

[1] We use preprocessing and the pretrained model as provided by PyTorch Hub.

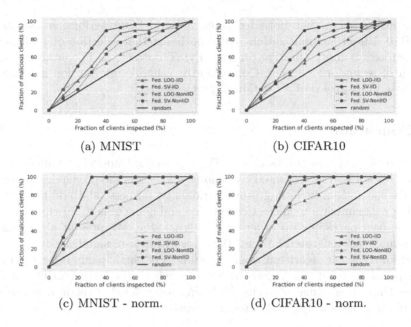

Fig. 3. Experiment results of (a) (b) backdoor detection; (c) (d) backdoor detection with normalized LOO/SV.

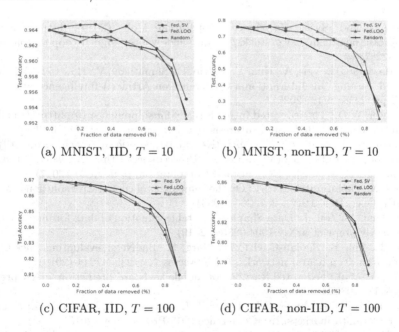

Fig. 4. Data summarization experiments on MNIST (top) and Cifar10 (bottom).

We also observe that both federated SV and LOO perform worse on the CIFAR10 dataset summarization. We hypothesize that selection of good participant subsets is more effective on the MNIST dataset, as it contains a larger portion of redundant samples. Consequently, valuable information is less likely to be lost by dismissal of a fraction of participants.

6   Conclusion

This chapter proposes the federated SV, a principled notion to value data for the process of FL. The federated SV uniquely possesses the properties desired by a data value notion, including group rationality, fairness, and additivity, while enjoying communication-efficient calculation and being able to capture the effect of participant participation order on the data value. We present algorithms to approximate the federated SV and these algorithms are significantly more efficient than the exact algorithm when the number of participants is large. Finally, we demonstrate that the federated SV can reflect the actual utility of data sources through a range of tasks, including noisy label detection, adversarial participant detection, and data summarization.

References

1. WeBank and Swiss Re signed cooperation MoU (2019). https://markets.businessinsider.com/news/stocks/webank-and-swiss-re-signed-cooperation-mou-1028228738#
2. Bagdasaryan, E., Veit, A., Hua, Y., Estrin, D., Shmatikov, V.: How to backdoor federated learning. In: International Conference on Artificial Intelligence and Statistics, pp. 2938–2948 (2020)
3. Brouwer, W.D.: The federated future is ready for shipping (2019). https://medium.com/@_doc_ai/the-federated-future-is-ready-for-shipping-d17ff40f43e3
4. Chessa, M., Loiseau, P.: A cooperative game-theoretic approach to quantify the value of personal data in networks. In: Proceedings of the 12th workshop on the Economics of Networks, Systems and Computation, p. 9. ACM (2017)
5. Deng, X., Papadimitriou, C.H.: On the complexity of cooperative solution concepts. Math. Oper. Res. **19**(2), 257–266 (1994)
6. Ghorbani, A., Zou, J.: Data Shapley: equitable valuation of data for machine learning. arXiv preprint arXiv:1904.02868 (2019)
7. Gu, T., Liu, K., Dolan-Gavitt, B., Garg, S.: BadNets: evaluating backdooring attacks on deep neural networks. IEEE Access **7**, 47230–47244 (2019)
8. Hard, A., et al.: Federated learning for mobile keyboard prediction. arXiv preprint arXiv:1811.03604 (2018)
9. Heckman, J.R., Boehmer, E.L., Peters, E.H., Davaloo, M., Kurup, N.G.: A pricing model for data markets. In: iConference 2015 Proceedings (2015)
10. Jia, Y., et al.: Efficient task-specific data valuation for nearest neighbor algorithms. Proc. VLDB Endow. **12**(11), 1610–1623 (2019)
11. Jia, R., et al..: Towards efficient data valuation based on the Shapley value. arXiv preprint arXiv:1902.10275 (2019)

12. Jia, R., et al..: Towards efficient data valuation based on the Shapley value. In: AISTATS (2019)
13. Jia, R., Sun, X., Xu, J., Zhang, C., Li, B., Song, D.: An empirical and comparative analysis of data valuation with scalable algorithms. arXiv preprint arXiv:1911.07128 (2019)
14. Kang, J., Xiong, Z., Niyato, D., Xie, S., Zhang, J.: Incentive mechanism for reliable federated learning: a joint optimization approach to combining reputation and contract theory. IEEE Internet Things J. **6**(6), 10700–10714 (2019)
15. Kang, J., Xiong, Z., Niyato, D., Yu, H., Liang, Y.C., Kim, D.I.: Incentive design for efficient federated learning in mobile networks: a contract theory approach. In: 2019 IEEE VTS Asia Pacific Wireless Communications Symposium (APWCS), pp. 1–5. IEEE (2019)
16. Kleinberg, J., Papadimitriou, C.H., Raghavan, P.: On the value of private information. In: Proceedings of the 8th Conference on Theoretical Aspects of Rationality and Knowledge. pp. 249–257. Morgan Kaufmann Publishers Inc. (2001)
17. Kolesnikov, A., et al.: Big Transfer (BiT): general visual representation learning. arXiv preprint arXiv:1912.11370 (2019)
18. Koutris, P., Upadhyaya, P., Balazinska, M., Howe, B., Suciu, D.: Query-based data pricing. J. ACM (JACM) **62**(5), 43 (2015)
19. Krizhevsky, A., Hinton, G., et al.: Learning multiple layers of features from tiny images (2009)
20. LeCun, Y., Cortes, C.: MNIST handwritten digit database (2010). http://yann.lecun.com/exdb/mnist/
21. Lee, J.S., Hoh, B.: Sell your experiences: a market mechanism based incentive for participatory sensing. In: 2010 IEEE International Conference on Pervasive Computing and Communications (PerCom), pp. 60–68. IEEE (2010)
22. Leroy, D., Coucke, A., Lavril, T., Gisselbrecht, T., Dureau, J.: Federated learning for keyword spotting. In: ICASSP 2019–2019 IEEE International Conference on Acoustics, Speech and Signal Processing (ICASSP), pp. 6341–6345. IEEE (2019)
23. Maleki, S.: Addressing the computational issues of the Shapley value with applications in the smart grid. Ph.D. thesis, University of Southampton (2015)
24. McMahan, B., Moore, E., Ramage, D., Hampson, S., Arcas, B.A.: Communication-efficient learning of deep networks from decentralized data. In: Artificial Intelligence and Statistics, pp. 1273–1282 (2017)
25. Mihailescu, M., Teo, Y.M.: Dynamic resource pricing on federated clouds. In: 2010 10th IEEE/ACM International Conference on Cluster, Cloud and Grid Computing (CCGrid), pp. 513–517. IEEE (2010)
26. Shapley, L.S.: A value for n-person games. In: Contributions to the Theory of Games, vol. 2, no. 28, pp. 307–317 (1953)
27. Song, T., Tong, Y., Wei, S.: Profit allocation for federated learning. In: 2019 IEEE International Conference on Big Data (Big Data), pp. 2577–2586. IEEE (2019)
28. Upadhyaya, P., Balazinska, M., Suciu, D.: Price-optimal querying with data APIs. PVLDB **9**(14), 1695–1706 (2016)
29. Wang, G., Dang, C.X., Zhou, Z.: Measure contribution of participants in federated learning. In: 2019 IEEE International Conference on Big Data (Big Data), pp. 2597–2604. IEEE (2019)
30. Yu, H., et al.: A fairness-aware incentive scheme for federated learning. In: Proceedings of the AAAI/ACM Conference on AI, Ethics, and Society, pp. 393–399 (2020)

A Gamified Research Tool for Incentive Mechanism Design in Federated Learning

Zichen Chen[1], Zelei Liu[1], Kang Loon Ng[1], Han Yu[1(✉)], Yang Liu[2], and Qiang Yang[2,3]

[1] Nanyang Technological University, Singapore, Singapore
{zcchen,zelei.liu,c170109,han.yu}@ntu.edu.sg
[2] WeBank, Shenzhen, China
yangliu@webank.com
[3] Hong Kong University of Science and Technology, Hong Kong, Hong Kong
qyang@cse.ust.hk

Abstract. Federated Learning (FL) enables multiple participants to collaboratively train AI models in a privacy-preserving manner, which incurs cost during the training processing. This can be a significant issue especially for business participants [8]. These costs include communication, technical, compliance, risk of market share erosion and free-riding problems (i.e., participants may only join FL training with low-quality data) [6]. Motivating participants to contribute high-quality data continuously and maintain a healthy FL ecosystem is a challenging problem. The key to achieving this goal is through effective and fair incentive schemes. When designing such schemes, it is important for researchers to understand how FL participants react under different schemes and situations.

In this chapter, we present a multi-player game to facilitate researchers to study federated learning incentive schemes – FedGame (A demonstration video of the platform can be found at: https://youtu.be/ UhAMVx8SOE8. Additional resources about the platform will continuously be made available over time at: http://www.federated-learning. org/.), by extending our previous work in [5]. FedGame allows human players to role-play as FL participants under various conditions. It serves as a tool for researchers or incentive mechanism designers to study the impact of emergent behaviors by FL participants under different incentive schemes. It can be useful for eliciting human behaviour patterns in FL and identifying potential loopholes in the proposed incentive scheme. After learning the behaviour pattern, FedGame can, in turn, further test any given incentive scheme's competitiveness again schemes based on real decision patterns.

Keywords: Federated learning · Incentive mechanism

1 Categories of Incentive Schemes

Before going into the details of the FedGame's design, we first present some existing research in incentive scheme related to our game design. The existing

Q. Yang et al. (Eds.): Federated Learning, LNAI 12500, pp. 168–175, 2020.
https://doi.org/10.1007/978-3-030-63076-8_12

approaches most closely related to our FL settings comes from the field of profit-sharing games [8,9]. In general, there are three categories of widely adopted profit-sharing schemes:

1. Egalitarian: any unit of utility produced by a data federation is divided equally among the data owners who help produce it.
2. Marginal gain: the payoff of a data owner in a data federation is the utility that the team gained when the data owner joined.
3. Marginal loss: the payoff of a data owner in a data federation is the utility that the team would lose if the data owner were to leave.

Equal division is an example of egalitarian profit-sharing [7]. Under this scheme, the available profit-sharing budget is equally divided among all participants. Under the Individual profit-sharing scheme [7], each participant's contribution to the community is used to determine his share of the profit.

The Labour Union game-based [2] profit-sharing scheme is a marginal gain scheme. It shares the profit based a participant's marginal contribution to the utility of the community formed by his predecessors. Each participant's marginal contribution is computed based on the sequence they joined the collective.

The Shapley game-based profit-sharing scheme [1] is also a marginal contribution based scheme. It is designed to eliminate the effect of the sequence of joining the collective by the participants in order to fairly estimate their marginal contributions. It averages the marginal contribution for each participant under all different permutations of its order of joining the collective relative to other participants. [3] computes a Shapley value to split rewards among data owners. Such computations tend to be expensive.

2 System Architecture

The architecture of FedGame is shown in Fig. 1. In the game, a number of AI players and Federations are created to simulate the FL environment. A human player plays the role of a business (with an arbitrary amount of data and resources allocated to him at the beginning of the game) joining the federation. His business is assumed to be from the same market sector as the AI players', which means contributing his data to the federation might result in an FL model that helps himself as well as his competitors [5].

Key information such as resource quantity, data quality, data quantity and payment are involved in decision-making. AI players follow existing approaches to determine how much data they want to contribute during the FL model training [8]. The human players decide how to allocate their resources that they want to contribute to the training of FL model independently. The Federations will receive payoffs from the virtual marketplace based on the market share their FL models occupy. Participants will be rewarded with a portion of their federation's payoff according to the incentive scheme adopted by Federation during a game session. The players' in-game behaviour data are recorded.

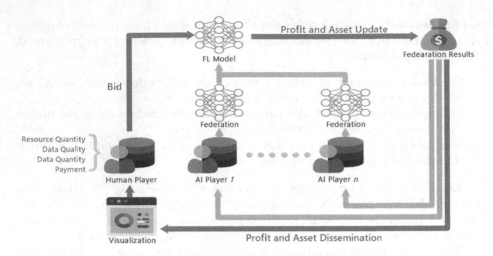

Fig. 1. *FedGame* system architecture.

3 Interaction Design

Each game session ends after a fixed number of turns have passed. The ultimate goal for a player is to obtain as much payoff as possible at the end of a game session. In order to motivate participants to contribute high-quality data to FL model training and truthfully report private cost types, the game first focuses on illustrating the FL environment from the perspective of business enterprises. A player can decide to join, leave or remain in a Federation at any point in the game. The game system provides functions for game designers to modify existing incentive schemes or add new incentive schemes by creating new levels in the game. Each time when a player enters the game, he/she will be randomly assigned with a set of starting characteristics in terms of the amount and quality of the local data and local computational resources. This will be done through the randomization of allocated variables to players. This design aims to provide opportunities for the players to adapt their behaviors.

Each Federation will be initialized with a fixed amount of credit for paying out incentives. The credit will change over time based on the market share its FL model occupies. A player can choose not to join any Federation and just train models with their local dataset, or participate in a Federation. The process for joining a Federation involves three different stages: 1) Bidding, 2) FL model training, and 3) Profit-sharing. In the bidding stage, participants bid to join a given Federation with his stated resources, data quality, data quantity and expected payout. At the end of the bidding stage, the Federation processes the bids and accepts the players as participants it deems to offer good cost-benefit trade-offs into the training stage. In the FL model training stage, the game simulates the training of the FL model. In the profit-sharing stage, the

Federation delivers payoffs to each participant following the incentive scheme it adopts before transitioning to the next bidding stage.

Under different incentive schemes, players have to consider a boarder range of factors during the game and adapt to their strategy. Currently, FedGame supports the following incentive schemes [8,9].

Linear: a participant i's share of the total payoff $P(t)$ is proportional to the usefulness of its contributed data in a given round t, denoted as $\hat{u}_i(t)$. The payoff is computed as:

$$\hat{u}_i(t) = \frac{u_i(t)}{\sum_{i=1}^{N} u_i(t)} P(t), \tag{1}$$

where $u_i(t)$ is i's share of $P(t)$ among his peers computed following a given scheme.

Equal: the federation profit $P(t)$ is equally divided among its N participants at a given round t. Thus, we have:

$$u_i(t) = \frac{1}{N}. \tag{2}$$

Individual: a participant i's share of the total payoff is proportional to its marginal contribution to the federation profit, $u_i(t)$:

$$u_i(t) = v(\{i\}), \tag{3}$$

where $v(P)$ is a function evaluating the utility of federation profit P.

Union: participant i's share of the total payoff $P(t)$ follows the Labour Union game [2] payoff scheme and is proportional to the marginal effect on the FL model by predecessors F if i were to be removed. Under this scheme, i's share of the profit is determined by:

$$u_i(t) = v(F \cup \{i\} - v(F)). \tag{4}$$

Shapley: the federation profit P is shared among participants according to their Shapley values [1]. Each participant i's payoff is:

$$u_i(t) = \sum_{P \subseteq P_j \setminus \{i\}} \frac{|P|!(|P_j| - |P| - 1)!}{|P_j|} [v(P \cup \{i\}) - v(P)] \tag{5}$$

where a Federation is divided into m parties (P_1, P_2, ..., P_m).

At the same time, the system variables which make up the context within which the players make decisions are also recorded to support further analysis of participant behaviors.

4   System Settings

Figure 2 illustrates how a user can interact with the FedGame system. The player with detailed information on market condition and model performance is

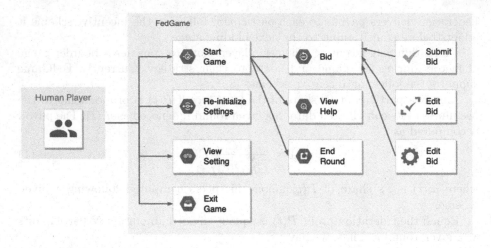

Fig. 2. Use case diagram for *FedGame*.

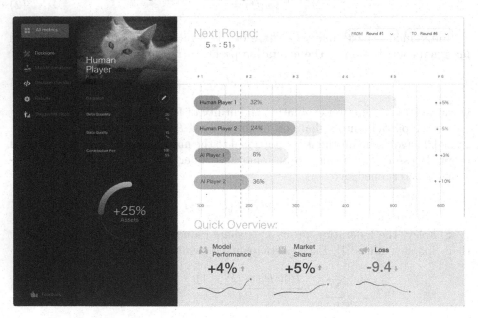

Fig. 3. An example of the *FedGame* user interface.

able to start a new bid and record new data about his/her in-game behaviors. The game system can track the decision made by the players and record their behaviors for further analysis.

Figure 3 shows a screenshot for a player of the FedGame system. The game visualizes information including Federation information, game session overview, player's statistics, and game session summary to facilitate decision-making.

It provides a continuous real-time view of the participants' data quality, quantity, change of market share, profit/loss, and participants joining each Federation. This simulates the information available to a sophisticated business joining FL to help researchers study possible reactions to given incentive mechanisms.

Below is an example sequence of activities in a game session:

1. Start Game: starts a new game instance.
2. Reinitialize Settings: a new Settings.xml file with default settings is created in the directory.
3. View Settings: a window part containing the current settings (from the Settings.xml file) is displayed to the player.
4. Exit Game: the application will be closed.
5. Bid: a window part containing decision selections is selectable to the player. User is able to select the Federation to bid for, amount of resource, data quality, data quantity, payment during the bidding stage.
6. Submit Bid: bid is created with the specified amount.
7. Edit Bid: bid or training object is edited with the specified amount.
8. Remove Bid: bid or training object is removed.
9. View Help: a window containing a simple textual guide detailing background and instructions of the game is displayed.
10. End Round: after the player selects end round, the system will process and simulate the FL environment.

The game system is configured using a text file that follows the XML format. Specified game settings, such as the number of players, types of Federations can be adjusted in FedGame through this configuration file. This facilitates game designers to modify the FL environment the players are exposed to. Besides the environment variables, designers can adjust the time for FL model training, and the time taken for each round of training. Modification of these variables will allow for a shorter or longer game duration which can influence participants' behaviour.

5 Tracking Environment Variables

The recording of a human players' decisions is a significant reference for researchers to design a new FL incentive schemes. Information, parameters and fields are recorded in a database for analyzing human behaviors. At each point of time whereby the players ends a round of game, environment variables are stored into the local database.

The initial FL environment will be set up following predefined settings defined in the XML file. This file can be modified by the player or the person presiding over the experiment to decide the type of FL environment to construct. Variables are initialized in a random manner. Examples of these variables can be seen in Table 1.

The game system mainly alternates between the bidding stage and the training stage during the game. In the bidding stage, the player can perform the

Table 1. List of environment variables

Variable	Brief description
Resource quantity	• Resource quantity will be randomly allocated between the minimum and maximum specified quantity, normally between 1 to 10 (integer) • Resource determines whether a player can bid for a Federation, more resource means wider spread or faster local training
Data quality	• Data quality will be randomized between the minimum and maximum range specified, normally between 0 to 1 (decimal)
Data quantity	• Data quantity will be randomized between the minimum and maximum range specified, normally between 0 to 1 (decimal)

operations as described in the previous section. Simultaneously, simulation on AI players' bidding actions is performed following each agent's assigned strategy. A bidding list is then created for each player who will be evaluated by the respective Federations subsequently. After a round of game, environment variables will be recorded and stored into the local database.

At the end of the game, the system is able to access the specified database and update the environment variables that were previously recorded throughout the progression of the game to a central storage.

6   Conclusions and Future Work

In this chapter, we reviewed existing literature on incentive schemes under profit-sharing games which are used to develop our gamified platform for supporting incentive mechanism design research in federated learning. The system is, to the best of our knowledge, the first game for studying participants' reactions under various incentive mechanisms under federated learning scenarios. Data collected can be used to analyse behaviour patterns exhibited by human players, and inform future FL incentive mechanism design research.

Current FedGame is able to support the basic foundation to illustrate FL participation behaviour. There is still much room for improvement. One task is to add or formulate more complex actions for human behaviour analysis. More controllable variables can be added to simulate different federation set-ups. For example, participants' data quality can be verified by the federation through additional pre-training based on small samples from each participant. These additional variables can both serve as a new FL paradigm/assumption or part of proposed incentive mechanism. We also plan to further extend FedGame to support non-monetary incentive schemes under the emerging trust-based self-organizing federated learning paradigm [4].

Another task is adding new incentive schemes when FL settings become more complicated. Specifically, some incentive schemes can only work under particular

FL settings. It might be a privacy assumption or extra processing procedures. Furthermore, in current setting, human players can play against AI players, which means that we can improve our system by training agents to mimic real human behaviour patterns.

Acknowledgment. This research is supported, in part, by Nanyang Technological University, Nanyang Assistant Professorship and NTU-WeBank JRI (NWJ-2019-007).

References

1. Augustine, J., Chen, N., Elkind, E., Fanelli, A., Gravin, N., Shiryaev, D.: Dynamics of profit-sharing games. Internet Math. **11**(1), 1–22 (2015)
2. Gollapudi, S., Kollias, K., Panigrahi, D., Pliatsika, V.: Profit sharing and efficiency in utility games. In: Proceedings of the 25th Annual European Symposium on Algorithms (ESA 2017) (2017)
3. Jia, R., et al.: Towards efficient data valuation based on the Shapley value. In: PMLR, pp. 1167–1176 (2019)
4. Lyu, L., et al.: Towards fair and privacy-preserving federated deep models. IEEE Trans. Parallel Distrib. Syst. **31**(11), 2524–2541 (2020)
5. Ng, K.L., Chen, Z., Liu, Z., Yu, H., Liu, Y., Yang, Q.: A multi-player game for studying federated learning incentive schemes. In: Proceedings of the 29th International Joint Conference on Artificial Intelligence (IJCAI 2020), pp. 5179–5281 (2020)
6. Yang, Q., Liu, Y., Cheng, Y., Kang, Y., Chen, T., Yu, H.: Federated Learning. Morgan & Claypool Publishers (2019)
7. Yang, S., Wu, F., Tang, S., Gao, X., Yang, B., Chen, G.: On designing data quality-aware truth estimation and surplus sharing method for mobile crowdsensing. IEEE J. Sel. Areas Commun. **35**(4), 832–847 (2017)
8. Yu, H., et al.: A fairness-aware incentive scheme for federated learning. In: Proceedings of the 3rd AAAI/ACM Conference on AI, Ethics, and Society (AIES 2020), pp. 393–399 (2020)
9. Yu, H., et al.: A sustainable incentive scheme for federated learning. IEEE Intell. Syst. **35**(4) (2020). https://doi.org/10.1109/MIS.2020.2987774

Budget-Bounded Incentives
for Federated Learning

Adam Richardson[1], Aris Filos-Ratsikas[2], and Boi Faltings[1(✉)]

[1] Artificial Intelligence Laboratory, Ecole Polytechnique Fédérale de
Lausanne (EPFL), Lausanne, Switzerland
{adam.richardson,boi.faltings}@epfl.ch
[2] Department of Computer Science, University of Liverpool, Liverpool, UK
aris.filos-ratsikas@liverpool.ac.uk

Abstract. We consider federated learning settings with independent,
self-interested participants. As all contributions are made privately, participants may be tempted to free-ride and provide redundant or low-
quality data while still enjoying the benefits of the FL model. In Federated Learning, this is especially harmful as low-quality data can degrade
the quality of the FL model.

Free-riding can be countered by giving incentives to participants
to provide truthful data. While there are game-theoretic schemes for
rewarding truthful data, they do not take into account redundancy of
data with previous contributions. This creates arbitrage opportunities
where participants can gain rewards for redundant data, and the federation may be forced to pay out more incentives than justified by the value
of the FL model.

We show how a scheme based on *influence* can both guarantee that
the incentive budget is bounded in proportion to the value of the FL
model, and that truthfully reporting data is the dominant strategy of
the participants. We show that under reasonable conditions, this result
holds even when the testing data is provided by participants.

Keywords: Federated learning · Data valuation · Incentives

1   Incentives in Federated Learning

Federated Learning [1] allows a set of participants to jointly learn a predictive
model without revealing their data to each other. In this chapter, we assume that
a coordinator communicates with the participants and distributes the Federated
Learning (FL) model equally to all of them. Participants can contribute actual
data or changes that improve the current FL model based on the data, which
may be more compact.

There is then clearly an incentive to free-ride: a participant can benefit from
the joint model without contributing any novel data, for example by fabricating

Supported by EPFL.

Q. Yang et al. (Eds.): Federated Learning, LNAI 12500, pp. 176–188, 2020.
https://doi.org/10.1007/978-3-030-63076-8_13

data that fits the current model, or using random noise. We call such strategies that are not based on actual data *heuristic* strategies. A participant may also wrongly report its data, for example by obfuscating it to achieve differential privacy [10]. There is no way for the coordinator to tell if data has been manipulated, and given that it can strongly degrade the FL model, it is important to protect the process against it. Even worse, a malicious participant could intentionally insert wrong data and poison the FL model; we do not consider malicious behavior in this chapter and assume that participants have no interest in manipulating the FL model.

Free-riding can avoided by *incentives* that compensate for the effort of a contributing participant. For federated learning, an incentive scheme will distribute rewards to participants in return for providing model updates, data, or other contributions to the learning protocol. Incentives should influence two behavior choices faced by participants:

- *observation strategy*: make the necessary effort to obtain truthful data and compute the best possible model update, rather than use a *heuristic* strategy to make up data with no effort, and
- *reporting strategy*: report the data *truthfully* to the coordinator, rather than perturb or obfuscate it.

We call participant behavior that is truthful in both regards *truthful* behavior. We observe that both properties can be satisfied if contributions are rewarded according to their *influence* [9] on the FL model. Influence is defined formally as the effect of the contribution on the loss function of the FL model:

- if the contribution is a model update, the improvement in the loss function through applying the update;
- if the contribution is data, the improvement in the loss function after adding the data to the training set.

For simplicity, we will refer to both cases as the contribution of a data point, even if data is often supplied in batches or in the form of a model update. The incentives for a batch of data is given as the sum of the incentives for the data points contained in it.

Clearly, influence is a good measure from the point of view of the coordinator, since it rewards contributions that make the FL model converge as fast as possible. The total expense is bounded by a function of the total reduction in the loss function, and so the coordinator can obtain the necessary budget for the rewards. It also allows participants to decide on their level of privacy protection and accept the corresponding reduction in their reward.

On the other hand, it is less clear what behavior such incentives induce in the participants. In this chapter, we answer the following questions:

- We show that when the coordinator evaluates contributions on truthful test data, the *dominant strategy* for participants is to invest effort in obtaining true data and to report it accurately. Thus, it avoids both aspects of free-riding.

- We show that participants will provide their data as soon as possible, so that there is no risk of participants holding back data hoping that it will gain higher rewards later.
- We show that when some or all of the testing data is supplied by particpants, truthful behavior is a *Bayes-Nash equilibrium* of the induced game. Furthermore, if a minimum fraction of the testing data is known to be truthful, truthful reporting is the dominant strategy for participants.

2   Related Work

The topic of learning a model when the input data points are provided by strategic sources has been the focus of a growing literature at the intersection of machine learning and game theory. A related line of work has been devoted to the setting in which participants are interested in the outcome of the estimation process itself, e.g., when they are trying to sway the learned model closer to their own data points [6,8]. Our setting is concerned with the fundamental question of eliciting accurate data when data acquisition is costly for the participants, or when they are not willing to share their data without some form of monetary compensation. Another line of work considers settings in which the participants have to be compensated for their loss of privacy [7].

A similar question to the one in our chapter was considered by [5], where the authors design strategy-proof mechanisms for eliciting data and achieving a desired trade-off between the accuracy of the model and the payments issued. The guarantees provided, while desirable, require the adoption of certain strong assumptions. The authors assume that each participant chooses an *effort level*, and the variance of the accuracy of their reports is a strictly decreasing convex function of that effort. Furthermore, these functions need to be known to the coordinator. In this chapter, we only require that the cost of effort is bounded by a known quantity. Furthermore, our strategy space is more expressive in the sense that, as in real-life scenarios, data providers can choose which data to provide and not just which effort level to exert.

Our ideas are closely related to the literature of *Peer Consistency* mechanisms [11] such as the Bayesian Truth Serum or the Correlated Agreement mechanism, or the *Peer Truth Serum for Crowdsourcing* [12,16]. The idea behind this literature is to extract high-quality information from individuals by comparing their reports against those of randomly chosen peers. This approach has been largely successful in the theory of eliciting *truthful* information. The main problem with using such mechanisms for federated learning is that they also pay for redundant data that does not improve the model. If multiple participants submit exactly the same data, the coordinator would still have to pay the full reward to each of them. Thus, it is not possible to bound the budget of the coordinator.

Recently, Liu and Wei [2] proposed an incentive scheme for federated learning based on the correlated agreement mechanism [17]. However, it also does not satisfy budget-balance and allows arbitrage where participants gain rewards by replicating the existing FL model.

More generally, the issue of economics of federated learning and the importance of budget-balance has recently been discussed in [3], where particular attention is paid to keep participants from dropping out of the federation due to insufficient rewards.

Finally, [13] recently considered a setting where the value of the provided data is determined via the *Shapley value*. Their approach does not support rewarding data incrementally, as is required for federated learning, but computes rewards only when all data has been received. However, it is worth noting that they consider the influence approximation of [14] for approximating the Shapley value.

3   Incentives Based on Influence

In our setting, there is a *coordinator* that wants to learn a model parametrized by θ, with a non-negative loss function $L(z, \theta)$ on a sample $z = (x, y)$. The samples are supplied by a set $\mathcal{A}$ of *participants*, with participant i providing point $z_i = (x_i, y_i)$. To simplify the exposition, we consider the contribution of a single data point as the most general case, but the results in this chapter also apply to batches of data points or model updates based on batches of data points, as is common in federated learning.

We will denote by $\mathcal{A}_{-i}$ the set of participants excluding participant i. Given a set of test data $Z = \{z_i\}_{i=1}^n$, the empirical risk is $R(Z, \theta) = \frac{1}{n} \sum_i L(z_i, \theta)$. The coordinator uses a scoring function $s(z)$ to determine the reward it pays for the data z.

3.1   Computing Influence

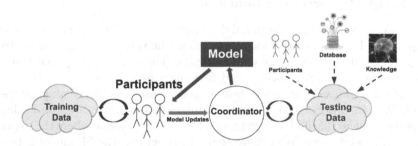

Fig. 1. The setting in this chapter: self-interested strategic participants observe data, translate it into model updates, and report to a coordinator. The coordinator maintains and broadcasts a joint FL model. To evaluate the quality of the contributions, the coordinator constructs an independent test set via other participants, a database, or other forms of prior knowledge. The coordinator scores model updates and rewards participants according to their influence on this test set.

The *influence* [9] of a data point is defined as the difference in loss function between the model trained with and without the data point. We generalize the notion to data sets and model updates as the analogous difference between loss functions. We consider payments to participant i that are proportional to the influence $I(D)$ of its contribution D: $pay_i(D) = \alpha I(D)$, where α is the same for all participants.

Computing loss functions requires access to a set of test data. In many federated learning settings, the coordinator actually never has access to data, but only model updates. In this case, it needs to ask participants to perform this evaluation. Figure 1 illustrates the process.

We distinguish two cases: the easier case where the center has access to independent and trusted test data, where we show that truthful behavior is a dominant strategy, and the more complex case where the center needs the cooperation of the strategic participants to perform this evaluation, and truthful behavior is a game-theoretic equilibrium.

Influence can be approximated [14] quite accurately (see the example in Fig. 2) and this can greatly speed up computation and allows to protect privacy using multiparty computation [4]. Good approximations exist for linear and logistic regression models, and to some extent also for complex models such as neural networks. This approximation is based on taking the Taylor expansion of the loss function and down-weighting a training point to remove it from the dataset in a smooth manner. We find that taking only the first term of the expansion is not sufficient because then the expected influence of a point over the whole training set will be 0. Taking up to the second term of the expansion is sufficient for accuracy, speed, and good theoretical properties. Figure 2 shows that this second-order approximation for a linear regression example tracks the true influence extremely closely.

3.2 Budget Properties of Influence

In general, the share of an additional data point in a model based on $n-1$ earlier datapoints is $1/n$. Many loss functions, such as the variance or the cross entropy, decrease as $1/n$ with the number of samples. The influence is proportional to the derivative of the loss function and thus decreases as $1/n^2$.

Figure 2 shows an example of the actual decrease of influence on a regression model. We can observe two phases: an initial phase, where additional data is necessary to make the model converge, and a converged phase where the expected influence is close to zero. We believe that this is because the FL model is never a perfect fit to the data, but will always leave some remaining variance. Once this variance is reached, additional data will not help to reduce it, and no further incentives should be given to provide such data.

Using influence as an incentive has the following properties:

- the expected reward is either close to 0, or it decreases as $1/n^2$. Therefore, it is always best for participants to report data as early as possible.
- the expected reward for redundant or random data is zero.
- for the coordinator, the total expense is proportional to the decrease in the loss function.

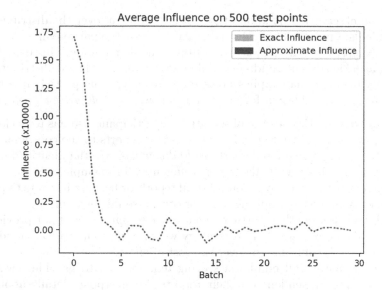

Fig. 2. Empirically observed decrease of influence on a typical regression model as more and more data is collected. Each batch corresponds to 100 data points. Both the exact influence and the 2nd order approximation are shown.

The last point has to be put in relation to the value of the model. If the value f of the model is increasing linearly with its loss R, i.e. $f(R) = C - \beta R$, choosing $\alpha = \beta$ means that the budget matches the cost exactly.

If the value increases faster, to avoid a loss the coordinator will have to choose α to be at most the average β over the loss reduction it intends to achieve. This means that the cost of obtaining the data may exceed its value during the initial phase, and the coordinator has to take some risk during the initial phase. If, on the other hand, it increases more slowly, the coordinator runs no risk, but may stop collecting data before the minimum variance is reached.

3.3 Assumptions

Our approach differs from other chapters on this topic in that we make relatively few assumptions about participant beliefs and effort models. We consider the participant and coordinator models as follows:

Participant: In the federated learning model, participants obtain data and contribute it to the federation, often in the form of a model update. For generality, we consider that participants contribute data points in some form.

Observation Strategy: Each participant i must decide to either exert effort $e_i(o)$ to observe data point o, exert 0 effort and obtain a data point based on some heuristic, for example a random or constant point[1] When the participant decides

---

[1] It is straightforward to extend the results in this chapter to a setting where increased effort results in increased quality, but this would require to characterize the exact relation which depends on the application.

to make an observation, it knows the expected effort δ_i over the distribution of observable data points. This value can vary amongst the participants. An observation $o_i = g(\phi_i|\psi_i)$, where ϕ_i is drawn from some shared underlying distribution Φ, ψ_i is a hidden latent random variable drawn from a shared distribution Ψ, and g is a function that applies noise to ϕ_i given ψ_i. The participants believe that their noise is unbiased, formulated as follows: $\forall \phi \in \Phi$, $\forall i$, $\mathbb{E}_\Psi[g(\phi|\psi_i)] = \phi$.

Reporting Strategy: Besides the observation, a participant also has to decide on a *reporting strategy* $r(o)$ that specifies what data it reports to the coordinator. We would like the participant to report *truthfully*, where r is the identity function. However, a participant may also report differently, for example because it hopes to obtain a higher reward by a non-truthful report, or because it wants to protect the privacy of its data by adding noise or otherwise misreporting it.

Finally, we assume that participants are free to *opt-out*, and not provide any data nor obtain any reward. This strategy would in particular be adopted when the rewards are insufficient to cover the cost of effort.

The coordinator will employ a scoring function $s(\cdot)$ to provide rewards to the participants, dependent on their reports; we postpone details about this scoring function until the next section. The scoring function is chosen to influence the strategy choices of participants among different options. Participants are rational, so they will choose the strategy that maximizes their expected utility.

We make one further assumption about participant beliefs. For this we introduce the notion of *risk-monotonicity*, which is the notion that a model learner is monotonic in the true risk over the number of data points in the training set. While [15] show that not all empirical risk minimizers are risk-monotonic in the number of training points, their counter-examples are adversarially constructed. As participants have no prior information about the distributions, we consider it reasonable to make the following formal assumption:

> *The participants believe the coordinator's model is risk-monotonic with respect to the true distribution Φ, i.e. a participant expects that a point drawn from Φ will not worsen the model's expected risk when evaluated on Φ.*

Coordinator: The coordinator wishes to construct a model because they believe they can extract some profit from this model. We assume the profit is a function $f(R)$ of the model risk. The expected utility of the coordinator is then the profit $f(R) - c(R)$, where $c(R)$ is the expected cost of constructing a model with risk R. We assume that $f(R)$ is monotonically decreasing, as discussed in Sect. 3.2.

Given a profit function $f(R)$, the utility of the coordinator is at least $f(R) - \sum_i \alpha_c \mathrm{Infl}(o_i)$. The coordinator needs to choose α_c to ensure that this profit is positive. At the same time, α_c determines the reward paid to participants, and must at least cover their cost of participation. Otherwise, participants may decide to opt out, and there is a risk that the federation could be left with too little data. Therefore, the coordinator must tune α_c to achieve both budget balance and sufficient participation.

For evaluating the model risk R, we consider two cases: *(a)* the coordinator may possess an *independent test set*, or *(b)* it may have to *acquire a test set* from participants.

4   Game-Theoretic Incentives for Participants

As the score of the data provided by a participant depends on the data provided by others, the choice of participant strategies is a game-theoretic problem.

Following standard game-theoretic terminology, we will say that a participant supplying point r_j is *best responding* to the set of strategies r_{-j} chosen by the other participants, if the strategy that it has chosen maximizes the quantity $\mathbb{E}[s(r_j|r_{-j}) - e_i(r_j)]$ over all possible alternative reports r'_j, where the expectation is over the distribution of reports of the other participants. We will say that a vector of strategies (i.e., a strategy profile) $(r_1, \ldots, r_n)$ is a *Bayes-Nash equilibrium (BNE)* if, for each participant j, r_j is a best response. If r_j is a best response to any set of strategies of the other players, we will say that r_j is a *dominant strategy*.

An *incentive scheme* is a function that maps data points z_i to payments $s(z_i)$; intuitively, a good incentive scheme should overcome the cost of effort (as otherwise participants are not incentivized to submit any observations) but also, crucially, to reward based on the effect that the data point z_i has on improving the accuracy of the trained model. For this reason, we will design incentive schemes via the use of influences. Let $Z_{-j} = \{z_i\}_{i \neq j}$ and let

$$\hat{\theta} = \arg\min_{\theta} R(Z, \theta) \quad \text{and} \quad \hat{\theta}_{-j} = \arg\min_{\theta} R(Z_{-j}, \theta).$$

We will assume that the coordinator is in possession of an *test set* $T = \{z_k\}$. Then the *influence* of z_j on the test set is defined as

$$\mathrm{Infl}(z_j, T, \theta) = R(T, \hat{\theta}_{-j}) - R(T, \hat{\theta}).$$

We will simply write $\mathrm{Infl}(z_j)$, when T and θ are clear from the context. Then, we can design the following incentive scheme:

– Case 1: The coordinator possesses an independent test set: $s(r_i) = \alpha_c \cdot \mathrm{Infl}(r_i) - \epsilon$, where $\epsilon > 0$ is a very small value.
– Case 2: The coordinator draws its test set from the reported data; they are rewarded in the same way as data used for the FL model, but not used in learning the model.

4.1   Using Independent and Truthful Test Data

For the lemmas and theorems in this section, we make the following assumptions:

- Observation noise is unbiased and non-trivial, as stated in the previous section.
- participants have no prior knowledge of the true distribution Φ or the model of the coordinator.

Theorem 1. *A participant having made no observation of the data believes the expected influence of any particular report to be 0.*

Proof. Let $\mathcal{D}$ be the domain of all possible sets of reports. The coordinator defines some non-negative loss function $\mathcal{L} : \mathcal{D} \to \mathbb{R}_0^+$, which serves as a blackbox that incorporates both training and testing. Given some set of reports $\{z\} \in \mathcal{D}$, define $B(\mathcal{L}|\{z\})$ as the random variable that represents the ex-ante belief of a participant on the value of $\mathcal{L}(\{z\})$. Lack of knowledge about both $\mathcal{L}$ and Φ induces the relation $B(\mathcal{L}|\{z\}_0) = B(\mathcal{L}|\{z\}_1)$ for all $\{z\}_0, \{z\}_1 \in \mathcal{D}$. For some report r and some set of other reports $\{z\}$, the influence score is defined as $\mathrm{infl}(\{z\}, r) = \mathcal{L}(\{z\}) - \mathcal{L}(\{z\} \cup r)$. Then a participant believes that its score will be $B(\mathcal{L}|\{z\}) - B(\mathcal{L}|\{z\} \cup r)$. In expectation, this score is $\mathbb{E}[B(\mathcal{L}|\{z\}) - B(\mathcal{L}|\{z\} \cup r)] = \mathbb{E}[B(\mathcal{L}|\{z\})] - \mathbb{E}[B(\mathcal{L}|\{z\} \cup r)] = 0$

Lemma 1. *A participant A_i believes that, almost certainly, given a finite number of reports, $\mathbb{E}_\Phi[\mathbb{E}_\Psi[\mathit{Infl}(o_i|\{o_j\}_{j \neq i})]] > 0$ when evaluated on $\{z_{test}\}$ with z_{test} in the distribution of observations.*

Proof. Define $B_0(\mathbb{E}_\Phi[\mathbb{E}_\Psi[L(z_{test}, z)]]) = \mathbb{E}_\Phi[L(z'_{test}, z)] + a(g, \Psi)$ as a participant's belief about $\mathbb{E}_\Phi[\mathbb{E}_\Psi[L(z_{test}, z)]]$, where z'_{test} is drawn from Φ, and a is unknown, but does not depend on L because the participants have no knowledge of L, and therefore no way of knowing if L introduces some bias given Ψ. It similarly follows that a participant's belief $B_1(\mathbb{E}_\Psi[\mathrm{Infl}(o_i|\{o_j\}_{j \neq i})] = \mathrm{Infl}(\phi_i|\{o_j\}_{j \neq i}) + b(g, \Psi)$. Therefore, it is only necessary to show that $\mathbb{E}_\Phi[\mathrm{Infl}(\phi_i|\{o_j\}_{j \neq i})] > 0$ when evaluated on $z' \in \Phi$. This follows directly from participant assumptions about risk-monotonicity.

The following theorem asserts that as long as the test set consists of truthful information, the dominant strategy for participants is to either be truthful of opt out. In the case where the coordinator possesses an independent test set, this condition is satisfied trivially.

Theorem 2. *Suppose that (a) the noise is unbiased and non-trivial, (b) the participants do not have knowledge of the distribution or the model and (c) the test set consists of truthful information. Then,*

- *for any $\alpha_c > 0$, for every participant the dominant strategy is either being truthful or dropping out, and*
- *there is a large enough α_c such that for every participant, almost certainly, being truthful is the dominant strategy.*

Proof. By Theorem 1, we have that $\alpha_c \mathrm{Infl}(h_i) = 0$, therefore the expected utility of heuristic reporting is negative. By Lemma 1, the participant believes that $\mathbb{E}_{\Phi}[\mathbb{E}_{\Psi}[\mathrm{Infl}(o_i|\{o_j\}_{j\neq i})]] > 0$ almost certainly, therefore if $\alpha_c > \frac{\delta_i}{\mathbb{E}_{\Phi}[\mathbb{E}_{\Psi}[\mathrm{Infl}(o_i|\{o_j\}_{j\neq i})]]}$, then the participant believes he or she will receive a positive utility almost certainly. If this inequality is not satisfied, the participant will receive a negative utility regardless of the choice of strategy and will opt out. There is always a large enough α_c such that the inequality is satisfied and the participant will be truthful.

We have thus shown that our incentive scheme induces truthful behavior as the dominant strategy for all participants that do not opt out, and that furthermore given a large enough payment no participants will opt out.

4.2 Using Participant Reports as Test Data

We have shown in Theorem 2 that under some reasonable assumptions, truthful reporting is a dominant strategy for the participants. However, this requires a truthful test set, which might not always be at the disposal of the coordinator. There are also good reasons for the coordinator to collect test data from participants: it allows it to cover a broader spectrum of cases, or to accommodate concept drift. We first observe that, even if we collect the reports as test data, truthful behavior is a Bayes-Nash Equilibrium:

Theorem 3. *Suppose that (a) the noise is unbiased and non-trivial, (b) the participants do not have knowledge of the distribution or the model and (c) the test set consists of data provided by participants under the incentive scheme. Then,*

- *for any $\alpha_c > 0$, there is a Bayes-Nash Equilibrium where every participant is either truthful or drops out, and*
- *there is a large enough α_c such that, almost certainly, there is a Bayes-Nash Equilibrium where all participants are truthful.*

Proof. If we assume that all participants that do not drop out are truthful, then the test set is made up of truthful data. By Theorem 2, truthful behavior is the best response for all participants, so it forms a Bayes-Nash equilibrium.

An equilibrium is a weaker notion than dominant strategies, so it is interesting to ask if the coordinator can make truthful behavior the dominant strategy even when test data has to be obtained from participants. Clearly, if all test data is supplied by participants, this is not possible: consider the example where all but one participant i submit test data according to a synthetic model M', but only participant i observes true data according to a different true model M. Then it will be better for participant i to report incorrectly according to model M', so truthful behavior cannot be a dominant strategy.

However, it turns out that if only a fraction of the test data is supplied by untrusted agents, we can place a bound on this fraction so that truthful behavior is still a dominant strategy. To obtain such a result, we need to exclude consideration of the cost of obtaining data, since we do not know what is the relative cost of obtaining true vs. heuristic data, and focus on the reporting strategy only.

Let Φ_1 be the distribution of truthful reports and Φ_2 be the distribution of heuristic reports. We assume they describe an input-output relationship such that $\Phi(x,y) = q(x)p(y|x)$, and $q_1(x) = q_2(x)$. This assumption merely asserts that the data we are collecting is drawn from the same domain regardless of the distribution of the output. Distributions Φ_1 and Φ_2 determine, in expectation, models M_1 and M_2 respectively. Let us now define $R_{i,j}$ as the expected risk of model M_i evaluated on distribution Φ_j. Given some fixed training data set with points drawn from a mixture of Φ_i and Φ_j, let $I_{i,j}$ be the expected influence of a data point sampled from distribution Φ_i on a test point from distribution Φ_j. Using the standard mean-squared-error loss function, we have that $R_{i,j} = R_{j,j} + \mathbb{E}[(M_i - M_j)^2]$. We then have the following:

Theorem 4. *As long as the test data contains at most a fraction*

$$p < \frac{I_{2,2}/R_{2,2}}{I_{1,1}/R_{1,1} + I_{2,2}/R_{2,2}} + \frac{I_{1,1} - I_{2,2}}{r(I_{1,1}/R_{1,1} + I_{2,2}/R_{2,2})}$$

of non-truthful reports, truthful reporting remains the dominant strategy for participants that do not choose to opt out.

Proof. Suppose we sample x_1 points from Φ_1 and x_2 points from Φ_2 to form our test set T, where $x_1 + x_2 = n$, and call the resulting distribution Φ_c. Now note that as $R_{1,2} - R_{1,1} = r$, and influence is proportional to the empirical risk, the influence of a datapoint following M_1 but tested on a sample from Φ_2 is decreased as follows:

$$I_{1,2} = I_{1,1}(1 - r/R_{1,1})$$

and so the expected influence when evaluating on the mixture (x_1, x_2) is

$$I_{1,c} = I_{1,1}(1 - r/R_{1,1}\frac{x_2}{n}) = I_{1,1}(1 - pr/R_{1,1})$$

$$I_{2,c} = I_{2,2}(1 - r/R_{2,2}\frac{x_1}{n}) = I_{2,2}(1 - r(1-p)/R_{2,2})$$

To ensure that reporting samples from Φ_1 carry a higher expected reward, we want to satisfy:

$$I_{1,c} > I_{2,c}$$

$$I_{1,1} - I_{2,2}(1 - r/R_{2,2}) > pr(I_{1,1}/R_{1,1} + I_{2,2}/R_{2,2})$$

$$p < \frac{I_{1,1} - I_{2,2}(1 - r/R_{2,2})}{r(I_{1,1}/R_{1,1} + I_{2,2}/R_{2,2})}$$

$$= \frac{I_{2,2}/R_{2,2}}{I_{1,1}/R_{1,1} + I_{2,2}/R_{2,2}} + \frac{I_{1,1} - I_{2,2}}{r(I_{1,1}/R_{1,1} + I_{2,2}/R_{2,2})}$$

If $I_{2,2}/R_{2,2} = I_{1,1}/R_{1,1}$, the first term is $= 1/2$. The second term is a correction: if $I_{1,1} > I_{2,2}$, more non-truthful reports are tolerated as the influence when improving the first model is stronger, otherwise it is the other way around.

A coordinator could use this result to decide how much test data to obtain from participants. As the underlying phenomenon could evolve over time, it is advantageous for the coordinator to include some contributed data in its test set so that such evolution can be tracked. To evaluate the bound, the coordinator could compare the statistics of scores obtained with trusted test data with those obtained using contributed test data, and thus estimate the parameters I, as well as the empirical risks of models fitted to the trusted and contributed data to estimate the parameters R. It could thus obtain a stronger guarantee on the quality of the test data.

5 Conclusion

When federated learning is extended to allow self-interested participants, free-riding participants that submit low-quality or redundant data can have significant negative impact on the result. Thus, it is important to provide incentives that reward truthful data providers for their effort.

As the economics of a federated learning system can be complex [3], it is important that the incentive scheme works with a bounded budget that is tied to the quality of the resulting data. We have shown that a scheme based on influence satisfies this criterion. At the same time, we have shown that it induces the desired truthful behavior as dominant strategies in participants, and that this holds even when some of the testing data is obtained from non-truthful participants.

An important question for future work is how to compute the incentives while maintaining privacy of the data. In the current scheme, a participant has to submit its contribution, whether data or a model update, before the influence can be computed. For limited cases, we have already shown how to compute an influence approximation privately [4], but the general question remains open.

References

1. Yang, Q., Liu, Y., Chen, T., Tong, Y.: Federated machine learning: concept and applications. ACM Trans. Intell. Syst. Technol. **10**(2), Article 12 (2019). 19 p. https://doi.org/10.1145/3298981
2. Liu, Y., Wei, J.: Incentives for federated learning: a hypothesis elicitation approach. In: ICML Workshop on Incentives in Machine Learning (2020)
3. Yu, H., et al.: A sustainable incentive scheme for federated learning. IEEE Intell. Syst. **35**(4) (2020). https://doi.org/10.1109/MIS.2020.2987774
4. Richardson, A., Filos-Ratsikas, A., Rokvic, L., Faltings, B.: Privately computing influence in regression models. In: AAAI 2020 Workshop on Privacy-Preserving Artificial Intelligence (2020)

5. Cai, Y., Daskalakis, C., Papadimitriou, C.: Optimum statistical estimation with strategic data sources. In: Grünwald, P., Hazan, E., Kale, S., (eds.) Proceedings of The 28th Conference on Learning Theory, Proceedings of Machine Learning Research, Paris, France, vol. 40, pp. 280–296. PMLR (2015)
6. Caragiannis, I., Procaccia, A., Shah, N.: Truthful univariate estimators. In: International Conference on Machine Learning, pp. 127–135 (2016)
7. Chen, Y., Immorlica, N., Lucier, B., Syrgkanis, V., Ziani, J.: Optimal data acquisition for statistical estimation. In: Proceedings of the 2018 ACM Conference on Economics and Computation, pp. 27–44. ACM (2018)
8. Chen, Y., Podimata, C., Procaccia, A.D., Shah, N.: Strategyproof linear regression in high dimensions. In: Proceedings of the 2018 ACM Conference on Economics and Computation, pp. 9–26. ACM (2018)
9. Cook, R.D., Weisberg, S.: Characterizations of an empirical influence function for detecting influential cases in regression. Technometrics $22(4)$, 495–508 (1980)
10. Dwork, C.: Differential privacy: a survey of results. In: Agrawal, M., Du, D., Duan, Z., Li, A. (eds.) TAMC 2008. LNCS, vol. 4978, pp. 1–19. Springer, Heidelberg (2008). https://doi.org/10.1007/978-3-540-79228-4_1
11. Faltings, B., Radanovic, G.: Game theory for data science: eliciting truthful information. In: Synthesis Lectures on Artificial Intelligence and Machine Learning, vol. 11, no. 2, pp. 1–151 (2017)
12. Faltings, B., Jurca, R., Radanovic, G.: Peer truth serum: incentives for crowdsourcing measurements and opinions. CoRR abs/1704.05269 (2017)
13. Jia, R., et al.: Towards efficient data valuation based on the Shapley value. In: Proceedings of the 22nd International Conference on Artificial Intelligence and Statistics (AISTATS) (2019)
14. Koh, P.W., Liang, P.: Understanding black-box predictions via influence functions. In: Precup, D., Teh, Y.W. (eds.) Proceedings of the 34th International Conference on Machine Learning, Proceedings of Machine Learning Research, International Convention Centre, Sydney, Australia, vol. 70, pp. 1885–1894. PMLR (2017)
15. Loog, M., Viering, T., Mey, A.: Minimizers of the empirical risk and risk monotonicity. In: Advances in Neural Information Processing Systems, pp. 7476–7485 (2019)
16. Radanovic, G., Faltings, B., Jurca, R.: Incentives for effort in crowdsourcing using the peer truth serum. ACM Trans. Intell. Syst. Technol. (TIST) $7(4)$, 48 (2016)
17. Shnayder, V., Agarwal, A., Frongillo, R., Parkes, D.C.: Informed truthfulness in multi-task peer prediction. In: Proceedings of the 2016 ACM Conference on Economics and Computation, pp. 179–196 (2016)

Collaborative Fairness in Federated Learning

Lingjuan Lyu[1(✉)], Xinyi Xu[1], Qian Wang[2], and Han Yu[3(✉)]

[1] National University of Singapore, Singapore, Singapore
{lyulj,xuxinyi}@comp.nus.edu.sg
[2] Wuhan University, Wuhan, China
qianwang@whu.edu.cn
[3] Nanyang Technological University, Singapore, Singapore
han.yu@ntu.edu.sg

Abstract. In current deep learning paradigms, local training or the *Standalone* framework tends to result in overfitting and thus low utility. This problem can be addressed by Distributed or Federated Learning (FL) that leverages a parameter server to aggregate local model updates. However, all the existing FL frameworks have overlooked an important aspect of participation: collaborative fairness. In particular, all participants can receive the same or similar models, even the ones who contribute relatively less, and in extreme cases, nothing. To address this issue, we propose a novel Collaborative Fair Federated Learning (CFFL) framework which utilizes reputations to enforce participants to converge to different models, thus ensuring fairness and accuracy at the same time. Extensive experiments on benchmark datasets demonstrate that CFFL achieves high fairness and performs comparably to the *Distributed* framework and better than the *Standalone* framework.

Keywords: Collaborative learning · Fairness · Reputation

1 Introduction

In machine learning practice, often organizations or companies (herein described as participants) need to conduct collaborate learning in order to achieve more accurate analysis, as the limited local data owned by a single participant generally results in an overfitted model that might deliver inaccurate results when applied to the unseen data, i.e., poor generalizability. In this context, federated learning (FL) emerged as a promising collaboration paradigm. The objective of FL is to facilitate joint concurrent and distributed training of one global model on locally stored data of the participants, by sharing model parameters in iterative communication rounds among the participants.

However, in most of the current FL paradigms [5,8,14,22], all participants can receive the same FL model in each communication round and in the end regardless of their contributions in terms of quantity and quality of their shared

© Springer Nature Switzerland AG 2020
Q. Yang et al. (Eds.): Federated Learning, LNAI 12500, pp. 189–204, 2020.
https://doi.org/10.1007/978-3-030-63076-8_14

parameters. This is potentially unfair, because while the contributions of the participants may vary, their final 'rewards' are the same, i.e., the jointly trained model. In practice, such variations in the contributions may be due to a number of reasons, the most obvious is that the quality of the data owned by different participants is different [27]. In this regard, the data from some participants may produce good model updates while data from some other participants may even lead to updates that impair the model performance. For example, several banks may want to work together to build a credit score predictor for small and medium enterprises. However, larger banks with more data may be reluctant to train their local models based on high quality local data for fear of smaller banks benefiting from the shared FL model and eroding their market shares [23]. Furthermore, this setting can be vulnerable to free-riders as the framework is not equipped to evaluate the contributions. Free-riders can simply share "useless" model parameters and hide in the crowd, but in the end receive the "reward". Without the promise of collaborative fairness, participants with high quality and large datasets may be discouraged from collaborating, thus hindering the formation and progress of a healthy FL ecosystem. Most of the current research on fairness focuses on an different concept of fairness, i.e., mitigating the model's predictive bias towards certain attributes [1,4]. The problem of treating FL participants fairly according to their contributions remains open [23].

For any proposed solution or framework to be practical, it is essential that it achieves fairness *not* at the cost of model performance. In this chapter, we address the problem of treating FL participants fairly based on their contributions towards building a healthy FL ecosystem. Our proposed framework is termed as Collaborative Fair Federated Learning (CFFL) framework. In contrast with the existing work such as [25] which requires external monetary rewards to incentivize good behaviour, our framework makes fundamental changes to the current FL paradigm so that instead of receiving the same FL model in each communication round, the participants will receive models with qualities commensurate with their contributions. CFFL ensures collaborative fairness by introducing reputations and evaluating the contribution of each participant in the collaborative learning process. We state that our CFFL is more suitable to horizontally federated learning (HFL) to businesses (H2B) [12], such as companies, hospitals or financial institutions to whom collaborative fairness is of significant concern.

Overall, our framework aims to enforce collaborative fairness in FL by adjusting each participant's local model performance according to their contributions [11,13]. Extensive experiments on benchmark datasets demonstrate that our CFFL delivers the highest fairness, with the accuracy of the most contributive participant comparable to that of *Distributed* frameworks, and higher than that of the *Standalone* framework. In the following sections, we interchangeably use Distributed/Federated to refer to the *Distributed* framework. A short version of this chapter appeared at FL-IJCAI'20 [10].

2   Related Work

We first relate our work to prior efforts on fairness in FL, which can be summarized as the following lines of research.

One research direction focuses on promoting collaborative fairness by using incentive schemes combined with game theory, based on the reasoning that participants should receive payoffs commensurate with their contributions. The representative works include [2,17,24,25]. However, these works still allow all participants to receive the same final FL model.

Another research direction addresses fairness issues in FL by optimizing for the performance of the device with the worst performance (largest loss/prediction error). In particular, Mohri et al. [15] proposed a minimax optimization scheme called *Agnostic Federated Learning* (AFL), which optimizes for the performance of the single worst device by weighing devices adversarially. A follow-up work called q-Fair Federated Learning (q-FFL) [9] generalizes AFL by reducing the variance of the model performance across devices. Similar to the idea behind AFL, in q-FFL, devices with higher loss are given higher relative weight to encourage less variance in the final accuracy distribution [9]. This line of work inherently advocates egalitarian equity, which can potentially deteriorate the collaborative fairness. Consequently, these methods are unable to detect and isolate possible free-riders, since they actively optimize the performance of the poorest-performing participants.

Different from all the above works, the most recent work by Lyu et al. [13] and another concurrent but independent work by Sim et al. [20] are better aligned with collaborative fairness in FL, where model accuracy is used as rewards for FL participants. Lyu et al. [13] enforce different participants to converge different local models, and Sim et al. [20] proposed a method to inject carefully computed Gaussian noise into the model parameters of the participants. In [13], they adopted a mutual evaluation of local credibility mechanism, where each participant privately rates the other participants in each communication round. However, their framework is mainly designed for a decentralized block-chain system, which may not be directly applicable FL settings which usually require a server. On the other hand, in [20], the Shapley value [18] is computed given each participant's local data, which may not be practical in FL setting with a large number of participants as the exact computation of Shapley values incurs exponential runtime in the number of participants.

In this chapter, we follow the intuition in [13], and extend their work to the general FL setting, in which a trusted server takes the role of a quality controller by controlling how much each participant can download in each communication round. In this way, each participant will be allocated with carefully selected model parameters which lead to his/her individual model to converge to performance commensurate with his/her contributions.

3   The CFFL Framework

3.1   Collaborative Fairness

In our framework, we achieve collaborative fairness by letting participants to converge to different final models based on their contributions. Under this context, we define collaborative fairness as:

Definition 1. *Collaborative fairness. In an FL system, a high-contribution participant should be rewarded with a better performing local model than a low-contribution participant. Mathematically, fairness can be quantifiably represented by the correlation coefficient between the contributions of participants and their respective final model accuracies.*

3.2   Fairness via Reputation

In our CFFL framework, instead of downloading the global model from the server as in all previous works, we modify the learning process by only allowing participants to download the *allocated aggregated updates* according to their reputations. The server keeps a reputation list for all the participants, and updates it according to the quality of the uploaded gradients of each participant in each communication round. In more detail, to quantify the reputation of participant j, the server separately evaluates the quality of uploaded parameters by j, via the accuracy on a public validation set V. The upload rate – θ_u – denotes the proportion of parameters of which gradients are uploaded, i.e., if $\theta_u = 1$, gradients of all parameters are uploaded; if $\theta_u = 0.1$, gradients of only 10% the parameters are uploaded instead. We further denote the selected set of gradients as S, which corresponds to θ_u gradients selected by the *"largest values"* criterion: sort gradients in Δw_j, and upload θ_u of them, starting from the largest. Consequently, if $\theta_u = 1$, $\Delta(w_j)^S \triangleq \Delta w_j$, so in each round participant j uploads gradients on all parameters, and therefore the server can derive participant j's entire updated model w_j, as all participants are initialized with the same parameters in the beginning. The server then computes the validation accuracy of participant j based on w_j and $\Delta(w_j)^S$ as $vacc_j \leftarrow V(w_j, \Delta(w_j)^S)$. If $\theta_u \neq 1$, the server integrates participant j's uploaded gradients $\Delta(w_j)^S$ into an auxiliary model w_g to compute participant j's validation accuracy as $vacc_j \leftarrow V(w_g, \Delta(w_j)^S)$. Here, the auxiliary model w_g is maintained by the server to aggregate local model updates and calculate reputations of participants, so its parameters are *not* broadcast to individual participants as in the standard FL systems.

Subsequently the server normalizes $vacc_j$ and passes the normalized $vacc_j$ through a $sinh(\alpha)$ function in Eq. (1) to calculate the reputation c_j of participant j in the current communication round.

$$c_j = sinh(\alpha * x) \tag{1}$$

x stands for the normalized $vacc_j$. The higher x, the more informative participant j's uploaded gradients, and thus a higher reputation should be rewarded. $sinh(\alpha)$ is introduced as a *punishment function*, and α denotes the *punishment factor*, which serves to distinguish the reputations among participants based on how informative their uploaded gradients are, in order to achieve better fairness. Based on c_j and participant j's past reputation c_j^o, the server calculates an updated reputation c_j', thus iteratively and adaptively updating the reputation of each participant. The high-contribution participant will be highly rated by the server, while the low-contribution participant can be identified and even isolated from the collaboration, preventing the low-contribution participants from dominating the whole system, or free-riding.

This updated reputation, c'_j determines how many aggregated updates each participant will be allowed to download in the subsequent communication round. The higher the c'_j, the more aggregated updates will be allocated to participant j.

We remark that the aggregated updates refer to the collection of gradients from all participants, and are used as a form of reward in each communication round. The detailed realization of CFFL is given in Algorithm 1. In each communication round, each participant sends θ_u fraction of clipped gradients to the server, and server updates the reputations according to individual validation accuracies, and then determines the number of aggregated updates to allocate to each participant. We adopt gradient clipping to mitigate noisy updates from abnormal examples/outliers.

3.3   Quantification of Fairness

In this chapter, we quantify collaborative fairness via the correlation coefficient between participant contributions (X-axis: test accuracies of standalone models which characterize their individual learning capabilities on their own local datasets) and participant rewards (Y-axis: test accuracies of final models received by the participants).

Participants with higher standalone accuracies empirically contribute more. Therefore, the X-axis can be expressed by Eq. 2, where $sacc_j$ denotes the standalone model accuracy of participant j:

$$x = \{sacc_1, \cdots, sacc_n\} \tag{2}$$

Similarly, Y-axis can be expressed by Eq. 3, where acc_j represents the final model accuracy of participant j:

$$y = \{acc_1, \cdots, acc_n\} \tag{3}$$

As the Y-axis measures the respective model performance of different participants after collaboration, it is expected to be positively correlated with the X-axis for a good measure of fairness. Hence, we formally quantify collaborative fairness in Eq. 4:

$$r_{xy} = \frac{\sum_{i=1}^{n}(x_i - \bar{x})(y_i - \bar{y})}{(n-1)s_x s_y} \tag{4}$$

where $\bar{x}$ and $\bar{y}$ are the sample means of x and y, s_x and s_y are the corrected standard deviations. The range of fairness falls within $[-1, 1]$, with higher values implying good fairness. Conversely, negative coefficient implies poor fairness.

Algorithm 1. Collaborative Fair Federated Learning

Input: reputable participant set R; auxiliary model w_g kept by server; local model w_j; local model updates Δw_j; upload rate θ_u; validation set V; local epochs E; c_j^o: reputation of previous round; D_j: data owned by each participant; data shard vector $n = \{n_1, \cdots, n_{|R|}\}$; class shard vector $class = \{class_1, \cdots, class_{|R|}\}$.

Role: participant j

if $j \in R$ then

  Runs SGD on local data by using current local model w_j and computes gradient vector $\Delta w_j \leftarrow$ SGD(w_j, D_j)

  Clips gradient vector: $\Delta w_j \leftarrow clip(\Delta w_j)$

  Sends the selected gradients $\Delta(w_j)^S$ of size $\theta_u * |\Delta w_j|$ to the server, according to the "largest values" criterion: sort gradients in Δw_j, and upload θ_u of them, starting from the largest;

  Downloads the allocated updates from the server, which is then integrated with all its local updates as: $w_j' \leftarrow w_j + \Delta w_j + \Delta w_g^j - \frac{n_j}{max(n)}\Delta(w_j)^S$ (imbalanced data size) or $w_j' \leftarrow w_j + \Delta w_j + \Delta w_g^j - \frac{class_j}{max(class)}\Delta(w_j)^S$ (imbalanced class number).

end if

Role: Server

  Updates aggregation:

  if data size is imbalanced then

    $\Delta w_g \leftarrow \sum_{j \in R}\Delta(w_j)^S \times \frac{n_j}{sum(n)}$.

  end if

  if class number is imbalanced then

    $\Delta w_g \leftarrow \sum_{j \in R}\Delta(w_j)^S \times \frac{class_j}{max(class)}$.

  end if

  if $\theta_u = 1$ then

    for $j \in R$ do

      $vacc_j \leftarrow V(w_j + \Delta(w_j)^S)$.

      Updates local model of participant j kept by the server: $w_j' \leftarrow w_j + \Delta(w_j)^S$ for next round of reputation evaluation.

    end for

  else

    for $j \in R$ do

      $vacc_j \leftarrow V(w_g + \Delta(w_j)^S)$.

    end for

    Updates temp model maintained by server $w_g' = w_g + \Delta w_g$ for next round of reputation evaluation.

  end if

  for $j \in R$ do

    $c_j \leftarrow sinh(\alpha * \frac{vacc_j}{\sum_{j \in R} vacc_j})$, $c_j' \leftarrow c_j^o * 0.5 + c_j * 0.5$

  end for

  Reputation normalisation: $c_j' \leftarrow \frac{c_j'}{\sum_{j \in R} c_j'}$

  if $c_j' < c_{th}$ then

    $R \leftarrow R \setminus \{j\}$, repeat reputation normalisation.

  end if

  for $j \in R$ do

    if data size is imbalanced then

      $num_j \leftarrow \frac{c_j'}{max(c)} * \frac{n_j}{max(n)} * |\Delta w_g|$

    end if

    if class number is imbalanced then

      $num_j \leftarrow \frac{c_j'}{max(c)} * \frac{class_j}{max(class)} * |\Delta w_g|$

    end if

    Groups num_j aggregated updates into Δw_g^j according to the "largest values" criterion, and allocates an adjusted version $\Delta w_g^j - \frac{n_j}{max(n)}\Delta(w_j)^S$ (imbalanced data size) or $\Delta w_g^j - \frac{class_j}{max(class)}\Delta(w_j)^S$ (imbalanced class number) to participant j.

  end for

---

4   Experiments

4.1   Datasets

We implement experiments on two benchmark datasets, MNIST[1] and Adult Census[2]. The MNIST dataset, for handwritten digit recognition, consists of 60,000 training examples and 10,000 test examples. The Adult Census dataset, contains 14 demographic attributes, including age, race, education level, marital status, occupation, etc. This dataset is typically used for a binary prediction task: whether the annual income of an individual is over or under 50,000 dollars. It consists of total 48,843 records, with 24% (11687) positive records (greater than 50,000), and 76% (37155) negative records (less than 50,000). To mitigate the imbalance, we randomly sample 11687 negative records to create a balanced dataset. Following this, we then use an 80–20 train-test split. For both experiments, we randomly set aside 10% of training examples as the validation set.

4.2   Baselines

To demonstrate the effectiveness of our CFFL, we compare it with the following two representative baseline frameworks: Federated Averaging (FedAvg) from [14] and Distributed Selective Stochastic Gradient Descent (DSSGD) from [19] for FL.

Standalone framework assumes participants train standalone models on local datasets without collaboration. This framework delivers minimum utility, because each participant is susceptible to falling into local optima when training alone. In addition, we remark that there is no concrete concept of collaborative fairness in the *Standalone* framework, because participants do *not* collaborate under this setting.

Distributed framework enables participants to train independently and concurrently, and by sharing their gradient updates or model parameters to achieve a better global model. We implement two commonly adopted frameworks for distributed/federated learning. The first one is a standard approach in FL: Federated Averaging (FedAvg) [14]. The other one is called Distributed Selective SGD (DSSGD) proposed by Shokri *et al.* [19], who showed that DSSGD empirically outperfoms the centralized SGD and argued it is because updating only a small fraction of parameters at each round acts as a regularization technique to avoid overfitting by preventing the neural network weights from jointly "remembering" the training data. Hence, we also include DSSGD for the analysis of the *Distributed* framework and omit the centralized framework.

Furthermore, we investigate different upload rates $\theta_u = 0.1$ and $\theta_u = 1$ [19], where gradients are uploaded according to the "largest values" criterion in [19]. Using the upload rate less than 1 has two advantages: reducing overfitting and saving communication overhead.

---

[1] http://yann.lecun.com/exdb/mnist/.
[2] http://archive.ics.uci.edu/ml/datasets/Adult.

4.3   Experimental Setup

In order to evaluate the effectiveness of our CFFL in realistic settings of heterogeneous data distributions in terms of dataset size and class number, we investigate the following two scenarios:

Imbalanced Data Size. To simulate dataset size heterogeneity, we follow a power law to randomly partition total {3000, 6000, 12000} MNIST examples among {5, 10, 20} participants respectively. Similarly, for Adult dataset, we randomly partition {4000, 8000, 12000} examples among {5, 10, 20} participants respectively. In this way, each participant has a distinctly different number of examples, with the first participant has the least and the last participant has the most. We remark that the purpose of allocating on average 600 MNIST examples for each participant is to fairly compare with Shokri *et al.* [19], where each participant has a small number of 600 local examples to simulate data scarity which necessitates collaboration.

Imbalanced Class Numbers. To examine data distribution heterogeneity, we vary the class numbers present in the dataset of each participant, increasing from the first participant to the last. For this scenario, we only investigate MNIST dataset as it contains 10 classes. We distribute classes in a linspace manner, for example, participant-{1, 2, 3, 4, 5} own {1, 3, 5, 7, 10} classes from MNIST dataset respectively. Specifically, for MNIST with total 10 classes and 5 participants, the first participant has data from only 1 class, while the last participant has data from all 10 classes. We first partition the training set according to the labels, then we sample and assign subsets of training set with corresponding labels to the participants. Note that in this scenario, each participant still has the same number of examples, *i.e.*, 600 examples.

Model and Hyper-Parameters. For MNIST *Imbalanced data size* experiment, we use a two-layer fully connected neural network with 128 and 64 units respectively. The hyperparameters are: local epochs $E = 2$, local batch size $B = 16$, and local learning rate $lr = 0.15$ for number of participants $P = 5$ and $lr = 0.25$ for $P = \{10, 20\}$, with exponential decay $\gamma = 0.977$, gradient clipping between $[-0.01, 0.01]$, and a total of 30 communication rounds. For MNIST *Imbalanced class numbers* experiment, we use the same neural network architecture. The hyperparameters are: local epochs $E = 1$, local batch size $B = 16$, and local learning rate $lr = 0.15$ for $P = \{5, 10, 20\}$, with exponential decay $\gamma = 0.977$, gradient clipping between $[-0.01, 0.01]$, and a total of 50 communication rounds. For Adult, we use a single layer fully connected neural network with 32 units. The hyperparameters are: local epochs $E = 2$, local batch size $B = 16$, and local learning rate $lr = 0.03$ for $P = \{5, 10, 20\}$, with exponential decay $\gamma = 0.977$, gradient clipping between $[-0.01, 0.01]$, and a total of 30 communication rounds.

In addition, for both datasets, to reduce the impact of different initializations and avoid non-convergence, we use the same model initialization w_0 for all participants. Note that all participants carry out subsequent training locally and individually.

For all the experiments, we empirically set the reputation threshold via grid search as $c_{th} = \frac{1}{|R|} * \frac{1}{3}$ for *imbalanced data size*, and $c_{th} = \frac{1}{|R|} * \frac{1}{6}$ for *imbalanced class numbers*, where R is the set of participants with reputations higher than the threshold. For the *punishment factor*, we empirically choose $\alpha = 5$. We use the Stochastic Gradient Descent (SGD) optimizer throughout.

Communication Protocol. In standard FL, the global model is given to all participants, both during and at the end of the training. Such a setup forbids the calculation of our definition of fairness via the pearson coefficient, when all participants have the same 'reward'. To mitigate this, we follow [19] to adopt the round-robin communication protocol for DSSGD and FedAvg. In each communication round, participants upload *parameter updates* and download *parameters* in sequence, so that their received models differ from each other in test accuracies. We then use the test accuracies for the calculation of fairness.

4.4   Experimental Results

Fairness Comparison. Table 1 lists the calculated fairness of DSSGD, FedAvg and CFFL over MNIST and Adult under varying participant number settings from $\{5, 10, 20\}$, and different upload rates θ_u from $\{0.1, 1\}$.

From the high values of fairness (some close to the theoretical limit of 1.0), we conclude that CFFL achieves good fairness, and the results confirm the intuition behind our notion of fairness: the participant who contributed more is rewarded with a better model. We also observe that DSSGD and FedAvg yield significantly lower fairness than our CFFL. This is expected since neither their communication protocols nor the learning algorithms incorporate the concept of fairness.

Table 1. Fairness [%] of DSSGD, FedAvg and CFFL under varying participant number settings (P-k), and upload rate θ_u.

Dataset	MNIST					Adult				
Framework	FedAvg	DSSGD		CFFL		FedAvg	DSSGD		CFFL	
θ_u	NA	0.1	1	0.1	1	NA	0.1	1	0.1	1
P5	3.08	90.72	84.61	**99.76**	99.02	−3.33	15.61	35.71	98.44	**99.37**
P10	−50.47	−78.18	90.67	98.55	**98.74**	44.27	62.30	56.60	**92.00**	91.95
P20	60.41	−81.77	80.45	**98.52**	98.51	−34.32	60.30	58.01	**80.56**	79.52

Accuracy Comparison. Table 2 reports the corresponding accuracies on MNIST and Adult datasets of $\{5, 10, 20\}$ participants when $\theta_u = 0.1$. For CFFL, we report the best accuracy achieved among the participants, because they receive models of different accuracies and we expect the most contributive participant to receive a model with the highest accuracy comparable to or even better than that of DSSGD and FedAvg. For the *Standalone* framework, we show the accuracy of this same participant. We observe that CFFL obtains comparable

Table 2. Maximum accuracy [%] over MNIST and adult of varying participant number settings, achieved by DSSGD, FedAvg, *Standalone* framework, and our CFFL ($\theta_u = 0.1$).

Framework	MNIST			Adult		
	P5	P10	P20	P5	P10	P20
DSSGD	93.28	94.20	82.36	81.94	82.78	82.07
FedAvg	**93.62**	**95.32**	**96.26**	**82.58**	**83.14**	**83.16**
Standalone	90.30	90.88	90.64	81.93	82.31	82.07
CFFL	91.83	93.00	93.25	81.96	82.63	82.72

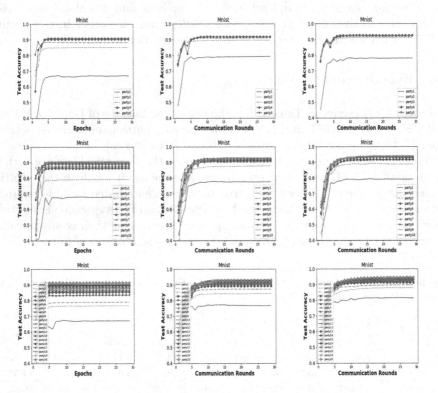

Fig. 1. Individual convergence for MNIST using *Standalone* framework and our CFFL. The 3 rows correspond to $\{5, 10, 20\}$ participants, the 3 columns correspond to {Standalone, CFFL with $\theta_u = 0.1$, CFFL with $\theta_u = 1$}.

accuracy to DSSGD and FedAvg, and even better accuracy than DSSGD for P20. More importantly, our CFFL always attains higher accuracies than the *Standalone* framework. For example, for MNIST dataset with 20 participants, our CFFL achieves 93.25% test accuracy, which is much higher than the *Standalone* framework (90.64%). Under this setting, DSSGD achieving the lowest accuracy may be attributed to the instability and fluctuations during training.

The above fairness results in Table 1, and accuracy results in Table 2 demonstrate that our proposed CFFL achieves both *high fairness and comparable accuracy* under various settings (Fig. 2).

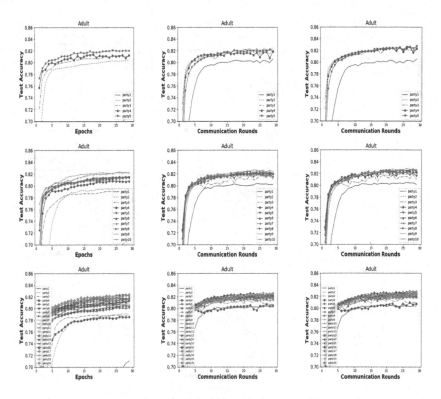

Fig. 2. Individual convergence for adult using *Standalone* framework and our CFFL. The 3 rows correspond to $\{5, 10, 20\}$ participants, the 3 columns correspond to {Standalone, CFFL with $\theta_u = 0.1$, CFFL with $\theta_u = 1$}.

Individual Model Performance. To examine the impact of our CFFL on individual convergence, we plot the test accuracy over training process in Fig. 1. It displays the test accuracies of the models of the participants for the *Standalone* framework and CFFL with upload rate of $\{0.1, 1\}$ in MNIST over 30 communication rounds. We observe that in CFFL, each participant consistently delivers better accuracy than their standalone model, implying that all participants stand to gain improvements in their model performance with collaboration. More importantly, the figure clearly demonstrates that CFFL enforces the participants to converge to different local models, which are still better than their standalone models, thus *achieving both fairness and improvement in model performance*. We do observe slight fluctuations at the beginning of training. This can be attributed to that in CFFL, participants are allocated with different aggregated updates from the server. We also note that including pretraining of few epochs at each participant before collaboration will not alter the overall convergence behaviour, but providing relatively better fairness, especially in settings with more participants.

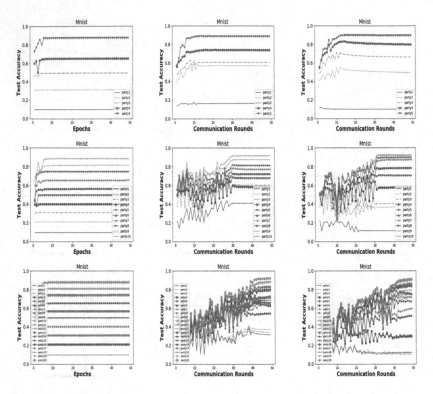

Fig. 3. Individual model accuracy for MNIST class imbalanced scenario, where classes are distributed in a linspace manner (for example, participant-$\{1, 2, 3, 4, 5\}$ own $\{1, 3, 5, 7, 10\}$ classes respectively). 3 columns correspond to $\{$Standalone, CFFL $\theta_u = 0.1$, CFFL $\theta_u = 1.\}$

For *Imbalanced class numbers*, Fig. 3 shows individual model accuracies in the *Standalone* framework and our CFFL. We see that all participants achieve higher model accuracies in CFFL than their standalone counterparts. Similar to the scenario of *Imbalanced data size*, all participants converge to different final models, but with more obvious accuracy gaps, resulting in higher fairness. Moreover, it takes longer time for participants to converge when there are more participants participating in the system. The fluctuations and the longer convergence time may be attributed to the increased heterogeneity in the participants' datasets.

5 Discussions

Robustness to Free-Riders. There may exist free-riders in FL systems, and they aim to benefit from the global model without really contributing. Typically, free-riders may pretend to be contributing by generating and uploading random or noisy updates. In standard FL systems, there is no specific safeguard against this, so the free-riders can enjoy the system's global model at virtually no cost. Conversely, CFFL can automatically identify and isolate free-riders. This is because the empirical utility (on the validation set) of the random or carefully crafted gradients is generally low. As collaborative training proceeds, the free-riders will receive gradually lower reputations, and eventually be isolated from the system when their reputations fall below the reputation threshold. Through our additional experiments (including 1 free rider who always uploads random values as gradient updates), we observe that our CFFL can always identify and isolate the free rider in the early stages of collaboration, without affecting either accuracy or convergence.

Choice of Reputation Threshold. With a reputation threshold c_{th}, the server can stipulate a minimum empirical contribution for the participants. Reputation mechanism can be used to detect and isolate the free-rider(s). A key challenge lies in the selection of an appropriate threshold, as fairness and accuracy may be inversely affected. For example, too small a c_{th} might allow low-contribution participant(s) to sneak into the federated system without being detected and isolated. On the contrary, too large a c_{th} might isolate too many participants to achieve meaningful collaboration. In our experiments, we empirically search for suitable values for different scenarios.

Coarse-Grained Fairness. The main design of this chapter targets at a fine-grained concept of fairness, in which, each participant corresponds to a different model. Another alternative is to consider coarse-grained fairness, in which, multiple participants can be categorised into a group with the same contribution level, and participant groups at different contribution levels should receive the different number of model updates, while participants in the same group receive the same number of model updates [26].

Will Reputation Help Robustness? In addition to the free-rider(s) considered in this chapter, recent works pointed out that reputation score is also helpful to defend against malicious participants in the system [16,28]. In particular, Regatti et al. [16] demonstrated that using reputation scores computed on an auxiliary dataset with a larger step size for gradient aggregation is robust to any number of Byzantine adversaries. Hence, it is promising to integrate sophisticated reputation design into FL to help build a fair and robust system.

Fairness in Vertically FL (VFL). This chapter mainly investigated how to ensure fairness in horizontally federated learning (HFL), in which datasets owned by each participant share similar features but concern different users [6]. Another interesting type of FL is called vertically federated learning (VFL), which is applicable to the cases in which participants have large overlaps in the sample space but differ in the feature space, *i.e.*, different participants hold different attributes of the same records [21]. In VFL [3], there may only be one participant who owns labels for the given learning task. It would be interesting to study how to formulate and achieve fairness in VFL, and whether our fairness solution in HFL can be adapted to this paradigm.

Fairness in Heterogeneous FL. For simplicity, our current design only considered homogeneous FL architectures, *i.e.*, the same model architecture is shared with all participants. It would be interesting to study how to extend the fairness concept to FL with heterogeneous model architectures, or even different families of learning algorithms [7]. In this scenario, instead of sharing gradients, participants share local model predictions on the public data, *i.e.*, through transfer learning and knowledge distillation. A potential solution to ensure fairness would be scoring their shared predictions.

6   Conclusion and Future Work

This chapter initiates the research problem of collaborative fairness in server-based FL, and revolutionizes FL by enforcing participants to download different ratios of the aggregated updates, and converge to different final models. A novel collaborative fair federated learning framework named CFFL is proposed. Based on empirical individual model performance on the public validation set, a notion of reputation is introduced to mediate participant rewards across communication rounds. Experimental results demonstrate that our CFFL achieves comparable accuracy to two *Distributed* frameworks, and always achieves better accuracy than the *Standalone* framework, confirming the effectiveness of CFFL of achieving both *fairness* and *utility.* We hope our preliminary study will shed light on future research on collaborative fairness. A number of avenues for further work are appealing. In particular, we would like to study how to quantify fairness in more complex settings involving vertically FL, heterogeneous FL, and other types of learning tasks such as speech, Natural Language Processing (NLP), etc. It is expected that our system can find wide applications in real world.

References

1. Cummings, R., Gupta, V., Kimpara, D., Morgenstern, J.: On the compatibility of privacy and fairness. In: Adjunct Publication of the 27th Conference on User Modeling, Adaptation and Personalization, pp. 309–315 (2019)
2. Gollapudi, S., Kollias, K., Panigrahi, D., Pliatsika, V.: Profit sharing and efficiency in utility games. In: ESA, pp. 1–16 (2017)
3. Hardy, S., et al.: Private federated learning on vertically partitioned data via entity resolution and additively homomorphic encryption. CoRR. arXiv:1711.10677 (2017)
4. Jagielski, M., et al.: Differentially private fair learning. arXiv preprint arXiv:1812.02696 (2018)

5. Kairouz, P., et al.: Advances and open problems in federated learning. arXiv preprint arXiv:1912.04977 (2019)
6. Kantarcioglu, M., Clifton, C.: Privacy-preserving distributed mining of association rules on horizontally partitioned data. IEEE Trans. Knowl. Data Eng. **16**(9), 1026–1037 (2004)
7. Li, D., Wang, J.: FedMD: heterogenous federated learning via model distillation. arXiv preprint arXiv:1910.03581 (2019)
8. Li, T., Sahu, A.K., Talwalkar, A., Smith, V.: Federated learning: challenges, methods, and future directions. CoRR. arXiv:1908.07873 (2019)
9. Li, T., Sanjabi, M., Smith, V.: Fair resource allocation in federated learning. In: ICLR (2020)
10. Lingjuan Lyu, X.X., Wang, Q.: Collaborative fairness in federated learning (2020). https://arxiv.org/abs/2008.12161v1
11. Lyu, L., Li, Y., Nandakumar, K., Yu, J., Ma, X.: How to democratise and protect AI: fair and differentially private decentralised deep learning. IEEE Trans. Dependable Secure Compu. (2020)
12. Lyu, L., Yu, H., Yang, Q.: Threats to federated learning: a survey. arXiv preprint arXiv:2003.02133 (2020)
13. Lyu, L., et al.: Towards fair and privacy-preserving federated deep models. IEEE Trans. Parallel Distrib. Syst. **31**(11), 2524–2541 (2020)
14. McMahan, B., Moore, E., Ramage, D., Hampson, S., Arcas, B.A.: Communication-efficient learning of deep networks from decentralized data. In: Artificial Intelligence and Statistics, pp. 1273–1282 (2017)
15. Mohri, M., Sivek, G., Suresh, A.T.: Agnostic federated learning. In: International Conference on Machine Learning, pp. 4615–4625 (2019)
16. Regatti, J., Gupta, A.: Befriending the byzantines through reputation scores. arXiv preprint arXiv:2006.13421 (2020)
17. Richardson, A., Filos-Ratsikas, A., Faltings, B.: Rewarding high-quality data via influence functions. arXiv preprint arXiv:1908.11598 (2019)
18. Shapley, L.S.: A value for n-person games. In: Contributions to the Theory of Games, vol. 2, no. 28, pp. 307–317 (1953)
19. Shokri, R., Shmatikov, V.: Privacy-preserving deep learning. In: Proceedings of the 22nd ACM SIGSAC Conference on Computer and Communications Security, pp. 1310–1321. ACM (2015)
20. Sim, R.H.L., Zhang, Y., Chan, M.C., Low, B.K.H.: Collaborative machine learning with incentive-aware model rewards. In: ICML (2020)
21. Vaidya, J., Clifton, C.: Privacy preserving association rule mining in vertically partitioned data. In: KDD, pp. 639–644 (2002)
22. Yang, Q., Liu, Y., Chen, T., Tong, Y.: Federated machine learning: concept and applications. ACM Trans. Intell. Syst. Technol. (TIST) **10**(2), 1–19 (2019)
23. Yang, Q., Liu, Y., Cheng, Y., Kang, Y., Chen, T., Yu, H.: Federated Learning. Morgan & Claypool Publishers (2019)
24. Yang, S., Wu, F., Tang, S., Gao, X., Yang, B., Chen, G.: On designing data quality-aware truth estimation and surplus sharing method for mobile crowdsensing. IEEE J. Sel. Areas Commun. **35**(4), 832–847 (2017)
25. Yu, H., et al.: A fairness-aware incentive scheme for federated learning. In: Proceedings of the 3rd AAAI/ACM Conference on AI, Ethics, and Society (AIES 2020), pp. 393–399 (2020)
26. Zhang, J., Li, C., Robles-Kelly, A., Kankanhalli, M.: Hierarchically fair federated learning. arXiv preprint arXiv:2004.10386 (2020)

27. Zhao, L., Wang, Q., Zou, Q., Zhang, Y., Chen, Y.: Privacy-preserving collaborative deep learning with unreliable participants. IEEE Trans. Inf. Forensics Secur. **15**, 1486–1500 (2019)
28. Zhao, Y., et al.: Privacy-preserving blockchain-based federated learning for IoT devices. IEEE Internet Things J. (2020)

A Game-Theoretic Framework
for Incentive Mechanism Design
in Federated Learning

Mingshu Cong[1,2](✉), Han Yu[3], Xi Weng[4], and Siu Ming Yiu[2]

[1] LogiOcean Technologies, Shenzhen, China
miranda.cong@logiocean.com
[2] The FinTech and Blockchain Lab, The University of Hong Kong,
Pok Fu Lam, Hong Kong
smyiu@cs.hku.hk
[3] School of Computer Science and Engineering,
Nanyang Technological University, Singapore, Singapore
han.yu@ntu.edu.sg
[4] Guanghua School of Management, Peking University, Beijing, China
wengxi125@gsm.pku.edu.cn
http://www.logiocean.com

Abstract. Federated learning (FL) has great potential for coalescing isolated data islands. It enables privacy-preserving collaborative model training and addresses security and privacy concerns. Besides booming technological breakthroughs in this field, for better commercialization of FL in the business world, we also need to provide sufficient monetary incentives to data providers. The problem of FL incentive mechanism design is therefore proposed to find out the optimal organization and payment structure for the federation. This problem can be tackled by game theory.

In this chapter, we set up a research framework for reasoning about FL incentive mechanism design. We introduce key concepts and their mathematical notations specified under the FML environment, hereby proposing a precise definition of the FML incentive mechanism design problem. Then, we break down the big problem into a demand-side problem and a supply-side problem. Based on different settings and objectives, we provide a checklist for FL practitioners to choose the appropriate FL incentive mechanism without deep knowledge in game theory.

As examples, we introduce the Crémer-McLean mechanism to solve the demand-side problem and present a VCG-based mechanism, PVCG, to solve the demand-side problem. These mechanisms both guarantee truthfulness, i.e., they encourage participants to truthfully report their private information and offer all their data to the federation. Crémer-McLean mechanism, together with PVCG, attains allocative efficiency, individual rationality, and weak budget balancedness at the same time, easing the well-known tension between these objectives in the mechanism design literature.

Supported by LogiOcean Co., Ltd.

Q. Yang et al. (Eds.): Federated Learning, LNAI 12500, pp. 205–222, 2020.
https://doi.org/10.1007/978-3-030-63076-8_15

Keywords: Federated learning · Mechanism design · Game theory

1 Introduction

In most industries, data are segregated into isolated data islands, among which direct data sharing is restricted by laws and regulations such as the General Data Protection Regulation (GDPR) [6]. *Federated learning* (FL) [12] has emerged in recent years as an alternative solution to train AI models based on distributedly stored data while preserving data privacy. Commercial FL platforms have been developed, e.g., *TensorFlow Federated* (TFF) from Google and *FATE* from WeBank. Industries such as finance, insurance, telecommunications, healthcare, education, and urban computing have great potential to benefit from FL technologies.

In real application scenarios of FL, where data providers are profit-seeking business entities, FL may not be economically viable because of the *free rider problem*, i.e., a rational data provider may hold back its data while expecting others to contribute all their data to the federation. Without proper incentives, it is hard to prevent such free-riding activities because the FL model, as a virtual product, has characteristics of *club goods*, i.e., it is non-rivalrous in consumption.

In order to incentivize data providers to offer their best datasets to federated learning, we need to pay data providers enough monetary reward to cover their costs. The marginal monetary reward for contributing more data should be no less than the marginal cost hence incurred. Also, we aim to maintain a balanced budget and optimize for social welfare. At least three sources of *information asymmetry* intertwined in this problem: 1) the datasets owned by each data provider, 2) costs incurred to each data provider, and 3) model users' valuations on the trained FL model. An *FL incentive mechanism*, formulated as a function that calculates payments to participants, is designed to overcome these information asymmetries and to obtain the above-mentioned objectives. The problem of *FL incentive mechanism design* is to find the optimal FL incentive mechanism.

In this chapter, we first propose a game-theoretic model for analyzing the FL incentive mechanism design problem. We provide a checklist to specify heterogenous game settings and mechanism design objectives, together with four benchmark theorems that help FL practitioners to choose the appropriate FL incentive mechanism. Then, under our research framework, we provide two examples of FL incentive mechanisms, one on the demand side and the other on the supply side. The proposed Crémer-McLean mechanism and Procurement-VCG (PVCG) mechanism encourage FL participants to truthfully report their type parameters and offer their best datasets to the federation. These mechanisms also provide theoretical guarantees for incentive compatibility, allocative efficiency, individual rationality, and weak budget balancedness.

2   Problem Setup

In this section, we set up a game-theoretic environment for our following discussions. For readers unfamiliar with game theory and mechanism design, this section also provides necessary background knowledge.

2.1   The Game-Theoretic Environment

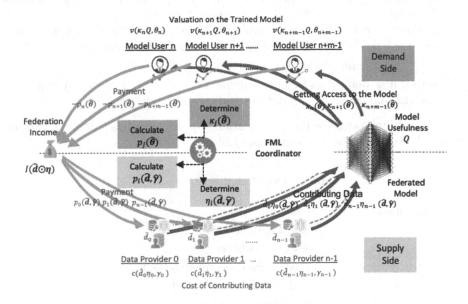

Fig. 1. The circular flow diagram of federated learning.

The environment of FL incentive mechanism design is set up as follows:

- There exists a set of n *data providers*, denoted by $N = (0, \ldots, n - 1)$, and another set of m *model users*, denoted by $M = (n, \ldots, n + m - 1)$;
- Each data provider $i \in N$ owns a dataset $\bar{d}_i$. It claims it owns a dataset $\hat{d}_i$. The federation accepts a dataset $d_i \leq \hat{d}_i$ from this data provider. We call $\eta_i = d_i \oslash \hat{d}_i$ the *acceptance ratio*, where $\oslash$ denotes element-wise division.
- Trained on datasets $\boldsymbol{d} = (d_0, \ldots, d_{n-1})$ from all data providers, the usefulness of the federated model is $Q(\boldsymbol{d})$. Model users may be granted limited access to the federated model such that the usefulness of the federated model to model user j is $\kappa_j Q(\boldsymbol{d})$, where κ_j is called the *access permission*.
- Each data provider $i \in N$ has a *cost type* $\gamma_i \in \Gamma_i$. Its cost of contributing data d_i is $c(d_i, \gamma_i)$. The collection of cost types of all data providers forms the *cost type profile* $\gamma = (\gamma_0, \ldots, \gamma_n)$. Data provider i may report a different cost type $\hat{\gamma}_i$.

- Each model user $j \in M$ has a *valuation type* $\theta_j \in \Theta_j$. Its valuation on the trained federated model is $w(\kappa_j Q(\boldsymbol{d}), \theta_j) = v(\boldsymbol{d}, \kappa_j, \theta_j)$. The collection of valuation types of all model users forms the *valuation type profile* $\boldsymbol{\theta} = (\theta_n, \ldots, \theta_{n+m-1})$. Model user j may report a different valuation type $\hat{\theta}_j$.
- The payment to data provider $i \in N$ is $p_i \geq 0$. The payment to model user $j \in M$ is $p_j \leq 0$. We denote $\boldsymbol{p}^s = (p_0, \ldots, p_{n-1})$ and $\boldsymbol{p}^d = (p_n, \ldots, p_{n+m-1})$. The *federation income* is $I = -\sum_{j=n}^{n+m-1} p_j$; the *federation expenditure* is $E = \sum_{i=0}^{n-1} p_i$; the *federation profit* is $P = \sum_{l=0}^{n+m-1} p_l$.
- Participants' preferences are represented by *quasi-linear utility functions* $u_i(\cdot) = p_i(\cdot) - c_i(\cdot), i \in N$ and $u_j(\cdot) = p_j(\cdot) + v_j(\cdot), j \in M$.
- The social effect of federated learning is measured by *social surplus*, defined as $S(\cdot) = \sum_{j=n}^{n+m-1} v_j(\cdot) - \sum_{i=0}^{n-1} c_i(\cdot)$, which includes consumer surplus $S^d = \sum_{j=n}^{n+m-1} v_j(\cdot)$ and producer surplus $S^d = -\sum_{i=0}^{n-1} c_i(\cdot)$.
- There is user-defined *unfairness functions* $\varpi^s(\boldsymbol{p}^s, \boldsymbol{c})$ and $\varpi^d(\boldsymbol{p}^s, \boldsymbol{v})$ that measures the unfairness among data providers and model users.

Figure 1 illustrates the flows of economic resources in this federated learning game. Table 1 lists the mathematical symbols.

Table 1. List of mathematical symbols

Symbol	Meaning
i	Index of data provider
j	Index of model user
$\bar{d}_i$, $\hat{d}_i$, or d_i	Owned/claimed/accepted dataset
$Q(\boldsymbol{d})$	Usefulness of federated model
γ_i or $\hat{\gamma}_i$	True/reported cost type
θ_j or $\hat{\theta}_j$	True/reported valuation type
p_i, p_j	Payment to participants
$\eta_i(\cdot)$	Acceptance ratio of datasets
$\kappa_j(\cdot)$	Access permission to the federated model
$c(d_i, \gamma_i)$	Individual cost function
$v(\boldsymbol{d}, \kappa_j, \theta_j)$	Individual valuation function
$u(\cdot)$	Utility function
$I(\cdot), E(\cdot), P(\cdot)$	Federation income/expenditure/profit
$S(\cdot), S^d(\cdot), S^s(\cdot)$	Social surplus/consumer surplus/producer surplus
$\varpi^s(\cdot), \varpi^d(\cdot)$	Unfairness functions

2.2   Definition of the FL Incentive Mechanism Design Problem

With these concepts and notations introduced so far, we present a formal definition for the problem of *FML incentive mechanism design*.

Definition 1 (FL Incentive Mechanism Design). *FL incentive mechanism design is to design the optimal $p^s(\cdot)$, $\eta(\cdot)$, $p^d(\cdot)$, $\kappa(\cdot)$, as functions of claimed $\hat{d}$ and reported $\hat{\gamma}$, $\hat{\theta}$, in order to achieve a set of objectives in Sect. 2.3.*

There are three sources of intertwined information asymmetry, $\hat{d}$, $\hat{\gamma}$ and $\hat{\theta}$, in the FL incentive mechanism design problem. When all variables are considered simultaneously, this problem becomes extremely complicated. As a tradition in the economic literature, we separate this big problem into a demand-side subproblem and a supply-side sub-problem. Formally, we introduce the following assumption:

Assumption 1 (Separation between Data Supply and Model Demand). *The data supply market and the model demand market are separated. When an FL participant is both a data provider and a model user, its decision as a data provider does not affect his decision as a model user, or vice versa.*

With Assumption 1, we can define the two subproblems as follows.

Definition 2 (Supply-Side FL Incentive Mechanism Design). *Given that the federation Income $I(Q)$ and the model quality $Q(\hat{d} \odot \eta)$ are exogenous functions, the supply-side FL incentive mechanism design is to design the optimal $p_i(\hat{d}, \hat{\gamma})$ and $\eta_i(\hat{d}, \hat{\gamma})$, $i = 1, \ldots, n$, as functions of claimed datasets $\hat{d}_i$, $i = 0, \ldots, n-1$ and reported cost types γ_i, $i = 1, \ldots, n$, in order to achieve some desirable objectives in Sect. 2.3.*

Definition 3 (Demand-Side FL Incentive Mechanism Design). *Given that the model quality Q is an exogenous constant, the demand-side FL incentive mechanism design is to design the optimal $p_j(\hat{\theta})$ and $\kappa_j(\hat{\theta})$, $j = 1, \ldots, m$, as functions of reported benefit types $\hat{\theta}$, $j = 1, \ldots, m$, in order to achieve some desirable objectives in Sect. 2.3.*

2.3 Objectives of FL Incentive Mechanism Design

Below is a list of desirable properties of FL incentive mechanism design. For detailed explanations of these objectives, refer to [10].

- *(Incentive Compatibility, IC)* IC is attained if in equilibrium, all participants report their types truthfully, i.e., $\hat{\theta} = \theta$. Different types of equilibriums correspond to different IC conditions, which can be one of *Nash Incentive Compatibility (NIC)*, *Dominant Incentive Compatibility (DIC)*, *Baysian Incentive Compatibility (BIC)*, or *Perfect Bayesian Incentive Compatibility (PBIC)*.
- *(Individual Rationality, IR)* A mechanism is *individually rational (IR)* if this mechanism does not make any player worse off than if he quits the federation, i.e.,

$$u_i(\hat{d}, \hat{\gamma}) \geq 0, \forall i \in N \quad \text{and} \quad u_j(\hat{\theta}) \geq 0, \forall j \in M. \tag{1}$$

In games of incomplete information, IR can be ex-ante IR, interim IR or ex-post IR.

- *(Budget Balance, BB)* A mechanism is *weakly budget balanced (WBB)* if for all feasible outcomes, the sum of payments is less than or equal to zero. i.e.,

$$\sum_{l=1}^{n+m-1} p_l(\hat{\boldsymbol{d}}, \hat{\boldsymbol{\gamma}}, \hat{\boldsymbol{\theta}}) \leq 0, \forall \hat{\boldsymbol{d}}, \hat{\boldsymbol{\gamma}}, \hat{\boldsymbol{\theta}}. \tag{2}$$

It is *strongly budget balanced (SBB)* if the equity holds. In games of incomplete information, BB can be ex-ante BB, interim BB or ex-post BB.
- *(Social Optimization)* *social optimization* can be *social surplus maximization (SSM)* when social surplus is maximized or *profit maximization (PM)* if the federation profit is maximized. Social surplus maximization implies *allocative efficiency (AE)*.
- *(Fairness)* We desire to minimize the unfairness function.

3   Specifications of FL Incentive Mechanisms

3.1   Non-standard Game Settings

Besides game settings in Sect. 2.2, several non-standard game settings also need to be specified when we design FL incentive mechanisms. These non-standard game settings include:

- *(Level of Information Asymmetry)* On the demand side, there may be or may not be *information asymmetry* on valuation types. On the supply side, there may be a) no information asymmetry, b) information asymmetry on datasets only, c) about cost types only, or d) about both.
- *(Mode of System Evolution)* If the FL game is played for only once, it corresponds to a static mechanism. If the FL game is played repeatedly or parameters change over time, it corresponds to a dynamic mechanism.
- *(Belief Updates)* In a dynamic FL game, as time passes by, agents update their beliefs based on *heuristic belief updates* or *Bayesian belief updates*, according to which agents update their information based on some heuristic rules or Bayesian rules, respectively.
- *(Controllable Parameters)* The FL coordinator may determine $\boldsymbol{p}^s(\cdot)$, $\boldsymbol{\eta}(\cdot)$, $\boldsymbol{p}^d(\cdot)$, and $\boldsymbol{\kappa}(\cdot)$, but in some situations, some of these parameters are not controllable. For example, it may not be possible to set up access control on the FML model so that $\boldsymbol{\kappa}(\cdot)$ is not controllable, or it may not be possible to reject datasets offered by data providers so that $\boldsymbol{\eta}(\cdot)$ is not controllable. Also, there are cases where *price discrimination* is not possible so that the unit price of data/model services has to be the same for all data providers/model users.
- *(Functional Forms)* On the supply side, exact forms of the federation income function $I(Q)$, the model quality function $Q(\boldsymbol{d})$, and the individual cost functions $c(d_i, \gamma_i)$ need to be specified. On the demand side, the form of the individual valuation function $w(\kappa_j Q, \theta_j)$ need to be specified.

3.2   Measures of Objectives

As a general rule, objectives in Sect. 2.3 cannot be attained simultaneously, so we would like to know how well each objective is achieved by a given FL incentive mechanism. There are also cases where the constraints of some objectives are approximately achieved. The performance of an FL incentive mechanism on achieving these objectives can be evaluated according to the following measures.

- *(Data offering rate, DOR)* DOR is defined as the total data offered by all data providers to the total data owned by all data providers, i.e.,

$$DOR = \frac{\sum_{i=0}^{n-1} \hat{d}_i}{\sum_{i=0}^{n-1} \bar{d}_i}. \tag{3}$$

  The data offering rate varies from 0.0 to 1.0, with 1.0 indicating all data being offered. When a payment scheme is incentive-compatible, the data offering rate is 1.0.

- *(Individual rationality index, IRI)* Rational data providers are not expected to stay in the federation if their costs cannot be covered by payments. The individual rationality indicator IR_i for data provider i is defined as $IR_i = 1$ if $p_i - c_i \geq 0$ and $IR_i = 0$ otherwise.

  The ideal case is that the payment scheme satisfies individual rationality for all participants. For general cases, we measure the individual rationality index (IRI), defined as the average of individual rationality indicators, i.e., $IRI = \sum_{i=0}^{n-1} w_i \times IR_i$, where $w_i, i \in N$ are user-defined weights for the relative importance of data owner I, e.g., $w_i = \frac{d_i}{\sum_{l=0}^{n-1} d_l}$.

  The individual rationality index varies from 0.0 to 1.0, with 1.0 indicating individual rationality constraints satisfied for all participants.

- *(Budget surplus margin, BSM)* The budget surplus is the difference between the total income received from model users and the total payments paid to data owners. In practice, the budget surplus is the profit made by the coordinator. Budget surplus margin is the ratio of the budget surplus to total revenue of the federation, i.e.,

$$BSM = \frac{-\sum_{j=n}^{n+m-1} p_j - \sum_{i=0}^{n-1} p_i}{-\sum_{j=n}^{n+m-1} p_j}. \tag{4}$$

  The budget surplus margin varies from $-\infty$ to 1.0, with 0.0 indicating a break-even point, and positive/negative values indicating net profits/losses, respectively.

- *(Efficiency Index, EI)* In federated learning, allocative efficiency is achieved when social surplus is maximized. The efficiency index(EI) is the ratio of realized social surplus to the maximum possible social surplus, i.e.,

$$EI = \frac{S(\hat{d}, \gamma, \theta, \eta(\hat{d}, \hat{\gamma}, \hat{\theta}), \kappa(\hat{d}, \hat{\gamma}, \hat{\theta}))}{\max_{\eta, \kappa} S(\bar{d}, \gamma, \theta, \eta, \kappa)} \tag{5}$$

EI varies from $-\infty$ to 1.0, with 1.0 indicating allocative efficiency.

– *(Fairness Index, FI)* In FL, we want the payment of a unit of contributed data to be the same for all data providers. We set the unfairness function to be the variance of the normalized unit price, i.e., rescaled to $[0.0, 1.0]$, i.e.,

$$\varpi(\boldsymbol{p}^s, \boldsymbol{d}) = Var\{\frac{p_i/d_i}{\sum_{i=0}^{n-1} p_i / \sum_{i=0}^{n-1} d_i}\}. \tag{6}$$

The normalized unit price is invariant with the change of measure.
The fairness index (FI) is the realized unfairness function rescaled to $[0.0, 1.0]$, i.e.,

$$FI = \frac{1}{1 + \varpi(\boldsymbol{p}^s, \boldsymbol{d})}, \tag{7}$$

which varies from 0.0 to 1.0, with 1.0 indicating the absolute fairness.

Table 2. Checklist for specifications of FL incentive mechanisms

	Game settings	Specifications
Demand-side settings	Information asymmetry on valuation types	Yes/No
	Access permission control on FL model	Yes/No/Partial
	Price discrimination	Yes/No
	Specification of individual valuation functions	Specification
Supply-side settings	Information asymmetry on datasets	Yes/No
	Information asymmetry on cost types	Yes/No
	Ability to reject data owners	Yes/No/Partial
	Price discrimination	Yes/No
	Specification of individual cost functions	Specification
	Specification of the federation income function	Specification
	Specification of the model quality function	Specification
Other settings	Mode of system evolution	Static/Dynamic
	Belief updates	No/Heuristic/Bayesian
	Objectives	Measures
Objectives	IC	Data offering rate
	IR	Individual rationality index
	BB	Budget Surplus Margin
	Social optimization	Efficiency index
	Fairness	Fairness index

3.3   A Checklist for FL Incentive Mechanisms

Designing FL incentive mechanisms often requires deep knowledge in game theory, a field unfamiliar to most FL practitioners. Nevertheless, for FL practitioners to apply an FL incentive mechanism, they only need to make sure the game settings of the targeted mechanism is a good approximation of the real-world scenario. Besides, they would like to know how well the mechanism achieves the objectives listed in Sect. 2.3. We recommend that a checklist of specifications, e.g., Table 2, is provided with every FL incentive mechanism so that FL practitioners can easily choose the right mechanism without understanding the inner workings of these mechanisms.

3.4 Benchmarks for Choosing FL Incentive Mechanisms

When choosing FL incentive mechanisms, simpler game settings and fewer objectives are preferred. There is well-known tension between the multiple objectives listed in Sect. 2.3 [8]. We can prove that when game settings become more complicated or more objectives are optimized, the expected social surplus attained by the optimal mechanism is reduced. Formally, we have the following benchmark theorems. For proofs of these theorems, refer to [4].

Theorem 1 (More controllable parameters, better social optimization). *The more parameters can be controlled by the FL coordinator, the larger is the expected social surplus attained by the optimal FL incentive mechanism.*

Theorem 2 (Less information asymmetry, better social optimization). *When the IC constraint is concerned, the more accurate is the prior belief on $\bar{d}$, γ and $\boldsymbol{\theta}$, the larger is the expected social surplus attained by the optimal FL incentive mechanism.*

Theorem 3 (More constraints, worse social optimization). *The more constraints (such as IC, IR, BB), the smaller is the expected social surplus attained by the optimal FL incentive mechanism.*

According to these theorems, it would always be helpful if the FL coordinator can better estimate the datasets and type parameters of FL participants. Also, objectives in Sect. 2.3 compete with each other. If an objective is not a concern for an FL scenario, the FL coordinator should not choose an FL incentive mechanism optimized for that objective.

4 A Demand-Side FL Incentive Mechanism - Crémer-McLean Mechanism

In this section and the next section, we provide two examples of FL incentive mechanisms, on the demand side and the supply side, respectively.

4.1 Crémer-McLean Theorem

The demand-side mechanism introduced in this section is an application of the famous Crémer-McLean mechanism [5]. In order to apply Crémer-McLean mechanism, we put two assumptions on the prior distribution Prior($\boldsymbol{\theta}$). For more discussions on these assumptions, refer to [2].

Assumption 2 (Crémer-McLean condition). *The prior distribution of $\boldsymbol{\theta}$ satisfies the "Crémer-McLean condition" if there are no $j \in M$, $\theta_j \in \Theta_j$ and $\lambda_j : \Theta_j \backslash \{\theta_j\} \mapsto \mathbb{R}_+$ for which*

$$Prior(\boldsymbol{\theta}_{-j}|\theta_j) = \sum_{\theta_j' \in \Theta_j \backslash \{\theta_j\}} \lambda(\theta_j')Prior(\boldsymbol{\theta}_{-j}|\theta_j'), \quad \forall \boldsymbol{\theta}_{-j} \in \boldsymbol{\Theta}_{-j}. \quad (8)$$

214 M. Cong et al.

The Crémer-McLean condition is often referred to as *correlated types*. To understand this, one can understand agent j's belief about other agents' types $\text{Prior}(\theta_{-j}|\theta_j)$ as a vector with as many entries as Θ_{-j} has elements. Each θ_j corresponds to such a vector. The Crémer-McLean condition requires that none of these vectors can be written as a convex combination of other vectors. Note that the Crémer-McLean condition is obviously *violated* when agent j's conditional beliefs are independent of his type, i.e., all these vectors are identical.

The assumption of correlated types is reasonable for the FL scenario. It is highly possible that when the FL model brings high value to one model user, it also brings high value to other model users.

Assumption 3 (Identifiability condition). *The prior distribution of θ satisfies the "identifiability condition" if, for all other prior distributions $\text{Prior}'(\theta) \neq \text{Prior}(\theta)$ such that $\text{Prior}'(\theta) > 0$ for all $\theta \in \Theta$, there is at least one model user j and one valuation type $\theta_j \in \Theta_j$ such that for any collection of nonnegative coefficients $\lambda(\theta_j'), \theta_j' \in \Theta_j$, we have*

$$\text{Prior}'(\theta_{-j}|\theta_j) \neq \sum_{\theta_j' \in \Theta_j} \lambda(\theta_j')\text{Prior}(\theta_{-j}|\theta_j') \tag{9}$$

for at least one $\theta_{-j} \in \Theta_{-j}$.

Intuitively, this condition says that for any alternative prior distribution $\text{Prior}'(\theta) > 0$, there is at least one agent and one type of that agent such that this agent cannot randomize over reports in a way that makes the conditional distribution of all other types under $\text{Prior}'(\theta)$ indistinguishable from the conditional distribution of all other types under $\text{Prior}(\theta)$. In practice, we do not need to worry about this assumption because identifiability is generic in the topological sense, i.e., for almost all prior distributions, we can assume the identifiability condition holds. We have the following proposition, of which the proof can be found in [9].

Proposition 1 (Genericity of identifiability). *Suppose there are at least three agents ($m \geq 3$). Also, if $m = 3$, then at least one of the agents has at least three types. Then almost all prior distributions $\text{Prior}(\theta)$ are identifiable.*

Provided Assumption 2 and 3, we can guarantee the existence of an interim truthful and interim individual rational demand-side mechanism that attracts full consumer surplus. Here, interim incentive compatibility means truth-telling is superior to other strategies in expectation under the conditional prior distribution of other agents' types, i.e.,

$$\mathbb{E}_{\text{Prior}(\theta_{-j}|\theta_j)}[w(\kappa_j(\theta_j, \theta_{-j})Q, \theta_j) + p_j(\theta_j, \theta_{-j})] \tag{10}$$

$$\geq \mathbb{E}_{\text{Prior}(\theta_{-j}|\theta_j)}[w(\kappa_j(\hat{\theta}_j, \theta_{-j})Q, \theta_j) + p_j(\hat{\theta}_j, \theta_{-j})], \quad \forall j \in M, \theta \in \Theta, \hat{\theta}_j \in \Theta_j;$$

interim individual rationality means the expected utilities of all agents are nonnegative, under the conditional prior distribution of other agents' types, i.e.,

$$\mathbb{E}_{\text{Prior}(\theta_{-j}|\theta_j)}[w(\kappa_j(\theta_j, \theta_{-j})Q, \theta_j) + p_j(\theta_j, \theta_{-j})] \geq 0, \quad \forall j \in M, \theta \in \Theta. \tag{11}$$

The *Crémer-McLean Theorem* is:

Theorem 4 (Crémer-McLean Theorem). *When the Crémer-McLean condition and the identifiability condition hold for* $Prior(\boldsymbol{\theta})$, *for any decision rule* $\boldsymbol{\kappa}(\hat{\boldsymbol{\theta}})$, *there exists an interim incentive compatible and interim individually rational payment rule* $\boldsymbol{p}(\hat{\boldsymbol{\theta}})$ *that extracts full consumer surplus, i.e.,* $-\sum_{j=n}^{n+m-1} p_j(\hat{\boldsymbol{\theta}}) = \sum_{j=n}^{n+m-1} w(\kappa_j(\hat{\boldsymbol{\theta}})Q, \theta_j)$.

As an application of this theorem, we can set $\kappa_j(\hat{\boldsymbol{\theta}}) \equiv 1$, i.e., every model user gets full access permission to the FL model. In this case, $w(\kappa_j(\hat{\boldsymbol{\theta}})Q, \theta_j) = w(Q, \theta_j)$, and we can find an interim incentive compatible and interim individually rational payment rule $\boldsymbol{p}(\hat{\boldsymbol{\theta}})$ such that $-\sum_{j=n}^{n+m-1} p_j(\hat{\boldsymbol{\theta}}) = \sum_{j=n}^{n+m-1} w(Q, \theta_j)$.

As an example, consider the following payment rule:

$$p_j(\hat{\boldsymbol{\theta}}) = -w(Q, \hat{\theta}_j) + \beta[\alpha - ln(\text{Prior}(\hat{\boldsymbol{\theta}}_{-j}|\hat{\theta}_j))], \tag{12}$$

where β and α are two constants. We can prove that when β is large enough, $p_j(\hat{\boldsymbol{\theta}})$ is interim incentive compatible. To understand this, noticing that if model user j reports a $\hat{\theta}_j$ lower than his true θ_j.

To see this, noticing that the Lagrange equation for model user j to maximize its utility is

$$\frac{\partial}{\partial \text{Prior}(\hat{\boldsymbol{\theta}}_{-j}|\hat{\theta}_j)}\{\mathbb{E}_{\text{Prior}(\hat{\boldsymbol{\theta}}_{-j}|\theta_j)}p_j(\hat{\boldsymbol{\theta}}) + \lambda[\sum_{\hat{\boldsymbol{\theta}}_{-j}} \text{Prior}(\hat{\boldsymbol{\theta}}_{-j}|\hat{\theta}_j) - 1]\}$$

$$= -\frac{\partial \mathbb{E}_{\text{Prior}(\hat{\boldsymbol{\theta}}_{-j}|\theta_j)}w(Q, \hat{\theta}_j)}{\partial \text{Prior}(\hat{\boldsymbol{\theta}}_{-j}|\hat{\theta}_j)} - \beta \cdot \frac{\text{Prior}(\hat{\boldsymbol{\theta}}_{-j}|\theta_j)}{\text{Prior}(\hat{\boldsymbol{\theta}}_{-j}|\hat{\theta}_j)} + \lambda = 0, \tag{13}$$

where λ is the Lagrange multiplier for the constraint $\sum_{\hat{\boldsymbol{\theta}}_{-j}} \text{Prior}(\hat{\boldsymbol{\theta}}_{-j}|\hat{\theta}_j) \equiv 1$. When β is large enough compared to $\frac{\partial \mathbb{E}_{\text{Prior}(\hat{\boldsymbol{\theta}}_{-j}|\theta_j)}w(Q, \hat{\theta}_j)}{\partial \text{Prior}(\hat{\boldsymbol{\theta}}_{-j}|\hat{\theta}_j)}$, solving the Lagrange equation in Eq. 13 results in

$$\frac{\text{Prior}(\hat{\boldsymbol{\theta}}_{-j}|\theta_j)}{\text{Prior}(\hat{\boldsymbol{\theta}}_{-j}|\hat{\theta}_j)} \simeq \frac{\lambda}{\beta}, \forall \hat{\boldsymbol{\theta}}_{-j}. \tag{14}$$

Therefore, $\text{Prior}(\hat{\boldsymbol{\theta}}_{-j}|\theta_j)$ has to be equivalent to $\text{Prior}(\hat{\boldsymbol{\theta}}_{-j}|\hat{\theta}_j)$, i.e., $\hat{\boldsymbol{\theta}}_{-j} = \boldsymbol{\theta}_{-j}$.

If we set $\alpha = \mathbb{E}_{\text{Prior}(\boldsymbol{\theta})}ln[\text{Prior}(\boldsymbol{\theta}_{-j}|\theta_j)]$, the payment rule in Eq. 12 is ex-ante individual rational and extracts full consumer surplus ex ante. We can use automated mechanism design to find a *Crémer-McLean mechanism* that is also ex-post individual rational and extracts full consumer surplus ex post, as explained in the following sub-section.

4.2   Training Crémer-McLean Mechanism

The Crémer-McLean payments can be calculated by automated mechanism design techniques, e.g., refer to [1]. The method presented in this section is slightly different from that in [1], compared to which our method extracts full consumer surplus ex post instead of ex ante.

The Crémer-McLean payments $p(\theta)$ should simultaneously satisfy the three constraints in the following equation set 15, corresponding to ex-post full consumer surplus extraction, interim incentive compatibility and ex-post individual rationality, respectively.

$$\begin{cases} -\sum_{j=n}^{n+m-1} p_j(\theta) = \sum_{j=n}^{n+m-1} w(Q, \theta_j), \ \forall \theta; \\ \sum_{\theta'_{-j}} [w(Q, \theta_j) + p_j(\theta_j, \theta'_{-j})] \mathrm{Prior}(\theta'_{-j}|\theta_j) \geq 0, \ \forall j \in M, \theta_j \in \Theta_j; \\ \sum_{\theta'_{-j}} [p_j(\theta_j, \theta'_{-j}) - p_j(\hat{\theta}_j, \theta'_{-j})] \mathrm{Prior}(\theta'_{-j}|\theta_j) \geq 0, \ \forall j \in M, \theta_j \in \Theta_j. \end{cases} \quad (15)$$

Crémer-McLean Theorem guarantees that there is a solution $p(\theta)$ to Eq. 15. In order to find such a solution, we can minimize the following LOSS in Eq. 16, because it is easy to see that $p(\theta)$ is a solution to Eq. 15 i.f.f. it minimizes the LOSS in Eq. 16 to 0. With such a LOSS function, we can easily learn the demand-side Crémer-McLean payments by applying standard backpropagation algorithms.

$$LOSS = \{ \sum_{j=n}^{n+m-1} [w(Q, \theta_j) + p_j(\theta)] \}^2 \quad (16)$$

$$+ \sum_{j=n}^{n+m-1} ReLu\{ -\sum_{\theta'_{-j}} [w(Q, \theta_j) + p_j(\theta_j, \theta'_{-j})] \mathrm{Prior}(\theta'_{-j}|\theta_j) \}$$

$$+ \sum_{j=n}^{n+m-1} ReLu\{ -\sum_{\theta'_{-j}} [p_j(\theta_j, \theta'_{-j}) - p_j(\hat{\theta}_j, \theta'_{-j})] \mathrm{Prior}(\theta'_{-j}|\theta_j) \},$$

where $\theta, \theta', \hat{\theta}$ are drawn randomly from the prior distribution of θ.

5   A Supply-Side FL Incentive Mechanism - PVCG

As a counterpart of Crémer-McLean mechanism, which is optimal on the demand side, we introduce an optimal supply-side procurement auction in this section. This proposed procurement auction, accompanied by the demand-side Crémer-McLean mechanism, maximizes producer surplus by incentivizing data providers to offer all their data to the federation and truthfully report their cost types. For more discussions on PVCG, refer to [3].

As explained in Sect. 2.3. When designing the supply-side mechanism, we assume the federation income $I(Q)$ and the model quality $Q(\hat{d} \odot \eta)$ are exogenous functions. For example, when Crémer-McLean mechanism is adopted on the demand side, we know the federation income is:

$$I(Q) = -\sum_{j=n}^{n+m-1} p_j(\theta) = \sum_{j=n}^{n+m-1} w(\kappa_j(\theta)Q, \theta_j), \quad (17)$$

where θ is assumed to be an exogenous parameter, so we can ignore it when we focus on the supply side. Because the federation income indirectly depends on $Q(\hat{d} \odot \eta)$, we also write $I(\hat{d} \odot \eta) = I(Q(\hat{d} \odot \eta))$.

5.1   The Procurement Auction

One can carry out the proposed procurement auction and compute the payments to data providers by following the following steps.

Step 1. Data providers claim datasets to offer and bid on cost types

As the first step, every data provider submits a sealed bid for their respective claimed datasets and cost types. The claimed dataset $\hat{d}_i$ is the best dataset that data provider i claims it can offer to federated learning. It may differ from the dataset $\bar{d}_i$ actually owned by data provider i. Similarly, the reported cost type $\hat{\gamma}_i$ may differ from the true cost type γ_i.

Step 2. The coordinator chooses the optimal acceptance ratios

Then, the coordinator decides how many data to accept from each data provider. It chooses $d_i \leq \hat{d}_i, i = 0, \ldots, n - 1$ that maximize the social surplus. Equivalently, the coordinator calculates the optimal *acceptance ratio* $\eta_i \in [0, 1]^{\dim(d_i)} = d_i \oslash \hat{d}_i$ such that $d_i = \hat{d}_i \odot \eta_i$, where $[0, 1]$ denotes the interval between 0 and 1.

The optimal acceptance ratios $(\eta_0^*, \ldots, \eta_{n-1}^*) = \eta^*$ are calculated according to the following formula:

$$\eta^* = \mathrm{argmax}_{\eta \in [0,1]^{\dim(x_i) \times n}} \{S(\hat{x} \odot \eta, \hat{\gamma})\} \tag{18}$$

$$= \underset{\eta \in [0,1]^{\dim(d_i) \times n}}{\mathrm{argmax}} \quad I(\hat{d} \odot \eta) - \sum_{i=0}^{n-1} c_i(\hat{d}_i \odot \eta_i, \hat{\gamma}_i).$$

Because different $(\hat{d}, \hat{\gamma})$ results in different η^*, η^* is written as $\eta^*(\hat{d}, \hat{\gamma})$. Correspondingly, the maximum producer surplus is denoted by $S^*(\hat{d}, \hat{\gamma}) = I(\hat{d} \odot \eta^*(\hat{d}, \hat{\gamma})) - \sum_{i=0}^{n-1} c_i(\hat{d}_i \odot \eta_i^*(\hat{d}, \hat{\gamma}), \hat{\gamma}_i)$.

It is worth noting that although $S^*(\hat{d}, \hat{\gamma})$ and $S(d, \gamma)$ both represent producer surplus, they are different functions. The first parameter d in $S(\cdot)$ is the accepted dataset, whereas the first parameter $\hat{d}$ in $S^*(\cdot)$ is the claimed dataset. d and $\hat{d}$ are related by $d = \hat{d} \odot \eta^*$.

Step 3. Data providers contribute accepted datasets to federated learning

In this step, data providers are required to contribute the accepted dataset $\hat{d} \odot \eta^*$ to federated learning. Since in the first step, data provider i has claimed the ability to offer a dataset no worse than $\hat{d}_i$, if it cannot contribute $\hat{d}_i \odot \eta_i^* \leq \hat{d}_i$, we impose a high punishment on it. With the contributed datasets, data providers collaboratively produce the output virtual product, bringing income $I(\hat{d} \odot \eta^*)$ to the federation.

Step 4. The coordinator makes transfer payments to data providers according to the PVCG sharing rule

In this final step, the coordinator pays data providers according to the PVCG sharing rule. The PVCG payment

$$p_i(\cdot) = \tau_i(\cdot) + h_i^*(\cdot) \tag{19}$$

is composed of two parts, the *VCG payment* τ_i and the *optimal adjustment payment* h_i^*. The VCG payment is designed to induce truthfulness, i.e., the reported capacity limits $\hat{d}$ and reported cost type $\hat{\gamma}$ are equal to the true capacity limits $\bar{d}$ and true cost type γ. The adjustment payment is optimized so that ex-post individual rationality and ex-post weak budget balancedness can also be attained.

With η^* calculated in Step 2, the VCG payment τ_i to data provider i is:

$$\tau_i = S^*(\hat{d}, \hat{\gamma}) - S_{-i}^*(\hat{d}_{-i}, \hat{\gamma}_{-i}) + c(\hat{d}_i \odot \eta_i^*(\hat{x}, \hat{\gamma}))$$
$$= [I(\hat{d} \odot \eta^*(\hat{d}, \hat{\gamma})) - I(\hat{d}_{-i} \odot \eta^{-i*}(\hat{d}_{-i}, \hat{\gamma}_{-i}))]$$
$$- \sum_{k=0,\neq i}^{n-1} [c(\hat{d}_k \odot \eta_k^*(\hat{d}, \hat{\gamma}, \hat{\theta}), \hat{\gamma}_k) - c(\hat{d}_k \odot \eta_k^{-i*}(\hat{d}_{-i}, \hat{\gamma}_{-i}, \hat{\theta}), \hat{\gamma}_k)], \tag{20}$$

where $(\hat{d}_{-i}, \hat{\gamma}_{-i})$ denotes the claimed datasets and the reported cost types excluding data provider i. η^{-i*} and $S_{-i}^*(\hat{d}_{-i}, \hat{\gamma}_{-i})$ are the corresponding optimal acceptance ratios and maximum producer surplus. Note that η^{-i*} is different from η_{-i}^*: the former maximizes $S(\hat{d}_{-i} \odot \eta_{-i}, \hat{\gamma}_{-i})$, whereas the latter is the component of η^* that maximizes $S(\hat{d} \odot \eta, \hat{\gamma})$. $\tau = (\tau_0, \ldots, \tau_{n-1})$ is a function of $(\hat{d}, \hat{\gamma})$, written as $\tau(\hat{d}, \hat{\gamma})$.

The *adjustment payment* $h_i(\hat{d}_{-i}, \hat{\gamma}_{-i})$ is a function of $(\hat{d}_{-i}, \hat{\gamma}_{-i})$. The optimal adjustment payments $(h_0^*(\cdot), \ldots, h_{n-1}^*(\cdot)) = h^*(\cdot)$ are determined by solving the following *functional equation* (a type of equation in which the unknowns are functions instead of variables; refer to [11] for more details):

$$\sum_{i=0}^{n-1} \mathrm{ReLu}[-(S^*(d, \gamma) - S_{-i}^*(d_{-i}, \gamma_{-i})) - h_i(d_{-i}, \gamma_{-i})]$$
$$+ \mathrm{ReLu}\{\sum_{i=0}^{n-1}[(S^*(d, \gamma) - S_{-i}^*(d_{-i}, \gamma_{-i}) + h_i(d_{-i}, \gamma_{-i})] - S^*(d, \gamma)\} \tag{21}$$
$$\equiv 0, \qquad \forall (\bar{d}, \gamma) \in \mathrm{supp}(\mathrm{Prior}(d, \gamma)),$$

where $\mathrm{supp}(\mathrm{Prior}(d, \gamma))$ is the *support* of the *prior distribution* $\mathrm{Prior}(d, \gamma)$ of the true parameters (d, γ). Support is a terminology from *measure theory*, defined as $\mathrm{supp}(\mathrm{Prior}(d, \gamma)) = \{(d, \gamma) | \mathrm{Prior}(d, \gamma) > 0\}$. In general, there is no closed-form solution to Eq. 21, so we employ neural network techniques to learn the solution, as is explained in the following sub-section.

Through rigorous mathematical derivation, we can prove that with some reasonable assumptions, the PVCG payment rule thus calculated is dominant incentive compatible, allocative efficient, ex-post individual rational, and ex-post weak budget balanced. For detailed proofs of these properties, refer to [3].

5.2 Learning the Optimal Adjustment Payments

We can prove that the solution $h^*(\cdot)$ to Eq. 21, if existing, is also a solution to the following minimization problem:

$$h^*(\cdot) = \operatorname{argmin}_{h(\cdot)} \mathbb{E}_{(\bar{x},\gamma,\theta)}\{\text{LOSS}\}, \tag{22}$$

where the expectation is over the prior distribution of $(\bar{x},\gamma,\theta)$. Here, we bring back the valuation type θ because we want the adjustment payments applicable to all possible θ. Note that different θ results in different federation income function $I(\hat{d} \odot \eta)$. Hence the maximum producer surplus also depends on θ.

LOSS is defined as

$$\text{LOSS} = \text{Loss1} + \text{Loss2} = 0, \tag{23}$$

where

$$\text{Loss1} = \sum_{i=0}^{n-1} \text{ReLu}[-(S^*(\bar{x},\gamma,\theta) - S^*_{-i}(\bar{x}_{-i},\gamma_{-i},\theta))$$
$$- h_i(\bar{x}_{-i},\gamma_{-i},\theta)] \quad \text{and} \tag{24}$$

$$\text{Loss2} = \text{ReLu}[\sum_{i=0}^{n-1}[(S^*(\bar{x},\gamma,\theta) - S^*_{-i}(\bar{x}_{-i},\gamma_{-i},\theta))$$
$$+ h_i(\bar{x}_{-i},\gamma_{-i},\theta)] - S^*(\bar{x},\gamma,\theta)]. \tag{25}$$

This fact informs us that we can learn the optimal adjustment payments $h^*(\cdot)$ by minimizing the expected LOSS function. Also, we know neural networks can approximate arbitrary continuous functions to arbitrary precisions [7]. Therefore, we construct n neural networks $\text{NET}_i^h, i \in N$ to approximate $h_i(\cdot), i \in N$. Output nodes of these n networks, denoted by $\text{NET}_i^h.o, i \in N$, are combined into a single *composite neural network* in Fig. 2 with the loss function in Eq. 23–25.

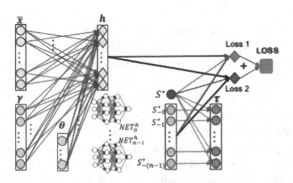

Fig. 2. The structure of the composite neural network of PVCG

The training data $(\bar{d}^t, \gamma^t, \theta^t), t = 0, 1, \ldots, T$ are drawn from their prior distribution $\mathrm{Prior}(\bar{d}, \gamma, \theta)$ and T is the sample size. For the tth sample, $\tau^t = \tau(\bar{d}^t, \gamma^t, \theta^t)$, $S^{*t} = S^*(\bar{d}^t, \gamma^t, \theta^t)$, and $S^{*t}_{-i} = S^*(\bar{d}^t_{-i}, \gamma^t_{-i}, \theta^t)$. Since we only need synthetic data to train this network, we can generate as many data as needed. As a result, LOSS can be minimized to its theoretical minimum almost perfectly in experiments.

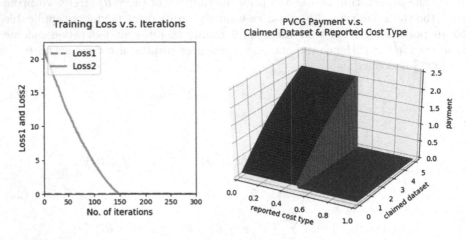

Fig. 3. Training loss v.s. iterations (left) and PVCG payment v.s. reported capacity limit & reported cost type (right)

To illustrate the effectiveness of this neural network method, we learned the adjustment payments for a hypothetical scenario. We set the individual valuation functions and individual cost functions as follows:

$$v(d) = \theta_i \sqrt{n(\sum_{k=0}^{n-1} d_k)} \text{ and } c_i(d_i, \gamma_i) = \gamma_i d_i, i \in N. \tag{26}$$

We report the experiment results for $n = 10, m = 2$, $\mathrm{Prior}(\bar{x}_i) = \mathrm{Uniform}[0, 5], i \in N$, $\mathrm{Prior}(\gamma_i) = \mathrm{Uniform}[0, 1], i \in N$, and $\mathrm{Prior}(\theta_j) = [0, 1], j \in M$. We let $\mathrm{NET}^h_i, i \in N$ each have three 10-dimensional hidden layers.

The loss curve is shown in the left figure of Fig. 3. The training loss fast converges to 0, as expected. After we obtain the trained networks $[\mathrm{NET}^h_i], i \in N$, we can use trained networks to calculate PVCG payments $p(\hat{d}, \hat{\gamma}, \hat{\theta})$ for any reported $(\hat{d}, \hat{\gamma}, \hat{\theta})$. For illustration, we draw p_0, the payment to data provider 0, with respect to $\hat{d}_0$ and $\hat{\gamma}_0$ in the right figure in Fig. 3, fixing parameters of other participants at $\hat{d}_i \equiv 2.5, \hat{\gamma}_i \equiv 0.5, i \in N, \neq 0, \hat{\theta}_j \equiv 0.5, j \in M$.

We can see that p_0 increases with $\hat{d}_0$. This indicates that the more data a data provider claim, the more data are accepted from this data provider; hence, it receives higher payments. Also, p_0 remains constant with γ_0 when γ_0 is below a threshold and sharply drops to around 0 when γ_0 passes the threshold.

This implies that the payment to a data provider should only be affected by its contribution to the federated learning process rather than its cost, but if a data provider's cost is too high, the optimal social choice is to exclude this data provider from the federation and thus pay it nothing.

6 Summary

In this chapter, we set up a game-theoretic framework for studying FL incentive mechanisms. We introduced the key concepts, mathematical symbols, definitions, and key assumptions that are necessary for readers to understand the FL incentive mechanism design problem and its objectives. Then, we suggest breaking down the original complicated problem into two sub-problems: a demand-side problem and a supply-side problem. We provide a checklist for FL practitioners to quickly understand the specifications and objectives of any given FL incentive mechanism so that real-world FL practitioners can choose the most appropriate mechanism without understanding its internal workings.

As examples, we introduced two FL incentive mechanisms designed under our proposed framework: the Crémer-McLean mechanism on the demand side and a VCG-based procurement auction, PVCG, on the supply side. These mechanisms both guarantee truthfulness, i.e., they encourage participants to truthfully report their private information and offer all their data to the federation. The Crémer-McLean mechanism, together with PVCG, attains allocative efficiency, individual rationality, and weak budget balancedness at the same time, easing the tension between these objectives.

References

1. Albert, M., Conitzer, V., Lopomo, G.: Assessing the robustness of Cremer-McLean with automated mechanism design. In: Twenty-Ninth AAAI Conference on Artificial Intelligence (2015)
2. Börgers, T., Krahmer, D.: An Introduction to the Theory of Mechanism Design. Oxford University Press, Oxford (2015)
3. Cong, M., Weng, X., Yu, H., Qu, J., Yiu, S.M.: Optimal procurement auction for cooperative production of virtual products: Vickrey-Clarke-Groves Meet Crémer-McLean. CoRR. arXiv:2007.14780 (2000)
4. Cong, M., Weng, X., Yu, H., Qu, Z.: FML incentive mechanism design: concepts, basic settings, and taxonomy. In: the 1st International Workshop on Federated Machine Learning for User Privacy and Data Confidentiality (FL-IJCAI 2019) (2019)
5. Crémer, J., McLean, R.P.: Optimal selling strategies under uncertainty for a discriminating monopolist when demands are interdepen0 denty. Econometrica **53**, 345–361 (1985)
6. EU: Regulation (EU) 2016/679 of the European parliament and of the council of 27 April 2016 on the protection of natural persons with regard to the processing of personal data and on the free movement of such data, and repealing directive 95/46. Off. J. Eur. Union (OJ) **59**(1–88), 294 (2016)

7. Funahashi, K.I.: On the approximate realization of continuous mappings by neural networks. Neural Netw. **2**(3), 183–192 (1989)
8. Jackson, M.O.: Mechanism theory. Available at SSRN 2542983 (2014)
9. Kosenok, G., Severinov, S.: Individually rational, budget-balanced mechanisms and allocation of surplus. J. Econ. Theory **140**(1), 126–161 (2008)
10. Narahari, Y.: Game Theory and Mechanism Design, vol. 4. World Scientific, Singapore (2014)
11. Rassias, T.: Functional Equations and Inequalities, vol. 518. Springer, Dordrecht (2012). https://doi.org/10.1007/978-94-011-4341-7
12. Yang, Q., Liu, Y., Chen, T., Tong, Y.: Federated machine learning: concept and applications. ACM Trans. Intell. Syst. Technol. (TIST) **10**(2), 12 (2019)

Applications

Application

Federated Recommendation Systems

Liu Yang[2], Ben Tan[1], Vincent W. Zheng[1(✉)], Kai Chen[2], and Qiang Yang[1,2]

[1] WeBank, Shenzhen, China
{btan,vincentz}@webank.com
[2] Hong Kong University of Science and Technology, Hong Kong, China
{lyangau,kaichen,qyang}@cse.ust.hk

Abstract. Recommender systems are heavily data-driven. In general, the more data the recommender systems use, the better the recommendation results are. However, due to privacy and security constraints, directly sharing user data is undesired. Such decentralized silo issues commonly exist in recommender systems. There have been many pilot studies on protecting data privacy and security when utilizing data silos. But, most works still need the users' private data to leave the local data repository. Federated learning is an emerging technology, which tries to bridge the data silos and build machine learning models without compromising user privacy and data security. In this chapter, we introduce a new notion of federated recommender systems, which is an instantiation of federated learning on decentralized recommendation. We formally define the problem of the federated recommender systems. Then, we focus on categorizing and reviewing the current approaches from the perspective of the federated learning. Finally, we put forward several promising future research challenges and directions.

1 Introduction

The recommender system (RecSys) plays an essential role in real-world applications. It has become an indispensable tool for coping with information overload and is a significant business for a lot of internet companies around the world. In general, the more data RecSys use, the better the recommendation performance we can obtain. The RecSys need to know as much as possible from the user to provide a reasonable recommendation. They collect the private user data, such as the behavioral information, the contextual information, the domain knowledge, the item metadata, the purchase history, the recommendation feedback, the social data, and so on. In pursuit of better recommendations, some recommender systems integrate multiple data sources from other organizations. All these informative user data is centrally stored at the database of each organization to support different kinds of recommendation services.

Liu Yang and Ben Tan are both co-first authors with equal contribution. This work was done during Liu Yang's internship at WeBank.

Q. Yang et al. (Eds.): Federated Learning, LNAI 12500, pp. 225–239, 2020.
https://doi.org/10.1007/978-3-030-63076-8_16

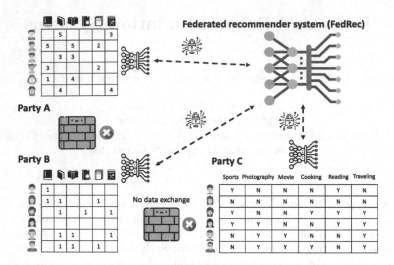

Fig. 1. The illustration of a Federated Recommender System. FedRec addresses the data silo issue and builds recommender systems without compromising privacy and security.

However, data centralization in RecSys could lead to serious privacy and security risks. For example, recommenders may unsolicitedly collect users' private data and share the data with third parties for profits. Besides, user privacy may also leak during data transmission. Moreover, in recent years, several acts protecting the privacy and security have come out, such as the General Data Protection Regulation (GDPR)[1]. The protection of privacy and security is an integral part of the RecSys. There have been pilot studies to protect user privacy and data security in the RecSys [6]. These approaches typically utilize obfuscation or cryptography techniques. Some of them add noises in different procedures of the recommendation. Others encrypt data before transmitting it to the recommender. However, most of them still need private data to leave their local data repository. How to enable recommendations across data silos securely and privately remains a challenging task.

Federated learning is an emerging technology for decentralized machine learning [13]. It protects parties' data privacy in the joint training of machine learning models. Parties could be mobile devices or organizations [26]. User private data is stored locally at each party. Only the intermediate results, *e.g.*, parameter updates, are used to communicate with other parties. Federated learning allows knowledge to be shared among multiple parties without compromising user privacy and data security. Compared with the conventional data-centralized machine learning approaches, federated learning reduces both the privacy risks and costs. This area has been paid more and more attention recently, in both academia and industry.

---

[1] GDPR is a regulation in EU law on data protection and privacy in the European Union and the European Economic Area. https://gdpr.eu/.

In this chapter, we introduce a new notion of Federated Recommender System (FedRec), as shown in Fig. 1. Compared to the conventional RecSys, FedRec primarily protects user privacy and data security through decentralizing private user data locally at each party. According to the data structure of recommendation tasks, we conclude the FedRec categorization. Moreover, we illustrate with typical real-world scenarios for each categorization and explain the existing solutions according to each scenario. When building real-world FedRec, people could encounter different challenges. On the one hand, the prevalent RecSys is so complicated and continuously improved with the state-of-the-art machine learning algorithms. On the other hand, there exist many open questions as new challenges that recommendations bring to federated learning. For these challenges, we categorize them at two levels, *i.e.*, algorithm-level and system-level, and discuss the solutions in the existing works.

Overall, our contributions are threefold: 1) We propose the notion of FedRec and provide a categorization method according to the data structure of the RecSys; 2) We make a first survey on the existing works about FedRec in terms of each category; 3) We give a discussion about the challenges that exist in the FedRec.

2   Federated Recommender System

To protect privacy in RecSys, we introduce the new notion of the Federated Recommender System (FedRec). FedRec adopts the data decentralization architecture. Parties keep their private data locally and train recommendation models collaboratively in a secure and privacy-preserving way. Each party could be a RecSys or data provider. A RecSys party basically contains the rating information, the user profiles, and the item attributes. A data provider party owns more user profiles or item attributes. In the following parts of this section, firstly, we define the FedRec. Secondly, we conclude the categories of FedRec in terms of its data structure. In each category, we give the problem definition, describe typical real-world scenarios, and discuss corresponding related works.

2.1   Definition of Federated Recommender System

Define N parties, K of whom are recommender systems, *i.e.*, $\mathcal{G}_{k\in\{1,...,K\}} = \{\mathcal{U}_k, \mathcal{I}_k, \boldsymbol{R}_k, \boldsymbol{X}_k, \boldsymbol{X}_k'\}$. $\mathcal{U}_k = \{u_k^1, u_k^2, ..., u_k^{n_k}\}$ and $\mathcal{I}_k = \{i_k^1, i_k^2, ..., i_k^{m_k}\}$ stand for the user set and item set respectively. $\boldsymbol{R}_k \in \mathbb{R}^{n_k \times m_k}$ is the rating matrix. $\boldsymbol{X}_k \in \mathbb{R}^{n_k \times d_k}$ and $\boldsymbol{X}_k' \in \mathbb{R}^{m_k \times d_k'}$ represent the user profiles and item attributes respectively. The other H parties are data providers containing user profiles, *i.e.*, $\mathcal{D}_{h\in\{1,...,H\}} = \{\mathcal{U}_h, \boldsymbol{X}_h\}$, or item attributes, *i.e.*, $\mathcal{D}_h = \{\mathcal{I}_h, \boldsymbol{X}_h'\}$.

Definition 1. *FedRec aims to collaboratively train recommendation model(s) among multiple parties without direct access to the private data of each other:*

$$\underset{\tilde{\theta}_k}{\arg\min} \sum_{k=1}^{K} L(\boldsymbol{R}_k, f_{\tilde{\theta}_k}^{fed}(\mathcal{U}_k, \mathcal{I}_k | \mathcal{G}_k, z(\mathcal{G}_{k' \in \{1,\dots,K\} \setminus \{k\}}),$$

$$z(\mathcal{D}_{h \in \{1,\dots,H\}}))), \tag{1}$$

where $L(\cdot,\cdot)$ is a loss function, $f_{\tilde{\theta}_k}^{fed}(\cdot,\cdot)$ is the prediction model for the kth FedRec, and $z(\cdot)$ stands for the data processing technique that exchanges intermediate results between parties instead of the raw data.

We expect that the performance of FedRec is better than the performance of each RecSys training with its own data, while very close to the performance of simply aggregating all parties' data together without considering data privacy and security:

$$|V(f_{\tilde{\theta}_k}^{fed}) - V(f_{\theta_k})| > \delta \quad and \quad |V(f_{\tilde{\theta}_k}^{sum}) - V(f_{\tilde{\theta}_k}^{fed})| \leq \epsilon, \tag{2}$$

where $\delta \in \mathbb{R}^+$, $\epsilon \in \mathbb{R}^*$, and $V(\cdot)$ is the evaluation function utilized by RecSys. The prediction model f_{θ_k} is obtained via separately training the model with the recommender's own data:

$$\underset{\theta_k}{\arg\min} L(\boldsymbol{R}_k, f_{\theta_k}(\mathcal{U}_k, \mathcal{I}_k | \mathcal{G}_k)). \tag{3}$$

The recommender $f_{\tilde{\theta}_k}^{sum}$ is obtained via training the recommendation model with all parties' data simply consolidated together:

$$\underset{\tilde{\theta}_k}{\arg\min} \sum_{k=1}^{K} L(\boldsymbol{R}_k, f_{\tilde{\theta}_k}^{sum}(\mathcal{U}_k, \mathcal{I}_k | \mathcal{G}_{k' \in \{1,\dots,K\}},$$

$$\mathcal{D}_{h \in \{1,\dots,H\}})). \tag{4}$$

2.2   Categorization of Federated Recommender System

We categorize the typical scenarios of FedRec according to the data structure of the RecSys. RecSys mainly consists of two types of entities, *i.e.*, users and items. Shared users or items naturally connect the parties of FedRec. As shown in Fig. 2(a), 2(b) and 2(c), we divide FedRec into **Horizontal FedRec, Vertical FedRec** and **Transfer FedRec** according to the sharing situation of users and items. In this subsection, we describe the details of each category and provide typical scenarios for illustration. Related works about FedRec are discussed under the corresponding categories.

Horizontal Federated Recommender System. As shown in Fig. 2(a), the horizontal FedRec is introduced where items are shared, but users are different between parties. Under this setting, the parties could be in the form of individual users or sets of users.

Definition 2. *Given N parties and each party contains a set of users or an individual user, i.e., $\mathcal{G}_{i\in\{1,...,N\}} = \{\mathcal{U}_i, \mathcal{I}_i, \boldsymbol{R}_i, \boldsymbol{X}_i, \boldsymbol{X}_i'\}$, $\mathcal{U}_i \neq \mathcal{U}_j, \mathcal{I}_i = \mathcal{I}_j, \forall \mathcal{G}_i, \mathcal{G}_j, i \neq j$, horizontal FedRec aims to train a recommender model by integrating users' historical behaviors on shared items from different parties, without revealing user's privacy:*

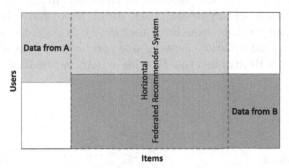

(a) Horizontal FedRec. Items are shared, but users are different between parties.

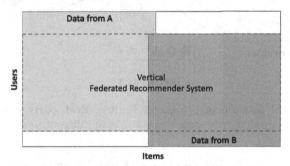

(b) Vertical FedRec. Users are shared, but items are different between parties.

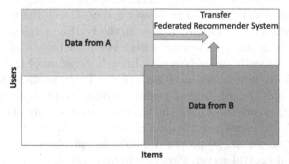

(c) Transfer FedRec. Neither users nor items are shared between parties.

Fig. 2. The categorization of federated recommender systems.

$$\arg\min_{\tilde{\theta}} \sum_{k=1}^{N} L(\boldsymbol{R}_k, f_{\tilde{\theta}}^{fed}(\mathcal{U}_k, \mathcal{I}_k | z(\mathcal{G}_{k' \in \{1,\dots,K\} \setminus \{k\}}))). \tag{5}$$

Typical Scenario of Horizontal FedRec. As shown in Fig. 3, users enjoy a personalized movie recommendation service provided by a movie recommender. But they do not want their private data to be collected. Inside the recommender, to preserve the data privacy of each user, we prefer to have the training data distributed on the local devices. Each user device is regarded as a party containing the rating information between one specific user and all items. Those devices can build a RecSys together to achieve both personalization and privacy requirements.

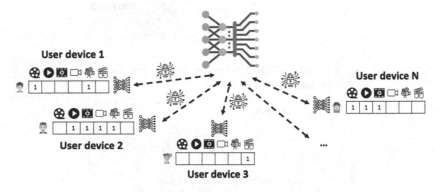

Fig. 3. The typical scenario of Horizontal FedRec. Each party is the device of an individual user. They share the same items but have different users.

Several current works focus on this scenario. [4] proposed a Federated Collaborative Filter (FCF) algorithm based on matrix factorization. In traditional RecSys, the matrix factorization algorithms work by decomposing the user-item rating matrix into the product of two lower matrices, *i.e.*, the user latent factors matrix and the item latent factors matrix. In the FedRec setting, FCF introduces a central server to maintain the shared item latent factors, while the user latent factors are stored locally on each device. In each iteration of training, the server distributes the item latent factors to each party. Then, parties update their user latent factor by local rating data and send the item latent factor updates back to the server for aggregation. During the training process, only the model updates are transmitted. No users' private data is collected. To avoid interaction with a third-party central server, [8] provided a fully-decentralized matrix factorization approach without central server. Parties communicate directly with each other to update the model. Besides, [5] proposed another decentralized method of matrix factorization. Local models are exchanged in the neighborhood, not with an arbitrary party. This approach further improves the performance of the algorithm. Moreover, [2] proposed a federated meta-learning framework for the recommendation. It regards the recommendation for each user as one separate task and designs a meta-learner to generate each task parameters. This framework utilizes a support set to generate the recommendation model on each party and computes the loss gradient on a query set. In addition, [11] offered another federated meta-learning algorithm for recommendation. It needs no separate support and query sets. The latter one performs relatively well within considerably fewer episodes in the experiments. Furthermore, [16] proposed a distributed factorization machine algorithm, which is known as DiFacto. It addresses the efficiency problem when scaling to large amounts of data and large numbers of users.

All the works mentioned above do not adopt other security methods. They own a privacy advantage compared to the data-centralized approaches. However, privacy risks still exist when transferring plain-text model parameters. A few works further utilize the obfuscation methods based on the data-centralized architecture. The obfuscation methods contain the anonymization, the randomization, and the differential privacy techniques. Among them, the differential privacy (DP) technique is a popular method. It incorporates random noise to anonymize data and protect privacy. It also offers a provable privacy guarantee and low computation costs. [19] proposed the private social recommendation (PrivSR) algorithm by utilizing the DP technique. This approach is based on a matrix factorization method with the friends-impacting regularizer. Since an inference attack can be conducted from the contribution of one particular user, the DP noise is added into the objective function to perturb the individual's involvement. [14] proposed the federated online learning to the rank algorithm by using users' online feedback. It trains the ranking model on local devices in a way that respects the users' privacy and utilizes the DP technique to protect model privacy on the server. DP noise is injected into the communicated values before transmitted to the server, which is different from the PrivSR. However, DP also introduces additional noise. These works involve a trade-off between performance and privacy.

To avoid performance loss, the other works make use of the cryptography techniques instead of the obfuscation methods. The cryptography methods contain homomorphic encryption (HE), secure multi-party computation (SMC) protocols, *etc.* They guarantee good security protection without the loss of accuracy. HE techniques have been widely utilized because it allows computing over encrypted data without access to the secret key. [1] proposed the secure federated matrix factorization algorithm (FedMF) with HE schemes. Each user encrypts the item latent factor updates with HE before transmitting. Besides, the item latent factor is aggregated and maintained by the central server under the encrypted form. No information of latent factors and updates will be leaked to the introduced server. [15] provided an efficient privacy-preserving item-based collaborative filtering algorithm. An SMC protocol is designed to compute the summation of private values of each party without revealing them. Then with this protocol, the PrivateCosine and PrivatePearson algorithm are implemented to calculate the item correlations. Final recommendations are generated using the correlations without revealing privacy.

Vertical Federated Recommender System. The vertical FedRec is shown in Fig. 2(b). Two parties shared the same user set, but different item set or feature spaces. Under this setting, the parties could be different recommenders or data providers.

Definition 3. *Given two parties, one of whom is a RecSys, i.e., $\mathcal{G}_A = \{\mathcal{U}_A, \mathcal{I}_A, \boldsymbol{R}_A, \boldsymbol{X}_A, \boldsymbol{X}'_A\}$, the other one is a data provider or the other recommender. Taking a data provider as an example, we have $\mathcal{D}_B = \{\mathcal{U}_B, \boldsymbol{X}_B\}$, and $\mathcal{U}_A = \mathcal{U}_B = \mathcal{U}$. The vertical FedRec aims to train a recommender model by exploiting the side information of users from the data provider or other recommenders. The training process is completed in a secure and privacy-preserving manner:*

$$\arg\min_{\tilde{\theta}} L(\boldsymbol{R}_A, f_{\tilde{\theta}}^{fed}(\mathcal{U}, \mathcal{I}_A, z(\boldsymbol{X}_B)|z(\mathcal{D}_B))). \tag{6}$$

Typical Scenario of Vertical FedRec. As illustrated in Fig. 4, the participants contain a RecSys, and a data provider. For instance, one party is a book RecSys and the other party is a data provider who can offer rich user profiles. They have a large set of users in common. The vertical FedRec helps to build a better book recommendation service without data privacy leakage.

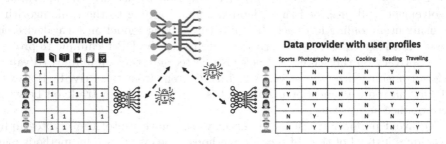

Fig. 4. The typical scenario of Vertical FedRec. One party is a book recommender, while the other one is a data provider with user profiles. They share the same users but have different items.

Several existing works have been designed for such a feature distributed learning problem where party A and B hold different feature sets. [10] proposed an asynchronous stochastic gradient descent algorithm. Each party could use an arbitrary model to map its local features to a local prediction. Then local predictions from different parties are aggregated into a final output using linear and nonlinear transformations. The training procedure of each party is allowed to be at various iterations up to a bounded delay. This approach does not share any raw data and local models. Therefore, it has fewer privacy risks. Besides, for a higher level of privacy, it can easily incorporate the DP technique. Similar to horizontal FedRec, there are also works that further utilize cryptography techniques. [3] presented a secure gradient-tree boosting algorithm. This algorithm adopts HE methods to provide lossless performance as well as preserving privacy. And [7] proposed a secure linear regression algorithm. MPC protocols are designed using garbled circuits to obtain a highly scalable solution.

Parties of vertical FedRec could also be two recommenders with different item sets. For instance, a movie RecSys and a book RecSys have a large user overlapping but different items to recommend. It is assumed that users share a similar taste in movies with books. With FedRec, the two parties want to train better recommendation algorithms together in a secure and privacy-preserving way. [21] proposed a secure, distributed item-based CF method. It jointly improves the effect of several RecSys, which offer different subsets of items to the same underlying population of users. Both the predicted ratings of items and their predicted rankings could be computed without compromising privacy nor predictions' accuracy.

Transfer Federated Recommender System. As Shown in Fig. 2(c), in the transfer federated recommender system, neither users nor items are shared between parties. In most cases, the parties are different recommender systems.

Definition 4. *Given two parties, who are different recommender systems, i.e.,* $\mathcal{G}_S = \{\mathcal{U}_S, \mathcal{I}_S, \boldsymbol{R}_S, \boldsymbol{X}_S, \boldsymbol{X}_S'\}$ *as the source-domain party,* $\mathcal{G}_T = \{\mathcal{U}_T, \mathcal{I}_T, \boldsymbol{R}_T, \boldsymbol{X}_T, \boldsymbol{X}_T'\}$ *as the target-domain party, and* $\mathcal{U}_S \neq \mathcal{U}_T, \mathcal{I}_S \neq \mathcal{I}_T$. *Generally,* $\boldsymbol{R}_S$ *contains much more rating information than* $\boldsymbol{R}_T$. *Transfer FedRec aims to train a recommender model by transferring knowledge from the source-domain party to the target-domain party, without revealing user privacy:*

$$\arg\min_{\tilde{\theta}} \sum_{k \in \{S,T\}}^{N} \lambda_k L(\boldsymbol{R}_k, f_{\tilde{\boldsymbol{\theta}}_k}^{fed}(\mathcal{U}_k, \mathcal{I}_k | z(\mathcal{G}_{k' \in \{S,T\} \setminus \{k\}}))), \tag{7}$$

where λ_k *is the weight for balancing the performance of two parties.*

Typical Scenario of Transfer FedRec. As shown in Fig. 5, a popular book recommender system in region A wants to help another new movie recommender system in region B to collaboratively learn a movie recommendation model. In this case, both users and items of the two parties are different.

Since both users and items are different between parties, it's challenging to construct a federated recommender system directly. However, federated transfer learning [20] offers a feasible scheme. A limited set of co-occurrence samples is used as a "bridge" to transfer knowledge from the source domain to the target domain. At first, parties update their neural networks using local data. Then, they together optimize the loss on the co-occurrence samples. The secret sharing technique is adopted to design a secure and efficient algorithm. Similarly, this algorithm can be applied in the transfer FedRec scenario via co-occurrence users or items.

As we have reviewed, horizontal FedRec managing RecSys across individuals or user sets is important and attracts lots of research attention. Vertical FedRec and transfer FedRec building RecSys among organizations are typical tasks in recommendation businesses. Yet, vertical and transfer FedRec are still underexplored areas with a lot of opportunities.

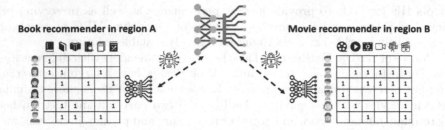

Fig. 5. The typical scenario of Transfer FedRec. One party is a book recommender, while the other one is a movie recommender in the different region. They share neither users nor items.

3   Challenges and Future Directions

In this section, we discuss the possible challenges when constructing FedRec. An industrial FedRec is more than the recommendation algorithms. It should also contain a comprehensive design of the system. Therefore, our discussion about the challenges is divided into the algorithm level and the system level. At the algorithm level, we discuss the possible difficulties of designing different federated recommender algorithms using popular models in the current recommendation area. Meanwhile, at the system level, we list several critical challenges of designing FedRec in terms of the characteristics of RecSys. Besides, we discuss current solutions for all the problems mentioned.

3.1   Algorithm-Level Challenges

Federated Deep Model for Recommendation. Deep recommendation models could cause severe problems when utilizing non-linear activation functions. Complex functions, *e.g.*, tanh and relu activation functions, are not well supported by HE. This limitation seriously affects the deep models' application in FedRec. For solving this problem, [9] utilized low degree polynomials as the approximation of activation functions. There exists a trade-off between the model performance and the degree of polynomial approximation. This work provides the polynomial approximations with the lowest degrees as possible for three common activation functions, *i.e.*, ReLU, Sigmoid, and Tanh.

Federated Graph Model for Recommendation. Protecting the privacy of structure information in the graph is the main difficulty of federalizing the graph-based models. The Graph-based models for recommendations utilize the relation information between users and items to enrich their representations. The relation information is more complicated than the feature information. Different secure methods are adopted to protect the privacy of the graph in the present works. For instance, [22] utilized a graph sampling method to improve both the efficiency and privacy of the privacy-preserving association rules mining approaches.

Users decide locally and privately, whether to become part of the sample. They are in control of their data and maintain sensitive item sets. Users with common interests are represented by the user groups. Neither the recommender nor other users know about the specific item sets of one particular user.

Federated Reinforcement Learning Model for Recommendation. The challenge of federalizing reinforcement learning models is to delicately design the state, action, and reward to catch the instant user interest and decide what to share among parties. Although reinforcement learning has an vital role in RecSys, its application in FedRec is still underexplored. Yet, there have been several works about federated reinforcement learning applied in other areas. [18] provided the lifelong federated reinforcement learning architecture for robots to perform lifelong learning of navigation in cloud robotic systems. A knowledge fusion algorithm and transfer learning approach are designed to fuse the robots' prior knowledge and make robots quickly adapt to the new environments.

3.2 System-Level Challenges

Design of Recall and Ranking in FedRec. The main challenge in the system level is to design privacy-preserving recall and ranking procedures with real-time feedback. RecSys sequentially adopts these two procedures to obtain the final recommendations. Conventionally, RecSys centrally collects the users' private data, and these two steps are designed to carry out on the central server. However, concerning user privacy, FedRec should modify the original design.

We discuss two extreme cases. The first case is server-side recall and participant side ranking. Firstly, each party sends the encrypted "noisy" model parameters to the server. Then recall procedure is carried out on the server-side. The resulted top-N items are then sent back to each party. Then, the ranking procedure is carried out at each party. There is a chance of privacy leakage because the server knows the exact results of recall. Several works have tried to address this problem. For example, [12] utilizes the private stream searching technique to obtain the result delivery without exposing its contents. The second case is participant-side recall and ranking. The server sends all item attributes and content to each party. Then, the whole recall and ranking procedures are carried out on the participant side. This design contains no leak of user privacy but will result in copious communication costs. Besides, it requires lots of computation resources and local storage for each party. However, with the fast development of 5G technology[2] in recent years, the communication cost problem could be alleviated to some extent.

Communication Cost in FedRec. Communication cost is one of the major problems that affect the performance of federated learning. Because of the

---

[2] 5G is the fifth generation wireless technology for digital cellular networks.

high-dimensional features and real-time requirement of RecSys, the communication cost problem is much serious in FedRec. Pilot works have tried to compress the high-dimensional features. Communication-mitigated federated learning (CMFL) [23] assumes that some local optimizations are not helpful to the global convergence, therefore reducing the total bits transferred in each update via data compression. CMFL identifies irrelevant updates made by each party and precludes them from updating. In more detail, it provides clients with feedback information regarding the global tendency of model updating. Each client checks if its update aligns with this global tendency and is relevant enough to model improvement.

Flexibility and Scalability in FedRec. As the number of parties keeps increasing, the challenge is to design better model-parallel and model-updating scheduling schema to guarantee convergence of the FedRec models. Many of the federated learning systems adopt a synchronous client-server architecture [17,25], which is inflexible and unscalable. In the RecSys, millions of users consume the recommendation services. Too many parties checking in at the same time can congest the network on the central server. It is hard to guarantee that all parties could participate in the whole process of federated training. As a result, the performance of the federated model severely suffers. Various solutions have been designed to address this challenge. Based on the client-server architecture, [25] proposed a new asynchronous federated optimization algorithm. The central server immediately updates the global model whenever receiving a local model from one arbitrary party. And the communication between parties and the central server is non-blocking. Abandoning the client-server architecture, [8] proposed the gossip learning algorithm, which can be regarded as a variant of federated learning with a fully decentralized architecture. Parties directly communicate with each other for collaborative training.

Non-IID Data in FedRec. The "long tail" phenomenon is common in RecSys and makes the non-IID data problem inevitable in FedRec. The performance of federated learning severely degrades due to the highly skewed non-IID. As the distance between the data distribution at each party becomes more significant, the accuracy of the model decreases accordingly. To alleviate the non-IID problem, a data-sharing strategy has been proposed by reducing the distance [27]. This approach shares a global data set of a uniform distribution over all classes among parties. In the initialization stage, a warm-up model, trained on the globally shared data, is distributed to each party instead of a random model. Then, the shared data and private data are used together to train the local model at each party.

Malicious Participants Cooperation in FedRec. In reality, the parties in the RecSys have a high probability of being untrustworthy [6]. These parties do not follow the frequently used assumption that both the participants and the central server are honest-but-curious. They may behave incorrectly in gradient collecting or parameter updating, while the servers may be malicious as well. Therefore, the honest parties could have a privacy leak in these scenarios. Among the existing solutions, [24] proposed the DeepChain as one possible solution, which combines the Blockchain[3] and federated learning. Based on the Blockchain technique, DeepChain provides a value-driven incentive mechanism to force the participants to behave correctly, which preserves the privacy of local gradients and guarantees the auditability of the training process. Smart contracts, *i.e.*, the trading contract and the processing contract, are utilized to guide the secure training process.

4   Conclusion

In this chapter, we investigate the user privacy and data security in RecSys. The risk of security and privacy is mainly raised by the central collection and storage of users' private data. Considering the growing privacy concern and related acts like GDPR, we introduce the new notion of the federated recommender system (FedRec). With FedRec, multiple parties could collaboratively train better recommendation models with users' private data maintained locally at each party. We categorize FedRec according to the data structure of RecSys. Many existing works focus on the horizontal FedRec scenarios, while the vertical and transfer FedRec have been given less attention. Besides, many current prevailing recommendation algorithms have not been applied in FedRec, either. Therefore, FedRec is a promising direction with huge potential opportunities. In our future work, we will concentrate on implementing an open-source FedRec library with rich recommendation algorithms and overcoming the system-level challenges as they arise.

References

1. Chai, D., Wang, L., Chen, K., Yang, Q.: Secure federated matrix factorization. arXiv preprint arXiv:1906.05108 (2019)
2. Chen, F., Dong, Z., Li, Z., He, X.: Federated meta-learning for recommendation. arXiv preprint arXiv:1802.07876 (2018)
3. Cheng, K., Fan, T., Jin, Y., Liu, Y., Chen, T., Yang, Q.: SecureBoost: a lossless federated learning framework. arXiv preprint arXiv:1901.08755 (2019)
4. Ammad-ud din, M., et al.: Federated collaborative filtering for privacy-preserving personalized recommendation system. arXiv preprint arXiv:1901.09888 (2019)
5. Duriakova, E., et al.: PDMFRec: a decentralised matrix factorisation with tunable user-centric privacy. In: Proceedings of the 13th ACM Conference on Recommender Systems (2019)

---

[3] A blockchain is a growing list of records, called blocks, that are linked using cryptography.

6. Friedman, A., Knijnenburg, B.P., Vanhecke, K., Martens, L., Berkovsky, S.: Privacy aspects of recommender systems. In: Ricci, F., Rokach, L., Shapira, B. (eds.) Recommender Systems Handbook, pp. 649–688. Springer, Boston, MA (2015). https://doi.org/10.1007/978-1-4899-7637-6_19

7. Gascón, A., et al.: Secure linear regression on vertically partitioned datasets. IACR Cryptology ePrint Archive (2016)

8. Hegedűs, I., Danner, G., Jelasity, M.: Decentralized recommendation based on matrix factorization: a comparison of gossip and federated learning. In: Cellier, P., Driessens, K. (eds.) ECML PKDD 2019. CCIS, vol. 1167, pp. 317–332. Springer, Cham (2020). https://doi.org/10.1007/978-3-030-43823-4_27

9. Hesamifard, E., Takabi, H., Ghasemi, M.: CryptoDL: deep neural networks over encrypted data. arXiv preprint arXiv:1711.05189 (2017)

10. Hu, Y., Niu, D., Yang, J., Zhou, S.: FDML: a collaborative machine learning framework for distributed features. In: Proceedings of the 25th ACM SIGKDD International Conference on Knowledge Discovery & Data Mining (2019)

11. Jalalirad, A., Scavuzzo, M., Capota, C., Sprague, M.: A simple and efficient federated recommender system. In: Proceedings of the 6th IEEE/ACM International Conference on Big Data Computing, Applications and Technologies (2019)

12. Jiang, J., Gui, X., Shi, Z., Yuan, X., Wang, C.: Towards secure and practical targeted mobile advertising. In: Proceedings of the 11th International Conference on Mobile Ad-hoc and Sensor Networks (2015)

13. Kairouz, P., et al.: Advances and open problems in federated learning. arXiv preprint arXiv:1912.04977 (2019)

14. Kharitonov, E.: Federated online learning to rank with evolution strategies. In: Proceedings of the 20th ACM International Conference on Web Search and Data Mining (2019)

15. Li, D., et al.: An algorithm for efficient privacy-preserving item-based collaborative filtering. Future Gener. Comput. Syst. **55**, 311–320 (2016)

16. Li, M., Liu, Z., Smola, A.J., Wang, Y.X.: DiFacto: distributed factorization machines. In: Proceedings of the 9th ACM International Conference on Web Search and Data Mining (2016)

17. Li, Q., Wen, Z., He, B.: Federated learning systems: vision, hype and reality for data privacy and protection. arXiv preprint arXiv:1907.09693 (2019)

18. Liu, B., Wang, L., Liu, M., Xu, C.: Lifelong federated reinforcement learning: a learning architecture for navigation in cloud robotic systems. IEEE Robot. Autom. Lett. **4**, 4555–4562 (2019)

19. Meng, X., et al.: Personalized privacy-preserving social recommendation. In: Proceedings of the 32nd AAAI Conference on Artificial Intelligence (2018)

20. Sharma, S., Chaoping, X., Liu, Y., Kang, Y.: Secure and efficient federated transfer learning. arXiv preprint arXiv:1910.13271 (2019)

21. Shmueli, E., Tassa, T.: Secure multi-party protocols for item-based collaborative filtering. In: Proceedings of the 11st ACM Conference on Recommender Systems (2017)

22. Wainakh, A., Grube, T., Daubert, J., Mühlhäuser, M.: Efficient privacy-preserving recommendations based on social graphs. In: Proceedings of the 13th ACM Conference on Recommender Systems (2019)

23. Wang, L., Wang, W., Li, B.: CMFL: mitigating communication overhead for federated learning. In: Proceedings of the 39th IEEE International Conference on Distributed Computing Systems (2019)

24. Weng, J.S., Weng, J., Li, M., Zhang, Y., Luo, W.: DeepChain: auditable and privacy-preserving deep learning with blockchain-based incentive. IACR Cryptology ePrint Archive (2018)
25. Xie, C., Koyejo, S., Gupta, I.: Asynchronous federated optimization. arXiv preprint arXiv:1903.03934 (2019)
26. Yang, Q., Liu, Y., Chen, T., Tong, Y.: Federated machine learning: concept and applications. ACM Trans. Intell. Syst. Technol. **10**, 1–19 (2019)
27. Zhao, Y., Li, M., Lai, L., Suda, N., Civin, D., Chandra, V.: Federated learning with non-IID data. arXiv preprint arXiv:1806.00582 (2018)

Federated Learning for Open Banking

Guodong Long[✉][iD], Yue Tan[iD], Jing Jiang[iD], and Chengqi Zhang[iD]

Australian Artificial Intelligence Institute (AAII), Faculty of Engineering
and IT (FEIT), University of Technology Sydney (UTS), Ultimo, Australia
{guodong.long,jing.jiang,chengqi.zhang}@uts.edu.au, yuetan031@gmail.com

Abstract. Open banking enables individual customers to own their banking data, which provides fundamental support for the boosting of a new ecosystem of data marketplaces and financial services. In the near future, it is foreseeable to have decentralized data ownership in the finance sector using federated learning. This is a just-in-time technology that can learn intelligent models in a decentralized training manner. The most attractive aspect of federated learning is its ability to decompose model training into a centralized server and distributed nodes without collecting private data. This kind of decomposed learning framework has great potential to protect users' privacy and sensitive data. Therefore, federated learning combines naturally with an open banking data marketplaces. This chapter will discuss the possible challenges for applying federated learning in the context of open banking, and the corresponding solutions have been explored as well.

Keywords: Federated learning · Heterogeneous federated learning · Few-shot federated learning · One-class federated learning · Open banking · Data marketplace

1 Introduction

As a subspecies to the open innovation [7,8] concept, open banking is an emerging trend in turning banks into financial service platforms, namely banking as a service. From a financial technology perspective, open banking refers to: [14] 1) the use of open application programming interfaces (APIs) that enable third-party developers to build applications and services around the financial institution, 2) greater financial transparency options for account holders ranging from open data to private data, and 3) the use of open-source technology to achieve the above. [6] Open banking can be naturally evolved into a new ecosystem of data marketplaces where participants can buy and sell data.

As stated by McKinsey & Company [6], open banking could bring benefits to banks in various ways, including better customer experience, increased revenue streams, and a sustainable service model for under-served markets. Open banking will form a new ecosystem for financial services by sharing banking data across organizations and providing new services. However, there are inherent risks in sharing banking data, which is sensitive, privacy-concerned, and valuable. It is

© Springer Nature Switzerland AG 2020
Q. Yang et al. (Eds.): Federated Learning, LNAI 12500, pp. 240–254, 2020.
https://doi.org/10.1007/978-3-030-63076-8_17

critical to developing processes and governance underpinning the technical connections. Moreover, the European Union's General Data Protection Regulation (GDPR) [12] enforces organizations to pay great attention when sharing and using customers' data.

In the new financial ecosystem, a number of small and medium-sized enterprises will provide novel applications using artificial intelligence (AI) technology. Intelligent applications are already driving a dramatic shift in how financial institutions attract and retain active customers. In recent times AI has become widely applied to review small loan applications fast and automatically. In this AI wave, the machine learning (ML) model with a deep neural network architecture has been a huge success in many financial applications. Imagine the open banking scenario in the near future, with a vast amount of customer data derived from various financial service providers that can be integrated and utilized to train a comprehensive AI model superior to all existing models. Federated learning (FL) is a decentralized ML framework that is able to collaboratively train an AI model while preserving user privacy. It is naturally suited to distributed data ownership settings in an open banking scenario.

In the context of open banking, federated learning needs to be adapted and enhanced to solve a few practical challenges, such as broad heterogeneity across users, limited times to access personal data, narrow scope of one user, and managing incentives for data contributors. In the following sections, we will briefly introduce applications of open banking, and then discuss the practical challenges with corresponding techniques that present solutions.

2 Applications of Open Banking

2.1 Open Innovation and Open Banking

Open innovation is "a distributed innovation process based on purposively managed knowledge flows across organizational boundaries, using pecuniary and non-pecuniary mechanisms in line with the organization's business model" [7]. The flows of knowledge may involve various ways to leverage internal and external resources and knowledge. Open banking is a kind of open innovation in the banking industry. By leveraging both internal and external knowledge, many innovative applications will emerge to benefit the whole finance industry, including both banks and third-party companies.

Open Banking. [6] can be defined as a collaborative model in which banking data is shared through APIs between two or more unaffiliated parties to deliver enhanced capabilities to the marketplaces. The potential benefits of open banking are substantial including customer experience, revenue, and new service models. It will also improve the finance industry by including more small and medium-sized players with innovative ideas and fine-grained service for different segmentations of customers. In addition to well-known players like Mint, examples include alternative underwriters ranging from Lending Club in the United States to M-Shwari in Africa to Lenddo in the Philippines, and payments disruptors like Stripe and Braintree.

The United Kingdom's. The Competition and Markets Authority issued a ruling in August 2016 that required the UK's nine biggest UK retail banks at that time – HSBC, Barclays, RBS, Santander, Bank of Ireland, Allied Irish Bank, Danske Bank, Lloyds, and Nationwide – to allow licensed startups direct access to their data down to the level of account-based transactions. By August 2020 there were 240 providers regulated by the Financial Conduct Authority enrolled in open banking. They include many providers of financial apps that help manage finances as well as consumer credit firms that use open banking to access account information for affordability checks and verification.

Australia launched an open banking project on 1 July 2019 as part of a Consumer Data Rights (CDR) project of the Australian Treasury department and the Australian Competition and Consumer Commission (ACCC). The CDR is envisaged to become an economy-wide system that will enable the safe and secure transfer of consumer data. CDR legislation was passed by the Australian Parliament in August 2019. From 1 July 2020 Australia's bank customers have been being able to give permission to accredited third parties to access their savings and credit card data. This enables customers to search for better deals on banking products and to track their banking in one place.

China's state media reports that China's financial authorities plan to launch new regulations and policies for the open banking sector and open APIs. Economic Information Observer said that Chinese authorities will "unveil policies in relation to the regulation of open API's and accelerate the formulation of regulatory standards in relation to open banking in China". Chinese authorities will also strengthen the regulation of client-end software provided by financial institutions, and expand filing for mobile financial apps from trial areas to the whole of the country. Some Internet giants have already dived into this new trend. For example, Tencent Cloud and WeBank collaborate to launch a Fintech Lab to explore open banking in China. PwC China also has an investigation report with a high-level design for the open banking ecosystem in China [40].

2.2   Open Banking Related Applications

Open banking has significantly advanced along various pathways [30]. They include enhancing intelligent applications in existing areas of banking, such as fraud detection, assessment of loan or credit card, customer retention, and personalized service. Below we will introduce the recent developments in open banking related applications worldwide.

Payment Management: In February 2020 payments organization Nacha announced a rollout of an online platform, namely Phixius, that integrates technology, rules, and participants to exchange payment-related information across ecosystem participants. It is associated with the current reliance on proprietary bilateral data-sharing agreements, which limits broader efficiency. The platform is intended to enable companies to exchange payment-related information to improve fraud protection, automate manual processes, and improve customer experiences. Moreover, digital payments company Payrailz announced a partnership with a credit union and FinTech collaborator, namely Constellation Digital Partners, to develop an elevated joint payment solution for credit union clients.

API Integration: The UK's Starling Bank has been expanding its Business Marketplaces for small businesses by integrating multiple ecosystem participants including Mortgage lender Molo, a freelance career management portal, and accounting system PayStream. These participants can access Starling Bank account data via an API, and it enables the financial institution to connect businesses with integrated solutions. Moreover, in February 2020 the Commonwealth Bank of Australia launched a free app that enables small businesses to consolidate data from various platforms, such as Xero and Google Analytics. This solution, Vonto, is designed to offer transparent and quick insights, connecting small business owners with 10 "key insights" each morning, including cash flow, social media engagement, and website traffic. The UK's Simply Asset Finance collaborates with open banking platform AccountScore, to enable Simply to wield an API to unlock borrower data for deeper underwriting capabilities. The companies said they will use the rich data set to assist lending decisions.

2.3 Federated Learning for Open Banking

Federated learning is a decentralized machine learning framework that can train a model without direct access to users' private data. The model coordinator and user/participant exchange model parameters that can avoid sending user data. However, the exchanging of model parameters, or gradients in machine learning terminology, may cause data leakage [12]. Therefore, differential privacy [11] technology is essential for federated learning to protect privacy from gradient-based cyber-attack [1].

Data sharing is the key idea in open banking. As there are inherent risks during data sharing, it is critical to develop processes and governance underpinning the new trend [6]. Customers are more likely to not sell the data, but to use the data to train a model in the local device. Moreover, as required by the GDPR, the shared data for a particular financial service, e.g. credit card application, cannot be used for another purpose, e.g. model training. It is therefore a natural solution to integrate federated learning with an open banking data marketplaces.

Privacy concerns are top priority in federated learning. In most cases, malicious attackers pretend to be a model coordinator of federated learning and can then use gradient-based privacy attack methods to guess what user data look like, to cause privacy leakage. Therefore, differential privacy, secure aggregation [4], and homomorphic encryption are widely used methods for data protection in the federated learning framework. This chapter does not discuss details of privacy-preserving techniques and data encryption as they have been well studied in many literature reviews [26, 32].

Incentive management is a practical challenge in open banking. Studies of this problem are two-fold: 1) how to incentivize data owners to participate in federated learning by contributing their data, and 2) how to measure each participant's contribution. Different forms of incentives are possible, such as user-defined utility and money-based rewards, and have been well discussed in the literature [20,21,36,39].

Data heterogeneity is an inherent challenge in a large-scale system across many organizations. In open banking, the user may come from different banks with different feature spaces. The same user may have different pieces of information in multiple banks. To utilize these data in federated learning, the major issue is to align the heterogeneous structured data via horizontal/vertical federated learning and federated transfer learning [35].

Statistical heterogeneity is caused by the diverse nature of user behaviors. Each user's data may vary in its hidden distribution. This kind of heterogeneity challenge widely exists in a large-scale machine learning system.

Model heterogeneity is the scenario that different participants may choose and run a model with personalized model architectures. It is critical to solving the problem of how a central server can aggregate information across participants with heterogeneous models.

Charging by access times is possible in federated learning. Access to a user's profile is not unlimited and could be charged by times. This raises the question of how the model trainer can complete the training process by accessing a user's profile in a few rounds, namely federated learning with few-shot round communications.

Only positive labels arise because each user usually only has one-class data while the global model trains a bi-class or multi-class classifier. For example, if we want to train a fraud detection model, we find that most users only have non-fraud data. Training on participants' data with only positive labels is a challenge known as a one-class problem. Aggregating these one-class classifiers is also a new challenge in federated learning.

In the following sections, we discuss the statistical heterogeneity, model heterogeneity, access limits, and one-class problems that are rarely discussed in other places.

3   Problem Formulation

The learning process of federated learning is decomposed into two parts that occur in different places: server (coordinator) and nodes (participants). These two parts are linked to each other via a specifically designed mechanism. In particular, the participant i can train a local model h_i using its own dataset $D_i = \{(x_{i.}, y_{i.})\}$. The model h_i is initialized by a globally shared model parameter W which is then fine-tuned to a new local model with parameters W_i using the data from node i.

It is proposed that the coordinator in federated learning can learn a global model controlled by W that could be shared with all participants on distributed nodes. Through a few rounds of communication, the global model has been gradually improved to better suit all participants, and the final global model is an optimal solution that could directly be deployed on each participant for further use. In particular, the optimal global model is expected to minimize the total loss of all participants, and it is defined as below.

$$\sum_{i=1}^{n} p_i \cdot L(D_i, W) = \sum_{i=1}^{n} p_i \cdot L_i \tag{1}$$

where $L(.)$ is the loss function for each participant's learning task, W is the model parameters, and p_i is the weight to represent each node's importance. In general, p_i is decided by considering the node's data set size $|D_i|$ so that each instance, regardless of the location or data owner, has equal importance contributing to the overall loss. Sometimes, we use L_i as a brief denotation of the $L(D_i, W)$.

4 Statistical Heterogeneity in Federated Learning

One challenge of federated learning is statistical heterogeneity in which users have different data distribution. Statistical heterogeneity is an inherent characteristic of a user's behaviour. It is also identified as a non-IID problem. Conventional machine learning is built upon the IID assumption of a uniform dataset. The stochastic gradient descent (SGD) optimization used in vanilla federated learning is not specifically designed and optimized for tackling non-IID data. As described in Fig. 1, each participant's data are generated from different distributions. Each local model should then be initialized by the global model that represents a particular distribution.

From the Bayes theorem perspectives, the classifications are highly linked to several distributions: $p(x)$, $p(y)$, $p(x|y)$ and $p(y|x)$. The variance of any distribution across participants will cause inconsistency in learning that will eventually damage the performance of a federated learning task. To solve this challenge, the simplest solution is to enhance existing distributed machine learning to be more

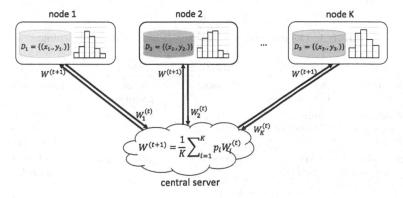

Fig. 1. Statistical heterogeneity problem in federated learning

robust for tolerating heterogeneity across data nodes [23], or to re-weight the contribution of each node according to the similarity of global and local models [19]. However, that solution still uses one global model to service all variety of participants. A better solution is to increase the number of global models from one to multiple (Sect. 4.1). We can cluster or group the participants so that same-group participants with the same or similar distributions will contribute one of the global models, and each group will have a unique global model. Personalized federated learning (Sect. 4.2) is a recent method that tries to increase the number of global models to be equivalent to the number of participants, and then each participant will have a unique model including both a commonly shared part and personalized information.

4.1   Clustered Federated Learning

A machine learning model could be treated as a function to approximate the distribution. In general, two models with similar parameters or functions are more likely to produce a similar outcome regarding the same input. Therefore, measuring models' similarity is an indirect way to measure distribution. Below are the related methods for clustered federated learning.

Xie *et al.* [34] addresses the non-IID challenge of federated learning and proposes a multi-center aggregation approach. The non-IID problem in federated learning is defined as a joint optimization problem of multiple centers/clusters across participants. It can simultaneously learn multiple global models from participants with non-IID data, and the clustering and model learning are jointly optimized in a stochastic expectation maximization framework. In particular, the loss function of the federated learning framework is defined as below.

$$\sum_{i=1}^{n} p_i \cdot \min_k ||W_i - W^{(k)}||^2 \tag{2}$$

where the similarity of two models is measured by the L2 distance between the i-th participant's model W_i and the global model $W^{(k)}$ of the cluster k (Table 1).

Table 1. Comparison of clustering-based federated learning

Methods	Motivation	Clustering	Factors	Measurement
Multi-center FL[34]	Better initialisation	K-means	Model parameters	L2-distance
Hierarchical clustering-based FL [5,31]	Similar distribution	Hierarchical clustering	Gradients	Cosine similarity & L1/L2 distance
Hypothesis clustering-based FL [13,25]	Better hypothesis	K-means	Test accuracy	The loss of hypothesis

In some cases using Convolutional Neural Networks (CNN) as basic model architecture, two neurons from different models may have similar functions but with different neuron indices. Therefore, neuron matching of two CNN models cannot be simply applied to index-based matching, and it needs to be carefully considered for functionality matching. A proper neuron matching mechanism in the context of federated learning can improve the performance [33]. It could be further applied to clustering-based federated learning that considers matching neurons in both averaging and clustering steps.

[31] proposes to distinguish participants based on their hidden data generating distribution by inspecting the cosine similarity $\alpha_{i,j}$ between their gradient updates r_i and r_j. Based on the measurement in Eq. 3, a hierarchical clustering method is proposed to iteratively split participants into multiple groups, in which pairs of participants with larger similarity are more likely to be allocated to the same group. Below is the equation to calculate the similarity between a pair of participants i and j. Moreover, [5] discussed using different measurements.

$$\alpha_{i,j} := \alpha(\nabla r_i(W_i), \nabla r_j(W_j)) := \frac{<\nabla r_i(W_i), \nabla r_j(W_j)>}{||\nabla r_i(W_i)|| \ ||\nabla r_j(W_j)||} \quad (3)$$

where the W_i and W_j are the model parameters of participants i ad j respectively.

Mansour $et\ al.$ in [25] use a performance indicator to decide the cluster assignment for each node. In particular, given K clusters with model F_k controlled by W, the participant i will be assigned to cluster k whose model will generate the minimal loss L using the test data set D_i from participant i. The overall loss can be rewritten as follows.

$$\sum_{i=1}^{n} p_i \cdot \min_k \{L(D_i, W_k)\} \quad (4)$$

in where $W_{(k)}$ is the parameters of the k-th global model/hypothesis. The paper gives a comprehensive theoretical analysis of the given method. Then, [13] conducts convergence rate analysis in the same method. [27] proposes a similar solution from a mixture of distribution perspectives.

4.2   Personalized Modelling

When a service provider wants to provide a service that is the best for each individual customer, the model trained in the central server needs to be personalized or customized. The simplest solution is to treat the global model as a pre-trained model, and then use local data to fine-tune the global model, which will derive a personalized model. However, in most cases, each participant just has a limited number of instances, and the fine-tuning operation will cause overfitting or increase the generalization error. Another solution is to treat each customer as a target task and the pre-trained global model as a source task, then to apply transfer learning [28] or domain adaptation [3] methods to fine-tune each personalized model. These methods will further leverage the global information to improve the fine-tuning process for each participant. [25] discusses two approaches, namely Data Interpolation and Model Interpolation, to learn a personalized federated learning model by weighting two components between local and global servers in terms of data distributions or models respectively.

Personalization Layers. In general, a model can be decomposed into two parts: a representation learning part and a decisive part. For example, CNN is composed of convolution layers for representation extraction and fully-connected layers for classification decision. In a federated learning setting, heterogeneity could impact one of the two parts. [2] proposes to share representation layers across participants, and then keep decision layers as a personalized part. [24] thinks representation layers should be the personalized part, and then the decision layers could be shared across participants.

Mixture Models. If we cannot clearly identify which parts in the model will be impacted by the heterogeneity, we can roughly mix the global model and local models to incorporate both common knowledge and personalized knowledge. [9] proposes a mixture model of global and local models in a federated setting. The local model can preserve the personalized information and the global model provides common information. In particular, the loss is designed as below.

$$\sum_i^n p_i \cdot \{L(D_i, W) + \lambda L(D_i, W_i)\} \tag{5}$$

where λ is the mixing weight, $L(D_i, W)$ and $L(D_i, W_i)$ are the loss of participant i using global and local model's parameters W and W_i respectively.

Personalized Models with Constraints. In FedAVG, the pre-trained global model will be deployed to each participant for direct use. However, each participant could use their own data to fine-tune the pre-trained global model to generate a personalized model. [10,16] enables participants to pursue their personalized models with different directions, but use a regularization term to limit each personalized model to not far away from the "initial point", the global model. A regularization term will be applied to each participant's personalized model to limit the distance of personalized changes. The model is to be optimized using the loss function below.

$$\sum_{i=1}^n p_i \cdot \{L(D_i, W_i) + \frac{\lambda}{2}||W_i - W||^2\} \tag{6}$$

where L is the loss function decided by dataset D_i and the i-th participant's model parameter, and W is the global model's parameter. The regularization term could be attached to the global model or local model respectively. Moreover, it could be added to the federated learning process [23].

[41] allows each participant to take one more gradient descent step from the global model. This one step optimization is toward a personalized model. The loss is changed as below.

$$\sum_{i}^{n} p_i \cdot L_i(W - \nabla L_i(W)) \tag{7}$$

where L_i is the loss function of the i-th participant that is controlled by the weights W and data set D_i.

5　Model Heterogeneity

5.1　Model Architecture Heterogeneity

Model heterogeneity will ruin the model aggregation operator that is the core part of federated learning. To enable the aggregation, we need to find a way to transform heterogeneous models into homogeneous models. As shown in Fig. 2, the participants in a federated learning system could have heterogeneous models with different architectures. Therefore, the global model W' is also different from each local model W. It will become a challenge to aggregate the heterogeneous model in the federated setting.

Knowledge distillation is such a technology to "compress" or "distill" a large model into a small model. It was proposed by Hinton *et al.* [17] in 2015. It can extract information from a "teacher" model W' into a simpler "student" model W. Given the same inputs, the objective function is to control the student model to produce similar outputs (probability vector) with the teacher model while considering ground truth. The loss function is defined below.

$$L_s(\{(x, y')\}, W) + \lambda \cdot L_h(\{(x, \hat{y})\}, W) \tag{8}$$

where $\hat{y}$ and y' represent the label from ground truth and teacher model's predicted probability of labels, W is the parameters for the student model, L_s is a soft loss function to measure the dissimilarity or distance between two distributions of predicted labels from teacher model and student model respectively,

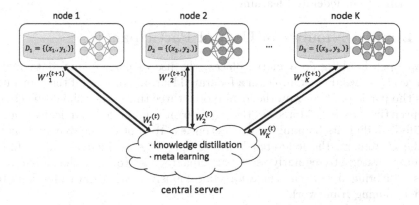

Fig. 2. Mode heterogeneity problem in federated learning

L_h is a loss function between predicted labels and ground truth, and λ is an importance weight of L_s and L_h.

In [22], each participant owns a private dataset and a public dataset is shared across all participants and servers. A local model is trained in a transfer learning framework by leveraging both public and private datasets. Then, a decentralized knowledge distillation will be applied to exchange information between participants and the coordinator. In particular, each participant calculates the prediction probability for all instances in the public dataset, and then sends it to the coordinator for prediction averaging. The averaged prediction probability could be viewed as the output of a teacher model (teacher) that is an ensemble learning of many local models, and the teacher model's outputs will be sent back to each participant to train a student model in a knowledge distillation process. In this work, the heterogeneous local models exchange prediction probability acquired on the public dataset, and knowledge distillation allows exchanging information in a model agnostic way.

The authors in [15] leverage distillation in a semi-supervised setting to reduce the size of the global model. The distillation mechanism also potentially adds privacy guarantees by replacing some sensitive model parameters during the distillation process. In [18], a new federated distillation (FD) is proposed to improve communication efficiency for an on-device machine learning framework. The proposed FD exchanges the model output rather than the model parameters, which allows the on-device ML to adopt large local models. Prior to operating FD, the non-IID datasets are rectified via federated augmentation, where a generative adversarial network is used for data augmentation under the trade-off between privacy leakage and communication overhead.

This technique can be used to bridge the gap between a global model and a local model for a specific client. In [37], the pre-trained global model is treated as the teacher, while the adapted model is treated as a student. The participant will train a unique local model with specific architecture that is different from the others. However, this solution assumes the federated model is pre-trained, and the knowledge distillation is just for the deployment stage or personalization step rather than federated learning.

6   Limited Number of Uses of Participants

In an open banking data marketplaces, the use of participants' data may be charged by times. For example, in a federated learning process, if the coordinator asks the participant to train the local model three times, they should be charged by three times as well. Moreover, the participant's data is a dynamically changing profile including its banking-related activities. To capture the dynamic changes of the customers, the federated learning may take an incremental or lifelong learning strategy to regularly use a participant's data to refine the global model. This will bring a new challenge for continuously sharing data in a long-term model training framework.

The pay-per-access mechanism can also be modeled as a few-shot federated learning problem in which the server can take very few communication rounds with each participant. Regardless of whether the federated learning is horizontal or vertical, the participants can help the coordinator to train a local model according to the global model's parameters at a particular moment. Thus, the coordinator will pursue highly efficient communication with participants using their data.

Some techniques can be used to solve the few-shot federated learning challenge in open banking. In [15], Guha *et al.* present one-shot federated learning that allows the central server to learn a global model over the network in a single round of communication. The proposed approach utilizes ensemble learning and knowledge aggregation to effectively and efficiently leverage information in large networks with thousands of devices. With this technique, the financial service provider can access the data from multiple data holders and finish model training in only one round of communication. This greatly improves the efficiency of communication and reduces the risk of sensitive data leakage.

7 Only Positive Labels in Each Participant

The one-class challenge is also a problem. For example, in a fraud detection or break contract, one user's data can only be labeled as fraud or not-fraud. Most users are labeled as the not-fraud class, which means that there are only a small number of users with the fraud class. Although each user can design and train personalized model based on its own financial data, the model may not be accurate enough as a result of the one-class problem. As shown in Fig. 3, the overall learning task is a bi-class problem although each participant has only a one-class learning task. The participant cannot properly train a bi-class classifier to be aggregated in the coordinator's model or global server.

In open banking scenarios, solutions to the one-class problem can fall into two categories. One is to embed the specific one-class classification algorithm into the imbalanced federated financial system from a task-level perspective. The other is to adjust the weights and incentive mechanism among users from a system-level

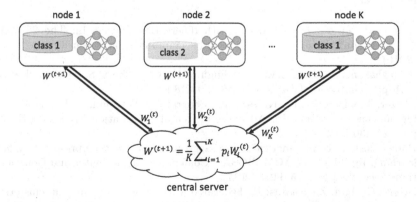

Fig. 3. One-class problem in federated learning

perspective. One-class classification is also known as anomaly detection in fraud detection applications, where outliers or anomalies are rare examples that do not fit in with the rest of the data.

In [38], the authors propose a federated learning-based proactive content caching (FPCC) scheme which is based on a hierarchical architecture where the server aggregates user-side updates to construct a global model. Based on a stacked auto-encoder, FPCC allows each user to perform training on its local data using hybrid filtering. In open banking, the users' similarity in a financial perspective can be calculated using the features generated from a stacked auto-encoder. In this way, it is easier to make fraud detection with imbalanced data distribution.

The authors in [29] addressed that federated learning setup allows an adversary to poison at least one of the local models and influence the outcome of one-class classification. Moreover, malicious behaviour can increase time-to-detection of the attacks. To solve these above issues, they designed a permitted blockchain-based federated learning method where the updates for the auto-encoder model are chained together on the distributed ledger. The trained auto-encoder can recognize the test samples of the baseline class while marking the other test samples that do not fit into the trained model as a potential negative class.

8   Summary

This chapter discusses the challenges of applying federated learning in the context of open banking. In particular, we focus on discussing the statistical heterogeneity (Sect. 4), model heterogeneity (Sect. 5), access limits (Sect. 6), and one-class problems (Sect. 7) that are rarely discussed in other places. This chapter explores various solutions to solve the aforementioned practical challenges in open banking, and then foresee the advancement of federated learning in the context of real-world scenarios.

References

1. Abadi, M., et al.: Deep learning with differential privacy. In: The 2016 ACM SIGSAC Conference on Computer and Communications Security, pp. 308–318 (2016)
2. Arivazhagan, M.G., Aggarwal, V., Singh, A.K., Choudhary, S.: Federated learning with personalization layers. arXiv:1912.00818 (2019)
3. Blitzer, J., Crammer, K., Kulesza, A., Pereira, F., Wortman, J.: Learning bounds for domain adaptation. In: Advances in Neural Information Processing Systems, pp. 129–136 (2008)
4. Bonawitz, K., et al.: Practical secure aggregation for privacy-preserving machine learning. In: The 2017 ACM SIGSAC Conference on Computer and Communications Security, pp. 1175–1191 (2017)
5. Briggs, C., Fan, Z., Andras, P.: Federated learning with hierarchical clustering of local updates to improve training on Non-IID data. arXiv:2004.11791 (2020)

6. Brodsky, L., Oakes, L.: Data Sharing and Open Banking. McKinsey Company, New York (2017)
7. Chesbrough, H., Vanhaverbeke, W., West, J.: New Frontiers in Open Innovation. OUP Oxford, Oxford, (2014)
8. Chesbrough, H.W.: Open Innovation: The New Imperative for Creating and Profiting from Technology. Harvard Business Press, Brighton (2003)
9. Deng, Y., Kamani, M.M., Mahdavi, M.: Adaptive personalized federated learning. arXiv:2003.13461 (2020)
10. Dinh, C.T., Tran, N.H., Nguyen, T.D.: Personalized federated learning with Moreau envelopes. arXiv:2006.08848 (2020)
11. Dwork, C.: Differential privacy: a survey of results. In: Agrawal, M., Du, D., Duan, Z., Li, A. (eds.) TAMC 2008. LNCS, vol. 4978, pp. 1–19. Springer, Heidelberg (2008). https://doi.org/10.1007/978-3-540-79228-4_1
12. European Parliament, Council of the European Union: General data protection regulation (GDPR). Technical report. The European Parliament and The Council of The European Union (2016). https://eur-lex.europa.eu/eli/reg/2016/679/oj
13. Ghosh, A., Chung, J., Yin, D., Ramchandran, K.: An efficient framework for clustered federated learning. arXiv:2006.04088 (2020)
14. Open Banking Working Group and others: The open banking standard. Technical report, working paper, Open Data Institute (2018)
15. Guha, N., Talwalkar, A., Smith, V.: One-shot federated learning. arXiv:1902.11175 (2019)
16. Hanzely, F., Richtárik, P.: Federated learning of a mixture of global and local models. arXiv:2002.05516 (2020)
17. Hinton, G., Vinyals, O., Dean, J.: Distilling the knowledge in a neural network. arXiv:1503.02531 (2015)
18. Jeong, E., Oh, S., Kim, H., Park, J., Bennis, M., Kim, S.L.: Communication-efficient on-device machine learning: federated distillation and augmentation under Non-IID private data. arXiv:1811.11479 (2018)
19. Jiang, J., Ji, S., Long, G.: Decentralized knowledge acquisition for mobile internet applications. World Wide Web, pp. 1–17 (2020)
20. Kang, J., Xiong, Z., Niyato, D., Xie, S., Zhang, J.: Incentive mechanism for reliable federated learning: a joint optimization approach to combining reputation and contract theory. IEEE Internet Things J. **6**(6), 10700–10714 (2019)
21. Khan, L.U., et al.: Federated learning for edge networks: resource optimization and incentive mechanism. arXiv:1911.05642 (2019)
22. Li, D., Wang, J.: FedMD: heterogenous federated learning via model distillation. arXiv:1910.03581 (2019)
23. Li, T., Sahu, A.K., Zaheer, M., Sanjabi, M., Talwalkar, A., Smith, V.: Federated optimization in heterogeneous networks. arXiv:1812.06127 (2018)
24. Liang, P.P., Liu, T., Ziyin, L., Salakhutdinov, R., Morency, L.P.: Think locally, act globally: federated learning with local and global representations. arXiv:2001.01523 (2020)
25. Mansour, Y., Mohri, M., Ro, J., Suresh, A.T.: Three approaches for personalization with applications to federated learning. arXiv:2002.10619 (2020)
26. Mirshghallah, F., Taram, M., Vepakomma, P., Singh, A., Raskar, R., Esmaeilzadeh, H.: Privacy in deep learning: a survey. arXiv:2004.12254 (2020)
27. Mohri, M., Sivek, G., Suresh, A.T.: Agnostic federated learning. arXiv:1902.00146 (2019)
28. Pan, S.J., Yang, Q.: A survey on transfer learning. IEEE Trans. Knowl. Data Eng. **22**(10), 1345–1359 (2009)

29. Preuveneers, D., Rimmer, V., Tsingenopoulos, I., Spooren, J., Joosen, W., Ilie-Zudor, E.: Chained anomaly detection models for federated learning: an intrusion detection case study. Appl. Sci. **8**(12), 2663 (2018)
30. PYMNTS: Open banking targets SMB apps, payments data. Technical report, PYMNTS.com (2020). https://www.pymnts.com/news/b2b-payments/2020/open-banking-targets-smb-apps-payments-data/
31. Sattler, F., Müller, K.R., Samek, W.: Clustered federated learning: model-agnostic distributed multi-task optimization under privacy constraints. arXiv:1910.01991 (2019)
32. Shokri, R., Shmatikov, V.: Privacy-preserving deep learning. In: The 22nd ACM SIGSAC Conference on Computer and Communications Security, pp. 1310–1321 (2015)
33. Wang, H., Yurochkin, M., Sun, Y., Papailiopoulos, D., Khazaeni, Y.: Federated learning with matched averaging. In: International Conference on Learning Representations (2020)
34. Xie, M., Long, G., Shen, T., Zhou, T., Wang, X., Jiang, J.: Multi-center federated learning. arXiv:2005.01026 (2020)
35. Yang, Q., Liu, Y., Chen, T., Tong, Y.: Federated machine learning: concept and applications. ACM Trans. Intell. Syst. Technol. (TIST) **10**(2), 1–19 (2019)
36. Yang, Q., Liu, Y., Cheng, Y., Kang, Y., Chen, T., Yu, H.: Federated learning. Synth. Lect. Artif. Intell. Mach. Learn. **13**(3), 1–207 (2019)
37. Yu, T., Bagdasaryan, E., Shmatikov, V.: Salvaging federated learning by local adaptation. arXiv:2002.04758 (2020)
38. Yu, Z., et al.: Federated learning based proactive content caching in edge computing. In: 2018 IEEE Global Communications Conference (GLOBECOM), pp. 1–6. IEEE (2018)
39. Zhan, Y., Li, P., Qu, Z., Zeng, D., Guo, S.: A learning-based incentive mechanism for federated learning. IEEE Internet Things J. (2020)
40. Zhang, L., Tao, X.: Open banking: what? Difficult? And how? Technical report, PwC China (2019). https://wemp.app/posts/05e3ed49-126e-408d-bf8a-ba1f86d86c88?utm_source=bottom-latest-posts
41. Zhao, Y., Li, M., Lai, L., Suda, N., Civin, D., Chandra, V.: Federated learning with Non-IID data. arXiv:1806.00582 (2018)

Building ICU In-hospital Mortality Prediction Model with Federated Learning

Trung Kien Dang[1], Kwan Chet Tan[2], Mark Choo[2], Nicholas Lim[2],
Jianshu Weng[2(✉)], and Mengling Feng[1]

[1] Saw Swee Hock School of Public Health,
National University Health System and National University of Singapore,
Singapore, Singapore
kiendang@u.nus.edu, ephfm@nus.edu.sg
[2] AI Singapore, Singapore, Singapore
{tankwanchet,markchoo,js}@aisingapore.org
nicholas.limchoonkang@gmail.com

Abstract. In-hospital mortality prediction is a crucial task in the clinical settings. Nevertheless, individual hospitals alone often have limited amount of local data to build a robust model. Usually *domain transfer* of an in-hospital mortality prediction model built with publicly-accessible dataset is conducted. The study in [6] shows quantitatively that with more datasets from different hospitals being shared, the generalizability and performance of *domain transfer* improves. We see this as an area that Federated Learning could help. It enables collaborative modelling to take place in a decentralized manner, without the need for aggregating all datasets in one place. This chapter reports a recent pilot of building an in-hospital mortality model with Federated Learning. It empirically shows that Federated Learning does achieve a similar level of performance with centralized training, but with additional benefit of no dataset exchanging among different hospitals. It also compares the performance of two common federated aggregation algorithms empirically in the Intensive Care Unit (ICU) setting, namely **FedAvg** and **FedProx**.

Keywords: In-hospital Mortality Prediction · Federated Learning · eICU

1 Introduction

Mortality prediction is a crucial task in the clinical settings. When a patient is admitted, predicting their mortality at the end of ICU stay or within a fixed period of time (e.g. 28 days, one month, or three months) is one way of estimating the severity of their condition. This information is essential in managing treatment planning and resource allocation. In practice, severity scores such as

This work was done when author Nicholas Lim was attached to AI Singapore as an apprentice.

Q. Yang et al. (Eds.): Federated Learning, LNAI 12500, pp. 255–268, 2020.
https://doi.org/10.1007/978-3-030-63076-8_18

SOFA [19], SAPS II [10] and APACHE II [8] are often calculated for patients at ICU admission for that purpose. Many of these scores were constructed by first building a mortality prediction model and then simplifying it into a scoring system. The effectiveness of severity scores are also often accessed by their correlation with patients' mortality. Thus, developing a good mortality prediction model works towards obtaining a more effective severity score [6].

Typically individual hospitals alone have a limited amount of local data to build a robust model. Usually, a hospital would *domain transfer* an existing in-hospital mortality prediction model that is built with publicly-accessible dataset or other hospitals' datasets. The study in [6] shows quantitatively that with more datasets from different hospitals being shared, the generalizability and performance of *domain transfer* improves. This also highlights the importance of data sharing in the development of high performance predictive models in the clinical settings.

Nevertheless, it is extremely common in healthcare that hospitals quarantine their datasets (often citing reasonable privacy concerns) and develop models internally. Even though hospitals are convinced of the value of data sharing, analysis in a centralized manner, which requires datasets from all participating hospitals or centers to be gathered in one place, incurs an increased risk in data privacy and security since sensitive datasets are now shared with external participants. In addition, moving datasets to a centralized location, either physically or over the network, introduces another attack vector for data leakage. Besides the privacy and security risk, the administrative effort to coordinate data sharing is also non-trivial since each participant usually has its own policies regarding data usage and data ownership. A method that enables collaborative modelling to take place in a decentralized manner, without the need for aggregating all datasets in one place, would thus make multi-center studies much more feasible.

Federated Learning is an emerging machine learning paradigm that enables building machine learning models collaboratively using distributed datasets. It was originally proposed by Google to build a query suggestion model for Gboard [9]. Each device trains a model with its own local dataset, and sends model parameters to a coordinator for aggregation into a common model usable by all participating devices. Since then, it has been extended to a more general setting, where different participants have isolated data in silos [7, 21]. The number of participants involved could also be small, compared to the billion scale of devices in the original application of mobile devices [9]. In essence, with Federated Learning, individual participants train local models on local data alone and exchange model parameters (e.g. the weights and/or gradients) with different participants at some frequency. The local model parameters are then aggregated to generate a global model. Various federated aggregation methods have been proposed. The aggregation is typically done with a coordinator, though it could also be done without one.

Federated Learning makes multi-center studies in medical research more feasible by enabling model training in a decentralized manner without the need for the individual centers to expose their dataset. In this chapter, we present a recent pilot applying Federated Learning to training machine learning models to predict mortality at the end of ICU stay based on electronic health records (EHR) from multiple ICU centers. We utilize the eICU Collaborative Research Database (eICU-CRD) [16], which collected EHR of patients admitted to around 200 different ICUs in the United States in year 2014 and 2015.

We empirically evaluate that Federated Learning does achieve level of performance comparable with centralized training. This is aligned with the findings in [6], but with the additional benefit of not incurring data exchange among participants. We also evaluate that **FedAvg** [14] and **FedProx** [11] achieved similar performance. **FedAvg** and **FedProx** are two of the most commonly used federated aggregation algorithms. This could be due to the fact that there are relatively small number of participants involved in this pilot, and the statistical heterogeneity and system heterogeneity is comparatively less significant. **FedProx** is shown to perform better than **FedAvg** when the heterogeneity is more severe, e.g. settings with more mobile devices are jointly training a global model [11]. To the best of our knowledge, we are the first one to empirically compare **FedAvg** and **FedProx** in Federated Learning with EHR.

This pilot also points directions for future work. For example, we plan to further explore other federated aggregation methods besides **FedAvg** and **Fed-Prox** with more participants in the clinical settings. We also plan to explore applying Federated Learning to more complex problems in healthcare, e.g medical imaging. In this pilot, we apply two different imputation strategies, one with a supervised machine learning model based on present feature values and the other with a simple strategy (to impute with mean for numerical features and mode for categorical ones). These two achieve similar performance. We plan to further study suitable imputation strategies for Federated Learning.

The rest of this chapter is organised as follows. Section 2 provides a survey of the related work. Section 3 details the methodology used in this pilot, including the dataset used, the pre-processing of the dataset, and the various models built. Section 4 reports the results obtained. Conclusions and possible future directions are summarized in Sect. 5.

2   Related Works

2.1   Federated Aggregation Algorithms

The key idea of Federated Learning is that individual participants train local models on their local dataset alone and exchange model parameters (e.g. the weights and/or gradients) among different participants at some frequency. There is no exchange of local datasets among different participants. The local model parameters are then aggregated to generate a global model. The aggregation can be conducted under the facilitation of a coordinator, which usually does not contribute any dataset. It can also be done without a coordinator.

A number of federated aggregations methods have been proposed, with **FedAvg** [14] being one of the most commonly used. More formally, **FedAvg** tries to optimize the following distributed optimization problem:

$$\min_{\mathbf{w}} \left(F(\mathbf{w}) = \sum_{i=1}^{N} p_i F_i(\mathbf{w}) \right) \tag{1}$$

where N is the number of participants, and p_i is the weight of participant i and $\sum_{i=1}^{N} p_i = 1$. $F_i(\cdot)$ is the local objective function.

At each global communication round t, a global model structure is broadcast to all participants. Each participant performs local training, using mini-batch gradient descent, for E local epochs with B mini-batch size. After E local epochs, each participant sends the parameters from its most recently obtained model state to the coordinator. The coordinator then aggregates these parameters into a single global model, with individual participants' parameters weighted by p_i, which are typically proportional to the participants' data volume.

The above scenario assumes *full participation*, i.e. all the N participants participate in the training and all participants train with same E local epochs. This is not practical due to the system heterogeneity across different participants, e.g. resource constraints in terms of the computation power and network connections vary. This is known to cause *straggler's effort*, which means everyone waits for the slowest [11,12]. To address this, partial participation can be allowed, i.e. the coordinator only uses the first K participants' response to update the global model.

Furthermore, the global model may not converge in the presence of statistical heterogeneity, e.g. situations that dataset is not independently and identically distributed across different participants (i.e. a phenomenon called non-IID dataset) and a high number of local epochs are used.

More formally, in Federated Learning setting, the local dataset at participant i is drawn from distribution $\mathcal{P}_i$, i.e. $(X, y) \sim \mathcal{P}_i(X, y)$. When non-IID is referenced, it refers to the difference between $\mathcal{P}_i$ and $\mathcal{P}_j$, i.e. $\mathcal{P}_i \neq \mathcal{P}_j$. We have $\mathcal{P}_i(X, y) = \mathcal{P}_i(y|X)\mathcal{P}_i(X) = \mathcal{P}_i(X|y)\mathcal{P}_i(y)$. The deviation in any of the components could lead to a non-IID dataset. Different participants may also have different sizes of datasets, which could also contribute to non-IID data.

Some improvements to address the performance in the presence of non-IID data have been proposed, including **FedProx** [11]. **FedProx** allows participants to carry out different numbers of local epochs. Besides this, an additional *proximal term* is also introduced. Instead of just minimizing the local objective function $F_i(\cdot)$, a participant is now to minimize the following objective h_i:

$$h_i(\mathbf{w}, \mathbf{w}^t) = F_i(\mathbf{w}) + \frac{\mu}{2} \left\| \mathbf{w} - \mathbf{w}^t \right\|^2 \tag{2}$$

where $\mathbf{w}^t$ is the model parameters received from the coordinator after previous round of federated aggregation. The additional proximal term addresses the statistical heterogeneity by restricting the local updates to be closer to the latest global model. The convergence guarantee of **FedProx** is developed under the assumption of bounded dissimilarity in the network. Yet, **FedProx** is very sensitive to the value of μ, the hyperparameter scaling the effect of proximal term.

2.2 Federated Learning with EHR

Typically individual hospital alone have a limited amount of local data to build a robust model to predict in-hospital mortality. Usually, a hospital would *domain transfer* an existing in-hospital mortality prediction model that is built with publicly-accessible dataset or other hospitals' datasets. The study in [6] shows quantitatively that with more datasets from different hospitals being shared, the generalizability and performance of *domain transfer* improved. This highlights the importance of data sharing in the development of high performance predictive models in the clinical settings. And we see this as an area that Federated Learning could help.

Federated Learning with EHR data is a relatively new research topic. There is limited prior work. [15] and [2] experimented with applying **FedAvg** [14] and Differential Privacy [3] to predicting ICU mortality and length of stay. [13] introduced Federated-Autonomous Deep Learning (**FADL** for short), which is built on top of **FedAvg**. **FADL** was applied in predicting ICU mortality based on medication intake. **FADL**'s performance was shown to be an improvement over **FedAvg**'s and similar to that of conventional centralized training. **FADL** involves two phases - global training and local training. The global training requires training the first layer of neural network with datasets from all hospitals with fixed global rounds and local epochs per global round. Subsequently, the models are locally trained in parallel on their own datasets in the layers 2 and 3 of the neural network for a fixed number of epochs. As a result, each hospital has its own specialised model for prediction.

[5] achieved high predictive accuracy when applying Federated Learning to prediction of ICU mortality and length of stay by clustering patients into clinical meaningful groups. The clustering is done by first training a denoising autoencoder on each hospital's dataset and averaged at the coordinator, which is used to convert patient's features into privacy-preserving representations. The patient clustering is conducted based on those representations. Finally, each hospital individually learns models for different clusters identified. The learned cluster models are sent to the coordinator for weighted average based on the cluster size.

3 Methods

In this section, we provide a detailed account of the dataset used, the preprocessing done, and the design of various experiments.

3.1   eICU Data

eICU Collaborative Research Database (eICU-CRD) [16] has been commonly used in EHR studies. It is a multi-center database sourced from the Philips eICU programme. Its multi-center nature makes it a natural choice for conducting Federated Learning pilot.

All records in the eICU-CRD dataset (**eICU** for short in the rest of this chapter) have been de-identified, and contains 200,859 distinct unit stays. We follow the data extraction steps in [6]. We excluded records that have the following traits: non-ICU stays, ICU stays which do not have an APACHE IVa score, non-adult patient, bad data, or organ donor. Such exclusion criteria would avoid repeated sampling and remove records that have an administrative intention. To ensure a fair evaluation of hospitals' modelling performance, only hospitals with at least 500 stays have been retained. The final cohort contains 50, 099 ICU stays from 46 (out of 179) hospitals. We further retained top 20 hospitals for analysis based on the number of ICU stays each hospital has. The number of ICU stays each hospital has is listed in Table 1.

Table 1. ICU stays of the hospitals used in the pilot

Hospital ID	ICU stays	% of Total data	Hospital ID	ICU stays	% of Total data
73	3,005	9.09%	188	1,601	4.84%
264	2,833	8.57%	449	1,335	4.04%
338	2,320	7.02%	208	1,161	3.51%
443	2,279	6.89%	307	1,102	3.33%
458	2,101	6.36%	416	1,083	3.28%
420	1,937	5.86%	413	1,066	3.22%
252	1,898	5.74%	394	1,022	3.09%
300	1,856	5.61%	199	1,022	3.09%
122	1,823	5.51%	345	1,012	3.06%
243	1,632	4.94%	248	970	2.93%

For each ICU stay, we extracted a dataset from a fixed window of length $W = 24$ (h) starting on ICU admission. The features were extracted from a number of physiologic and laboratory measurements, e.g. glucose, bilirubin, urine output. Features extracted used consistent functional forms, e.g. the first, last, or sum (in the case of urine output). Besides these, we also extracted gender, age, race, and whether the hospital admission was for an elective surgery (binary covariate). No explicit data regarding treatment were extracted, e.g. use of vasopressors, mechanical ventilation, dialysis, etc. A total of 84 features were obtained.

In this pilot, each individual hospital is considered one participant in Federated Learning. They jointly train a global model without exposing local datasets. A coordinator is introduced to facilitate the federated aggregation in the 20-participant Federated Learning. The coordinator does not contribute any dataset.

3.2 Data Pre-processing

Missing Data Imputation. Missing values are present in **eICU**, with varying degrees across different hospitals. As different hospitals do not expose their local datasets to one another with Federated Learning, imputation of missing values is conducted locally at individual hospitals.

For each individual hospital, it is assumed that the data is missing at random, and a machine learning based imputation approach is applied [4]. Inspired by MissForest [20], we apply an iterative imputation scheme by training a supervised learning model on the observed values in the first step, followed by predicting the missing values. This then proceeds iteratively.

For a feature X_t, assume it has missing values at entries $i_{mis}^{(t)} \subseteq \{1, ..., n\}$. We can separate the dataset into four parts:

1. the observed values of feature X_t, denoted as $y_{obs}^{(t)}$
2. the missing values of feature X_t, denoted as $y_{mis}^{(t)}$
3. the features other than X_t with observations $i_{obs}^{(t)} = \{1, ..., n\} \setminus i_{mis}^{(t)}$, denoted as $x_{obs}^{(t)}$
4. the features other than X_t with observation $i_{mis}^{(t)}$, denoted as $x_{mis}^{(t)}$

We first sort the features according to the nullity (i.e. the amount of missing values) starting with the lowest one. For each feature X_t, the missing values are imputed by first fitting a supervised model with $x_{obs}^{(t)}$ as features and $y_{obs}^{(t)}$ as labels; and then predicting the missing value $y_{mis}^{(t)}$ by applying the trained model on $x_{mis}^{(t)}$. After that, the same imputation procedure is applied on the next feature with the second lowest nullity. This procedure is repeated on the remaining features with missing values iteratively. Note that in this scheme, the label in the original dataset (before imputation) is also treated as a feature that can be used to train a supervised model during the imputation procedure.

Figure 1 provides an illustration of the imputation procedure. In this example, feature $X2$ and $X3$ have missing values as shown in Fig. 1 (1). Feature $X3$ has a lower nullity than $X2$, i.e. $X3$ has one missing value while $X2$ has two. A supervised model is trained with the last three rows of $X1$ and $Target$ as features and $X3$ as the label as shown in Fig. 1 (2). The missing value of $X3$ is then imputed by applying the trained model on the first row of $X1$ and $Target$ in Fig. 1 (3). Now feature $X3$ is complete. And it is used together with $X1$ and $Target$ to train another supervised model to impute the missing values of $X2$ in Fig. 1 (4).

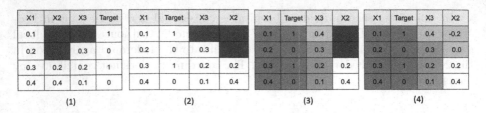

Fig. 1. Illustration of the imputation procedure

CatBoost [17] is used to build the supervised models due to its superior handling of both categorical and numerical features, which are both present in **eICU**.

Feature Alignment. For the categorical features (e.g. race) in **eICU**, One-Hot Encoding is applied. With Federated Learning, each hospital does not expose its dataset to others, One-Hot Encoding is conducted locally. Nevertheless, since different hospitals generate and collect data independently, it is possible that some categories in some common features in one hospital may not be present in other hospitals. For example, Hispanic is not present in certain hospital used in this pilot while it appears in other hospitals.

Therefore, an additional step to align features across different hospitals is necessary. Each hospital still conducts One-Hot Encoding locally. After that, the feature names from all participating hospitals are sent to the coordinator. No local dataset is sent to the coordinator. The coordinator would then align the features and send the universe of the categorical feature header back to all the hospitals. Upon receiving the aligned features, the individual hospitals would create additional features if necessary, and fill in zeros to represent non-presence of the related categories. An example of feature alignment is shown in Fig. 2.

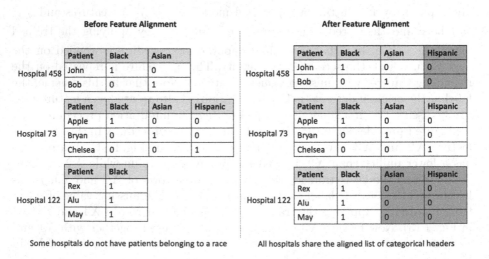

Fig. 2. Illustration of the feature alignment procedure

3.3   Experimental Design

Setup. The outcome we are predicting is in-hospital mortality, which is treated as a binary classification problem. The incidence of in-hospital mortality across all 20 hospitals is shown in Fig. 3.

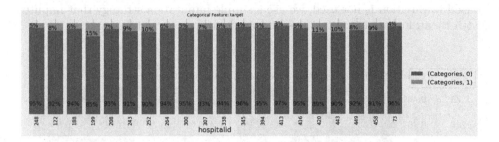

Fig. 3. Incidence of in-hospital mortality by hospitals

All the models built in the experiments are logistic regression (with regularization). Logistic regression is chosen because of its inherent explainability. Due to the heavy imbalance of the two classes, we use Area Under Precision-Recall Curve (**AUC-PR**) as the metric to measure the models' performance.

A series of experiments are conducted to evaluate the benefit of Federated Learning in clinical data analysis and to compare the performance of **FedAvg** and **FedProx**, which are two commonly used federated aggregation methods. The following set of experimental conditions are evaluated:

- **Local training**: A model is trained for each hospital using only its local training dataset (no other hospitals' data is used), and the evaluation is also done with a local testing dataset.
- **Centralized training**: A scenario is simulated where all hospitals' datasets are available in a central location. A centralized model is trained with a consolidated training dataset which is an aggregation of all 20 hospitals' local training datasets. The centralized model's performance is then evaluated with each individual hospital's local testing dataset.
- **Federated training**: All hospitals jointly train a global model with Federated Learning. Both **FedAvg** and **FedProx** have been implemented as federated aggregation methods, and their performance will be compared. For both aggregation methods, all hospitals jointly train a model with full participation, i.e. no hospital would drop out from the federated training half-way. For each round of federated training, all hospitals would train same number of local epochs, which is set to be $E = 5$.

4   Experiment Results

AUC-PRs for each hospital across eight methods: **local training, centralized training, federated training** with a combination of **FedAvg** or **FedProx**, and with or without the use of Catboost for imputation, are reported in Fig. 4. For better comparison, the same results are visualized in Fig. 5. When Catboost-based imputation is not used, we use a simple imputation strategy that imputes with mean for numerical features and mode for categorical features.

	Local	Centralized	FedAvg	FedProx	Local (Catboost)	Centralized (Catboost)	FedAvg (Catboost)	FedProx (Catboost)
73	0.481	0.569	0.583	0.593	0.499	0.573	0.6	0.589
264	0.497	0.506	0.525	0.527	0.486	0.474	0.505	0.504
338	0.463	0.472	0.478	0.467	0.448	0.436	0.474	0.464
443	0.679	0.684	0.681	0.675	0.676	0.683	0.677	0.679
458	0.638	0.646	0.663	0.646	0.652	0.714	0.643	0.65
420	0.638	0.69	0.669	0.671	0.644	0.7	0.698	0.699
252	0.4	0.496	0.501	0.491	0.398	0.486	0.493	0.486
300	0.359	0.396	0.452	0.443	0.339	0.409	0.43	0.432
122	0.331	0.429	0.415	0.417	0.332	0.595	0.381	0.386
243	0.365	0.414	0.445	0.449	0.325	0.424	0.449	0.43
188	0.433	0.537	0.514	0.502	0.465	0.625	0.578	0.554
449	0.398	0.53	0.529	0.535	0.336	0.562	0.523	0.523
208	0.32	0.46	0.442	0.429	0.299	0.424	0.403	0.396
307	0.734	0.876	0.864	0.864	0.717	0.876	0.864	0.896
416	0.3	0.415	0.409	0.496	0.317	0.492	0.492	0.492
413	0.136	0.412	0.422	0.415	0.465	0.438	0.424	0.432
394	0.692	0.722	0.621	0.627	0.688	0.688	0.666	0.599
199	0.756	0.764	0.756	0.761	0.746	0.708	0.733	0.721
345	0.29	0.602	0.608	0.608	0.289	0.486	0.571	0.596
248	0.171	0.241	0.222	0.222	0.182	0.228	0.217	0.218

Fig. 4. AUC-PRs of models built with different methods

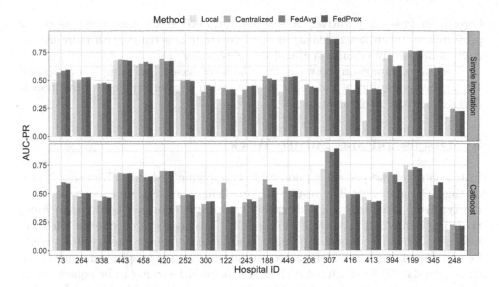

Fig. 5. Comparison of model performance

Overall, **centralized training** and **federated training** performed better than **local training**. Model trained with hospital 199 local dataset with Catboost-based imputation is the only **local training** model that achieves the best overall AUC-PR compared to both **centralized training** and **federated training**. The difference between **centralized training** and **federated training** is not noticeable. There are one or two hospitals where **centralized learning** yielded an improvement of more than 0.05 in AUC-PR over **federated training**:

- with Catboost-based imputation, **centralized training** achieves a noticeable improvement in AUC-PR over **federated training** (with both **FedAvg** and **FedProx**) for hospital 122 (the improvement is >0.2) and 458 (the improvement is >0.06).
- with simple imputation, **centralized training** achieves a noticeable improvement in AUC-PR over **federated training** (with both **FedAvg** and **FedProx**) for hospital 394 (the improvement is >0.09).

This observation highlights the benefits of Federated Learning in the clinical settings. It addresses the concerns of data privacy and takes away the need for exchanging datasets in the multi-center scenarios, yet it could achieve similar performance as what centralized training could do with aggregating data from multiple centers together.

Within **federated training**, **FedAvg** and **FedProx** perform on the same level. Around three fourths of the hospitals saw a difference within 0.01 in AUC-PR between **FedAvg** and **FedProx**, with or without Catboost imputation. This could be due to the fact that there are relatively small number of participants (20 hospitals) involved in this pilot, and the statistical heterogeneity and system heterogeneity is comparatively less significant. **FedProx** is shown to have better performance when heterogeneity is more severe, e.g. settings with more mobile devices are jointly training a global model together [11].

For the comparison between the Catboost-based and simple imputation strategies, no significant difference is observed in the performance of the models derived the respective strategies.

5   Discussion and Future Work

In this chapter, we present a pilot study of applying Federated Learning in predicting ICU mortality. The results are promising. The experiments showed that **centralized training** and **federated training** performed better than **local training** in predicting mortality in the ICU. This gives evidence to the effectiveness of collaborative model training in healthcare domain where hospitals would benefit from having a model trained on data from other hospitals in addition to their own data. The results also showed Federated Learning to be equally effective as centralized training. This highlights the potential of Federated Learning as a replacement for centralized learning in multi-center studies with enhanced data security and privacy without sacrificing model performance.

Nevertheless it also warrants further investigation into Federated Learning in the healthcare domain. In this pilot study, we only applied Federated Learning in training a logistic regression model to solve a binary classification task. We plan to explore applying Federated Learning to more complex problems in healthcare. One such area is medical imaging where deep neural networks have proved to be very effective in solving several non-trivial classification and segmentation tasks [1,18]. We also observed that **FedAvg** and **FedProx** perform on the same level. This could be due to the relatively small number of participants involved and the full participation assumption in this pilot. The statistical heterogeneity and system heterogeneity is therefore comparatively less significant. We plan to further explore various federated aggregation methods including **FedAvg**, **FedProx**, and other variants in more realistic clinical settings, e.g. more participants and partial participation. Additionally, the results showed that the current implementation of Catboost-based imputation does not provide improvement over simple imputation strategy. One possible direction is to develop an early stopping mechanism for Catboost-based imputation and identify non-essential features globally without different participants exposing dataset.

References

1. Akkus, Z., Galimzianova, A., Hoogi, A., Rubin, D.L., Erickson, B.J.: Deep learning for brain MRI segmentation: state of the art and future directions. J. Digit. imaging **30**(4), 449–459 (2017). https://doi.org/10.1007/s10278-017-9983-4
2. Beaulieu-Jones, B.K., Yuan, W., Finlayson, S.G., Wu, Z.S.: Privacy-preserving distributed deep learning for clinical data. arXiv preprint arXiv:1812.01484 (2018)

3. Dwork, C., Roth, A., et al.: The algorithmic foundations of differential privacy. Found. Trends Theoret. Comput. Sci. **9**(3–4), 211–407 (2014)
4. García-Laencina, P.J., Sancho-Gómez, J., Figueiras-Vidal, A.R.: Pattern classification with missing data: a review. Neural Comput. Appl. **19**(2), 263–282 (2010). https://doi.org/10.1007/s00521-009-0295-6
5. Huang, L., Shea, A.L., Qian, H., Masurkar, A., Deng, H., Liu, D.: Patient clustering improves efficiency of federated machine learning to predict mortality and hospital stay time using distributed electronic medical records. J. Biomed. Inform. **99**, 103291 (2019)
6. Johnson, A.E., Pollard, T.J., Naumann, T.: Generalizability of predictive models for intensive care unit patients. arXiv preprint arXiv:1812.02275 (2018)
7. Kairouz, P., et al.: Advances and open problems in federated learning. arXiv preprint arXiv:1912.04977 (2019)
8. Knaus, W.A., Draper, E.A., Wagner, D.P., Zimmerman, J.E.: APACHE II: a severity of disease classification system. Crit. Care Med. **13**(10), 818–829 (1985)
9. Konecný, J., McMahan, H.B., Ramage, D., Richtárik, P.: Federated optimization: distributed machine learning for on-device intelligence. CoRR abs/1610.02527 (2016), http://arxiv.org/abs/1610.02527
10. Le Gall, J.R., Lemeshow, S., Saulnier, F.: A new simplified acute physiology score (SAPS II) based on a European/North American multicenter study. Jama **270**(24), 2957–2963 (1993)
11. Li, T., Sahu, A.K., Zaheer, M., Sanjabi, M., Talwalkar, A., Smith, V.: Federated optimization in heterogeneous networks. In: Dhillon, I.S., Papailiopoulos, D.S., Sze, V. (eds.) Proceedings of Machine Learning and Systems 2020, MLSys 2020, Austin, TX, USA, 2–4 March 2020. mlsys.org (2020). https://proceedings.mlsys.org/book/316.pdf
12. Li, X., Huang, K., Yang, W., Wang, S., Zhang, Z.: On the convergence of FedAvg on Non-IID data. In: 8th International Conference on Learning Representations, ICLR 2020, Addis Ababa, Ethiopia, 26–30 April 2020. OpenReview.net (2020). https://openreview.net/forum?id=HJxNAnVtDS
13. Liu, D., Miller, T.A., Sayeed, R., Mandl, K.D.: FADL: federated-autonomous deep learning for distributed electronic health record. CoRR abs/1811.11400 (2018), http://arxiv.org/abs/1811.11400
14. McMahan, B., Moore, E., Ramage, D., Hampson, S., Arcas, B.A.Y.: Communication-efficient learning of deep networks from decentralized data. In: Artificial Intelligence and Statistics, pp. 1273–1282 (2017)
15. Pfohl, S.R., Dai, A.M., Heller, K.: Federated and differentially private learning for electronic health records. In: Machine Learning for Health (ML4H) at the 33rd Conference on Neural Information Processing System (NeurIPS 2019) (2019)
16. Pollard, T.J., Johnson, A.E., Raffa, J.D., Celi, L.A., Mark, R.G., Badawi, O.: The eICU collaborative research database, a freely available multi-center database for critical care research. Sci. Data **5**, 180178 (2018)
17. Prokhorenkova, L.O., Gusev, G., Vorobev, A., Dorogush, A.V., Gulin, A.: CatBoost: unbiased boosting with categorical features. In: Bengio, S., Wallach, H.M., Larochelle, H., Grauman, K., Cesa-Bianchi, N., Garnett, R. (eds.) Advances in Neural Information Processing Systems 31: Annual Conference on Neural Information Processing Systems 2018, NeurIPS 2018, 3–8 December 2018, Montréal, Canada, pp. 6639–6649 (2018). http://papers.nips.cc/paper/7898-catboost-unbiased-boosting-with-categorical-features

18. Ronneberger, O., Fischer, P., Brox, T.: U-Net: convolutional networks for biomedical image segmentation. In: Navab, N., Hornegger, J., Wells, W.M., Frangi, A.F. (eds.) MICCAI 2015. LNCS, vol. 9351, pp. 234–241. Springer, Cham (2015). https://doi.org/10.1007/978-3-319-24574-4_28
19. Singer, M., et al.: The third international consensus definitions for sepsis and septic shock (SEPSIS-3). Jama **315**(8), 801–810 (2016)
20. Stekhoven, D.J., Bühlmann, P.: MissForest' non-parametric missing value imputation for mixed-type data. Bioinformatics 28(1), 112–118 (2011). https://doi.org/10.1093/bioinformatics/btr597
21. Yang, Q., Liu, Y., Chen, T., Tong, Y.: Federated machine learning: concept and applications. ACM Trans. Intell. Syst. Technol. (TIST) **10**(2), 1–19 (2019)

Privacy-Preserving Stacking with Application to Cross-organizational Diabetes Prediction

Xiawei Guo[1]([✉]), Quanming Yao[1,2], James Kwok[2], Weiwei Tu[1],
Yuqiang Chen[1], Wenyuan Dai[1], and Qiang Yang[2]

[1] 4Paradigm Inc., Beijing, China
{guoxiawei,yaoquanming}@4paradigm.com
[2] Department of Computer Science and Engineering, HKUST, Kowloon, Hong Kong

Abstract. To meet the standard of differential privacy, noise is usually added into the original data, which inevitably deteriorates the predicting performance of subsequent learning algorithms. In this chapter, motivated by the success of improving predicting performance by ensemble learning, we propose to enhance privacy-preserving logistic regression by stacking. We show that this can be done either by sample-based or feature-based partitioning. However, we prove that when privacy-budgets are the same, feature-based partitioning requires fewer samples than sample-based one, and thus likely has better empirical performance. As transfer learning is difficult to be integrated with a differential privacy guarantee, we further combine the proposed method with hypothesis transfer learning to address the problem of learning across different organizations. Finally, we not only demonstrate the effectiveness of our method on two benchmark data sets, i.e., MNIST and NEWS20, but also apply it into a real application of cross-organizational diabetes prediction from RUIJIN data set, where privacy is of a significant concern.

1 Introduction

In recent years, data privacy has become a serious concern in both academia and industry [1,6–8]. There are now privacy laws, such as Europe's General Data Protection Regulation (GDPR), which regulates the protection of private data and restricts data transmission between organizations. These raise challenges for cross-organizational machine learning [14,22,23,30], in which data have to be distributed to different organizations, and the learning model needs to make predictions in private.

A number of approaches have been proposed to ensure privacy protection. In machine learning, differential privacy [8] is often used to allow data be exchanged among organizations. To design a differentially private algorithm, carefully designed noise is usually added to the original data to disambiguate the algorithms. Many standard learning algorithms have been extended for differential privacy. These include logistic regression [6], trees [10,11], and deep networks [1,25]. In particular, linear models are simple and easy to understand, and

© Springer Nature Switzerland AG 2020
Q. Yang et al. (Eds.): Federated Learning, LNAI 12500, pp. 269–283, 2020.
https://doi.org/10.1007/978-3-030-63076-8_19

their differentially private variants (such as privacy-preserving logistic regression (PLR)) [6]) have rigorous theoretical guarantees [2,6,14,16]. However, the injection of noise often degrades prediction performance.

Ensemble learning can often significantly improve the performance of a single learning model [31]. Popular examples include bagging [4], boosting [12], and stacking [29]. These motivate us to develop an ensemble-based method which can benefit from data protection, while enjoying good prediction performance. Bagging and boosting are based on partitioning of training samples, and use pre-defined rules (majority or weighted voting) to combine predictions from models trained on different partitions. Bagging improves learning performance by reducing the variance. Boosting, on the other hand, is useful in converting weak models to a strong one. However, the logistic regression model, which is the focus in this chapter, often has good performance in many applications, and is a relatively strong classifier. Besides, it is a convex model and relatively stable.

Thus, in this chapter, we focus on stacking. While stacking also partitions the training data, this can be based on either samples [5,20,26] or features [3]. Multiple low-level models are then learned on the different data partitions, and a high-level model (typically, a logistic regression model) is used to combine their predictions. By combining with PLR, we show how differential privacy can be ensured in stacking. Besides, when the importance of features is known a priori, they can be easily incorporated in feature-based partitioning. We further analyze the learning guarantee of sample-based and feature-based stacking, and show theoretically that feature-based partitioning can have lower sample complexity (than sample-based partitioning), and thus better performance. By adapting the feature importance, its learning performance can be further boosted.

To demonstrate the superiority of the proposed method, we perform experiments on two benchmark data sets (MNIST and NEWS20). Empirical results confirm that feature-based stacking performs better than sample-based stacking. It is also better than directly using PLR on the training data set. Besides, the prediction performance is further boosted when feature importance is used. Finally, we apply the proposed approach for cross-organizational diabetes prediction in the transfer learning setting. The experiment is performed on the RUIJIN data set, which contains over ten thousands diabetes records from across China. Results show significantly improved diabetes prediction performance over the state-of-the-art, while still protecting data privacy.

Notation. In the sequel, vectors are denoted by lowercase boldface, and $(\cdot)^\top$ denotes transpose of a vector/matrix; $\sigma(a) = \exp(a)/(1+\exp(a))$ is the sigmoid function. A function g is μ-strongly convex if $g(\alpha\mathbf{w} + (1 - \alpha)\mathbf{u}) \leq \alpha g(\mathbf{w}) + (1 - \alpha)g(\mathbf{u}) - \frac{\mu}{2}\alpha(1 - \alpha)\|\mathbf{w} - \mathbf{u}\|^2$ for any $\alpha \in (0, 1)$.

2 Related Works

2.1 Differential Privacy

Differential privacy [7,8] has been established as a rigorous standard to guarantee privacy for algorithms that access private data. Intuitively, given a privacy budget ϵ, an algorithm preserves ϵ-differentially privacy if changing one entry in the data set does not change the likelihood of any of the algorithm's output by more than ϵ. Formally, it is defined as follows.

Definition 1 ([7]). *A randomized mechanism M is ϵ-differentially private if for all output t of M and for all input data $\mathcal{D}_1, \mathcal{D}_2$ differing by one element, $Pr(M(\mathcal{D}_1) = t) \leq e^\epsilon Pr(M(\mathcal{D}_2) = t)$.*

To meet the ϵ-differentially privacy guarantee, careful perturbation or noise usually needs to be added to the learning algorithm. A smaller ϵ provides stricter privacy guarantee but at the expense of heavier noise, leading to larger performance deterioration [2,6]. A relaxed version of ϵ-differentially private, called (ϵ, δ)-differentially privacy in which δ measures the loss in privacy, is proposed [8]. However, we focus on the more stringent Definition 1 in this chapter.

2.2 Privacy-Preserving Logistic Regression (PLR)

Logistic regression has been popularly used in machine learning [13]. Various differential privacy approaches have been developed for logistic regression. Examples include output perturbation [6,7], gradient perturbation [1] and objective perturbation [2,6]. In particular, objective perturbation, which adds designed and random noise to the learning objective, has both privacy and learning guarantees as well as good empirical performance.

Privacy-preserving logistic regression (PLR) [6] is the state-of-the-art model based on objective perturbation. Given a data set $\mathcal{D} = \{\mathbf{x}_i, y_i\}_{i=1}^n$, where $\mathbf{x}_i \in \mathbb{R}^d$ is the sample and y_i the corresponding class label, we first consider the regularized risk minimization problem:

$$\min_{\mathbf{w}} 1/n \sum_{i=1}^{n} \ell(\mathbf{w}^\top \mathbf{x}_i, y_i) + \lambda g(\mathbf{w}), \tag{1}$$

where $\mathbf{w}$ is a vector of the model parameter, $\ell(\hat{y}, y) = \log(1 + e^{-y\hat{y}})$ is the logistic loss (with predicted label $\hat{y}$ and given label y), g is the regularizer and $\lambda \geq 0$ is a hyperparameter. To guarantee privacy, Chauduri et al. (2011) added two extra terms to (1), leading to:

$$\min_{\mathbf{w}} 1/n \sum_{i=1}^{n} \ell(\mathbf{w}^\top \mathbf{x}_i, y_i) + \mathbf{b}^\top \mathbf{w}/n + \Delta \|\mathbf{w}\|^2/2 + \lambda g(\mathbf{w}), \tag{2}$$

where $\mathbf{b}$ is random noise drawn from $h(\mathbf{b}) \propto \exp(\epsilon'/2\|\mathbf{b}\|)$ with $\mathbb{E}(\|\mathbf{b}\|) = 2d/\epsilon'$, ϵ' is a privacy budget modified from ϵ, and Δ is a scalar depending on λ, n, ϵ. The whole PLR procedure is shown in Algorithm 1.

Proposition 1 ([6]). *If the regularizer g is strongly convex, Algorithm 1 provides ϵ-differential privacy.*

Algorithm 1. PLR: Privacy-preserving logistic regression.

Require: privacy budget ϵ, data set $\mathcal{D}$;
  1: $\epsilon' = \epsilon - \log(1 + \frac{1}{2n\lambda} + \frac{1}{16n^2\lambda^2})$;
  2: **if** $\epsilon' > 0$ **then**
  3:    $\Delta = 0$;
  4: **else**
  5:    $\Delta = (4n(\exp(\epsilon/4) - 1))^{-1} - \lambda$ and $\epsilon' = \epsilon/2$;
  6: **end if**
  7: scale $\|\mathbf{x}\| \le 1$ for all $\mathbf{x} \in \mathcal{D}$;
  8: pick a random vector $\mathbf{b}$ from $h(\mathbf{b}) \propto \exp(\epsilon'\|\mathbf{b}\|/2)$;
  9: obtain $\mathbf{w}$ by solving (2);
 10: **return** $\mathbf{w}$.

While privacy guarantee is desirable, the resultant privacy-preserving machine learning model may not have good learning performance. In practice, the performance typically degrades dramatically because of the introduction of noise [2,6,24,25]. Assume that samples from $\mathcal{D}$ are drawn i.i.d. from an underlying distribution P. Let $L(\mathbf{w}; P) = \mathbb{E}_{(\mathbf{x},y) \sim P}[\ell(\mathbf{w}^\top\mathbf{x}, y)]$ be the expected loss of the model. The following Proposition shows the number of samples needed for PLR to have comparable performance as a given baseline model.

Proposition 2 ([6]). *Let* $g(\cdot) = \frac{1}{2}\|\cdot\|^2$, *and* $\mathbf{v}$ *be a reference model parameter. Given* $\delta > 0$ *and* $\epsilon_g > 0$, *there exists a constant* C_1 *such that when*

$$n > C_1 \max\left(\|\mathbf{v}\|^2\log(\tfrac{1}{\delta})/\epsilon_g^2, \, d\log(\tfrac{d}{\delta})\|\mathbf{v}\|/\epsilon_g\epsilon, \, \|\mathbf{v}\|^2/\epsilon_g\epsilon\right), \tag{3}$$

$\mathbf{w}$ *from Algorithm 1 meets* $Pr[L(\mathbf{w},P) \le L(\mathbf{v},P) + \epsilon_g] \ge 1 - \delta$.

2.3   Multi-Party Data Learning

Ensemble learning has been considered with differential privacy under multi-party data learning (MPL). The task is to combine predictors from multiple parties with privacy [23]. Pathak et al. (2010) first proposed a specially designed protocol to privately combine multiple predictions. The performance is later surpassed by [14,22], which uses another classifier built on auxiliary unlabeled data. However, all these combination methods rely on extra, privacy-insensitive public data, which may not be always available. Moreover, the aggregated prediction may not be better than the best single party's prediction. There are also MPL methods that do not use ensemble learning. Rajkumar and Agarwal (2012) used stochastic gradient descent, and Xie et al. (2017) proposed a multi-task learning method. While these improve the performance of the previous ones based on aggregation, they gradually lose the privacy guarantee after more and more iterations.

3 Privacy-Preserving Ensemble

In this section, we propose to improve the learning guarantee of PLR by ensemble learning [31]. Popular examples include bagging [4], boosting [12], and stacking [29]. Bagging and boosting are based on partitioning of training samples, and use pre-defined rules (majority or weighted voting) to combine predictions from models trained on different partitions. Bagging improves learning performance by reducing the variance. However, logistic regression is a convex model and relatively stable. Boosting, on the other hand, is useful in combining weak models to a strong one, while logistic regression is a relatively strong classifier and often has good performance in many applications.

3.1 Privacy-Preserving Stacking with Sample Partitioning (SP)

We first consider using stacking with SP, and PLR is used as both the low-level and high-level models (Algorithm 2). As stacking does not impose restriction on the usage of classifiers on each partition of the training data, a simple combination of stacking and PLR can be used to provide privacy guarantee.

Algorithm 2. PST-S: Privacy-preserving stacking with SP.

Require: privacy budget ϵ, data set $\mathcal{D}$;
1: partition $\mathcal{D}$ into disjoint sets $\mathcal{D}^l$ and $\mathcal{D}^h$, for training of the low-level and high-level models, respectively;
2: partition samples in $\mathcal{D}^l$ to K disjoint sets $\{\mathcal{S}_1, \ldots, \mathcal{S}_K\}$;
3: **for** $k = 1, \ldots, K$ **do**
4:    train PLR (Algorithm 1) with privacy budget ϵ on $\mathcal{S}_k$, and obtain the low-level model parameter $\mathbf{w}_k^l$;
5: **end for**
6: construct meta-data set $\mathcal{M}^s = \{[\sigma(\mathbf{x}^\top \mathbf{w}_1^l); \ldots; \sigma(\mathbf{x}^\top \mathbf{w}_K^l)], y\}$ using all samples $\{\mathbf{x}, y\} \in \mathcal{D}^h$;
7: train PLR (Algorithm 1) with privacy budget ϵ on $\mathcal{M}^s$, and obtain the high-level model parameter $\mathbf{w}^h$;
8: **return** $\{\mathbf{w}_k^l\}$ and $\mathbf{w}^h$.

Proposition 3. *If the regularizer g is strongly convex, Algorithm 2 provides ϵ-differential privacy.*

However, while the high-level model can be better than any of the single low-level models [9], Algorithm 2 may not perform better than directly using PLR on the whole $\mathcal{D}$ for the following two reasons. First, each low-level model uses only $\mathcal{S}_k$ (step 4), which is about $1/K$ the size of $\mathcal{D}$ (assuming that the data set $\mathcal{D}$ is partitioned uniformly). This smaller sample size may not satisfy condition (3) in Proposition 2. Second, in many real-world applications, features are not of equal importance. For example, for diabetes prediction using the RUIJIN data set

(Table 3), Glu120 and Glu0, which directly measure glucose levels in the blood, are more relevant than features such as age and number of children. However, during training of the low-level models, Algorithm 2 adds equal amounts of noise to all features. If we can add less noise to the more important features while keeping the same privacy guarantee, we are likely to get better learning performance.

3.2   Privacy-Preserving Stacking with Feature Partitioning (FP)

To address the above problems, we propose to partition the data based on features instead of samples in training the low-level models. The proposed feature-based stacking approach is shown in Algorithm 3. Features are partitioned into K subsets, and $\mathcal{D}^l$ is split correspondingly into K disjoint sets $\{\mathcal{F}_1, \ldots, \mathcal{F}_K\}$. Obviously, as the number of training samples is not reduced, the sample size condition for learning performance guarantee is easier to be satisfied (details will be established in Theorem 1)[1].

Algorithm 3. PST-F: Privacy-preserving stacking with FP.

Require: privacy budget ϵ, data set $\mathcal{D}$, feature importance $\{q_k\}_{k=1}^K$ where $q_k \geq 0$ and $\sum_{k=1}^K q_k = 1$;

1: partition $\mathcal{D}$ into disjoint sets $\mathcal{D}^l$ and $\mathcal{D}^h$, for training of the low-level model and high-level model, respectively;
2: partition $\mathcal{D}^l$ to K disjoint sets $\{\mathcal{F}_1, \ldots, \mathcal{F}_K\}$ based on features;
3: $\epsilon' = \epsilon - \sum_{k=1}^K \log(1 + q_k^2/2n\lambda_k + q_k^4/16n^2\lambda_k^2)$;
4: **for** $k = 1, \ldots, K$ **do**
5:     scale $\|\mathbf{x}\| \leq q_k$ for all $\mathbf{x} \in \mathcal{F}_k$;
6:     **if** $\epsilon' > 0$ **then**
7:         $\Delta_k = 0$ and $\epsilon_k = \epsilon'$;
8:     **else**
9:         $\Delta_k = q_k^2/4n(\exp(\epsilon q_k/4)-1) - \lambda_k$ and $\epsilon_k = \epsilon/2$;
10:    **end if**
11:    pick a random $\mathbf{b}_k$ from $h(\mathbf{b}) \propto \exp(\epsilon_k\|\mathbf{b}\|/2)$;
12:    $\mathbf{w}_k^l = \arg\min_{\mathbf{w}} 1/n \sum_{\mathbf{x}_i \in \mathcal{F}_k} \ell(\mathbf{w}^\top\mathbf{x}_i, y_i) + \mathbf{b}_k^\top\mathbf{w}/n + \Delta\|\mathbf{w}\|^2/2 + \lambda_k g_k(\mathbf{w})$;
13: **end for**
14: construct meta-data set $\mathcal{M}^f = \{[\sigma(\mathbf{x}_{(1)}^\top\mathbf{w}_1^l), \ldots, \sigma(\mathbf{x}_{(K)}^\top\mathbf{w}_K^l)], y\}$ using all $\{\mathbf{x}, y\} \in \mathcal{D}^h$, where $\mathbf{x}_{(k)}$ is a vector made from $\mathbf{x}$ by taking features covered by $\mathcal{F}_k$;
15: train PLR (Algorithm 1) with privacy budget ϵ on $\mathcal{M}^f$, and obtain the high-level model parameter $\mathbf{w}^h$;
16: **return** $\{\mathbf{w}_k^l\}$ and $\mathbf{w}^h$.

When the relative importance of feature subsets is known, Algorithm 3 adds less noise to the more important features. Specifically, let the importance[2] of $\mathcal{F}_k$ (with d_k features) be q_k, where $q_k \geq 0$ and $\sum_{k=1} q_k = 1$, and is independent

---

[1] $-q_k$ to partitions.
[2] When feature importance is not known, $q_1 = \cdots = q_K = 1/K$.

with $\mathcal{D}$. Assume that $\epsilon' > 0$ in step 6 (and thus $\epsilon_k = \epsilon'$). Recall from Sect. 2.2 that $\mathbb{E}(\|\mathbf{b}_k\|) = 2d_k/\epsilon_k = 2d_k/\epsilon'$. By scaling the samples in each $\mathcal{F}_k$ as in step 5, the injected noise level in $\mathcal{F}_k$ is given by $\mathbb{E}(\|\mathbf{b}_k\|)/\|\mathbf{x}\| = 2d_k/\epsilon' q_k$. This is thus inversely proportional to the importance q_k.

Remark 1. In the special case where only one feature group has nonzero importance, Algorithm 3 reduces Algorithm 1 on that group, and privacy is still guaranteed.

Finally, a privacy-preserving low-level logistic regression model is obtained in step 12, and a privacy-preserving high-level logistic regression model is obtained in step 15. Theorem 1 guarantees privacy of Algorithm 3. Note that the proofs in [2,6] cannot be directly used, as they consider neither stacking nor feature importance.

Theorem 1. *If all g_k's are strongly convex, Algorithm 3 provides ϵ-differential privacy.*

Analogous to Proposition 1, the following bounds the learning performance of each low-level model.

Theorem 2. $g_k = 1/2\| \cdot -\mathbf{u}_k\|^2$, *where $\mathbf{u}_k$ is any constant vector, and $\mathbf{v}_k$ is a reference model parameter. Let $a_k = q_k\|\mathbf{v}_k\|$. given $\delta > 0$ and $\epsilon_g > 0$, there exists a constant C_1 such that when*

$$n > C_1 \max \left(a_k^2 \log(1/\delta)/\epsilon_g^2, \, d \log(d/K\delta) a_k / q_k K \epsilon_g \epsilon, \, a_k^2/\epsilon_g \epsilon \right), \qquad (4)$$

$\mathbf{w}_k^l$ *from Algorithm 3 satisfies* $Pr[L(\mathbf{w}_k^l, P) \leq L(\mathbf{v}_k, P) + \epsilon_g] \geq 1 - \delta$.

Remark 2. When $K = 1$ (a single low-level model trained with all features) and $\mathbf{u}_k = \mathbf{0}$, Theorem 2 reduces to Proposition 2.

Note that, to keep the same bound $L(\mathbf{v}_k, P) + \epsilon_g$, since xs' are scaled by q_k, $\mathbf{v}_k$ should be scaled by $1/q_k$, so $\mathbb{E}(a_k) = \mathbb{E}(q_k\|\mathbf{v}_k\|)$ remains the same as q_k changes. Thus, Theorem 2 shows that low-level models on more important features can indeed learn better, if these features are assigned with larger q_k. Since stacking can have better performance than any single model [9,27] and Theorem 2 can offer better learning guarantee than Proposition 2, Algorithm 3 can have better performance than Algorithm 1. Finally, compared with Proposition 1, g_k in Theorem 2 is more flexible in allowing an extra $\mathbf{u}_k$. We will show in Sect. 3.3 that this is useful for transfer learning.

Since the learning performance of stacking itself is still an open issue [27], we leave the guarantee for the whole Algorithm 3 as future work. A potential problem with FP is that possible correlations among feature subsets can no longer be utilized. However, as the high-level model can combine information from various low-level models, empirical results in Sect. 4.1 show that this is not problematic unless K is very large.

3.3   Application to Transfer Learning

Transfer learning [21] is a powerful and promising method to extract useful knowledge from a source domain to a target domain. A popular transfer learning approach is hypothesis transfer learning (HTL) [17], which encourages the hypothesis learned in the target domain to be similar with that in the source domain. For application to (1), HTL adds an extra regularizer as:

$$\min_{\mathbf{w}} \sum_{\mathbf{x}_i \in \mathcal{D}_{\text{tgt}}} \ell(\mathbf{w}^\top \mathbf{x}_i, y_i) + \lambda g(\mathbf{w}) + \eta/2 \|\mathbf{w} - \mathbf{w}_{\text{src}}\|^2. \tag{5}$$

Here, η is a hyperparameter, $\mathcal{D}_{\text{tgt}}$ is the target domain data, and $\mathbf{w}_{\text{src}}$ is obtained from the source domain. Algorithm 4 shows how PST-F can be extended with HTL using privacy budgets ϵ_{src} and ϵ_{tgt} for the source and target domains, respectively. The same feature partitioning is used on both the source and target data. PLR is trained on each source domain data subset to obtain $(\mathbf{w}_{\text{src}})_k$ (steps 2–4). This is then transferred to the target domain using PST-F with $g_k(\mathbf{w}) = \frac{1}{2}\|\mathbf{w} - (\mathbf{w}_{\text{src}})_k\|^2$ (step 5).

Algorithm 4. PST-H: Privacy-preserving stacking with HTL.

Require: source data sets $\mathcal{D}_{\text{src}}$, target data set $\mathcal{D}_{\text{tgt}}$, and corresponding privacy budgets ϵ_{src} and ϵ_{tgt}, respectively.
   (source domain processing)
1: partition $\mathcal{D}_{\text{src}}$ to K disjoint sets $\{\mathcal{F}_1, \ldots, \mathcal{F}_K\}$ based on features;
2: **for** $k = 1, \ldots, K$ **do**
3:    train PLR with privacy budget ϵ_{src} on $\mathcal{F}_k$ and obtain $(\mathbf{w}_{\text{src}})_k$;
4: **end for**
   (target domain processing)
5: obtain $\{(\mathbf{w}_{\text{tgt}})_k^l\}$ and $\mathbf{w}_{\text{tgt}}^h$ from PST-F (Algorithm 1) by taking $g_k(\mathbf{w}) = 1/2\|\mathbf{w} - (\mathbf{w}_{\text{src}})_k\|^2$ and privacy budget ϵ_{tgt} on $\mathcal{D}_{\text{tgt}}$;
6: **return** $\{(\mathbf{w}_{\text{src}})_k\}$ for source domain, $\{(\mathbf{w}_{\text{tgt}})_k^l\}$ and $\mathbf{w}_{\text{tgt}}^h$ for target domain.

The following provides privacy guarantees on both the source and target domains. Recently, privacy-preserving HTL is also proposed in [28]. However, it does not consider stacking and ignores feature importance.

Corollary 1. *Algorithm 4 provides ϵ_{src}- and ϵ_{tgt}-differential privacy guarantees for the source and target domains.*

4   Experiments

4.1   Benchmark Datasets

Experiments are performed on two popular benchmark data sets for evaluating privacy-preserving learning algorithms [22, 25, 28]: MNIST [19] and NEWS20 [18] (Table 1). The MNIST data set contains images of handwritten digits. Here, we

Table 1. Summary of the MNIST and NEWS20 data sets.

MNIST			NEWS20		
#train	#test	#features	#train	#test	#features
3000	2000	100	4321	643	100

use the digits 0 and 8. We randomly select 5000 samples. 60% of them are used for training (with 1/3 of this used for validation), and the remaining 20% for testing. The NEWS20 data set is a collection of newsgroup documents. Documents belonging to the topic "sci" are taken as positive samples, while those in the topic "talk" are taken as negative. Finally, we use PCA to reduce the feature dimensionality to 100, as original dimensionality for MINIST/NEWS20 is too high for differentially private algorithms to handle as the noise will be extremely large. Note that we use PCA for simplicity of the ablation study. However, note that the importance scores should be obtained from side information independent from the data or from experts' opinions (as in diabetes example). Otherwise, ϵ-differential privacy will not be guaranteed.

The following algorithms are compared: (i) PLR, which applies Algorithm 1 on the training data; (ii) PST-S: Algorithm 2, based on SP; and (iii) PST-F: Algorithm 3, based on FP. We use $K = 5$ and 50% of the data for $\mathcal{D}^l$ and the remaining for $\mathcal{D}^h$. Two PST-F variants are compared: PST-F(U), with random FP and equal feature importance. And PST-F(W), with partitioning based on the PCA feature scores; and the importance of the kth group $\mathcal{F}_k$ is

$$q_k = \sum_{i: f_i \in \mathcal{F}_k} v_i / \sum_{j: f_j \in \mathcal{D}^l} v_j, \tag{6}$$

where v_i is the variance of the ith feature f_i. Gradient perturbation is worse than objective perturbation in logistic regression [2], thus is not compared.

The area-under-the-ROC-curve (AUC) [15] on the testing set is used for performance evaluation. Hyper-parameters are tuned using the validation set. To reduce statistical variations, the experiment is repeated 10 times, and the results averaged.

Varying Privacy Budget ϵ. Figure 1 shows the testing AUC's when the privacy budget ϵ is varied. As can be seen, the AUCs for all methods improve when the privacy requirement is relaxed (ϵ is large and less noise is added). Moreover, PST-S can be inferior to PLR, due to insufficient training samples caused by SP. Both PST-F(W) and PST-F(U) have better AUCs than PST-S and PLR. In particular, PST-F(W) is the best as it can utilize feature importance. Since PST-S is inferior to PST-F(U), we only consider PST-F(U) in the following experiments.

Varying Number of Partitions K. In this experiment, we fix $\epsilon = 1$, and vary K. As can be seen from Fig. 2(a)–(b), when K is very small, ensemble learning is not effective. When K is too large, a lot of feature correlation information is lost and the testing AUC also decreases.

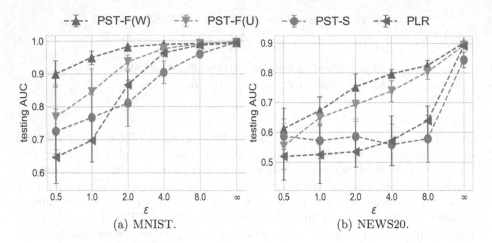

Fig. 1. Testing AUC vs ϵ. Here, "∞" corresponds to the non-privacy-preserving version of the corresponding algorithms.

Changing the Feature Importance. In the above experiments, feature importance is defined based on the variance from PCA. Here, we show how feature importance influences prediction performance. In real-world applications, we may not know the exact importance of features. Thus, we replace variance v_i by the ith power of α (α^i), where α is a positive constant, and use (6) for assigning weights. Note that when $\alpha < 1$, more importance features have larger weights; and vice versa when $\alpha > 1$. Note that PST-F(W) does not reduce to PST-F(U) when $\alpha = 1$, as more important features are still grouped together. Figure 2(c)–(d) show the testing AUCs at different α's. As can be seen, with proper assigned weights (i.e., $\alpha < 1$ and more important features have larger q_k's), the testing AUC can get higher. If less important features are more valued, the testing AUC decreases and may not be better than PST-F(U), which uses uniform weights. Moreover, we see that PST-F(W) is not sensitive to the weights once they are properly assigned.

Choice of High-Level Model. We compare different high-level models in combining predictions from the low-level models. The following methods are compared: (i) major voting (C-mv) from low-level models; (ii) weighted major voting (C-wmv), which uses $\{q_k\}$ as the weights; and (iii) by a high-level model in PST-F (denoted "C-hl"). Figure 3 shows results on NEWS20 with $\epsilon = 1.0$. As can be seen, C-0 in Fig. 3(b) has the best performance among all single low-level models, as it contains the most important features. Besides, stacking (i.e., C-hl), is the best way to combine predictions from C-{0-4}, which also offers better performance than any single low-level models.

Table 2. Testing AUC on all branches of RUIJIN data set. The best and comparable results according to pair-wise 95% significance test are high-lighted. Testing AUC of PLR on main center is 0.668 ± 0.026.

branch#	1	2	3	4	5	6	7	8
PST-H(W)	**0.747±0.032**	**0.736±0.032**	**0.740±0.040**	**0.714±0.040**	**0.766±0.039**	**0.707±0.017**	**0.721±0.0464**	**0.753±0.042**
PST-H(U)	0.678±0.049	**0.724±0.037**	0.652±0.103	**0.708±0.033**	0.653±0.070	0.663±0.036	**0.682±0.0336**	0.692±0.044
PPHTL	0.602±0.085	0.608±0.078	0.528±0.062	0.563±0.067	0.577±0.075	0.601±0.031	0.580±0.0708	0.583±0.056
PLR(target)	0.548±0.088	0.620±0.055	0.636±0.046	0.579±0.075	0.533±0.058	0.613±0.035	0.561±0.0764	0.584±0.045

branch#	9	10	11	12	13	14	15	16
PST-H(W)	**0.701±0.023**	**0.698±0.036**	**0.736±0.046**	**0.738±0.045**	**0.746±0.0520**	**0.661±0.094**	**0.697±0.023**	**0.604±0.012**
PST-H(U)	0.635±0.026	0.644±0.050	0.635±0.054	0.645±0.061	**0.718±0.0647**	0.644±0.044	0.647±0.061	0.567±0.036
PPHTL	0.547±0.066	0.517±0.075	0.565±0.059	0.547±0.089	0.592±0.0806	0.615±0.071	0.558±0.065	0.524±0.027
PLR(target)	0.515±0.065	0.555±0.061	0.553±0.066	0.520±0.088	0.619±0.0701	0.563±0.026	0.558±0.060	0.517±0.053

Table 3. Some features in the RUIJIN data set, and importance is suggested by doctors. Top (resp. bottom) part: Features collected from the first (resp. second) investigation.

Name	Importance	Explaination
mchild	0.010	Number of children
weight	0.012	Birth weight
bone	0.013	Bone mass measurement
eggw	0.005	Frequency of having eggs
Glu120	0.055	Glucose level 2 h after meals
Glu0	0.060	Glucose level immediately after meals
age	0.018	Age
bmi	0.043	Body mass index
HDL	0.045	High-density lipoprotein

4.2 Diabetes Prediction

Diabetes is a group of metabolic disorders with high blood sugar levels over a prolonged period. The RUIJIN diabetes data set is collected by the Shanghai Ruijin Hospital during two investigations (in 2010 and 2013), conducted by the main hospital in Shanghai and 16 branches across China. The first investigation consists of questionnaires and laboratory tests collecting demographics, life-styles, disease information, and physical examination results. The second investigation includes diabetes diagnosis. Some collected features are shown in Table 3. Table 4 shows a total of 105,763 participants who appear in both two investigations. The smaller branches may not have sufficient labeled medical records for good prediction. Hence, it will be useful to borrow knowledge learned by the main hospital. However, users' privacy is a major concern, and patients' personal medical records in the main hospital should not be leaked to the branches.

In this section, we apply the method in Sect. 3.3 for diabetes prediction. Specifically, based on the patient data collected during the first investigation in 2010, we predict whether he/she will have diabetes diagnosed in 2013. The main hospital serves as the source domain, and the branches are the target

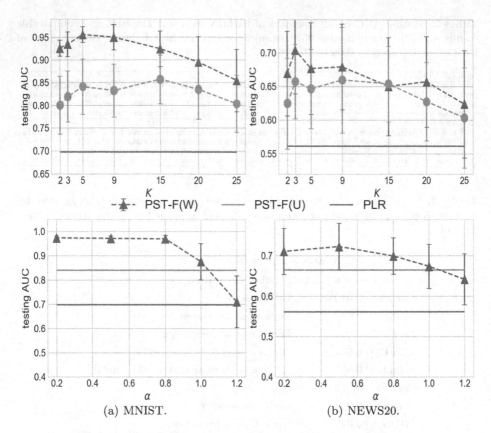

Fig. 2. Testing AUC with different K (first row) and different feature importance settings (second row).

domains. We set $\epsilon_{\mathrm{src}} = \epsilon_{\mathrm{tgt}} = 1.0$. The following methods are also compared: (i) PLR(target), which directly uses PLR on the target data; (ii) PPHTL [28]: a recently proposed privacy-preserving HTL method based on PLR; (iii) PST-F(U): There are 50 features, and they are randomly split into five groups, i.e., $K = 5$, and each group have equal weights; (iv) PST-F(W): Features are first sorted by importance, and then grouped as follows: The top 10 features are placed in the first group, the next 10 features go to the second group, and so on. q^k is set based on (6), with v_i being the importance values provided by the doctors. The other settings are the same as in Sect. 4.1.

Results are shown in Table 2. PPHTL may not have better performance than PLR(target), which is perhaps due to noise introduced in features. However, PST-F(U) improves over PPHTL by feature splitting, and consistently outperforms PLR(target). PST-F(W), which considers features importance, is the best.

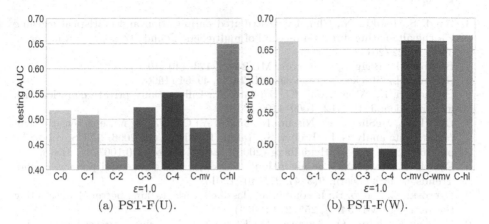

Fig. 3. Testing AUC of low-levels models and different combining methods on NEWS20 ($\epsilon = 1.0$), where C-0 to C-4 are performance of low-level models.

Table 4. Number of samples collected from the main hospital and 16 branches in the RUIJIN data set.

main	#1	#2	#3	#4	#5	#6	#7	#8
12,702	4,334	4,739	6,121	2,327	5,619	6,360	4,966	5,793

#9	#10	#11	#12	#13	#14	#15	#16
6,215	3,659	5,579	2,316	4,285	6,017	6,482	4,493

5 Conclusion

In this chapter, we propose a new privacy-preserving machine learning method, which improves privacy-preserving logistic regression by stacking. This can be done by either sample-based or feature-based partitioning of the data set. We provide theoretical justifications that the feature-based approach is better and requires a smaller sample complexity. Besides, when the importance of features is available, this can further boost the feature-based approach both in theory and practice. Effectiveness of the proposed method is verified on both standard benchmark data sets and a real-world cross-organizational diabetes prediction application.

Acknowledgments. We acknowledge the support of Hong Kong CERG-16209715. The first author also thanks Bo Han from Riken for helpful suggestions.

References

1. Abadi, M., et al.: Deep learning with differential privacy. In: SIGSAC, pp. 308–318. ACM (2016)
2. Bassily, R., Smith, A., Thakurta, A.: Private empirical risk minimization: efficient algorithms and tight error bounds. In: FOCS, pp. 464–473. IEEE (2014)

3. Boyd, S., Parikh, N., Chu, E.: Distributed optimization and statistical learning via the alternating direction method of multipliers. Found. Trends® Mach. Learn. **3**(1), 1–122 (2011)
4. Breiman, L.: Bagging predictors. ML **24**(2), 123–140 (1996)
5. Breiman, L.: Stacked regressions. ML **24**(1), 49–64 (1996)
6. Chaudhuri, K., Monteleoni, C., Sarwate, A.: Differentially private empirical risk minimization. JMLR **12**, 1069–1109 (2011)
7. Dwork, C., McSherry, F., Nissim, K., Smith, A.: Calibrating noise to sensitivity in private data analysis. In: Halevi, S., Rabin, T. (eds.) TCC 2006. LNCS, vol. 3876, pp. 265–284. Springer, Heidelberg (2006). https://doi.org/10.1007/11681878_14
8. Dwork, C., Roth, A.: The algorithmic foundations of differential privacy. Found. Trends® Mach. Learn. **9**(3–4), 211–407 (2014)
9. Džeroski, S., Ženko, B.: Is combining classifiers with stacking better than selecting the best one? ML **54**(3), 255–273 (2004)
10. Emekçi, F., Sahin, O., Agrawal, D., El Abbadi, A.: Privacy preserving decision tree learning over multiple parties. TKDE **63**(2), 348–361 (2007)
11. Fong, P., Weber-Jahnke, J.: Privacy preserving decision tree learning using unrealized data sets. TKDE **24**(2), 353–364 (2012)
12. Friedman, J., Hastie, T., Tibshirani, R.: Additive logistic regression: a statistical view of boosting. Ann. Stat. **28**(2), 337–407 (2000)
13. Hastie, T., Tibshirani, R., Friedman, J.: The Elements of Statistical Learning. SSS. Springer, New York (2009). https://doi.org/10.1007/978-0-387-84858-7
14. Hamm, J., Cao, Y., Belkin, M.: Learning privately from multiparty data. In: ICML. pp. ,555–563 (2016)
15. Hanley, J., McNeil, B.: A method of comparing the areas under receiver operating characteristic curves derived from the same cases. Radiology **148**(3), 839–843 (1983)
16. Kasiviswanathan, P., Jin, H.: Efficient private empirical risk minimization for high-dimensional learning. In: ICML, pp. 488–497 (2016)
17. Kuzborskij, I., Orabona, F.: Stability and hypothesis transfer learning. In: ICML, pp. 942–950 (2013)
18. Lang, K.: NewsWeeder: learning to filter netnews. In: ICML. Citeseer (1995)
19. LeCun, Y., Bottou, L., Bengio, Y., Haffner, P.: Gradient-based learning applied to document recognition. Proc. IEEE **86**(11), 2278–2324 (1998)
20. Ozay, M., Vural, F.: A new fuzzy stacked generalization technique and analysis of its performance. Technical report. arXiv:1204.0171 (2012)
21. Pan, J., Yang, Q.: A survey on transfer learning. TKDE **22**(10), 1345–1359 (2010)
22. Papernot, N., Abadi, M., Erlingsson, U., Goodfellow, I., Talwar, K.: Semi-supervised knowledge transfer for deep learning from private training data. In: ICLR (2017)
23. Pathak, M., Rane, S., Raj, B.: Multiparty differential privacy via aggregation of locally trained classifiers. In: NIPS, pp. 1876–1884 (2010)
24. Rajkumar, A., Agarwal, S.: A differentially private stochastic gradient descent algorithm for multiparty classification. In: AISTAT, pp. 933–941 (2012)
25. Shokri, R., Shmatikov, V.: Privacy-preserving deep learning. In: SIGSAC, pp. 1310–1321 (2015)
26. Smyth, P., Wolpert, D.: Linearly combining density estimators via stacking. ML **36**(1–2), 59–83 (1999)
27. Ting, K., Witten, I.: Issues in stacked generalization. JAIR **10**, 271–289 (1999)
28. Wang, Y., Gu, Q., Brown, D.: Differentially private hypothesis transfer learning. In: ECML (2018)

29. Wolpert, D.: Stacked generalization. Neural Netw. **5**(2), 241–259 (1992)
30. Xie, L., Baytas, I., Lin, K., Zhou, J.: Privacy-preserving distributed multi-task learning with asynchronous updates. In: SIGKDD, pp. 1195–1204 (2017)
31. Zhou, Z.H.: Ensemble Methods: Foundations and Algorithms. Chapman and Hall/CRC, New York (2012)

Author Index

Printed in the United States
By Bookmasters